ADVENTURES IN THINKING

EDITH D. NEIMARK
Rutgers University

Under the General Editorship of
JEROME KAGAN
Harvard University

HARCOURT BRACE JOVANOVICH, PUBLISHERS

San Diego   New York   Chicago   Austin   Washington, D.C.
London   Sydney   Tokyo   Toronto

Dedicated to the memory of my brother,
Joshua E. Neimark, and my parents,
Solomon J. and Regina Stein Neimark—thinkers all.

◆ Preface ◆

Instructors today are concerned with the perceived decline in thinking skills of American students and are seeking ways to reverse that decline. One attempt at correction has been a new crop of texts proposing simple remedies. As every good teacher knows, there are no simple remedies for deficient thinking. What is required is a change in attitudes and values as well as an augmentation of skills. The development of a thoughtful person is a long and difficult evolution that must be undertaken by the individual student. Nevertheless, a good teacher, armed with a good textbook, can facilitate the development of sound thinking by providing occasions to stimulate thought, by giving constructive criticism and direction, and by offering rewards for achievement along with encouragement when the going is rough. This book is designed to assist the instructor in fulfilling those facilitating roles. One hopes that after students have acquired a taste for the delights of intellectual pursuits nature will take its course and inspire them to continue on their own.

This book differs from similar texts in a number of ways. First, it deals with a greater variety of topics than the traditional texts because I believe that thinking is an integral component of an individual's approach to life. Training in thinking should help the student outside of the classroom as well as within it. For that reason, I have covered such topics as dealing with emotions, taking the perspective of another person, and the processes of evaluation and judgment.

Second, I have tried to address some of the serious issues confronting the young person entering adulthood. Students are deeply concerned with such issues and welcome help in confronting them. For this reason I have included discussion of social and ethical issues as well as exercises drawn from everyday experience.

Third, I have drawn upon a broad range of subject matters in order to emphasize that thinking applies to all realms of human endeavor and to appeal to a broad spectrum of student interests. Some skills that are fundamental to the sciences, such as model building and hypothesis testing, are equally valuable to the nonscientist as well. Although these skills are best taught within the context of a specific discipline, I have tried to present them in a relatively content free manner. Some basic concepts of statistics, probability, and logic have also been included with the same rationale—that an understanding of these topics is necessary for an educated citizen. Similarly, illustrations from art and literature have been included for the student who has evaded contact with the humanities.

Acknowledgments

Writing a book is always something of a voyage of discovery to new ideas and new material. That process has been advanced by the help of many colleagues, whose assistance is gratefully acknowledged. My greatest debt is to Ruth Gottdiener, who urged me to teach the course that inspired the book. I also wish to thank the Rutgers Committee on Instructional Development for supporting a research component of that first course. I would like to thank the following colleagues to whom I am indebted for advice, comments, and education: Richard D. Ashmore, Charlotte Avers, Anna Benjamin, Jean Burton, Rae Carlson, George Erdos, Carol Gilligan, Sandra Harris, Richard Henson, David Krantz, Michael Kubovy, Richard Lore, Lorraine McCune, Elliot Noma, Larry Pervin, Richard Quaintance, Ellin Scholnick, Beatrice Seagull, Fadlou Shehadi, Heather Strange, Lillian Troll, and Janet Wyckoff. A special thanks to Jean Natereli, who typed the manuscript in record time and with real devotion.

I would also like to thank the following reviewers, who offered critical evaluations as well as instructive suggestions: Jerome Kagan, Harvard University; Barbara Nodine, Beaver College; Susan Nummedal, California State University at Long Beach; and Finbar O'Connor, Beaver College.

Edith D. Neimark

◆ Contents ◆

CHAPTER 7

Evaluating Arguments   158

CHAPTER 8

Foundations of Induction:
Causation, Chance, and Information   186

CHAPTER 9

Model Building and Hypothesis Testing   211

CHAPTER 10

Problem Solving   237

CHAPTER 11

Decision and Choice   266

1

The Basics

You are about to embark on a lifelong adventure. As with all voyages, you will get more from the journey if you are prepared for it and are open to the experiences you encounter along the way. In visiting a new country, for example, you go prepared with the expectation that you may have to learn a new language, that the native customs will differ from your own, and that you will have to seize opportunities that may never reoccur. So, too, with becoming a thinker. You will not derive much from the journey if you stay within the confines of your room (in this case, your old habits), venturing forth only when the situation demands and then returning quickly. Start with a commitment to learning the new language and new ways of behaving. Examine your accustomed practices and beliefs in light of your new experiences with the expectation of modifying them to better conform with your emerging status as a thinker. While this may be difficult at first, and you may find that you need help on occasion, it should become easier and more enjoyable as you go along. Stick with it.

This book is divided into two parts: the first part attempts to provide a general orientation, while the second focuses on specific skills and conceptual machinery. The general orientation suggests ways of looking at and labeling your experiences and directing your own cognitive activities. Try to carry these suggestions beyond the confines of the course and its assignments into your everyday life. Make them part of your own habit and belief system. As you become more aware and directive of your own thinking, you will find yourself classifying occasions requiring thought and kinds of problems. You will become more attuned to seeking systematic means of dealing with them. The second part introduces you to a variety of existing classifications and systematic procedures. Although those introductions are, of necessity, brief and compressed, they should provide the basics for you to pursue on your own. Bon voyage.

• *1* •

What Is Thinking and How Does One Become a Thinker?

This introductory chapter will acquaint you with some of the essential ingredients of thought and some current views as to how it is promoted. As emphasized throughout this book, formulating one's purpose is always a good first step toward its attainment. Your purpose is to become a more effective thinker; my purpose is to help you attain that goal. In the final analysis, you will have to do all the work because thinking is an individual activity that no one else can do for you. All that any instructor can do is to provide occasions for engaging in thought, to suggest how to proceed, and to correct inadequacies. By way of preparation for your endeavor, get a notebook in which to record your progress and keep it handy as you proceed through this book, using it regularly. Exercises will be suggested throughout each chapter as well as at the end. Do them. As you do the assignments make marginal notes for yourself on the likely purpose of the exercise as well as the steps you go through in the course of completing the exercises. This will assist you in becoming more aware of the nature of thought and of your practices as a thinker. It will also provide a record of your development in the form of field notes and observations from which to derive hypotheses about where you are having difficulty as well as successful strategies to be used in the future.

With that essential equipment in hand, you are now ready to examine in more detail the nature of thinking and some of the ways it is promoted.

WHAT IS THINKING?

Starting off with a definition is so conventional as to be taken for granted. As an apprentice thinker, however, you should take nothing for granted. Let us, therefore, consider the function of a definition. Had you taken seriously the injunction to use your notebook, you may have listed some examples of thinking and examined them to identify a common property, or you may have consulted a dictionary. In either case, you quickly discover that no single common property is immediately apparent. A deeper analysis is required. That analysis is a necessary first step because identifying a defining property, or properties, is a prerequisite to focusing on them, rather than on some peripheral or irrelevant properties. To better appreciate the implications of that assertion, since you are taking nothing for granted, list what you take to be the defining properties of thinking. You may also want to list some clear, as well as some questionable examples of thinking, against which to test these properties.

This book is predicated upon the definition of thinking as a symbolic activity whose goal is understanding. That definition treats thinking as behavior, something one does, that differs from other behavior (such as, brushing one's teeth, running, or constructing a bookcase) with respect to two defining properties or necessary component activities. Those defining properties are (a) the manipulation of symbols (as contrasted with real-world actions upon objects) and (b) the imposition of meaning. Before delving into those properties, let us get some data as a background for discussion.

Five classic problems are presented in Box 1-1 for you to work on. In doing them do not focus exclusively upon the solution but also record your thought processes so that you can later examine them in relation to the proposed defining properties. What did you discover about the nature of thinking? Perhaps you immediately tried a solution and discovered that it did not work; for example, you may have connected the dots at the edge of the figure forming a square that exhausted the permitted four lines without including the center dot, or opened the link at the end of each chain length and discovered that you were opening and closing four links instead of three. After an initial failure, you probably asked yourself some questions, tried reformulating the problem, considered how you went astray, and made notes or diagrams. In the case of the last problem, instead of initial trial and error, you may have realized that there were too many possible solutions and looked for a systematic way to reduce the set of potential solutions to a manageable size. Clearly, you were generating and operating upon symbolic representations of the problem, in this case your notes, or instructions to yourself. You also, with increasingly explicit self-awareness, tried to make sense of the problem and to devise a systematic solution strategy. (For solutions to the problems, see the notes.[1]) All of these are manifestations of the defining properties of thought. In addition, you probably got some insight into a few of the structural features of difficult problems (that is, those aspects that led you astray).

Thinking as Symbolic Activity. Thinking is a *symbolic activity* because objects and events are detached from their presenting context and represented through the medium of ideas, images, words, implicit motor activity, or a variety of notational schemes such as numbers or diagrams independent of the specific context or of environmental supports. Mental activation takes place before, after, or in place of physical activity. Consider any mundane activity such as grocery shopping or rearranging the furniture. The actual conduct of those activities involves locomotion through space in an appropriate place, at an appropriate

---

BOX 1-1

Five Classic Problems

Do these problems and make notes on how you went about solving them.
Include all your steps, not just the ones that led to your success.

1. Without lifting your finger from the paper draw four straight lines so that
   every dot has a line going through it.

2. A man and his son were involved in an auto crash in which the father was
   killed and the son received severe head injuries. The son was rushed to
   a hospital where the neurosurgeon gasped, "I can't perform the operation; he is my son." How could that be?

3. You have four separate lengths of chain, each consisting of three links.
   Your task is to join them into one continuous necklace as cheaply as
   possible. It costs 3¢ to open a link and 2¢ to close it. You are allowed no
   more than 15¢.

4. At a celebration for two fathers and two sons each honoree has a cake.
   There are only three cakes. Explain how that can be.

5. If a unique number is substituted for each letter in the problem below
   the answer will be a correct arithmetic sum.

$$
\begin{array}{r}
S\ E\ N\ D \\
+\ \ M\ O\ R\ E \\
\hline
M\ O\ N\ E\ Y
\end{array}
$$

---

time, in relation to appropriate objects: for example, walking down the aisle of
a supermarket, pushing a cart, selecting items from a shelf, freezer, or bin, or,
in the case of moving furniture, pulling out the couch, shoving in a chair, and
so on. On the other hand, making up a grocery list or planning the arrangement
of furniture can be done anywhere and at any time in a rich variety of ways: for
example, with cardboard furniture surrogates on a piece of graph paper. Some
obvious instances of symbolic activity include mental calculation of sums, planning daily activities, selecting possible courses of action and rehearsing the one
finally selected, explaining some observations, or rationalizing your own behavior. You can, and should, come up with many more examples of your own.

    As should be evident from the foregoing examples, representing information
and operating upon it is a highly selective process. Certain features of the actual
situation, such as the size of the pieces of furniture are emphasized whereas
other features, such as the color or texture of the fabric, are ignored. To take

another example, in calculating a total bill you sum digits; actual currency is irrelevant. In planning a daily schedule you ignore routine activities like brushing your teeth, or getting from one place to another. Instead you focus upon the major events (a class, an appointment, a vital errand) and the various constraints of time or place to fit all of them in as efficiently as possible. Thoughts are not a literal copy of reality but an abstract transformation of it. How much transformation or abstraction takes place in any given instance can vary enormously depending on the demands of the task.

In the first four problems of Box 1-1, for example, too literal or too narrow a representation of the problem impedes solution; for example, treating the dots as an enclosed square, interpreting "father" and "son" as mutually exclusive labels, defining "neurosurgeon" as a man while ignoring that every son has two parents, all lead down a blind alley. Similarly, in the third problem transforming the goal into "find three links that can serve to form a necklace" promotes solution. In the last problem the content is already in symbolic form, but you must find a procedure for reducing all the possible letter-digit equivalents to a manageable size for testing. Chapter 2 will delve more deeply into the requisite selection process.

If you have summarized the meaning of this section for yourself as "thinking involves representing information and processing those representations" you are essentially correct. If you are in the habit of identifying main ideas and expressing them in your own words you are also well on the way to being a thinker. It may occur to you that computers also process information. In fact, computers satisfy the requirement of operating upon information with much greater speed and accuracy than do humans. Do computers think? Although most of us would have difficulty in justifying the conclusion, we would be in immediate agreement that computers don't think. What makes them machines in contrast to human thinkers is the absence of the second defining property of thinking: meaning-making.

Thinking as Meaning-Making. What I attempt to convey through that awkward term *meaning-making* is the underlying purpose that directs and motivates information processing. You do not passively register experience willy-nilly, but try to make sense of it so as to understand your experiences. What constitutes understanding? That is a hard question. I pose it to the reader now with the urging that you return to it throughout the course of the semester. You should find that your answer changes as you develop insight into your own thought processes. As a first step towards an answer it is important to note that meaning is not intrinsic to experience. Objects and events simply are; meaning is something that the experiencer imposes upon them. It is a personal construction. Your understanding of your own experience is like no one else's. For example, you may see a tree fall, someone may address you in sharp tones, or you may take your first sip of new Coke. Some possible responses to these examples might be, "The tree fell because of a bad storm, someone was angry with me, or new Coke is sweeter." All events are interpreted through labeling, placing them in some context, searching for causes, and then relating them to previous experience and existing knowledge.

In trying to describe what it is that you do in the process of understanding, two necessary components should emerge: one is an awareness of your own thought processes and of a deliberate direction of them; the second is the systematic application of procedures to achieve direction and to bring order out of the constant stream of sense impressions. Neither of these two component aspects of meaning-making is manifest in an all-or-none fashion. One is not aware of everything one does nor is one consistently systematic in thinking about it. There are degrees of awareness and of systematic ordering. In identifying these two components of meaning-making, I am suggesting (a) that they are central to a uniquely human characteristic of thought, but (b) they are not neatly separable from each other, and (c) your central purpose in becoming a better thinker will be to move toward a higher level of both continua. With that preface let us consider each aspect of meaning-making in more detail.

Degree of Awareness and Self-Regulation of Thought. [2]   To some extent all behavior is self-regulated, but the degree of deliberate conscious regulation varies, in part, as a function of the circumstances. In calling to a friend in another room, how loudly you call is automatically dictated by distance. In picking up a pencil, the direction of reach is determined by the location of the pencil; the grasp applied in lifting it differs from the grasp for seizing a wrench, a mug of beer, or any other object differing in shape and weight. There are countless other possible examples demonstrating that behavior is nicely adjusted to existing circumstances in an ongoing manner. One is frequently unaware of the adjustments. Well-established habits such as signing your name, walking home, or dialing a frequently used phone number are executed automatically. In reviewing your description of your thought process in solving the problems in Box 1-1, for example, you may find sparse reporting of why a particular solution was attempted or, even, of what was done. Such a finding would suggest either that you were behaving in an automatic manner or that you are not yet skilled at monitoring and describing your own thought processes.

As an initial aid to developing greater self-awareness it might be useful to do exercises in pairs. While one member of the pair is doing the exercise, the other member can observe what is being done (preferably, by taking notes) and speculate about the determinants of observed action. Those speculations can then be tested by direct specific questioning of the member doing the exercise: for instance, "Why did you open the end links?" rather than "Why did you do that?" The rationale for this suggestion is that initially it may be easier to examine another's behavior more objectively than your own, especially when examination is the sole task required. From the viewpoint of the member doing the exercise, questioning by an outside observer can help bring into awareness some aspects of the thinking process. More will be said about such dialogues in Chapter 3.

The next step up from regulation intrinsic to the task and unexpressed in consciousness is a level that was probably reflected in your performance on the problems of Box 1-1. At this level there is some awareness of the determinants of activity and of direction of them, especially when an attempt at solution fails and one tries to understand why. This may lead to a conjecture about the cause of failure and a hypothesis about improving the situation. That hypothesis is then tested and the initial conjecture is revised to encompass observed results. One is, in effect, evolving proto-theories, or theories in action, that develop through a process of trial-and-error accompanied by self-examination. The earmark of this level of self-regulation is that the theories produced are tied to the context of action and inspired by it: action precedes explanation and understanding rather than the reverse. Much of everyday behavior has this trial-and-error quality. One finds what works and sticks with it. Discrepancies, inconsistencies, and failures of habitual approaches or presuppositions often serve to instigate more careful scrutiny.

After mastery of a task in a particular context one may seek new challenges and try to generalize the presumed principle for success to new contexts and tasks. At that point the theory is formulated at the outset and serves to direct subsequent action. For example, in the first two or three problems of Box 1-1, your attention may have been focused on the specific problem, but in comparing them, you may have noted some structural similarity, for example, that in each problem some aspect of wording or material, if accepted uncritically, sent you down a blind alley. As a result of this insight, you may have developed a theory that some problems are difficult because they "set traps"—and approached the next problem with a deliberate search for a trap. If so, you were attaining a third level of self-regulation.

The distinguishing feature of the level of conscious regulation is that understanding precedes and directs action. At this level a newly encountered instance is identified as a likely member of a class of similar, previously encountered instances for which solution procedures are available: "Aha! It's one of those; I know how to deal with them!" (where "those" might refer to a trap-setting problem, determining valence or significance of difference between group means, or soothing hurt feelings). In knowing "how to deal with them" you invoke understanding, that is, a conscious identification of principles and the means for applying them that serve as the basis for a deliberate plan of attack on the new instance. That plan may well include not only a detailing of initial steps but, also, the anticipation of possible outcomes and means of dealing with each of them. To take an example close to home, in consulting an advisor about next year's schedule you don't go in "cold;" rather, you have some idea of your ultimate goal, the requirements remaining to be satisfied, the courses being offered, a tentative schedule, and some alternatives in the event that sections chosen may be closed. Such deliberate planning prior to action characterizes a thinker. Take it as your goal. An example of the levels of awareness is given in the first part of Box 1-2.

To augment your own understanding of levels of self-regulation and of self-awareness, examine some of your own skills (playing a musical instrument; programming a computer; or playing tennis, bridge, or chess) and identify the

BOX 1-2

An Example of Three Levels of Awareness and Instructions from an Expert on Self-regulation in Learning to Juggle

A. Understanding and Nasal Congestion

1. *Autonomous regulation.* You know how to blow your nose and do so when circumstances demand. It's no big deal, although it is a learned response unlike coughing or sneezing, which are automatic. All of these activities produce relief. Lingering longer in the shower, drinking lots of hot beverages and soups, or sleeping with more pillows are other means of producing relief from a stuffed-up head. The defining feature of all of them is that they are done without deliberate prior plan.

2. *Active regulation.* Discomfort inspires active experimentation. For example, if blowing one's nose produces a gurgling in the ear, a gentler blow focused upon one nostril at a time may be tried. Tickling and soreness in the throat lead to use of liquids and lozenges. Several varieties of each may be tried and compared to find which are most effective. Through this process of trial-and-error experimentation, one builds up a repertoire of palliatives for the particular cold and any future ones. You are aware of what works and doesn't as a result of experience.

3. *Conscious regulation.* A theory directs one's action. You plan your attack upon nasal congestion based upon a view of what is wrong and how it must be dealt with. The experienced discomfort is the result of one or both of two conditions: swollen, narrowed nasal passages; too much goo accumulating in those passages. Based upon that analysis there are two general lines of attack: (a) reduce the inflammation of nasal passages through the use of sprays, drops, or decongestants; and (b) promote drainage and reduction of the mucus. The latter goal is attained in a variety of mechanical means such as heat, steam, and other devices to promote flow or direct elimination through flushing with a saline solution, tilting the head, etc. There are also drugs that have some value. This level of understanding differs from the level of active regulation in that thinking precedes and determines action rather than vice versa.

Note that success, in the form of temporary relief, is attained at each level by exactly the same behavior. The difference lies in the determination of that behavior which shifts from involuntary to voluntary to deliberately planned and directed on the basis of understanding.

B. A Lesson in Juggling

Mr. Paul Cinquevalli, a pitch-and-toss champion

THE BEST WAY TO UNDERSTAND the essence of juggling is to learn to do it yourself. As in learning mathematics, the student of juggling starts from basic facts and skills and is led step by step to new and ever more complex permutations. Mastering these requires new perceptual skills, beyond the mere motor ability to catch and throw. To many a neophyte juggler, the balls seem to fall so quickly that catching them seems impossible. But with practice, the juggler learns to see the balls differently. Eventually, they actually look as if they were falling much more slowly.

Some adults, perhaps as many as five percent, can learn the three-ball cascade in minutes. Most people, however, acquire the basic idea with a little coaching and then need from one to sixty days of practice to achieve a reasonably stable pattern. The novice will be comforted to know that once learned, juggling, like bicycle riding, is almost impossible to forget.

Beware of spending too much time in one practice session. It is better to try for ten minutes on several different occasions than to frustrate yourself with a two-hour binge.

As for equipment, three lacrosse balls, tennis balls, or beanbags will do nicely.

STEP 1: ONE BALL

Practice throwing a ball from your right hand to your left and back again. The ball should be thrown higher than eye level but no higher than your arms can reach. Most people do best with a height just a bit above the tops of their heads. Try to make the ball follow the path of a figure eight lying on its side: you can do this by slightly "scooping" the ball before throwing it, and releasing it near the navel. Catch the ball at the side of your body, and then repeat the sequence of scoops, throws, and catches.

STEP 2: TWO BALLS

Put one ball in each hand. Throw the ball in the left hand as in Step 1, and then, just as the ball passes its high point, throw the right-hand ball. (Left-handed people should reverse this sequence and all succeeding steps.) The sequence of throws is thus left, then right, with a noticeable pause between throws. Two very common problems are not waiting long enough to release the second throw, and not throwing the balls to approximately equal heights.

At first it may be difficult to catch the balls. Don't worry. Try to focus instead on the accuracy of the throws and on their height. The catching skill will appear naturally as soon as the throws are on target. Keep the two throws in a plane parallel to your body. It is important to throw the second ball so that it passes the first with a bit of room to spare. If things seem hectic, try increasing the height of the throws.

STEP 3: TWO BALLS REVERSED

Next, reverse the order of throws so that the sequence is first right, then left. Throw the second ball as high as the first. Do not pass it directly across to the right hand. Do not throw the second, or left-hand, ball too soon.

STEP 4: THREE BALLS

Now put two balls in your right hand and one in your left. Try to complete Step 2 while simply holding the extra ball in your hand. Pause, and then go on to Step 3. The sequence should flow left, right, pause, right, left.

The third ball can make it difficult to catch the second throw. To solve this problem, throw the third ball before the second throw arrives (in fact, just after the second throw reaches its high point). The sequence is thus right, left, right. At first it may be difficult to persuade your right hand to make the second throw. Just concentrate on making the three throws; the catches are irrelevant at this point. Throw high, accurately, and *slowly*. It is important to make sure that your left-hand throws rise to the same height as your right-hand throws. Don't rush the tempo and don't forget the figure-eight pattern.

STEP 5: THREE BALLS REVERSED

Put two balls in your left hand, one in your right, and throw left, right, left.

STEP 6: FOUR THROWS

Starting with two balls in the right hand, throw right, left, right, left.

STEP 7: MORE AND MORE!

Continue in this way slowly to increase the number of throws you make. Concentrate on height and accuracy. If you find yourself moving forward to make the catches (and almost everyone does at the beginning), try harder not to throw the balls outward. Don't let your hands rise much above the level of your navel. Persist over a period of days and become a teacher yourself!

(After Buhler & Graham, 1984)

level at which you characteristically operate. Interview someone who is a "pro" at one of your skills to get a description of how he or she accomplishes some aspect of that skill (for example, you may ask, "How do you bid a hand with six low cards of one suit and only three cards, plus an ace in a second suit?"). Compare the expert's level of prior planning to your own. Studies comparing experts and novices typically report much more prior planning and deliberate regulation in terms of general principles on the part of experts (for example, see Chi, Glaser, & Rees, 1982). Expertise is not simply a matter of practiced skills; experts think differently from novices. Box 1-2 contains an expert's instructions on how to juggle. You should be able to develop some skill as a juggler by following them. Regardless of whether or not you follow the instructions, examine them from the standpoint of the level of self-regulation at which they are formulated. You can better appreciate it if you try to juggle through a trial-and-error process. Trial and error can lead to success, but understanding of the basis for success requires a higher degree of self-awareness and leads to a deeper level of skill.

Systematic Organization of Thinking. Meaningful thinking and understanding is organized with respect to a framework or set of principles. The quest for understanding is not simply collecting unrelated facts, but also relating them into an organized body of knowledge that provides the foundation for further enrichment of understanding. The quest for understanding requires tools with which to impose order upon experience and knowledge. Those tools may take the form of systematic procedures, models, theories, and general frameworks or other "conceptual machinery." The rules for juggling in Box 1-2 provide an example of systematic procedures for a limited task: juggling. The procedure for problem solving in Box 1-3 is an example of systematic procedures for a larger domain. Compare your procedure for solving the problems of Box 1-1 with that recommended in Box 1-3. Much of what you are learning in other courses consists of systematic procedures. It may be helpful to you to try to identify the procedures as such. First, however, you need greater familiarity with the concept.

In the course of your long career as a student you undoubtedly have developed systematic study habits, note taking procedures, and techniques for comprehending text. Describe one of your systematic study procedures in your notebook. Now that you have described it, consider your systematic procedure as a general tool and compare it with those of other class members or those prescribed in any of a number of good texts on improving study skills.[3] A good reader, for example, gains an overview of the material to be covered by scanning the heading and subheads of a chapter to identify the general content and its means of organization. While reading he or she monitors comprehension by identifying the main point of each section, summarizing it in his or her own words and relating it to previous material, anticipating future points, and searching for disconfirming instances to test assertions. If one of those self-administered tests reveals unsatisfactory comprehension, the appropriate passage is reviewed for clarification. If this procedure, or something similar to it, does not accurately describe your own reading practices, analyze how your practice differs and experiment with ways of making it more systematic.

The purpose of the preceding exercise was to heighten your initial understanding of what being a thinker requires. You may, at first, feel like the proverbial centipede who when asked to describe how it walked was rendered incapable of moving. Don't be discouraged. Understanding formulated at a higher level of self-regulation with respect to systematic procedures is a different kind of understanding than understanding at the level of successful execution of tasks. You may have learned many useful "short cuts" to success that served adequately, but attainment of success is not synonymous with understanding. The Tiger cartoon nicely illustrates the distinction between success and understanding. All this self-examination and explicit formulation of procedures may be very disconcerting at first as you replace old habits with new ones, but if you set yourself the goal of finding and using systematic procedures and organizing frameworks, you should find that it becomes more automatic. You should also find that it helps.

The Role of Knowledge.   This long section on the definition of thinking has been concerned exclusively with how one thinks without reference to what one thinks about. Obviously, there is no such thing as "pure thought"—function devoid of content. One has to think about something and, presumably, the more one knows in terms of available knowledge the more deeply one can think about it. Not only do experts think differently from novices, they also know more. I have no intention of downplaying the importance of knowledge; rather, I am suggesting that, to the extent that knowledge is not synonymous with understanding, knowledge alone is insufficient equipment for a thinker. Nor is one realm of knowledge more privileged than another as an avenue to thinking. Whatever your areas of interest, you can be a thinker with the knowledge available to you. Moreover, your skills as a thinker should assist you in future learning if you apply them consistently. Armed with a preliminary understanding of what thinking is we turn, now, to an examination of how it can be developed.

TIGER   By BUD LAKE

BOX 1-3

How to Solve It

Understanding the Problem

First.
You have to *understand* the problem.

What is the unknown? What are the data? What is the condition? Is it possible to satisfy the condition? Is the condition sufficient to determine the unknown? Or is it insufficient? Or redundant? Or contradictory?

Draw a figure. Introduce suitable notation.

Separate the various parts of the condition. Can you write them down?

Devising a Plan

Second.
Find the connection between the data and the unknown. You may be obliged to consider auxiliary problems if an immediate connection cannot be found. You should obtain eventually a plan of the solution.

Have you seen it before? Or have you seen the same problem in a slightly different form?

Do you know a related problem? Do you know a theorem that could be useful?

Look at the unknown! And try to think of a familiar problem having the same or a similar unknown.

Here is a problem related to yours and solved before. Could you use it? Could you use its result? Could you use its method? Should you introduce some auxiliary element in order to make its use possible?

Could you restate the problem? Could you restate it still differently?

TRAINING IN THINKING

The goal of training follows from the definition of thinking: (a) an enlarged repertoire of means for symbolic representation of knowledge, along with a greater facility in their use; (b) a deeper insight into one's own thought processes and a greater deliberate regulation of them; and (c) the acquisition of an arsenal of powerful systematic procedures for organizing and integrating knowledge in the pursuit of understanding. Practical means of attaining those goals, however, are by no means readily available; even likely routes toward their attainment are matters of dispute. It is possible to distinguish two theoretical approaches to the training of thinking which will be outlined below. One, which will be called a skills approach, focuses upon training in techniques for specific situations; the second, a styles approach, focuses upon changing the orientation of the individual who uses the skills. Each is relevant to at least one of the goals previously cited. Since the approaches are not incompatible, a combination of both would

Go back to definitions.

If you cannot solve the proposed problem try to solve first some related problem. Could you imagine a more accessible related problem? A more general problem? A more special problem? An analogous problem? Could you solve a part of the problem? Keep only a part of the condition, drop the other part; how far is the unknown then determined? how can it vary? Could you derive something useful from the data? Could you think of other data appropriate to determine the unknown? Could you change the unknown or the data, or both if necessary, so that the new unknown and the new data are nearer to each other? Did you use all the data? Did you use the whole condition? Have you taken into account all essential notions involved in the problem?

Carrying Out the Plan

Third.

Carry out your plan.

Carrying out your plan of the solution, *check each step.*

Can you see clearly that the step is correct? Can you prove that it is correct?

Looking Back

Fourth.

Examine the solution obtained.

Can you check the result? Can you check the argument?

Can you derive the result differently? Can you see it at a glance?

Can you use the result, or the method, for some other problem? (After Polya, 1957)

appear to be indicated. First, however, it is advisable to address a nagging doubt that may be troubling the reader: is thinking a trainable behavior?

Can Thinking Be Trained?   There is a popular tendency to equate thinking with intelligence and to assume that the former is a direct consequence of the latter. If that assumption were correct then raising intelligence should be the route to improving thinking. But, intelligence seems to have a large genetic component that is most obvious if one considers the extremes of the distribution: the severely retarded and the genius. One might argue they are born—not made. While there certainly is a kernel of truth in that position, it is too simplistic to accord with reality. The outstanding genius—a Mozart, a Gauss, an Einstein, or a Mill—gives early evidence of unusual ability in some domain which he or she continues to develop. How many equivalently gifted individuals failed to develop and attain prominence will never be known; possibly their number is large. Similarly, at the opposite extreme, there is no way of assessing how many persons were doomed to a limited existence by being inaccurately labeled as hopelessly subnormal. For the great bulk of humanity who fall between the two extremes, there is no question that education can and does make a profound difference in ultimate attainment. Thus, while native intelligence (whatever that may mean) may set an upper limit on the extent of possible advancement through training, there is still ample room for improvement between any present state and some theoretical upper limit.

Of greater relevance is the undisputed fact that much physical and intellectual growth takes place during the first 20 years of life. So long a period of maturation surely argues for plasticity. Moreover, given the many strands of development—for example, of language skills or reasoning ability, to cite but two aspects of cognitive development—and the as yet unknown relation among them, it would seem reasonable to assume that no two individuals are at the same stage of development with respect to all possible aspects of development. It would seem to follow, therefore, that no one training regimen is likely to work for all persons in exactly the same way. Rather, assuming (as most of us do) that training can be beneficial, what should be taught and how it should be taught might well be a function of the stage from which one starts and what strengths are already available upon which to build. Since the specifics of status will differ among individuals, you are advised to devote a page of your notebook to a personal assessment of your own strengths and weaknesses as a thinker.

To begin, consider the following: independence, initiative, self-expression, reasoning, judgment, self-awareness, self-confidence, self-discipline, talent, specific knowledge. Don't approach this assessment too globally, but consider specific things you do well ("I think on my feet," "I know when I don't know something and seek help") as well as areas that need improvement (identifying major points, drawing implications, disciplining yourself to tackle difficult tasks). This exercise is designed to make you aware of your specific needs. At the end of the semester it will serve as a basis for assessing your progress.

The Skills Approach. A *skill* is an organized pattern of behavior that is executed in a coherent fashion. There is an added implication that it is well executed, in part, as a result of practice. It is knowing how to do something. Most skills are acquired and subject to improvement through directed training. Some common examples of acquired skills include speaking a language, reading, riding a bicycle, playing a musical instrument, dealing with people, or operating a computer. Thinking may also be viewed as a skill that is, in principle, no different from other skills. Systematic organizing procedures, one of the defining characteristics of meaning-making, are best characterized as skills, as are procedures for symbolic representation. Even self-regulation may be considered a skill. Viewing the defining properties of thinking as skills has some very powerful implications: (a) they can be acquired, (b) they are acquired through training, (c) they are strengthened through practice, and (d) they are context related. The first three points are fairly obvious; the last may not be so obvious.

What I mean by context related is that there is a specificity to the skill: you learn how to ride a bicycle, play an instrument, or speak a language. While skills can differ in general applicability, it is nevertheless true that they are acquired in a particular context and are appropriately applied in specific situations. With respect to thinking skills, you can learn to solve arithmetic problems, like those algebra problems in Box 1-1. Polya's procedures for problem solving (Box 1-3) are directed toward all mathematical problems and could, conceivably, be applicable to real-life problems as well (for example, getting along with one's roommate or getting the computer program to run). Most of you have had the unsettling experience of studying for a test by reviewing each chapter along with the questions at the end and convincing yourself that you really know the material, only to discover on the exam that you cannot associate some question with the appropriate chapter and are hopelessly lost. You have the skill but can't apply it appropriately in a new context. The solution to that difficulty, of course, is to practice skills in a variety of contexts beyond those associated with the original learning. Another way of expressing the property of context relatedness is to note that skills involve specific knowledge that includes knowledge about their realm of applicability. The realm of applicability is less likely to be explicitly taught but is left for the learner to discover.

Most available texts on how to think[4] address themselves to skills for problem solving, increasing creativity, visual thinking, or more effective learning. They are worth consulting as supplements to the chapters in the second half of this book, which are addressed to those skills. Clearly, becoming a better thinker requires the acquisition of specific skills. Is there something more involved? Style approaches, by focusing upon characteristics of the thinker and his or her propensity for applying skills widely, suggest that there is.

The Styles Approach. A great many characterizations of *cognitive style* have been proposed. What they have in common is (a) an assumption that individuals differ in their accustomed orientation or general approach to cognitive tasks; (b) that features of style may be assessed and described in terms of relative standing along a continuum of variation; (c) that the individual's style is somewhat analogous to a personality trait in that it is a relatively stable characteristic persisting over time; and (d) that style affects substance, that is, performance on cognitive tasks. Sample items similar to those in existing cognitive style tests are given in Box 1-4. Do them and then compare your performance with that of other class members to get an appreciation of individual variation. (For help, see the notes.[5])

To score and interpret your own performance, start with B in Box 1-4. Trace the target figure on a piece of tracing paper and place it over the figure you outlined in the embedding context. Does it coincide? Did you find it readily, with difficulty, or not at all? How many instances of the target figure did you find? If you readily identified many instances of the target figure you have a field-independent style as contrasted to a field-dependent style. Presumably, you are

BOX 1-4

Some Style Test Items

A. Find the skater in the row below who is exactly like the skater to the left.

B. Find the simple form below in the complex figure to its right.

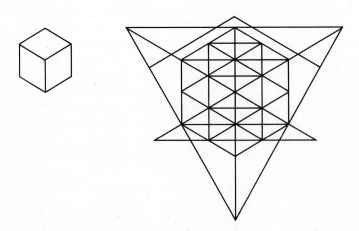

C. For each of the bottles pictured below imagine that it is half full of wine and closed tightly. Draw a line showing the fluid level. The first one has been completed as an example.

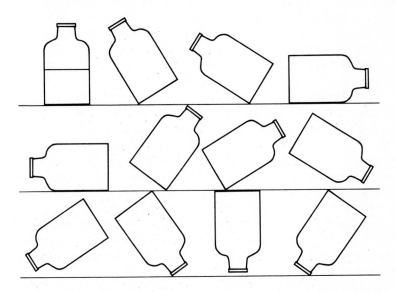

D. Answer yes or no to each of the items below:
   1. I find it difficult to handle questions requiring a comparison of different concepts.
   2. I have trouble making inferences.
   3. I have trouble organizing the information I remember.
   4. I find it difficult to handle questions requiring critical evaluation.
   5. I do well on essay tests.
   6. I look for reasons behind the facts.
   7. New concepts usually make me think of similar concepts.
   8. While studying, I attempt to find answers to questions I have in mind.
   9. I am usually able to design procedures for solving problems.
   10. After reading a unit of material I sit and think about it. (After Schmeck, Ribich, & Ramanaiah, 1977)

good at disembedding features from context and overcoming distraction or obfuscation. Quite possibly, you are more independent in forming opinions and conclusions. All of these field-independent qualities tend to be characteristic of good analytic thinkers. Because correlation does not imply causation, there is no guarantee that developing a field-independent style will lead to more effective thinking, but characteristics of a field-dependent style such as literalness and the inability to get beyond the immediate context are a shortcoming of many students. As a check on the consistency of this style consider your performance on C. How did you arrive at your answers? Did you imagine tilting a bottle or did you invoke a general principle? If you did each item separately and drew some tilted levels you are unduly influenced by context.

For the figure matching in A, trace the target and verify your match. Were you correct? How long did it take and how did you go about it? If you compared parts of each alternative with the corresponding part of the target to find a perfect match you were reflective (a style that promotes thinking); if you chose first and checked later, you were impulsive (a style not conducive to thinking). As a test of the generality of that characterization, do you, for example, weigh alternatives and seek relevant information before reaching a decision or do you act without prior reflection? The set of questions in D are part of a larger test of depth of processing and elaboration in individual learning processes. If you answered no to the first four questions and yes to the remaining six, you are assumed to have the learning style characteristic of good students: that is, you do not read superficially and deal with small units; rather, you analyze material, express it in your own words, and try to relate it to what you already know.

Some other dimensions of stylistic variation are listed below along with pertinent questions:

1. *Intellectual independence.* Do you assume that there is one right answer to every question that is known by some expert who should be consulted or do you try to find answers for yourself? Do you look for the justification of assertions or accept them?
2. *Responsibility.* Do you assume sole credit for your failures as well as successes or do you shift responsibility to another? Do you meet your commitments regardless of difficulty?
3. *Flexibility.* How are you at (a) compromising to settle disagreements, (b) appreciating an opponent's point of view, (c) generating alternatives, or (d) deciding what is right and wrong?
4. *Tolerance of ambiguity.* Can you accept uncertainty or the possibility that no ideal solution may exist? Do you believe that in disagreements each side may be partially correct? Can you withhold judgment until all the relevant evidence is available?

Now that you know where you stand on these brief style assessments, what can be done about it? To the extent that your cognitive style, like a personality trait, is not readily modifiable, you may have to learn to live with it. Certainly, simple exhortation to change is of no value, as you doubtless have discovered in trying to break even trivial bad habits like nail biting. On the other hand, people do change. Certainly, developmental evidence shows that children become more reflective, more independent, and more responsible as they become older. Much of this learning results from emulation of good examples. There is hope for becoming a more thoughtful person. At the very least, it is useful to assess your current status to identify weaknesses and capitalize on strengths. It is also helpful to discuss your assignments and experiences with other members of the group for reassurance that your difficulties are not unique and to become aware of other possible styles.

Becoming a thoughtful person has much in common with becoming a more mature person. As a young adult, you should be aware that you have more to learn and that the growth process never really ends. This book attempts to help you perfect useful skills, but its final value will be a function of the extent to which you take charge of your own education. You will have to do the assignments, to make them meaningful for you, and to stay abreast in a disciplined manner. Only you can develop for yourself a directing style that will enable you to continue your own education as a thinker beyond the limits of this course or of your formal education. That requires viewing yourself as a thinker, committing yourself to becoming more reflective, more self-aware and more systematic, and assuming the responsibility of directing your efforts toward those goals. Thinking is more than a collection of very useful skills; it is a way of life.

SUMMARY

This is probably the most difficult chapter in the entire book. It attempts to provide a framework for all that is to follow. To the extent that subsequent chapters fill in the framework, you will find it helpful to reread this chapter at the end of the first part, and again, at the end of the book. That review should help to integrate your own understanding of what thinking is all about.

Thinking was defined as a *symbolic activity* whose goal is understanding. The definition was amplified by identification of the defining properties of thought: (a) representation of experience through the symbolic media of ideas, images, words, implicit motor activity, or notational devices, such as numbers and diagrams, and operation upon those representations, and (b) the endowing of experience as represented with meaning. The process of *meaning-making* was further analyzed into two interrelated components: deliberate self-regulation and application of systematic organizing procedures. It was additionally noted that specific content knowledge is a necessary, but not sufficient, ingredient of thinking.

Having defined thought and, in so doing, specified the goals of the enterprise, attention was turned to the practical question of attaining those goals. After presenting some justification of the view that one can learn to be a better thinker, two approaches to attaining the goals were presented: a *skills approach* and a *styles approach.* The skills approach focuses upon the requisite skills and relevant knowledge to be employed. They certainly constitute all systematic organizing procedures as well as symbolic representation. The styles approach focuses upon the characteristics of the thinker and the personal orientations that motivate and maintain thought. The first approach is directed at describing or creating a skilled practitioner, the second at describing or creating a thoughtful person who seeks understanding. Both are relevant.

EXERCISES

1. Why must it be true that understanding is a personal construction?
2. How do you decide in the morning what you will wear that day? Make your answer relevant to issues raised in the text, that is, level of abstraction of representation, degree of awareness, and systematizing of the procedure. Could you write a computer program for the process? Do the same exercise for a different decision task such as scheduling daily activities. Do you have a general decision system or is it specific to the type of decision being made? (I once had a student whose notebook contained procedures for finding something edible among the dining hall selections, crossing a dangerous intersection, and a variety of other everyday tasks. They were amusing, but they also reflected her orderly and systematic approach to all endeavors.)
3. Identify some of your acquaintances who might be classified as clear thinkers, average thinkers, and fuzzy thinkers. Take one member of each category and describe examples of his or her thinking that served as the basis of your classification. Compare your list of defining properties for each category with the lists of other class members and revise your own list accordingly. This is an exercise you might want to return to during the course of the semester. You might also consider the extent to which you could emulate the clear thinkers.
4. Describe the kind of thinker you would ultimately like to be (i.e., the model you set as your goal). This is another exercise you might want to return to throughout the semester.
5. On the basis of your own experience can you distill some recommendations for training thinkers? As a help in getting started, you might want to recall some experiences that changed your way of thinking or led to new insights and consider why they had that effect.
6. For each of the following vignettes, diagnose the source of poor thinking. (For help, see the notes.[6])
   (a) On a visit to a friend in Chicago a man was asked the riddle: "It isn't my sister, it isn't my brother, and yet it's a child of my father and mother. Who is it?" After some consideration he gave up, asked for the answer, and was told, "It's me!". He was so enchanted with the riddle that on return home he gave it to his wife. She also gave up and asked for the answer which he told her was, "It's my friend in Chicago."

(b) The same gentleman in the preceding example, while in Chicago, discovered that he had left home without his slippers. He wrote to his wife to ask her to send them as follows: "Please send me your slippers." Since what he really wanted was *his* slippers what could his reasoning have been in sending such a message?

(c) While visiting in Chicago the man went swimming in Lake Michigan and almost drowned before being rescued. On being helped from the water he took an oath, "I swear never to go into the water again until I learn how to swim."

(d) Our hero asked a wise friend why buttered toast always falls buttered side down. The friend then conducted an experiment: he dropped a slice of buttered toast that landed buttered side up. He claimed to have disproved the hypothesis. "Not so," our hero replied, "You buttered the wrong side."

(e) The same two men later disputed the question from which end a human being grows. Our hero contended that growth proceeds from the feet up. As proof he offered the observation that some years ago he bought a pair of pants so long that they trailed on the ground but today they no longer did so. His friend countered with the following observation. "Yesterday I watched a parade and all the marchers had their feet on the ground; they differed in size only at the head end." (These vignettes are modified with permission of the publisher from counterparts in Ausuble, N. [1948]. *A treasury of Jewish folklore*. New York: Crown.)

7. At this stage of your career as a thinker you might want to anticipate evaluating at the end of the semester what you learned from this course. Design an experiment and begin collecting measures with which to evaluate your progress.

8. Whimbey and Lochhead (1982) suggest a very helpful technique for becoming more aware of one's own thought processes, refining them, and eliminating error. That procedure is to think aloud to a critical listener. You might try it with a friend, for example, on the problems below, where you take turns serving as solver or listener. Here are the problems; a sample dialogue is given for the first.

(a) There are three schools in town (A, B, C) located in the north, west, or central part of town (but not necessarily in that order). There are three boys, George, Tom, Herb, each of whom goes to a different school. Given the information below, determine who goes where:

> Tom lives in the north.
> Herb does not go to school B.
> George goes to school A in the central part of town.

Thinker: I need a way of systematically organizing the information.
Listener: What information?
Thinker: That there are three boys, three schools, and three parts of town. The solution will take the form of three triplets where each is a unique combination of boy, school, and part of town.

Listener: That is a good way of stating the problem.

Thinker: One triplet is supplied, George:A:Central. That leaves me with the possibilities Tom:B:West, Tom:B:North, Herb:B:West, Herb:B:North, Tom:C:West, Tom:C:North, Herb:C:West, Herb:C:North. But I'm told that Herb doesn't go to B so he must go to C. That means Tom goes to B. And, since Tom lives in the north, school B must be north. That leaves me with school C in the west, and I know that Herb goes to C.

LOCATION

		N	C	W
S **C** **H** **O** **O** **L**	A		George	
	B	Tom		
	C			Herb

Listener: Is that the only possible solution?

Thinker: Well, I know that since George goes to A and Herb does not go to B he must go to C leaving B for Tom. Since Tom lives in the north it is reasonable that that is where his school is located. Without that assumption there cannot be a unique solution.

(b) Mary, Jean, and Amy differ in age. One is a teacher, one is a florist, and one is a plumber. Mary is older than Amy but younger than Jean. The teacher is the oldest and the plumber is the youngest. What does each woman do? (For help, see the notes.[7])

(c) If the second letter in the word "west" comes after the fourth letter in the alphabet write yes; if it does not, write no.

(d) Complete the pattern below and generate a different problem with the same solution rule (see Note 7 for the answer):

27 24 22 19 17 14 12 9 __ __ __

9. This exercise concerns the assertion that behavior organized at the level of deliberate self-regulation differs qualitatively from behavior organized at a less conscious level.

(a) Compare your present understanding of the relation among the basic arithmetic processes of addition, subtraction, multiplication, and division to your understanding in the fourth grade.

(b) Does explicit evaluation of how and why you love another person change the nature of the relationship?

· *2* ·

Getting the Information In: Attending and Encoding In the Creation of Meaning

A little boy who had been working on a geography assignment rushed to his father in tears. According to the *Atlas* the area of the state of Massachusetts is 25,000 miles. But, he also knew that the diameter of the earth at the equator is 25,000 miles. How could a small part of the earth like the state of Massachusetts be as large as the whole earth at its widest part? Could the *Atlas* lie? Like any good thinker, the child was trying to organize his knowledge into a meaningful framework that led to an apparent paradox because he failed to note an important detail—area is measured in square miles. He treated area measurement units as equivalent to a linear measure applied to circumference. Such failures of attention, or inappropriate representation of information, are among the major sources of error in problem solving, and of ineffective thinking in general. The purpose of this chapter is to make you more aware of how you gather and represent information in order to assist you in refining these processes. Although it is somewhat arbitrary to differentiate the initial registering of information from its expression, I shall first discuss paying attention; next, I will show how the form in which information is expressed affects the understanding of it; and, finally, I will offer some suggestions about encoding information for several general purposes. You should note that encoding clearly qualifies as thinking because it involves a transformation of information for the purpose of capturing meaning.

PAYING ATTENTION

Although attending does not, in itself, constitute thinking, it is an important prerequisite. It can provide both a source for questions and a direction for answers. It is also central to awareness of thought processes. All organisms attend to what is of importance to them, such as the availability of food or the threat of danger. They are intrinsically attuned to some environmental features; for example, amphibia are sensitive to motion, ants to chemical traces, and nocturnal creatures to sound. Human beings attend not only to perceptual input but also to the ideas generated as we impose meaning relative to our background of experience. The trained biologist, psychologist, or artist, for example, is sensitive to nuances that might escape an untrained person. People seek training even in such direct pleasures as wine tasting in order to enhance their appreciation. In wine tasting one does not focus solely on color, aroma, or flavor. One also labels the attended features in words or other symbolic forms in order to compare the present experience with prior experiences. These critical observations lead quite naturally to classifying patterns and organizing observed regularities toward explicit understanding of what makes a "fine" wine. At that level thinking is clearly involved.

The work of any good writer provides abundant examples of acute observation. Notice how the author creates the scene, or the character, using phrases that capture its uniqueness and suggesting other related features. The good actor, similarly, creates a character through the use of expressions and gestures that convey not only the general mood but also the unique expressions of a particular individual. To appreciate the nature of this skill pretend that you are an actor or a writer. Evoke some familiar scene or person for an audience which is capable of identifying the subject of your portrayal. Their recognition—or failure—will provide a test of the adequacy of your portrayal.

If you take that experiment seriously you will probably find that you are making new discoveries. To strengthen your newfound role as acute observer, systematically scrutinize, over the next few days, familiar people and places for some feature that you had previously failed to notice—a person's smile, characteristic vocal inflection, preferred topic of conversation, or gait. When visiting places, note the number and kind of trees, signs of animal habitation, plant life, or bits of ornamentation. You doubtless will discover many features of your world to which you had been oblivious as, for instance, a discovery you may have made about tilted vessels in the first chapter.

Having become a more acute observer of your physical and interpersonal world should have inspired you to apply your skills to your intellectual world as well. As you read assignments in this and other courses note not only the ideas expressed but also how they are conveyed. Express the same ideas in different ways, not only by putting them into different words but also by changing the medium as, for example, replacing a verbal description with a diagram. Note the effect of these variations upon your understanding of the idea. This exercise is your introduction to the subject of encoding.

ENCODING

The term *encoding* is used to describe the process of representing experience or knowledge in symbolic form through the medium of words, pictures, gestures, mental images, and so on. Several features of the process of encoding should be noted. First, the term refers to a process rather than to the product of that process. The details of the process vary greatly because each individual engages in the process for his or her own purposes in his or her own way. The purpose of the process, on the other hand, is the same for all individuals, that is, to promote meaning. Finally, although encoding takes place early in the processing of information, it is not a primitive process nor is its role confined to early processing. Rather, it is a necessary component at all levels of knowledge and meaning.

The nature of the encoding process varies with the level of abstraction at which it operates. At the lowest level of dealing with specific objects and events, encoding usually takes the form of applying a name or a label to an experience by way of identification. Even the simplest act of labeling, however, implies a prior process of classification. Classification, in turn, may take place at a variety of levels of abstraction as one constructs classes of classes or shifts the basis of classification. These fundamental processes will be discussed in the next section on foundations of encoding.

The end product of the encoding process is a symbolic carrier of meaning that might be called a representation or a code. None of these terms does full justice to the rich variety of encoding products. They include not only individual symbols, signs, and words but also language itself as well as numbers, gestures, pictorial depictions, art, music, and literature. As should be clear from the examples cited, although encoding refers to the action of an individual, the resulting products often are socially shared and utilize socially shared codes. That observation suggests that particular carriers of meaning vary with respect to effectiveness in fulfilling their intended role, and that their associated meaning may undergo change over time and usage. Those observations are, in fact, correct as will be seen in a review of some examples from a variety of disciplines. The concluding portion of the chapter will offer advice on effective encoding.

FOUNDATIONS OF ENCODING

Although actual events or objects provide the occasion and instigation for encoding, the process of encoding transforms events or objects into concepts or ideas. How adequately the encoding conveys meaning is a function of the particular property of the concept emphasized and whether it is a defining feature or an irrelevant one. To provide a more systematic framework for suggestions about effective encoding, it is first useful to consider in more detail the general processes that underlie analysis of meaning. Toward that end, the processes of *naming, defining, classification,* and *hierarchical classification* will be considered.

Naming. "What's in a name?" asked Romeo. In that celebrated passage he notes that there is a certain arbitrariness in the assignment of names. Several "naming" devices are employed in our society to refer to a unique individual. Each of us has a surname, Smith, Ramos, Bauer, that designates family, and a given name, George, Mary, Esmeralda, Oscar, that designates specificity within the family. To the school's computer you are a student number; to the government, a social security number. Although all those names may be equivalent with respect to denotation (that is, identifying a particular individual in a population), they differ with respect to connotation. Many people consider it dehumanizing to be identified by a number and prefer a name. Use of the first name for that purpose normally connotes closeness or intimacy, but it can also connote an inferior status, for example children, servants, and patients are rarely addressed as Mr. or Ms.

Outside the realm of proper names descriptive adjectives produce different perceptions of the person or object being described. A child who is born out of wedlock, an illegitimate child in legal terms, may be called a "bastard" or a "love child." The former has negative connotations whereas the latter does not. You can think of many other examples to demonstrate that synonyms rarely, if ever, are equivalent in connotation: persons over 65 may be "old people," "senior citizens," or "golden agers;" persons of lower IQ may be "retardates," "exceptional children," or "developmentally delayed;" an instrument of massive destruction may be called a "peace keeper" to make it more acceptable; and old clothes fetch a higher price as "period costumes" than as "rags." However, try as one may to change the evaluation of a particular defining property, such as age or low IQ, there is no escaping its centrality. Thus, although a name *per se* may be relatively arbitrary within a language community, the conditions governing its usage are lawful.

Definitions.   A definition specifies the conditions under which a term is used appropriately. Although dictionary definitions commonly provide synonyms, somewhat equivalent terms at the same level of generality, definition as a general process always implies classification. By that I mean that any adequate definition must (a) place the term being defined (the definiendum) in the context of a superordinate class of which it is a member, and (b) differentiate it from other members of that class through specification of its distinguishing features (defining features or definiens). The word "dog," for instance, refers to a class of carnivorous mammals differing from other carnivorous mammals, such as cats, in characteristic features of physical structure and behavior (for example, barking). Dogs differ from each other with respect to a variety of features such as size, color, and disposition that are relevant when further differentiation within the class is desired.

To the extent that most concepts are characterized by a number of correlated characteristics, a common failing of working definitions lies in the selection of a salient, but irrelevant, characteristic. For instance, if you use mode of locomotion as a defining characteristic, as in defining birds as flying creatures, then flightless birds, such as ostriches or penguins, are improperly excluded and flying animals, such as bats or flying squirrels, are inappropriately included in the definition. Identification of an appropriate defining property is, in other words, sometimes a difficult task that illustrates the relation of a definition to the more basic process of classification. To become better acquainted with the nature of the difficulty in identifying defining features try defining the word "hassle" as a class exercise. Is it a verb or a noun? What differentiates the word "hassle" from the word "inconvenience?"

Classification.   Classification consists of grouping things together on the basis of some shared similarity. Everyone engages in the process of classifying from a very early age, for instance, edible things, throwable things, likable things, and so on. For purely personal classifications, such as "things that drive me up the wall," the classification rule need never be clearly formulated. You might, however, consider some of your own personal categories from the standpoint of identifying their defining property. Where a classification system is socially shared, on the other hand, variation among members of the group in identifying the classification rule can lead to confusion. Some lovely examples of this may be found in the young child's first words. At first the child may select some characteristic but irrelevant property such as where things are encountered before a more appropriate invariant feature is identified. For example, "tomato" may refer to juiciness rather than to the particular food having that property.

In the history of most sciences, the development of classification systems is a central enterprise. In this context they are often called taxonomies. Moreover, the basis of classification schemes may change as a result of technical or theoretical advances and the revised taxonomies themselves then provide a basis for additional advances. Before considering some scientific classification schemes, it is important to note an additional feature inherent in the process of classification that does not normally arise in definition—the existence of a continuum with respect to level of analysis. The continuum can go from general to specific or from concrete to abstract or molar, that is, defined by overall structure, to molecular, defined by the smallest independent elements. Classification as a process can proceed at many levels. One can sort pencils by color or sharpness. One can also form classes of classes in a procedure of hierarchical classification, a definition of which follows.

Hierarchical Classification.   Hierarchical classifications simultaneously order instances with respect to several levels of generality by forming classes of classes on the basis of several classification rules, each appropriate to a particular level of analysis. Ideally, each known instance, as well as possible novel instances to be encountered in the future, are uniquely located in the hierarchy. Several hierarchical classification systems will be discussed by way of example. For some, such as the Library of Congress classification for books, the ordering principle is an arbitrary convention; for others, it is based upon basic knowledge within the discipline. The periodic table of the elements is an example of such a classification.

The Library of Congress classification system assigns two letters referring to the broad area and to the subset within it—R for medicine, RC for internal medicine, RD for surgery, RS for drugs, and so on, followed by digits that further delimit the subset. The specific volume within the delimited subset is indicated by a letter, the first letter of the author's name, followed by digits and a date. This system encompasses the thousands of works already published as well as volumes yet to appear.

The biological classification system for animals, which was devised to correspond to order of appearance in evolution, utilizes defining properties that are more or less clear. Phyla, the most general differentiation, based upon the presence or absence of a notochord at some stage of development, are divided into classes based upon characteristics of reproduction, locomotion, and so on. Classes, in turn, are divided into orders which are classified into families. Families are further differentiated with respect to genus. At any given level, (for example, order), the members at that level all share the defining properties of the higher levels of class and phylum to which they belong, but differ with respect to the defining properties of lower levels, family, and genus. Box 2-1 provides an illustration.

Mendeleev's formulation of a periodic table of the elements was an important event in the history of chemistry.[1] It was a classification based not upon compounds, such as water, but upon their constituent elements, such as hydrogen and oxygen. Recent modification of the periodic table utilizes a more molecular classification principle. Each element is indexed by a subscript, its atomic number, which designates the number of protons in the nucleus, and a superscript, its mass number, which designates the number of protons and neutrons in the atomic nucleus. Carbon, for example, is written $_6C^{12}$; it has 6 protons (its atomic number) and 6 neutrons (for a mass number of $6 + 6 = 12$). Isotopes of an element have the same atomic number but differ with respect to mass number. For example, hydrogen appears in three forms: $_1H^1$, $_1H^2$ (deuterium), and $_1H^3$ (tritium). Defining properties have been identified by the classification system; this is evidenced by the fact that all elements sharing the same atomic number form the same compound with another element. Hydrogen, in whatever form, and oxygen form the compound water. Water formed by compounding with isotopes, such as heavy water of which deuterium is a constituent, are less stable. Moreover, the classification system has been successfully used to predict the existence of heretofore unknown elements and to describe the properties of those predicted elements.

What you should have learned from this section is that in the process of encoding one attends to many features of the event or object in question. The selection of defining features promotes understanding and the organization of knowledge.

CARRIERS OF MEANING: THEIR CREATION AND EFFECT

If asked to describe in one word what poets, composers, sculptors, choreographers, and playwrights do, your answer probably would be, "Create." It is unlikely that you would characterize the process of creation in which they engage as a process of encoding, but I would like to suggest that such is the case. It satisfies the definition of encoding in that the artist is transforming experience and conveying meaning symbolically through his or her particular medium. Classification and definition are important components of the process. It is, like all encoding, an individual process although the outcome of the process is a socially circulated product. The resultant work of art, to the extent that it successfully conveys the artist's intended meaning, expands the understanding of its viewer, listener, or reader. The same assertion applies to the work of scientists; the theories and taxonomies they create may properly be viewed as the end products of an encoding process. The symbolic representation of meaning by the successful artist or scientist is incorporated into the symbolic repertoire of the larger society, serving as an element in or stimulus for future encodings by others. Unfortunately, not all the current symbolic carriers of meaning are successful. Some serve to augment understanding while others serve to diminish it. In this section I shall try to show that the effect of a carrier of meaning is determined by the nature of the features selected for emphasis in the process of encoding.

Art as Encoding.   Box 2-2 contains some haiku[2] (a Japanese verse form of 17 syllables) and drawings of sumo wrestlers by Hokusai. The Japanese art forms illustrated follow very demanding conventions. Their effect is to convey an impression with a great economy of means, leaving a great deal of information to be filled in by one's imagination. The effect is attained by paring away contextual detail and emphasizing the defining features.

The painting, *Nude Descending a Staircase,* by Marcel Duchamp in Box 2-3 may not look like any nude you have ever seen before, but note the artist's intent. Duchamp set out not to portray a particular individual engaged in a particular activity but to convey a generic body in motion. It is totally appropriate, therefore, to omit all individualizing features, adornment, or, even, evidence as to the sex of the individual in focusing upon the interplay of planes, surfaces, and volumes in the course of movement. How successfully Duchamp attained his goal in a two-dimensional rendering should be evident from comparing the painting to the photographic sequence by Muybridge in the same box. Another means of rendering motion graphically was explored by Johansson (1974) who photographed a person moving in a dark room with small lights at the knee, ankle, elbow and other joints. That Johansson has correctly identified the most informative elements of motion is shown by the finding that observers of the resulting film can immediately and accurately identify the action on the basis of this minimal information.

To further your own understanding of the artist's purpose and the means of its attainment, look at some other examples of modern art[3] and compare your chosen examples with works from earlier periods in the history of art, for example, Impressionism, Renaissance, Baroque, or Primitive art. You will find obvious differences in the preferred subject matter along with some recurring themes. In fact, reworking the material of another artist is a favorite device of some artists

---

BOX 2-1

Biological Classifications

Red Maple (*Acer rubrum*)

CATEGORY	TAXON	CHARACTERISTICS
Kingdom	Plantae	Multicellular terrestrial organisms that have chlorophylls *a* and *b* contained in chloroplasts, have rigid cell walls, and show structural differentiation
Division	Anthophyta	Vascular plants with seeds and flowers; ovules enclosed in an ovary; the angiosperms
Class	Dicotyledones	Embryo with two seed leaves (cotyledons)
Order	Sapindales	Soapberry order; usually woody plants
Family	Aceraceae	Maple family, characterized by watery, sugary sap; opposite leaves; winged fruit; chiefly trees of temperate regions
Genus	*Acer*	Maples and box elder
Species	*Acer rubrum*	Red maple

(see variations on the Laocoön theme in Box 12-5). You will also find differences in the artistic conventions used to convey the themes. Many modern paintings, for example, use broad washes of bright color rather than subtle shadings. How does color choice enhance the impact of the information conveyed? For additional insights on graphic encoding, see McKim (1972).

In this classification scheme, each lower level subgroup shares the properties of the higher levels. You might generate some additional branches of the classification tree to augment your understanding of it. (After Curtis, 1983)

Human (*Homo sapiens*)

CATEGORY	TAXON	CHARACTERISTICS
Kingdom	Animalia	Multicellular organisms requiring complex organic substances for food
Phylum	Chordata	Animals with notochord, dorsal hollow nerve cord, gill pouches in pharynx at some stage of life cycle
Subphylum	Vertebrata	Spinal cord enclosed in a vertebral column, body basically segmented, skull enclosing brain
Superclass	Tetrapoda	Land vertebrates, four-limbed
Class	Mammalia	Young nourished by milk glands, skin with hair or fur, body cavity divided by a muscular diaphragm, red blood cells without nuclei, three ear bones (ossicles), high body temperature
Order	Primates	Tree dwellers or their descendants, usually with fingers and flat nails, sense of smell reduced
Family	Hominidae	Flat face; eyes forward; color vision; upright, bipedal locomotion
Genus	*Homo*	Large brain, speech, long childhood
Species	*Homo sapiens*	Prominent chin, high forehead, sparse body hair

Two poems are included in Box 2-4 as additional illustrations of encoding in another artistic medium. Most poems should be read aloud because the sound of the words is often as important as their meaning in conveying the intended effect. There are many poetic devices, among them onomatopeia (use of words whose sound suggests the meaning), personification (ascribing human

---

BOX 2-2

A. Five Japanese Haiku

"Silence"

On the tongue
    of the temple bell
        a butterfly sleeps
            —Buson

Abandoned by a wintry stream
    a dog's
        dead body
            —Shiki

The whole long day
    he sang, and is unsated still—
        the skylark
            —Basho

Did it yell
    till it became all voice?
        Cicada shell!
            —Basho

On a withered branch
    a crow roosts:
        autumn nightfall
            —Basho

The haiku is a 17 syllable Japanese verse form. It is difficult to translate into English as should be apparent from comparing translations of the classics given above. The first has been titled; the rest are left for you to title as an exercise in encoding the mood or impression expressed. (After Henderson, 1958)

B. Drawings of Sumo Wrestlers by Hokusai

---

characteristics to a thing or abstraction), metaphor (suggested likeness through use of a term usually used in another descriptive context), and allegory (use of symbolic figures and actions to convey moral truths). The selections in Box 2-4 illustrate some of these devices. Read them to determine which devices are used and how. Note how Frost conveys futility and waste without explicitly introducing

BOX 2-3

A. Marcel Duchamp, *Nude Descending a Staircase, No. 2.* 1912

(The Philadelphia Museum of Art, Arensberg Collection.)

B. Muybridge, *Woman Walking Downstairs*

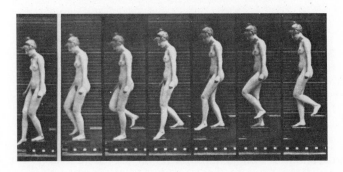

BOX 2-4

Two Poems

What is the author's purpose in each and what devices are used to achieve that purpose?

A. Driving Through Kansas

From yesterday to tomorrow.
Grain waving in the wind
Bending from ground hardened by sun
Mimics the ancient seas beneath the sod.
Congealed in muds that freeze and protect
Ancient forms swim in that ocean.
Ooze along successive floors.
Stretch original fingers.
Grand Canyon's depth does not exhaust that sea
Nor reflect one sunbeam off a wave
Rippling over the surface.
I turn to you and smile
Bending to hear what you say.
The covered ocean locked from sight
But frozen in those depths wait fossils
Which will not be eroded by any weather.
The geologist's hammer may split the layered rock
Exposing a perfect replica.
'Trilobite' he will say
Or 'Outrage.'
        Patricia Fillingham
(After Fillingham, 1983)

B. The Woodpile

Out walking in the frozen swamp one grey day,
I paused and said, 'I will turn back from here.
No, I will go on farther—and we shall see.'
The hard snow held me, save where now and then

---

those words, and how Fillingham similarly invites consideration of suppressed anger by her description of buried geologic features. Once again, instead of a literal depiction, the defining elements have been distilled and emphasized to convey meaning indirectly.

One foot went through. The view was all in lines
Straight up and down of tall slim trees
Too much alike to mark or name a place by
So as to say for certain I was here
Or somewhere else: I was just far from home.
A small bird flew before me. He was careful
to put a tree between us when he lighted,
And say no word to tell me who he was
Who was so foolish as to think what *he* thought.
He thought that I was after him for a feather—
The white one in his tail; like one who takes
Everything said as personal to himself.
One flight out sideways would have undeceived him.
And then there was a pile of wood for which
I forgot him and let his little fear
Carry him off the way I might have gone,
Without so much as wishing him good-night.
He went behind it to make his last stand.
It was a cord of maple, cut and split
And piled—and measured, four by four by eight.
And not another like it could I see.
No runner tracks in this year's snow looped near it.
And it was older sure than this year's cutting,
Or even last year's or the year's before.
The wood was grey and the bark warping off it
And the pile somewhat sunken. Clematis
Had wound strings round and round it like a bundle.
What held it though on one side was a tree
Still growing, and on one a stake and prop,
These latter about to fall. I thought that only
Someone who lived in turning to fresh tasks
Could so forget his handiwork on which
He spent himself, the labour of his axe,
And leave it there far from a useful fireplace
To warm the frozen swamp as best it could
With the slow smokeless burning of decay.
                    Robert Frost
(After Lathem, 1969)

Music provides many examples of encoding evocatively, albeit one not amenable to inclusion in a book. Programmatic music conveys ideas through "sound
pictures." Some lively examples are Saint-Saens's *Carnival of the Animals,* Pro-
kofiev's *Peter and the Wolf,* Tchaikovsky's *1812 Overture,* and, at a more abstract

level, Vivaldi's *The Four Seasons*. Popular songs provide simple and relatively transparent examples of musical devices. The love song, for instance, goes back into history but modern love songs differ from earlier ones in theme, tempo, beat, and typical accompaniment. Listen to some love ballads from medieval, Renaissance, or eighteenth, nineteenth, and early-to-late twentieth century music to sample some of these differences and the changing attitudes toward love reflected. As a final exercise consider how music, with its less literal elements presented sequentially through time, may be more appropriate for conveying some aspects of meaning whereas the visual arts, where elements are simultaneously present and distributed in space, are more appropriate for others.

Encoding in Science.   The artist conveys meaning by distilling the essential, defining features of the intended meaning and expressing them in an aesthetic manner. The work of the scientist has much in common with that of the artist. Both are concerned with conveying knowledge and meaning. Both do a great deal of analysis and classification to identify the basic feature defining meaning. Both create new carriers of meaning to convey their discoveries. However, where the artist may wish to invoke associated impressions, the scientist strives to convey information with maximal precision and economy. Let's consider some of the characteristic devices of science for this purpose.

Quantification is the preferred means of representing data. Wherever possible, phenomena are measured and recorded on the appropriate scale to promote both precision and objectivity. The creation of scales will be discussed in Chapter 5 and the treatment of measures will be discussed in Chapter 6. As a preliminary exercise in precision you might try to describe an object, event, or person in a variety of ways for identification by someone else. Note how much more effective it is to provide information about size, weight, and location in measurable terms rather than in verbal descriptions. As another example, if you recently have had a physical exam you are aware that the status of your health is expressed in a set of numbers for weight, pulse, and blood pressure and in the tracing of functions as shown in an EKG. Find additional examples of quantification.

Another basic task of science is the use of schematics to summarize relations among elements in order to describe structure or organization. Schematics have in common the property of abstraction, which is the removing of nonessential detail to focus upon defining properties and basic ingredients. Models and diagrams are familiar examples. Instances of models include maps of all kinds, structural depictions of the DNA molecule or of the atomic structure of chemical elements and compounds, planetarium reconstructions of planets and galaxies, or more purely conceptual representations such as the sets of equations defining an econometric model. You should be able to expand the list. Commonly encountered diagrams include wiring diagrams, blueprints, flow charts, tree diagrams of classification schemes and other hierarchies, and summary tables. These schematic devices also play an important role in the construction of theory.

One example is Darwin's use of an irregularly branching tree as a schematic to provide a solution to the thorny problem of establishing continuity among the various species, such as man and ape—through time some of the branches may have disappeared (see Gruber, 1981). Yet another example is the search for a periodic table of the elements relating their properties to their structure. Box 2-5 contains two structural diagrams, one a model of information transmission, the second a model for a theory of the structure of human memory. Examine them for an understanding of the processes portrayed. Note how the schematic representation leads you to focus upon basic ingredients and to raise questions about them and the relations among them. Ask yourself, "What is noise? Could it arise at input? If so, how would that affect attempts to filter out noise?" The subject of organizing models and their role will be discussed again in Chapter 8. We turn now to a consideration of some forms of encoding that do not promote understanding.

Clichés, Conventions, Propaganda, and Advertising. When sensory information is encoded it is transformed into a symbolic mode. Symbols, whose meaning is shared or conventionalized among a particular group, are called *signs*. The international sign code (for example, cigarette with a red diagonal through it for "No smoking") provides some especially clear examples. Words are signs, too, but they constitute rather tricky examples in that their meaning often undergoes change over time due to individual development or cultural changes. As an example of personal change, consider the enrichment of meaning that has probably already occurred in your understanding of such words as "love," "honor," "justice" and a host of other abstract nouns. Many words continue to change in meaning or to lose meaning through overuse. Examples of cultural change in meaning are abundantly available in the instances of slang terms. Consider, for instance, the word "hot" (as in "not so hot") or "cool" (as in "that's cool") where the meaning is removed from temperature sensations. Additional examples include ironic use of the opposite word to describe someone or something, for example, nicknames such as Speedy or Lightning for a slow-moving person or creature.

One mechanism operating in the evolution of meaning is a process of association in which part of a larger complex, but not necessarily the defining feature, stands in lieu of the whole. Some examples of this process are evident in signs of holidays, such as pine trees, wreaths, or Santas for Christmas; bunnies, chicks and colored eggs for Easter; and hearts for Valentine's day. Whoever first invented these devices was quite original. The description of the flag of the United States as the star-spangled banner, for instance, is poetic, but over many years of repeated usage it has become a cliché. Our language—and the personal label repertoire of every individual—is studded with clichés that we come, justifiably, to ignore. As a result, a resort to the use of clichés discourages attending or serious thought. The implication of that conclusion should be obvious: eschew clichés if you would be a thinker or want to command attention.

BOX 2-5

Schematic Diagrams

A. A Schematic of Information Transmission

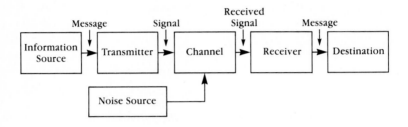

A message delivered into a transmitter (telephone or telex) is converted into a signal transmitted along a channel (telephone lines) where it may be subject to noise (a signal component not in the original message). Noise may take the form of interference (for example, static) or distortion. The received signal is converted back into a message at the receiver. (After Shannon, C. E., & Weaver, W. [1949]. *The mathematical theory of communication.* Urbana: The University of Illinois Press.)

Clichés are innocuous enough; their cousin, the stereotype, is not. The stereotype, like the cliché, represents a draining of originality by using a rigid referent, generally with the addition of a perjorative connotation. The carefree "darkie" who sang and danced but rarely engaged in productive effort is an example of a stereotype that has, happily, disappeared, perhaps to be replaced by others, such as the mugger or the welfare mother. We are all acquainted with a host of similar ethnic stereotypes. They function to derogate "them" and, by implication, glorify "us." They generally do so by selecting an irrelevant but salient feature that is not defining of the group and use it, inappropriately, as a group descriptor.

From early childhood each of us has been exposed to propaganda espousing a variety of causes from preventing litter to voting a specific way. We are also bombarded by advertising and by purported factual evidence of the dangers

B. A Schematic of Information Flow

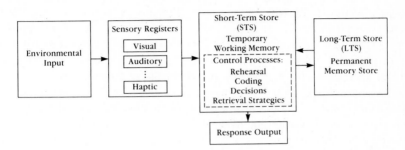

Information flow through the memory system is conceived of as beginning with the processing of environmental inputs in sensory registers (receptors plus internal elements) and entry into the short-term store (STS). While it remains there the information may be copied into the long-term store (LTS), and associated information that is in the long-term store may be activated and entered into the short-term store. If a triangle is seen, for example, the name "triangle" may be called up. Control processes in the short-term store affect these transfers into and out of the long-term store and govern learning, retrieval of information, and forgetting. (From Atkinson, R. C. and Shiffrin, R. M. [1971, August]. The control of short term memory. *Scientific American, 224*, 225, 82–90). Copyright © 1971 by Scientific American, Inc. All rights reserved.

of caffeine, cholesterol, food additives, and over- or underweight. Some of the devices of advertising are transparent to a sophisticated adult, for example, "30% more effective! Doctors recommend the pain relieving ingredient in. . . ." Others are more subtle, such as "Diamonds are the gift of love at all stages of life."

To understand the growth of clichés, stereotypes, and unexamined assumptions read the publications of some special interest groups which cater to movie fans, food faddists, investors, Jehovah's witnesses, or chocolate lovers, for the purpose of identifying the loaded words and implicit assumptions of that group. After having done so, complete the exercise by identifying the clichés, stereotypes, and implicit assumptions of your own reference group (athlete, student, housewife). Where possible, trace the origins of the clichés and stereotypes, along with some of the implications associated with your reference group.

The foregoing exploration of a variety of carriers of meaning differentiated the effective encoding of art and science from clichés, stereotypes, and propaganda. In every case only a part of the available information is used to convey meaning. The differentiating feature is that in effective encoding, the emphasized feature is a defining property of the class in relation to the directing purpose— change in locus of joints relative to motion, elements and atomic weights relative to the material in the universe, something not precisely identifiable but best captured through apt metaphor in the case of poetry. In the case of clichés and stereotypes, some irrelevant but frequently occurring element is selected—skin color as a determinant of behavior, the exchange of gifts and use of seasonal decor as the defining elements of the spirit of Christmas, or brand name as a determinant of the effect of aspirin. Carriers of meaning that emphasize defining features enhance understanding whereas those focusing upon irrelevant features impoverish understanding.

SELECTING AN APPROPRIATE ENCODING

This section offers three guidelines for effective encoding and some illustrations of their application:

1. *Purpose.* The first determinant of an appropriate encoding is the purpose to be served by it. Is precise meaning to be conveyed or general feeling tone? Is the purpose immediate or long range? Is the intended level general or specific? Here you might note that if it is your purpose to misinform or to evoke emotion rather than reason, stereotypes and propaganda are well suited.
2. *Defining features.* After having identified the purpose, decide what aspects of the information are centrally relevant so that you can emphasize them rather than associated, but irrelevant, features. This step always involves definition and classification.
3. *Vehicle.* Select a mode of encoding that best embodies the relevant information and purpose identified in the first two steps.

In the remainder of this section, some advice will be offered on ways of attaining precise, specific encoding, encoding to summarize what is important in large amounts of information, and encoding for retention. The subject is continued in Chapter 3 where effective communication and enhancement of personal understanding are discussed.

Precise Encoding of Specific Information.   Habits of inarticulate encoding are not likely to promote clear thinking. Consider the common utterance, "You know what I mean, it's like hard." What does that mean? The statement suggests that what is being described shares some common features with "hard" but differs in some unspecified, possibly unspecifiable, manner (if that were not the case "hard" would not be modified by "like"). Even "hard" is itself ambiguous in the absence of additional context: it refers to an unyielding surface or something difficult to understand. Clearly "like" and "you know what I mean" are empty phrases that can safely be ignored. They convey nothing except that the speaker is a member of a language community or age group who, by this means, asserts group membership.

Precision in identification of a referent is promoted by a process akin to definition: identification of the larger class and differentiation of the particular referent from other class members by identification of its unique properties. For example, in drawing attention to some fine detail such as a warbler in a tree, you first identify the tree, then the branch, and finally the bird's location on the branch. A similar encoding process is involved in describing a malfunction of your car. In identifying the appropriate equation to be applied in solving a physics problem or a statistics problem, you first identify the relevant concept or domain through precise encoding of the demands of the problem, for example, does it deal with velocity? a maximum likelihood estimate? Box 2-6 contains a set of drawings that have been widely used in an experimental task where one individual must instruct a partner, who is physically separated in another booth, on how to arrange the pictures in a specific sequence corresponding to his own. Repeat the experiment and record what you learn about encoding for precision. Your success will be advanced by approaching the task by utilizing the structural diagram of information transmission presented in Box 2-5. A common source of imprecise encoding is noise from idiosyncratic associations (that is, associations meaningful to the speaker that are not shared by the partner).

As a final example, consider the economic principle of diminishing returns. It applies to a large number of situations in which continuing investments of effort, money, or time do not produce commensurate returns. Many examples can be constructed: the first beer, cigarette, or chocolate tastes so good that a second is desired. The second may produce as much pleasure as the first but successive inputs become less and less satisfying. The same is true for time spent studying for an exam or applying cosmetics. Box 2-7 provides a general illustration that the relation between resource commitment and result is not linear; if it were, each successive input would yield the same return as preceding ones. Certainly the relation is not increasing; it is decreasing or, possibly, even, non-monotonic. Non-monotonic means that the direction of change is not in one direction; it may, for example, increase and then decrease or vice versa. Expressing the relation graphically not only captures the essence and generality of the asserted relation but also suggests testable implications that could lead to finer classification among classes of examples, such as situations leading to reduced returns as contrasted to those leading to deterioration.

Summary Encodings for Identification of Relevant Features.   Precise encoding applies a definition-like process to situations where central properties are more or less known and one wants to emphasize their unique features in

BOX 2-6

A Communication Experiment

The forms to be described by speaker to listener.

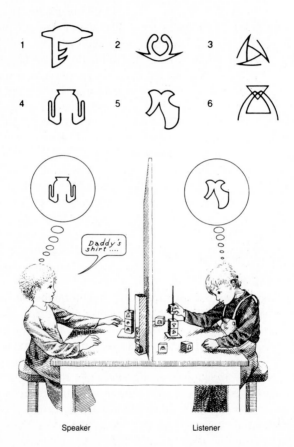

A communication problem. The speaker and listener have identical sets of blocks, but only the speaker knows which order they should be stacked in. He must tell his listener which blocks to stack so that their two stacks are identical.

From Krauss, R. M. & Glucksberg, S. (1977, February). Social and Nonsocial Speech. *Scientific American.* Copyright © 1977 by Scientific American, Inc. All rights reserved.

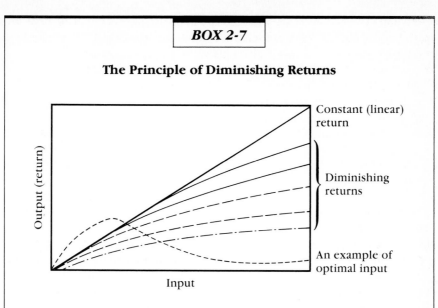

BOX 2-7

The Principle of Diminishing Returns

Constant (linear) return

Diminishing returns

An example of optimal input

Output (return)

Input

Some possible functions compatible with the principle of diminishing returns. The principle itself states that the result of additional units of input investment do not yield a constant return (output); rather, output amount declines.

conveying meaning. The information to be understood is relatively circumscribed. In many other instances, where there is a great deal of information, it is desirable to reduce it to manageable proportions in order to identify the relevant properties or dimensions. In those instances more extensive transformation is required to reduce information overload by removing irrelevancies. The process here is akin to classification, either at a single level or with respect to hierarchies. Darwin was faced with such a problem in making sense of his many observations of variation among species, as was Linnaeus in developing a classification scheme for plants, or Mendeleev in devising a periodic table of the elements. For this purpose an analogy, such as Darwin's image of the irregularly branching tree, the use of principles from some other discipline, such as applying the physics of the camera as to the eye, a summary table or an outline are helpful. The subject of constructing appropriate models for ordering information will be considered in greater detail in Chapter 9. Let's focus now on summary tables and outlines.

Most students develop the habit of underlining to identify important points in text. While this is a good preliminary device for small units, it does not address the problem of relating units for understanding of the whole, nor does it detach important points from the presenting context. A good device for those purposes is the outline, with which you probably are familiar. A good summary table also takes information out of its presenting context and arranges it economically to promote comparison of major elements with respect to several possible bases of comparison. Frequently, such an array suggests a summary generalization that would not otherwise have been apparent. For example, in understanding historical events, it is helpful to prepare a chronological table in which time is the horizontal row element and developments in several historical realms such as economic and cultural events serve as the vertical column entries. Similarly, to understand the disease process one might prepare a summary table with diseases charted as horizontal rows and with causes, contributing factors, and symptoms charted as vertical columns. Box 2-8 presents a summary table of stages of cognitive development. Note how the table, by emphasizing the basis of comparison (row elements), focuses the contrast among stages and identifies neglected research questions. Examine summary tables and graphs in your own texts to see how they direct attention to relevant properties and the relations among them. Where a text is unclear because too much unorganized information is presented, prepare a summary table of your own for clarification. This is also an excellent device in studying for exams.

Encoding for Remembering.   A widely held popular model of memory derives from a file cabinet analogy: information is stored unchanged in some place from which it is retrieved as needed. This simple model is not correct as is evident when one considers some of its implications: (a) storing information is equivalent to perceiving it, (b) nothing is lost from memory, (c) accumulating information eventually exhausts the filing space, (d) filed contents remain unchanged by preceding or following entries, and (e) retrieval is the reverse of storage. Although some of these implications are difficult to test, others are clearly wrong.[4] Memory is not a static, mechanical process but a complex dynamic one akin to thinking. Entries into memory require transformation for registration, storage, and retrieval, and their status undergoes change as a result of time and experience.

Consider the first implication above. Young children act as though it were true and seem genuinely surprised when they discover that attending to something does not automatically lead to remembering.[5] The physical analogy commonly invoked to account for forgetting is a trace that fades over time unless its strength is reinforced ("Use it or lose it!"). Perhaps the first device discovered to promote retention is rehearsal (for example, see Flavell, Beach, & Chinsky, 1966). Material that is repeated over and over is more likely to be recalled. The first implication is clearly wrong; you must do something to information in order to facilitate retention. If all that you did was rehearse, however, the third implication might be correct. Before considering how it is overcome, we might examine forgetting a bit more. Isolated bits of information, such as facts, dates, phone numbers, proper names seem to be much more vulnerable to forgetting than motor skills or fundamental knowledge (for example, about language or natural phenomena[6]). Moreover, the accessibility of stored knowledge is related to the nature of the test: recognition (as in a true-false or multiple-choice test) is a less demanding test of retention than is unprompted production, such as an essay exam.

A good device for overcoming storage limitations is to compress information into more manageable "chunks" (Miller, 1956). Consider the digit string: 9375648257; or a randomly selected word list: audit, inspiration, physic, spear, rub, creamery, much, transit, forever, quarry. One device for compressing such lists is arbitrary grouping: 937 564 8257, or audit-inspiration-physic, spear-rub-creamery, much-transit-forever-quarry. The grouped list can then be rehearsed, perhaps with a beat, intonation pattern, or other form of rhythmic stress, to augment the grouping. That will work but arbitrary groups don't fulfill the second requirement of a good mnemonic: natural staying power and ease of retrieval. That demand requires additional transformation of the material, generally in the direction of making it more meaningful. One means of increasing retention is to utilize intrinsic properties of the material, noting that the first four digits are odd and the next four even, putting the words into alphabetical order, categorizing into parts of speech, or creating a story or image (for example, hunting much quarry [on mass] transit [with a] spear rub[bed with] creamery . . .).

Another meaning-creating mode of chunking of lists is the creation of acronyms by forming a word of the first letter of each list element. As an example, Anderson (1980) offers seven techniques for remembering that are grouped into organizing and repeating procedures linked by the acronym ABC ROAD: *A*nalyze into chunks; *B*ind with images, associations or rules; *C*ue with associations; *R*epeat to establish associations; *O*verlearn; *A*ctively test recall; and *D*istribute practice. Another useful transformation is to change the form of the code, for instance, from words into images, or from digits into letters. The latter is especially useful for phone numbers (for example, "Call 800 USA LOAN"). Yet another useful device, invented by the ancient Greeks, is to use points along a familiar route (for example, your habitual route from home to class or a clockwise circuit around your room) as "pegs" on which to hang list items.[7] To use the earlier lists as an example, if the features of your room (starting at the door) are bookcase, closet, desk, lamp, chair, window, table, clock, bed, and chest, you would associate—perhaps by forming images—audit with bookcase, inspiration with closet, physic with desk, spear with lamp, and so on and cue your recall by mentally circling your room. In this manner you utilize familiar knowledge as a mechanism to promote retrieval of new information and make the storage sequence identical to the retrieval sequence.

These mnemonic techniques and many others found in the literature (see Note 7) are not presented as major milestones on the route to effective thinking. Rote memorization should be viewed as a default procedure to be resorted to

---

BOX 2-8

Summary of the Piagetian Stages, Some of Their Defining Characteristics and Average Age of Appearance

	Concrete Operations	
Stage Property	Sensorimotor	Preoperational Subperiod
Average Age of Appearance	0–1½ or 2 yrs.	2–7
Kind of Operations Available	None—motor schemes, which are not reversible, serve in lieu of operations. They are practical but not logical, for example, sucking, throwing, looking.	
Status of Semiotic Functions	No representation as such except where an internalized scheme or imitation serves this function, for example, closing eyes and lying down as a sleep symbol.	Development of imagery and symbolization through play, drawing, mental imagery, and language.
Elements of Thought	No real thought, hence no basis of distinguishing its elements.	Elements of thought tend to be objects and individuals in context.
Organizational Structure of Operations		

Note: based upon Piaget, 1970.

Concrete Operations	Formal Operations	
Concrete Operation Subperiod	Subperiod of Organization	Subperiod of Achievement
7–11	11–15	15–
Concrete operations, for example, classification (single and multiple), seriation, conservation.	Formal operations, for example, deduction, permutation correlation.	
Further refinement in forms and functions of language and of imagery, that is, appearance of anticipatory imagery in addition to reproductive imagery.	Not studied. Presumably further refinements in and abstractions of imagery and language over those attained in concrete operations.	
Elements of thought are properties and relations.	Elements of thought are propositions.	
Eight groupements: four parallel classes for dealing with operations on properties and four for operations upon relations.	The four group, or INRC group; the complete combinatorial scheme.	

only where better techniques are unavailable. What I suggest are general rules for encoding information to be remembered: transform the material into chunks and bind those chunks with the glue of meaning. Wherever possible the best device is to subsume something to be remembered into something that is already well known. A working inductive generalization such as "dark clouds precede a storm" summarizes all instances from which it derives and predicts all future ones; it is more easily remembered than a list of individual instances. Similarly, no one memorizes all possible sums, products, or integrations because they are readily derived as the need arises. In other words, where possible use laws, analogies, theories and other general frameworks as a program to generate knowledge. A good education that provides an understanding of basic principles supplies a general working framework that is superior to memorization. To encode for memory try to encode for understanding. The attainment of that goal is the subject of Chapter 3.

SUMMARY

The thinker does not merely soak up information like a sponge but actively transforms it through a process of selecting certain features for emphasis while ignoring others in the course of enhancing meaning. The process of scanning and registering features is called *attending*. It is not an automatic process but one which can be improved through training. The term *encoding* was used to describe the process of representing that which is attended symbolically through the vehicle of words, pictures, images, gestures, and so on.

Encoding may take the form of naming or it may involve a more extensive processing of information to transform it into knowledge. All encoding implies classification. *Classification* is a process of grouping instances into equivalent groups on the basis of a defining feature(s) or property selected for the purpose. *Naming, defining,* and *hierarchical classification* were also discussed with examples.

The end product of the encoding process is a *carrier of meaning*. A variety of examples of carriers of meaning selected from art, science, and popular usage were examined as illustrations of how the particular means of encoding affects the meaning conveyed. Effective encoding was shown to convey a great deal of information economically by emphasizing defining features or properties. In contrast, clichés and stereotypes distort meaning by emphasizing irrelevant features.

Finally, general guides were offered for the selection of appropriate encoding: (a) identify the purpose of the encoding, (b) select those features of the information relevant to it, and (c) choose a device that emphasizes the features relevant for the purpose. Precise encoding of specific information is best attained through emphasizing unique defining features in an exact neutral fashion. Reducing large amounts of information for the purpose of identifying defining features is promoted through the use of economical summary devices such as tables, graphs, or outlines. Promoting retention requires the creation of larger units or chunks that capitalize on meaningful aspects to reduce demands on memory storage.

EXERCISES

1. Paying attention should become a habit rather than the subject of an exercise. These exercises are designed to get you started. In the course of class discussion you may find yourself devising many more.
   (a) Give an objective description of some perceptual experience, such as a really good pizza or your favorite song as rendered by your favorite singer that adequately conveys its unique properties. Critique each other's descriptions from the standpoint of their adequacy in conveying the intended information. You might also record in your notebook how attending aided in precise encoding and vice versa.
   (b) Notice three things that you had not noticed previously and speculate why you may have overlooked them. There are many illustrative exercises available: How many buttons on your coat? How many windows in the front of your house? Try to draw a dollar bill from memory.
   (c) In the following game, divide the class into two groups who sit with their backs to each other (so you cannot look at each other). Next, select one member from each group of whom the members of the other group will provide a detailed description appropriate for a police WANTED circular or for someone with an Identikit to prepare a picture. Identify the person described on the basis of the description. The goal is to provide as succinct a description as possible.
2. Here is another poem. What is the author's purpose and how is it attained?
   > The golf links are so near the mill
   > that almost every day
   > the little children at their work
   > can watch the men at play.

   If you were unaware that this is a protest against child labor, reread it for the clues that you missed the first time.
3. You are perhaps familiar with Warhol's paintings of soup cans and may have wondered if they were art. Consider what his purpose might have been and how the depiction of soup cans advances this purpose. Some other artists whose work you might want to consider, again from the standpoint of the artist's purpose and how it is attained, are Johns, Lichtenstein, Wesselman, or Stuart Davis. You might also collect some drawings by children or adults who are not professional artists and analyze them from the standpoint of features selected for encoding and what they suggest about the artist's knowledge of the subject depicted.
4. Collect examples of clichés, stereotypes, and propaganda. Try to find subtle

instances in addition to obvious ones. Bring them in to assemble a class scrapbook. Organize the scrapbook so that it summarizes the class findings about the devices employed.

5. To understand encoding for precision, complete the following:

   (a) Prepare directions for getting somewhere, for example, from a dormitory to some other building on campus. State them in at least two ways (verbally, in a diagram). Compare class solutions and award a prize to the best entry.

   (b) Define each of the following terms in light of what you know about encoding for precision: cliché, encoding, organization, hassle, attention, style. What are the defining features? Why select them rather than some other characteristic feature?

   (c) Write a definition of some central concept in another course that conveys its meaning to class members unacquainted with the term.

6. Each of the exercises below requires summarizing of information.

   (a) Select one of the words in the list above and count the number of words used by each member of the class in defining the word. Devise a means of summarizing the resulting information. Is there any relation between definition length and judged adequacy of definition?

   (b) Prepare a summary table of information you are trying to master in some other course. This may take the form of a summary outline to be used in studying for a quiz. If several people use the same material, you can compare summaries to see if and how they differ and try to reconcile discrepancies.

   (c) Go to the library and find a text for some course you are taking and compare it to the assigned text with respect to treatment of a particular topic covered in both. You might take some physical concept such as cell mitosis, inertia, valence or a social science concept such as reinforcement or cultural diffusion. Note differences and similarities in the features identified and how they are related. Hint: if your assigned text is unclear on some point you can always consult another one.

7. To familiarize yourself with mnemonic devices, do the following:

   (a) Prepare a number of lists of words, digits, or nonsense syllables of comparable length and difficulty. Construct alternative mnemonics and learn one list with each. Compare their effectiveness as measured by the number of trials required to learn the list to one perfect repetition or the number of list items recalled the following day. You might repeat the experiment with a different kind of material to determine if some mnemonics work better for a particular kind of material than for other kinds.

   (b) Devise some mnemonic schemes for the following tasks: associating a name with a face (as in learning the names of all the students in the class or attendees at a party) or winning a game in which a number of cards, each with a different picture, are turned face down and you have to then find specific ones. Compare class solutions.

8. To understand hierarchical classification, complete the following:
   (a) The grammatical procedure of parsing a sentence breaks the sentence into the structure of its component parts as shown below. Find some long complex sentences and subject them to this form of analysis.

   Rewrite rules in a simple phrase structure grammar

   1. S   → Noun phrase (NP) + Verb phrase (VP)
   2. NP → Adjective (A) + Noun (N)
             Article (T) + Noun phrase (NP)
   3. VP → Verb (V) + Noun phrase (NP)
   4. T   → the
   5. N   → woman, child
   6. V   → kissed
   7. A   → ugly, squirming

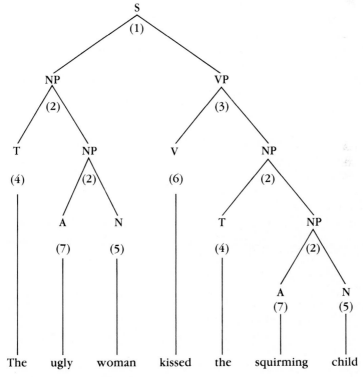

   A simple phrase structure grammar.

   (b) The second diagram (see page 52) shows a hypothesized memory structure of an individual's knowledge about animals. Apply it in diagramming the hierarchical classification summarizing your knowledge about some topic, for example, encoding, the last presidential election, or computers.

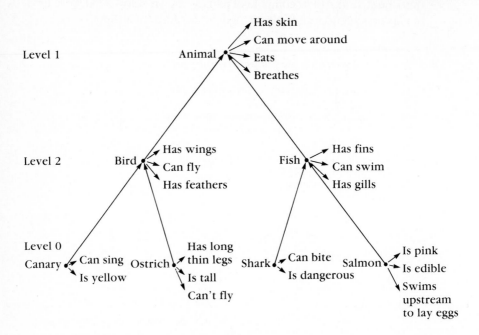

(c) Explicitly formalize some classification schemes that you use in dealing with some subject matter, in your personal evaluation of people (for example, who you would select for a friend) or commodities, from the standpoint of the defining properties of the classes and the form of the taxonomy.

9. Compare the pairs of synonyms below with respect to different connotations of each: (a) drinker, drunkard, alcoholic; (b) animal, mammal; (c) product, creation; (d) adored, beloved; (e) conflict, war; (f) critical, contentious.

· *3* ·

Using the Information: Communication and Understanding

The identification and encoding of information, the focus of the preceding chapter, is only half the story. The development of meaning cannot be fully achieved in solitude and detachment; rather, it requires the interchange of communication with others or with oneself. Over time and public exposure ideas are challenged, expanded, refined, or disproved. An important component of the process of refining ideas is developing the means for their expression. That goal is the subject of this chapter.

To some extent it is appropriate to speak of encoding as a means towards communication and understanding. The directing guidelines for encoding, once again, are fully applicable: (a) formulate the purpose, (b) identify the focal points and defining properties, and (c) devise an appropriate vehicle to embody the focal points for achieving the goal. There are, however, two additional considerations which, although they are by no means absent in the process of encoding information, assume greater prominence in the course of developing ideas for communication to others or enrichment of personal understanding. They are the role of an audience and the process of revision. Knowledge does not emerge full-blown, like Athena from the head of Zeus, and remain immutable thereafter; rather, it evolves through a dynamic interplay that I characterize as communication (either with others or with oneself), during which there may be modification of any or all of the directing elements, including purpose, central features, or conveying vehicle.

This chapter will begin by discussing how to communicate simple objective information such as is imparted in giving directions. It will go on to consider letter writing as an example of communication in which further interchange is anticipated or invited. A much more extended instance of written communication arises in writing a paper or an essay where a good deal of information from a variety of sources must be explored and integrated. To the extent that producing papers is a common student activity, helpful advice on the process will be offered, but there is a broader purpose to be served as well. In the service of thinking through difficult issues, there is no substitute for writing, as I shall demonstrate in the final discussion of understanding as communication with yourself. To the extent that writing and thinking are synonymous, there is no substitute for writing articulately and precisely.

COMMUNICATION

Recall the experiment in Box 2-6. Placing six objects in a prescribed order is not a difficult task. The difficulty arises in communicating to a listener which of the forms is required at each point. Because the participants are physically isolated from each other the simple device of pointing to the appropriate form is precluded. Adequate communication in this context requires that the speaker describe the form in a unique manner for the listener. Even preschoolers encode forms verbally, for example, "Daddy's shirt" or " 'Nother daddy shirt." Yet, when a preschool partner requests additional clarification the encoding is not modified appropriately. Older subjects arrive at understanding through an interchange of questions and answers. By doing the experiment you can appreciate the nature of the process of refining descriptors to facilitate communication. The experiment is a good introduction to giving instructions.

Giving Instructions.   In giving instructions the three guidelines for encoding of purpose, focal point and vehicle are so obviously relevant as to implicitly structure the communication. Some common devices for organizing instructions are to present the components sequentially, as in a computer program, or to organize around major topics. In a recipe, for example, there are the ingredients, the conditions for their assemblage (whether the oven should be preheated, the necessary temperature of the ingredients), the order of processing ingredients, and the necessary cooking time and temperature. In giving place directions you can give a step-by-step route, a general orientation of the area, key landmarks, and alternate routes.

Requisite features and the means of conveying them are often combined in direct oral communication through the process of establishing a common knowledge base. Do you know where . . . is? Do you know how to make. . . ? If direct interchange is precluded because the recipient is not physically present, as in writing a letter or preparing a handout for a group, it is necessary to do some role-playing of the absent audience to guess what is likely to be known and to provide backup information in case the guess is incorrect. In providing a route, for example, you might anticipate some concern on the part of the reader as to whether he or she is on the correct route. That anxiety can be allayed by providing identifying landmarks and travel time or distance. A possibility that an alternate route may be required because of road work, an accident, or traffic density might also be anticipated. Similarly, in providing a recipe you might want to anticipate possible problems such as separation of ingredients or poor texture by providing ways of identifying and correcting such problems. A review of some cookbooks, or instructions for assembly or repair of purchased articles, is useful to acquaint you with the means of communicating simple information. A good and a poor recipe are given in Box 3-1 along with incomprehensible operating instructions that came with a clock and a journal account of constructing directions. Collect some additional examples of your own.

The foregoing examples were simple in that the purpose was well defined and the audience was both limited and well known. In such cases, transferring one's own understanding to another does not pose a difficult problem of communication. Where the audience is physically present, as in a face-to-face or telephone conversation, any necessary revision can be supplied immediately. With an absent audience, as in writing a letter or a paper, ambiguities and uncertainties must be anticipated and the communication structured to preclude them. A common means of precluding confusion is to specify referents and to avoid vague language, such as "it" or "that," or to provide intervening steps, checkpoints, and alternatives. Those considerations usually lead to more precise encoding. Where the communication is more extended or more abstract, such as expressing ideas or arguments, deliberate planning is required and revision is inescapable. As an initial example of this form of communication, letter writing will be discussed; a discussion of formal writing will follow.

Letter Writing.   There was a time, historically, when letter writing was the sole means of communication over distance. With the advent of the telephone its role in communication among friends and relations has declined markedly; however, its importance in business communication has increased. For this reason it is worth examining the process of letter writing for both personal and business purposes.

The personal letter takes many forms and serves many purposes, from simple reminder to declaration of major decisions. In fact, the personal letter is a recognized literary form, as you can readily verify by browsing through collections of letters of eminent persons in the library.[1] Works of fiction, generally amusing ones, are sometimes conveyed in the form of letters. The sampling of letters in Box 3-2 are all drawn from an earlier era when letters played a more important role than they do today. The first two are drawn from a work that presented "model" letters by way of instruction; the remaining three are from a parent to a grown child. You might find it instructive to compare them with communications from your own parents to appreciate both the fixed characteristics as well as the changes which have developed over time in both style and substance of parental advice or reproof.

Although much of the information in a personal letter takes the form of imparting information or requests, and, in that sense, differs little from the communication involved in giving directions, there is an additional role of describing

BOX 3-1

A. Instructions for Making Peach Ice Cream

1903 Peach Ice Cream

---

   6 yolks
1¼ cup sugar
   1 cup hot milk
   6 yellow peaches
   1 quart cream

Stir yolks and sugar together, add milk,
grated peaches, and cream: freeze.

1984 Peach Ice Cream

---

   6 egg yolks, lightly beaten
1¼ cups sugar (or more, to taste)
   1 cup milk
   6 ripe peaches, peeled and pitted
   1 quart (4 cups) non-ultrapasturized
      heavy cream

1. Whisk the egg yolks and sugar together in a bowl until the mixture turns light yellow.
2. Combine the yolk-sugar mixture with the milk in a heavy-bottomed saucepan and set over medium-low heat. Whisk gently or stir with a wooden spoon until the mixture thickens. You are in fact making a custard. Thickening occurs well before boiling, at about 180 degrees. If you are in physical contact with the potential custard, you should be able to tell easily when thickening occurs, as you stir. Stirring helps spread heat evenly through the mixture. As the right temperature is reached, the mixture will be very hot to the touch, hotter than normal hot tap water.

   When the custard thickens, plunge the bottom of the pan into a basin of cold water to stop cooking. Push the custard through a *chinois* (a fine strainer) to purge any particles of scrambled yolk. This technique will save a custard that has started to boil. Nothing will save a custard that never thickened in the first place. Boldness is crucial the first time you try this. It is almost worth letting a custard scramble completely, once, so that you will forever know what egg yolks do across the whole possible range of cooking temperatures. Let the strained custard cool to room temperature.

3. Meanwhile, chop the peaches very finely, by hand or in a food processor with the metal blade. If you use the processor, do this in small batches, with short bursts of power, so as not to liquefy the peaches. Or use the grating blade. The idea is to leave shreds or specks of recognizable peach flesh in the ice cream. If the pieces are too large, they will freeze solid because of the water they retain. You should end up with roughly four cups of chopped peach.

4. Combine the custard, cream, and peaches. If possible, let the mixture stand for three hours so that the flavor develops. Pour into the canister of your ice cream freezer. If you are using the old-fashioned, hand-cranked variety, follow these uncharacteristically complete instructions from the original *"Settlement" Cook Book:*

"Scald and then chill can cover and dasher before using. Adjust can in tub, put in the mixture, then the dasher and cover, adjust the crank, and pack with finely chopped ice and rock salt; this must be higher around than the mixture is inside. Use three parts of ice to one part of rock salt for freezing, and use four parts ice to one part rock salt for packing afterwards. Ice cream must be frozen slowly and steadily. . . . Let stand five minutes, turn again five minutes; repeat until frozen. When mixture is frozen, remove ice and salt from top of can, wipe top and the cover; uncover and remove dasher, scrape it; beat the frozen mixture with a wooden spoon. Place heavy paper over it, put on cover, and place a cork in the hole. Do not strain off the water until the mixture is frozen. Repack the freezer, putting ice on the top, cover with carpet or newspaper, and stand in cool place several hours.

"A tightly covered tin can and a wooden pail may be substituted for an ice cream freezer, using a wooden spoon to scrape the mixture from sides and bottom of can as it freezes.

"The ice must be finely crushed. Place in a burlap bag and give a few blows with the broad side of an ax or hatchet."

Yield: Approximately two quarts

(Reprinted from Sokolov, R. Guides for the perplexed [1984, August]. With permission from *Natural History,* Vol. 93, No. 8; Copyright the American Museum of Natural History, 1984.)

BOX 3-1 *(con't)*

B. Instructions for an Analog Alarm Clock

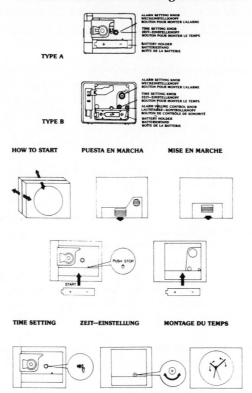

C. Journal Entry on the Construction of Directions

Today I had to give somebody who was totally unfamiliar with the area in which I live directions to my house. I imagined myself driving up Route 1 and the landmarks that I would see to indicate I was approaching my destination. I directed my friend along route 1 and local streets by my house. Since I realized it is extremely difficult to read and drive at the same time, I gave her some mnemonics to help her remember the diner on that intersection or the bank three blocks before the left turn. I also suggested that it might be helpful to map out her route ahead of time since she said she always gets lost going to an unfamiliar location. Once I explained that Route 1, Route 27, and the street I live on are all parallel and the other streets serve as connectors, this sequence made much more sense to her.

feelings about or meanings assigned to events. In this sense, the personal letter is a form of social sharing that not only invites and maintains closeness to another but also clarifies the writer's own sentiments. To explore this specific function of the personal letter, write a letter to someone about an incident that you would like to share with him or her. Write a second letter about the same event to someone with whom you share a very different relationship. The importance of the role of the intended audience as a determinant of context should be clear from a comparison of the two letters.

The business letter assumes great prominence in everyday life not only as a means of communication for an immediate purpose but also as a vehicle for official record (for example, "I paid that bill on 3/25"). Because of the added purpose of permanent official recording, you should remember that additional correspondence may ensue and that records will need to be maintained for reference. In the business letter, unlike the personal letter, feeling tone is not relevant and encoding for precision is of primary importance. All relevant data should be presented as exactly and efficiently as possible: names, dates, serial or account numbers are advisable inclusions. It is usually helpful to state the purpose explicitly at the outset: for example, "In response to your inquiry, I supply the following information. . . . This is a complaint about defective equipment. . . ." The differentiation between personal and business letters is further marked by conventional differences in the form of the inside address, salutation, and close. To appreciate some of the niceties of effective business letters you might get into the habit of reading the Letters to the Editor section of your local newspaper. Usually the quality of letters varies widely, providing good examples of what to avoid as well as what to emulate.

WRITING A PAPER

For many students producing a paper is a hectic process of going to the library, assembling a pile of references, and copying selections from them to be woven together into a patchwork of all but plagiarized snippets connected sequentially by threads of immediate associations. That is not the way to write a paper. Although general rules for producing a paper will not be offered in this chapter, a number of useful suggestions will be provided along with references to some good texts on the subject.[2]

Writing a paper is a concentrated process of meaning-making that requires a good deal of deliberate regulation and systematic organizing. It also requires time. No matter how much advance planning is devoted to writing, the work itself assumes a life of its own that needs time and incubation for development. In the course of writing, a good deal of rewriting and revision will take place as ideas evolve. You are well advised to allow enough time for every stage in the writing process.

Organization takes place on at least two different levels: (a) during the formulating and research stages that direct the writing and (b) during the writing

BOX 3-2

An Assortment of Letters

A. The following two letters are sample letters taken from a collection of 173 letters published in 1741 by Samuel Richardson under the title "Letters written to and for particular friends, on the most important occasions, directing not only the requisite style and forms to be observed in writing familiar letters; but how to think and act justly and prudently in the common concerns of human life." (After Isaacs, 1928)

*An Apprentice to an Uncle, about a Fraud committed by his
Fellow-Apprentice to their Master.*

Dear Uncle,

I am under greater uneasiness than I am able to express. My fellow-'prentice, for whom I had a great regard, and from whom I have received many civilities, has involved me in the deepest affliction. I'm unwilling to tell you, and yet I must not conceal it, that he has forfeited the confidence reposed in him, by a breach of trust, to which he ungenerously gained my consent, by a pretence I did not in the least suspect. What must I do? My master is defrauded: If I discover the injury, I am sure to ruin a young man I would fain think possessed of some merit; if I conceal the unjustice, I must at present share the guilt, and hereafter be partaker in the punishment. I am in the greatest agony of mind, and beg your instant advice, as you value the peace of

Your dutiful, tho' unfortunate Nephew.

The Uncle's Answer.

Dear Nephew,

Your letter, which I just now received, gives me great uneasiness: And as any delay in the discovery may be attended with consequences which will probably be dangerous to yourself, and disagreeable to all who belong to you; I charge you, if you value your own happiness, and my peace, to acquaint your master instantly with the injustice that has been done him; which is the only means of vindicating your own innocence, and preventing your being looked upon as an accomplice in a fact, to which I wish you may not be found to have been too far consenting. As to the unhappy young man who has been guilty of so fatal an indiscretion, I wish, if the known clemency and good-nature of your master may pardon this offence, he may let his forgiveness teach him the ingratitude and inhumanity of injuring a man, who is not only the proper guardian of his youth, but whose goodness deserves the best behaviour, tho' he be generous enough to excuse the worst. Let not a minute pass after you receive this, before you reveal the matter to your master. For I am in hopes, that your application to me, and your following my advice, will greatly plead in your behalf. I will very speedily call on your master; and am, as far as an honest regard for you can make me,

Your loving Uncle.

B. The following three letters are from *Selected English Letters, XV-XIX Centuries.* The first letter is from William Hazlitt to his son; the second from Lady Mary Wortley Montagu to her daughter, the Countess of Bute; and the third from Phillip Dormer Stanhope, Earl of Chesterfield to his son. (After Duckitt & Wragg, 1913)

To his son
Marriage, and the choice of a profession

[1822.]

. . . If you ever marry, I would wish you to marry the woman you like. Do not be guided by the recommendations of friends. Nothing will atone for or overcome an original distaste. It will only increase from intimacy; and if you are to live separate, it is better not to come together. There is no use in dragging a chain through life, unless it binds one to the object we love. Choose a mistress from among your equals. You will be able to understand her character better, and she will be more likely to understand yours. Those in an inferior station to yourself will doubt your good intentions, and misapprehend your plainest expressions. All that you swear is to them a riddle or downright nonsense. You cannot by any possibility translate your thoughts into their dialect. They will be ignorant of the meaning of half you say, and laugh at the rest. As mistresses, they will have no sympathy with you; and as wives, you can have none with them.

Women care nothing about poets, or philosophers, or politicians. They go by a man's looks and manner. Richardson calls them 'an eye-judging sex'; and I am sure he knew more about them than I can pretend to do. If you run away with a pedantic notion that they care a pin's point about your head or your heart, you will repent it too late. . . .

If I were to name one pursuit rather than another, I should wish you to be a good painter, if such a thing could be hoped. I have failed in this myself, and should wish you to be able to do what I have not—to paint like Claude, or Rembrandt, or Guido, or Vandyke, if it were possible. Artists, I think, who have succeeded in their chief object, live to be old, and are agreeable old men. Their minds keep alive to the last. Cosway's spirits never flagged till after ninety; and Nollekens, though nearly blind, passed all his mornings in giving directions about some group or bust in his workshop. You have seen Mr. Northcote, that delightful specimen of the last age. With what avidity he takes up his pencil, or lays it down again to talk of numberless things! His eye has not lost its lustre, nor 'paled its ineffectual fire'. His body is but a shadow: he himself is a pure spirit. There is a kind of immortality about this sort of ideal and visionary existence that dallies with Fate and baffles the grim monster, Death. If I thought you could make as clever an artist, and arrive at such an agreeable old age as Mr. Northcote, I should declare at once for your devoting yourself to this enchanting profession; and in that reliance, should feel less regret at some of my own disappointments, and little anxiety on your account!

BOX 3-2 *(con't)*

To the same
Fielding and other authors

Lovere, 22 Sept. [1755].

My Dear Child,

I received, two days ago, the box of books you were so kind to send; but I can scarce say whether my pleasure or disappointment was greatest. I was much pleased to see before me a fund of amusement, but heartily vexed to find your letter consisting only of three lines and a half. Why will you not employ Lady Mary as secretary, if it is troublesome to you to write? I have told you over and over, you may at the same time oblige your mother and improve your daughter, both which I should think very agreeable to yourself. You can never want something to say. The history of your nursery, if you had no other subject to write on, would be very acceptable to me. I am such a stranger to everything in England, I should be glad to hear more particulars relating to the families I am acquainted with: if Miss Liddel marries the Lord Euston I knew, or his nephew, who has succeeded him; if Lord Berkeley has left children; and several trifles of that sort, that would be a satisfaction to my curiosity. I am sorry for H. Fielding's death, not only as I shall read no more of his writings, but I believe he lost more than others, as no man enjoyed life more than he did, though few had less reason to do so, the highest of his preferment being raking in the lowest sinks of vice and misery. I should think it a nobler and less nauseous employment to be one of the staff officers that conduct the nocturnal weddings. His happy constitution (even when he had, with great pains, half demolished it) made him forget everything when he was before a venison pasty, or over a flask of champagne; and I am persuaded he has known more happy moments than any prince upon earth. His natural spirits gave him rapture with his cook-maid, and cheerfulness when he was starving in a garret. There was a great similitude between his character and that of Sir Richard Steele. He had the advantage both in learning, and, in my opinion, genius: they both agreed in wanting money in spite of all their friends, and would have wanted it, if their hereditary lands had been as extensive as their imagination; yet each one of them so formed for happiness, it is a pity he was not immortal. . . . This Richardson is a strange fellow. I heartily despise him, and eagerly read him, nay, sob over his works in a most scandalous manner. The first two tomes of *Clarissa* touched me, as being very resembling to my maiden days; and I find in the pictures of Sir Thomas Grandison and his lady, what I have heard of my mother, and seen of my father. . . .

---

and rewriting stages. The first stage involves identification of the purpose, audience, and vehicle for communication; research and note taking; use of directing questions; and systematic treatment of information. The second stage involves organization of information, including arrangement of note cards and use of an outline or diagram; writing; and rewriting and editing.

Every paper has a beginning, a middle, and an end; the beginning states the

**PHILIP DORMER STANHOPE, EARL
OF CHESTERFIELD**
1694-1773
To his son
Dancing

Dublin Castle, 29 Nov. 1745.

Dear Boy,

I have received your last Saturday's performance, with which I am very well satisfied. I know or have heard of no Mr. St. Maurice here; and young Pain, whom I have made an ensign, was here upon the spot, as were every one of those I have named in these new levies.

Now that the Christmas breaking-up draws near, I have ordered Mr. Desnoyers to go to you, during that time, to teach you to dance. I desire that you will particularly attend to the graceful motion of your arms; which with the manner of putting on your hat, and giving your hand, is all that a gentleman need attend to. Dancing is in itself a very trifling, silly thing; but it is one of those established follies to which people of sense are sometimes obliged to conform; and then they should be able to do it well. And though I would not have you a dancer, yet when you do dance, I would have you dance well; as I would have you do everything you do, well. There is no one thing so trifling, but which (if it is to be done at all) ought to be done well; and I have often told you that I wish you even played at pitch, and cricket, better than any boy at Westminster. For instance, dress is a very foolish thing; and yet it is a very foolish thing for a man not to be well dressed, according to his rank and way of life; and it is so far from being a disparagement to any man's understanding, that it is rather a proof of it, to be as well dressed as those whom he lives with: the difference in this case between a man of sense and a fop is, that the fop values himself upon his dress; and the man of sense laughs at it, at the same time that he knows he must not neglect it. There are a thousand foolish customs of this kind, which not being criminal, must be complied with, and even cheerfully, by men of sense. Diogenes the cynic was a wise man for despising them; but a fool for showing it. Be wiser than other people if you can; but do not tell them so.

It is a very fortunate thing for Sir Charles Hotham, to have fallen into the hands of one of your age, experience, and knowledge of the world: I am persuaded you will take infinite care of him. Goodnight.

purpose and provides a context or rationale as well as an outline of what is to follow and the end summarizes and offers a conclusion with respect to the initial question. After a preliminary formulation of the beginning, which directs information gathering for the body of the paper, the writer works most intensively on the middle and then goes back to adjust the beginning and end of the paper to accord with the changes. The process of adjustment might well require more than one round of shuttling among sections before the finished form of the written paper is attained. Three guides for effective encoding introduced earlier apply at both the planning and production level. They are identification of purpose and of major points, and choice of vehicle. The intended audience colors treatment of each guide.

Refining the Purpose.   In formulating the directing purpose of the paper a nested hierarchy of decisions must be made that will influence selection of central points and the means of conveying them. By this I mean that you select the thematic focus in terms of topic, supporting material, and intended conclusion. For example, if you are writing about anxiety, the Revolutionary War, twentieth century changes in U.S. balance of trade, or reproduction in simple organisms, decide first what aspect of the topic you will deal with: theories of anxiety, economic causes of the American revolution, the role of monetary policy, or the function of the various forms of reproduction. Then decide what point is to be made with respect to it: for example, each theory of anxiety deals well with some aspect of anxiety but none satisfactorily accounts for all of them, or some economic determinants of the Revolution played a larger role than others. In developing the theme, the chosen focus should maintain prominence in the sense that supporting points should be related to it explicitly.

A second directing decision concerns the nature of the audience. Novice writers often address an audience of one, themselves, or a course instructor. So narrowly directed a communication is usually opaque to a wider audience. In order to adjust the level it is necessary to consider what the audience can be expected to know and what must be explained or defined. Regardless of the nature of the audience illustrative examples are essential in clarifying points raised. The choice of particular examples is a function of the audience. Technical or highly specific examples may be enlightening for the professional level audience but are unfamiliar for a more general one. For example, fission, budding, and conjugation do not have the same meaning for a general audience that they have for biologists. For a nontechnical audience, analogies or additional background may be required. The form of the communication as well as its content will be influenced by the audience addressed. Although there are standard conventions in many special areas, such as prescribed journal form in the sciences, an informal and motivating style is more inviting for the average reader.

Gathering Information.   As a student in grade school you learned that the way to research a subject was to look it up in the encyclopedia. While that remains a good strategy for getting a quick overview, the implication that all knowledge is in books, like lifeless objects packed in boxes, is an unfortunate one, as is the related assumption that everything printed in books is necessarily true. Knowledge is living, growing, and changing, even in such seemingly established areas as literature or history. You can advance not only your own knowledge but also that of society—you need not be especially annointed to do so. It is helpful to bear this in mind when researching a topic, even one about which there is a great deal of published evidence. Even a novice can spot gaps, notice inconsistencies, or cast old problems in a new framework.

Given the immensity of materials available it is almost impossible to give advice for locating information on all possible subject topics. A preliminary background survey in a dictionary, encyclopedia, or basic text usually provides a general orientation. After that you can consult the appropriate specialized publications or a reference librarian. The reference librarian will instruct you in the use of the card catalogue for identifying relevant books by author or subject. Under subject headings you will find references not only to specific volumes but also to bibliographies and guides to the literature. The reference librarian can also direct you to specialized reference materials and computerized reference sources. Get an idea of the relevant material available before reading in detail.

To the extent that your topic has a single call number, or a limited number of them, it is also possible, under the Library of Congress system, to go to that section of the library and browse among the collection, sampling from selected volumes to get a "feel" for the topic. In areas where there are a great many research journals published on a regular basis throughout the world there are also journals that regularly abstract the research journals: *Biological Abstracts, Chemical Abstracts, Psychological Abstracts,* and so on. In some fields, such as art or medicine, the publication title is *Index* rather than *Abstracts,* for example, *Index Medicus.* There is also a publication, *Current Contents,* that reproduces the table of contents of current journals in a variety of areas. There also are special publications devoted to critical reviews of selected topics. Some examples are the *Advances* or the *Annual Review* series in a variety of disciplines. These publications include topical reviews of research in specific areas over a specified time period by experts who provide an evaluation of the work, complete with references.

Whatever the topic being researched, after reading a few references and scanning their bibliographies you can identify the authors and papers that are repeatedly cited. They, presumably, are the most influential sources. For additional references you can then look up other citations of influential authors in the appropriate *Citation Index.* That publication lists all papers in which the referenced author was cited; they constitute possible additional references. Bear in mind, however, that because many writers go through the same process that you go through when assembling their references, a relevant reference that is overlooked in the early stages of development of a topic may be consistently omitted thereafter. Many useful contributions are made by "discovering" a relevant contribution that was hitherto overlooked.

As noted earlier, not all knowledge is found in publications. There is growing appreciation of the fact that every individual is a library of unique information to be tapped through the "oral history" process. You might find it interesting to explore the possibilities of oral history by asking acquaintances or relatives, especially older ones, about their knowledge and experiences, what the world was like when they were your age, and so on. In fact, if you have difficulty conversing with a stranger or new acquaintance you might assume the role of an inquiring reporter and ask that person to instruct you in something he or she knows a lot about.

Another major source of knowledge is laboratory research about which more will be said in Chapter 9. For present purposes, it is often useful to adopt the role of a scientist in advancing your own understanding. Whatever the topic, anyone can raise searching questions and pursue them in a systematic manner. The two aspects of a scientific approach of relevance here are *use of directing questions* and *systematic treatment of information*.

Use of Directing Questions.   Having assembled a list of references, you may find that to read each in turn from start to finish will be both time consuming and unproductive. They should be scanned with the purpose of the paper firmly in mind. For example, you may ask yourself, "What were the roots of World War II? What are the central themes of nineteenth century feminist literature? How did the radio change American folkways?" Of course, there is always the possibility that you may discover, in the course of your reading, that the initial question is not interesting, currently unanswerable, or that it requires modification. You need to be prepared for those possible outcomes although the viability of your major focus is usually established during the initial information-gathering stage.

There are a number of general directing questions concerning supporting information to be raised in reading: What methods are employed in the area? What are the key concepts and major assumptions? Upon what evidence are they based? Who are the influential contributors and why? What is this all about? Why should anyone care to know about this topic? On what other issues does it shed light? The answers to all of these questions will assist in developing a framework within which to present the topic.

A third class of directing questions is more critically evaluative: Are there gaps, ambiguities, or inconsistencies in the available evidence? Are there implicit assumptions underlying conclusions, such as author bias or ethnocentrism, that preclude tenable alternative interpretations? How else might the evidence be interpreted? Which of the available interpretations best accounts for the evidence? Critical analysis and evaluation of content material is the feature that most often distinguishes a good paper from one that is pedestrian or superficial. The subject of evaluation will be pursued further in Chapter 5.

Systematic Treatment of Information.   Advance planning of systematic procedures for dealing with reference information repays the effort. First, it is poor policy to rely on memory which is subject to loss or distortion. Your basic facts should be reliable and capable of direct verification. Everyone can recall instances of "known facts" taken for granted that turn out to be incorrect. Second, it may be necessary to return to source material as decisions about what to include change over the course of revisions. Good notes can save extra trips to the library. Third, good notes can be useful at a later stage of organizing the material for writing the paper. For this purpose it is useful to devise an indexing scheme and to avoid tying notes too tightly to a particular source or index category. One device is to take notes on cards on which source and a variety of index categories are included. Cards have the additional advantage that they can be filed for later reference should the information be pertinent for a different question. To promote flexibility for revision or later use, it is a good idea not to tie the indexing categories too tightly to the paper or the course. Good thinkers avoid pigeonholing their knowledge in narrow categories that might render information inaccessible on later occasions or in different contexts. Remember the warning about being context bound from Chapter 1.

Organizing Information: The First Draft. Now that all the notes are assembled how do you get from them to a first draft? If the reader has taken seriously the advice of the first chapter to be deliberately directing and search for systematic procedures he or she will have used directing questions and developed a preliminary integrating framework. The initial focus, the purpose, sets some bounds in the sense that it is always good policy at the outset to state your purpose and to buttress it by supporting background about how it arose, why it is interesting, and so on. People differ, however, with respect to preferred strategy for arriving at an initial framework. Some will do the arranging directly with the note cards, others may need to do some writing or diagramming prior to that step to clarify the central ideas and establish connections among them, such as developing an outline, listing central ideas and questions, or arranging them in a tree or other hierarchical structure. Some of these devices are illustrated in Box 3-3. The goal of these efforts is to identify main topics and subtopics that will be indicated in the draft through the use of appropriate headings and subheadings. This form of structuring is always preferable to the common student practice of ordering information with respect to source, that is, detailing in turn what each reference contained. Such a procedure is analogous to serving the courses of a meal in the same packages from which they came from the supermarket; it doesn't make for an appetizing meal nor does it provide credit to the creativity of the chef.

A paper should offer the reader substance in an inviting presentation. Taking a hint from the preceding example, sometimes an analogy or analysis of a compelling example may provide a useful framework. For some purposes, such as presenting an experiment, the organizing structure is prescribed by convention: (a) statement of the problem and background of prior research, (b) method, (c) results, (d) discussion of results in relation to broader issues and alternative interpretations, and (e) conclusions. That general framework will often serve other purposes as well.

BOX 3-3

Planning a Communication

A. Chapter 1 Organized by Means of an Outline

I. What is thinking?
   A. Thinking as symbolic activity
   B. Thinking as meaning-making
   C. Degree of awareness and self-regulation
   D. Systematic organization of thinking
   E. The role of knowledge

II. Training of thinking
   A. Can it be trained?
   B. A skills approach
   C. A styles approach

B. Chapter 1 Organized as a Partial List of Ideas

1. Thinking has a structure:
   symbols
   transformation
   framework

   Thinking has a function:
   understanding

2. There are many kinds of thinking
   directed   undirected
           analytic synthetic
        purposeful playful

Writing and Revising.   It is advisable in a first draft not to be too concerned with polished prose or with creating wonderful sentences and paragraphs with which you become so enamored that it is difficult to part with them. For a first draft it is better to keep your eye on the big picture acknowledging that later revision can deal with the finer details.

When you reach the revision stage the first consideration is to ensure that the material of the paper is developed in a coherent, logical fashion. Are there gaps or inconsistencies to be resolved? Are there alternative interpretations that have not been addressed adequately? Are there any unwarranted assumptions? Are all the major points explicitly addressed? In answering those questions you can adopt the role of an intended reader, detaching yourself from your writing

3. Possibilities of improvement
   techniques
   orientation

C. Use of a Tree Structure to Organize Some of the Main Ideas of Chapter 1

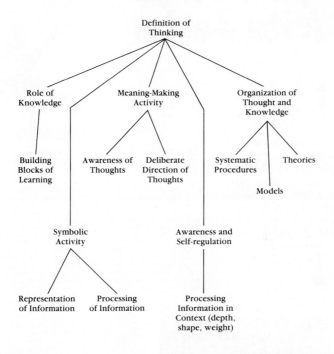

so as to view it through the eyes of another. Anticipate whether it will be as meaningful to the reader as it is to you. Have terms been adequately defined? Are appropriate examples provided? Are there ambiguities? Are implications drawn and sufficiently justified? What should the reader know after reading the paper that he or she did not know before?

The directing considerations for editing require that you have a clear understanding of the text in order to promote understanding on the part of the reader. That is rarely a neat two-step procedure. In the course of clarifying material for the reader it is possible you will discover gaps in your own understanding. The process of dialogue with an imaginary reader may necessitate additional revision or, even, a return to your source material; but, you may find that third step

BOX 3-4

Tips: How to Write Better

EDUCATION

Tips: How to Write Better

America's colleges and universities have a wide variety of writing requirements, and every instructor develops techniques to help students improve. But in surveying writing programs and teachers across the country, NEWSWEEK ON CAMPUS found that the basic advice they give students is surprisingly uniform. Here, distilled from the experts, are seven tips for better writing:

Writing is, at base, an exercise in thinking. Setting down thoughts on paper forces the writer to examine the logic—or lack of it— behind those thoughts

---

Read—as much as you can. Teachers of writing almost unanimously emphasize that reading and writing are inextricably linked. "I don't think you can write any better than you can read," says University of Texas English Prof. John Trimble, who adds that even many bright students are not very sophisticated readers. If you are already a reader, make it a point occasionally to sample books you wouldn't ordinarily try. Someone steeped in 20th-century pulp fiction, for instance, can get surprising enjoyment—and learn a great deal about the rich variety of the English language—from the works of 19th-century novelists. If you are not a regular reader, try to get into the habit. At the very least, set aside some regular time to read something that is not required by your studies.

■ **Organize before you start.** Writing is, at base, an exercise in thinking. The very act of setting down thoughts in words forces the writer to examine the real meaning of those words and the logic—or lack of it— that leads from one thought to another. It requires careful decisions on which information is unimportant to the task at hand and which is critical. And it demands attention to the most effective order in which to present the critical information. The clear message is that writing is much easier if you have first outlined just exactly what it is you want to say. An outline is not set in concrete: even the best writers revise their plans as they go along. But simply throwing a jumble of thoughts onto paper or a computer screen without prior consideration produces just a jumble of thoughts in a new medium—not good writing.

■ **Simplify.** As you write, beware of highfalutin word choice and pretentious phrasing. Always try for the simplest, clearest, most lucid way of expressing what you want to say. Beware, too, of jargon. It is a common misconception among students that adopting the specialized idiom of a particular discipline sounds more knowledgeable or important, and therefore makes their writing "better." This is not true. In fact, a student who can wrestle a complex idea into felicitous new phrasing demonstrates that he or she has mastered the idea *behind* the jargon.

■ **Revise and rewrite.** Professors say this is where college students most often fall short: once they see their words written or typed out, they think the job is done. Nothing could be farther from the truth. Start a writing assignment far enough ahead so that you will have time to do it again—and again, if necessary. Read closely for meaning. Are the words you have chosen the best

ILLUSTRATIONS BY KEITH BENDIS

words possible? If not, change them. Does each sentence you have written precisely convey the meaning you intended? If not, try again. "Good writing is extraordinarily time-consuming," observes Richard C. Marius, director of Harvard's Expository Writing Program. "You have to sit and shut out the rest of the world."

And remember: spelling and grammar *do* count—not because they satisfy what UT's Trimble calls "formalistic old fuddy-duddies," but because they help clarify and refine meaning. "I smelled the oysters going down the stairs for dinner"—a student solecism supplied by the University of Wisconsin's Madison campus writing lab—does not convey what the writer meant.

■ **Read your prose aloud.** This is a most useful way to determine whether your writing is

awkward or stilted. If it sounds strange or incomprehensible to your ear, it probably will strike the reader the same way. This is also an excellent exercise for checking the rhythms of your writing. If every single sentence is a simple declarative statement (or, alternatively, too long and convoluted), you will hear it immediately—and be able to vary your pace to make it better.

■ **Practice.** You learn to write by reading and writing as much as you can. English

courses are not the only places to work on your writing: strive for the same tight thinking, the same clarity and even elegance of expression by writing for your biology or business or art classes—even if no writing is formally required. It's not simply a matter of honing the skill. The discipline of writing also forces you to think in a way that enhances your learning. And although many students—and even some professors—contend that writing is not useful in disciplines outside English, that is arrant nonsense. It is no accident that an economist like John Kenneth Galbraith and scientists like Lewis Thomas and Stephen Jay Gould are renowned in their respective fields. They have mastered the art of communicating difficult disciplines to nonspecialists with grace, lucidity and wit.

■ **Seek criticism.** If you can't get harried professors to critique your writing, don't despair. Many schools maintain one-on-one tutorial programs that will help with everything from a term paper to a cover letter for a job application. Wisconsin's writing lab, for instance, operates much like a clinic: students make appointments with instructors who examine their work closely, then work with them on their weaknesses. Even if your school does not have such a resource, don't give up. Ask friends and classmates to read your work—and be honest in their reactions.

Remember, there are no set formulas for good writing. Many students arrive at college with the notion, imparted in high school, that the perfect essay is exactly five paragraphs long with five sentences within each paragraph. Too many "have no conception that you can think or write in any other way," says Princeton writing instructor Madeleine Picciotto. "That's what got them A's in high school—a certain kind of pompous, pretentious, automatic writing." In fact, of course, there is no easy formula. Good writing involves rigorous thought, a lot of work and—at its very best—the inspiration and courage to take some risks. Economist Galbraith, who cautions that he never achieves his wonderful "spontaneity" of expression before the seventh revision, quotes an editor he once worked for: "Anyone who says writing is easy is either a bad writer or an unregenerate liar."

MERRILL SHEILS *with* ALAN DEUTSCHMAN *in Princeton, N.J.,* TIM KELLEY *in Madison, Wis.,* BEN SHERWOOD *in Cambridge, Mass.,* *and* KELLY KNOX *in Austin, Texas*

> You learn to write by reading and writing as much as you can. Try practicing your skills even in courses where writing is not formally required

problems of attending to sentence structure, spelling, and punctuation have been largely resolved during this second stage. Some additional tips on good writing are offered in Box 3-4. An example of the process of revision is given in Box 3-5.

PROMOTING UNDERSTANDING

Much space has been devoted to the process of writing a paper because (a) it illustrates the close relation between personal understanding and communication to others, and (b) it serves as a framework for promoting personal understanding in other contexts. In order to communicate ideas to others it is first necessary to understand them yourself. That observation suggests that a good way to attain understanding is through explanation to another or through an internal dialogue. By answering self-imposed questions like "How does the first point relate to the second?" or "How do those two related ideas differ?" you refine and more precisely encode your own understanding. There is, however, much that you don't say to yourself because you already know it or believe that you know it. Everyone has encountered overoptimistic assessments in their knowledge or depth of preparation in the course of confidently embarking upon some performance only to discover inadequacies in its execution (for example, in taking an exam or delivering a talk). Gaps and inadequacies of understanding are more likely to be recognized when you attempt to impart knowledge to another and, in so doing, discover previously unconsidered questions. These observations suggest that the best test of your understanding is to express it to someone else, preferably in writing. Why should that be the case? In order to communicate you are forced to become more self-aware of the nature and determinants of understanding and more self-directing in encoding in an organized fashion that enhances meaning. Note, also, that this reasoning underlies the suggestion of Chapter 1 that you do exercises with a partner. When writing is the mode of encoding, contextual supports, such as demonstration, enactment, or pointing, are eliminated. In short, in written communication you are forced to manifest all the defining properties of thought outlined in Chapter 1 and to take nothing for granted. The remainder of this section is devoted to further examining the nature of understanding and to offering some advice on the means of promoting it through a personal journal and through good study techniques.

The Nature of Understanding. This section is a continuation of the discussion of encoding in Chapter 2 and might be called encoding for understanding. You will recall that encoding for precision emphasizes unique, relevant properties, the identification of which may require order imposing devices to promote assembling of information for effective scanning. To the extent that ordering devices constitute a form of chunking they can, and do, promote retention as well as precision. Encoding for understanding incorporates all of these means of transformation as well as the basic underlying process of classification in the service of a more encompassing goal, the apprehension of meaning relative to a broader framework. The framework may take the form of a theory, a model, an analogy, a value system, a set of causal principles, or various societal conventions. The way in which encoding of understanding differs from the simpler forms of encoding in Chapter 2 is that it proceeds simultaneously at several levels of generality rather than being confined to a single level. The basic process underlying it is the process of hierarchical classification. Understanding integral calculus, for example, entails not only knowing and using specific techniques of integration but, also, a deeper insight into the nature of integration that provides a basis for knowing when and why a given technique applies and for extrapolating beyond practiced problems.

Consider a common example: your friend is crying and you want to understand why. This may strike you as a ridiculous example in which no thinking is involved at all but look at the analysis of the cause of tears in Box 3-6. In practical situations something similar to the hierarchy presented in Box 3-6 is implicitly invoked in identifying a cause and applying an appropriate solution. Whether or not actual thinking is involved depends upon the explicit level of awareness of your behavior and its deliberate direction. What I am suggesting is that understanding at a nontrivial level requires awareness and explicit formulation of an appropriate hierarchical classification that serves as its broader framework. Because you are not accustomed to this view of the nature of understanding let us make it more familiar by showing its implications for practice in the development of understanding.

As a first step in that direction, return to the two recipes presented in Box 3-1. The first recipe was clearly lacking in sufficient detail; but the second does a good deal more than simply fill in the requisite detail. It is directed toward producing understanding in the reader, a goal that is attained by supplying information at several levels. In providing directions for producing ice cream through the intermediate step of producing a custard it places the directions in a broader context of custard production, whose bounds the reader is invited to explore. Armed with the theory of ice cream making from the second recipe one could go on to produce a variety of ice cream flavors by varying ingredients within the general procedure.

This example is illustrative of the difference in level of understanding between a novice and an expert. An expert organizes knowledge within a systematic general framework or theory at the highest level; specific theories are derived from the general theory at an intermediate level, and details of specific applications are derived at the level of the particular. The expert can operate at any level using other levels as an integrating framework. The novice, by way of contrast, tends to focus at a particular level (often the lowest) and has difficulty in moving back and forth among levels of generality because he or she lacks the

BOX 3-5

The Process of Revision As Applied to a Resume

BEFORE

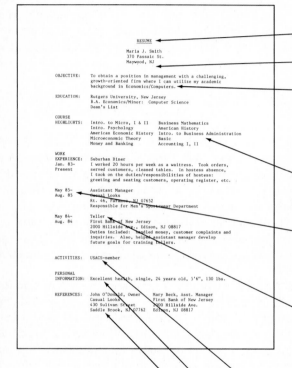

RESUME CRITIQUE

Eliminate any unnecessary words like "resume."

Don't forget to include your telephone number!

This sounds too general. Be more specific, if possible (if not, include a career objective in your cover letter).

Include your date of graduation, G.P.A. (if it's 3.0 or above), and your college affiliation.

Try to list about 5 or 6 courses that would be relevant to your field, or perhaps special electives that generally wouldn't be required within your major.

These dates are confusing, try moving them to the right side.

List most recent experience first. Whichever approach you choose, be consistent in your format.

Highlight positions you've held if you think they will catch the reader's eye.

Use action words to describe what you did and watch verb tense. Phrases like "duties and responsibilities include" can be eliminated since it doesn't convey pertinent information to the employer.

Abbreviations like this may confuse the employer. It would be helpful to write out the name of the organization and describe your involvement, if significant.

Personal information is unnecessary.

It is probably best to simply state "available upon request" unless your references are prominent figures in the field.

AFTER

MARIA J. SMITH

370 Passaic Street
Maywood, New Jersey 07777
(201) 555-4567

OBJECTIVE: An entry level position in Retail Purchasing Management
where I can utilize my analytical skills.

EDUCATION: B.A. in Economics, May 1986
Minor in Computer Science
Rutgers College, Rutgers University
New Brunswick, New Jersey

Dean's List-three semesters
Economics G.P.A.: 3.85/4.00

COURSE
HIGHLIGHTS: Retail Management
Principles in Retail Purchasing
Marketing Research and Analysis

RELATED
EXPERIENCE: Assistant Manager, May 1985–August 1985
Casual Looks, Paramus, New Jersey
-Increased department sales by 25%.
-Trained and Supervised 5 new employees.
-Handled basic accounting/bookkeeping.
-Organized effective displays, assisted customers.

Teller, May 1984–August 1984
First Bank of New Jersey, Edison, New Jersey
-Handled banking transactions and customer complaints.
-Managed daily cash flow of $10,000.
-Assisted with long range planning.

ADDITIONAL
EXPERIENCE: Waitress/Hostess, January 1983 to present
Suburban Diner, Paramus, New Jersey
-Financed 50% of college expenses through part-time
work
-Took orders, served customers, and filled in for
hostess.

COMPUTER
SKILLS: Basic, Fortran, Pascal
IBM-PC, Apple IIe, DEC 20

ACTIVITIES: Rutgers University Computer Science Club (USACS), member

INTERESTS: Swimming, Volleyball, Computers

REFERENCES: Available Upon Request

(After Jones, Galanos, & Lin, 1985)

BOX 3-6

A Hierarchical Classification of the Causes of Tears

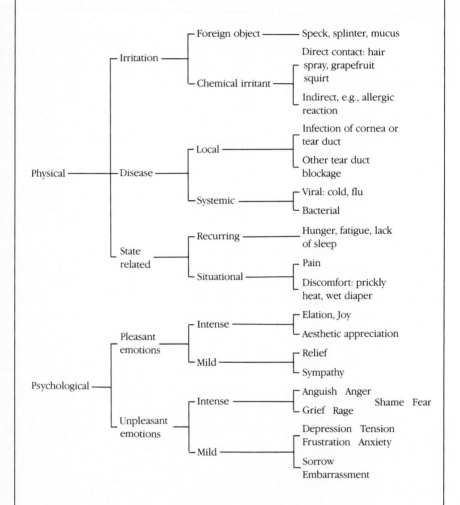

Note: This table is not exhaustive; it might be instructive to expand it. For infants one tends to enter the hierarchy at the state-related level; for adults one tends to enter it at the emotional level unless there is direct evidence of physical cause.

integrated framework of a hierarchy. To provide additional substance to this skeletal context you might examine any number of "educational" TV programs, or texts, in which many facts are presented without the organizing framework of a broader context. In the case of textbooks, find other texts on the same topic that do a far better job of filling in the context and compare them to basic texts with respect to presentation and explanation of material. Information placed within the framework of hierarchical structure does a far better job of promoting understanding. Thus, the moral of this story is that in order to understand, you must construct a broader framework of meaning. How is that achieved? The next section considers studying and learning for understanding; the question is pursued more broadly in Chapter 5.

Learning and Studying for Understanding.   As a child in grade school you may have been confronted at suppertime with queries from your parents about what you learned in school today. These queries may have been dismissed as another empty convention like, "How are you?" but they could have served to promote your understanding of what was learned by prompting summary and organization. Applying the convention of playing parent to yourself and asking, "What did I learn from this?" is a useful first step along the route to promoting your own understanding. The contribution is further enhanced through the use of additional questions, such as, how does it relate to what I already know? How would I explain it to someone else? It is suggested that such queries are a very useful habit to employ at the end of a chapter or the end of a lecture. The resulting summaries provide the ingredients for the next step of developing a coherent framework, that is, integrating the summaries into a hierarchical structure.

A familiar example of the need for summarizing and integrating arises in studying for exams. Many students review the underlined areas of the text, reread lecture notes, and perhaps, scan assignments as well. What many fail to do is to integrate the material from these three sources into a coherent unity. There are many routes to the goal of integration. One common form is to outline the text, to outline lecture notes, and then to integrate the two outlines. Another procedure might be to identify central concepts, themes, or topics and to create an organized summary of each, utilizing whatever material is appropriate for the purpose. The vehicle for representing your summary might take the form of an outline, a tree diagram, or a network like that of Exercise 8 at the end of Chapter 2. The form of the integrative summary is of less importance than its creation. Understanding is not the residue of traces stamped into memory but the product of an active process of meaning-making. The process of meaning-making is materially enhanced by transforming information through a process of seeking defining features, creating examples and noting similarities and differences among them, and by trying various ways of encoding your discoveries to find how best to communicate the meaning. That is thinking. It is also hard work.

Why coherently organized information is conducive to understanding may be illustrated by the simple analogy to a desk drawer. Anyone in the habit of tossing things of immediate or future relevance into a desk drawer rapidly discovers that the drawer fills to capacity until it is impossible to find anything in the mess. In fact, you never are sure as to what is or is not in the drawer. For all practical purposes its contents might just as well be lost. So, too, with knowledge. If it is meaningful to compare memory storage to the contents of a drawer and to assume that there are capacity limits to both, the observation that a carefully packed container holds far more than one that is randomly filled is supported by evidence on memory. Whatever limits may exist seem to be defined with respect to numbers of chunks. A rich, organized chunk takes up no more room than a single item. The great advantage of integrated knowledge lies not only in the increased storage provided but also in greater ease of retrieval on future occasions and in different contexts, such as in applying your knowledge.

The schematic memory network of Exercise 8 at the end of Chapter 2 illustrates an assumed connection among items of memory. Multiply connected items have many possible routes of retrieval; isolated items, like objects thrown into a drawer, are far more likely to be lost. Of course, to pursue the drawer analogy, form of storage is adjusted to frequency of use and value; indispensable, frequently used objects are carried about in the pocket or purse, valuable or irreplaceable ones may be kept in a vault. Provisional knowledge and ideas that may be revised or abandoned in the development of understanding warrant storage that is appropriate to their status. The personal journal is ideally suited to that purpose.

The Journal.   Most writers, scientists, and other accomplished thinkers develop the habit of keeping a journal in which they record ideas and observations that show promise for future development but are not yet in finished form. There are two great advantages to such journals: (a) since you know where to retrieve them they can't be lost either to you or to posterity (scholars continue to mine the journals of eminent persons[3]); (b) because of the privileged status of this semipermanent recording, the ideas and observations are preserved in a form that enables or invites additional use and transformation. As a student you might not have ideas that will eventuate into the great American novel or a new theory but you certainly are grappling with many important concepts and issues in the quest of understanding. You are also in the process of evolving your own philosophy of life. To the extent that these projects are not readily resolved but must be returned to, reexamined, and revised, you do need to be reminded of them and of the continuing need to deal with them. Moreover, the very fact of having a special vehicle, for this purpose the journal, helps promote your having ideas and observations to record. That observation is almost a corollary of Parkinson's law, that things proliferate to fill the space available to them, which is certainly true of attics and basements. You can also get into the habit of writing regularly—simply sit down and proceed.

With respect to the journal as a device for more effective learning, many students keep wide margins in their course notebook specifically for the purpose of noting in the margin questions that arise or self-instructions to relate the information to some other topic. Blank pages at the end of each day's lecture notes in which to record your own summary of the material are a related device. You probably have encountered courses in which the value of a journal was emphasized. If you took the injunction to keep a journal seriously you already have discovered its utility. Armed with the insights of Chapter 1 you are now better able to identify the cause of a journal's benefits: it promotes the process of becoming self-aware and self-directive in the quest for meaning. Thinkers keep a journal.

SUMMARY

This chapter focused on the essential role of *communication* in the development of understanding. The communication process was first examined in the relatively simple context of giving instructions and of letter writing. It was shown that the three guidelines for effective encoding discussed in Chapter 2 continue to apply. In addition, a new ingredient—the *intended audience*—assumes greater prominence in forging and transmitting meaning. By providing good and poor examples of instructions it was shown how effective communication can expand the understanding of the audience.

Producing a paper was considered a representative example of the process of communicating larger amounts of more detailed information. In pursuit of that goal *establishing an organizing framework* and *presenting information* in relation to it is central. Since the requisite organization is rarely, if ever, attained on the first attempt, repeated *revision* is inescapable. One should not only accept that fact but treat it as an opportunity for reassessment. Practical suggestions were offered for dealing with the various stages of writing a paper. They are *formulating the purpose, gathering information, processing and organizing the information, the first draft,* and *subsequent revision.*

Development of personal understanding was described as a communication with yourself that is enhanced through writing as though you were communicating to a larger audience. All the considerations of writing a paper continue to apply. The nature of understanding was described as establishing a broader framework that takes the form of a hierarchical classification in which material is organized at several levels of analysis. Practical suggestions for learning for understanding were derived from this analysis of the nature of understanding. The role of a journal in the evolution of understanding was stressed.

EXERCISES

1. Review your answer to Exercise 5 in Chapter 2 from the standpoint of what you learned in Chapter 3. How can you improve upon your answer? To what audience were your initial instructions addressed? In what way would they change for a more, or less, knowledgeable audience?

2. There is some interesting research[4] showing that children have difficulty in appreciating that instructions are inadequate. How do you detect that instructions are inadequate (as contrasted, for example, with deciding you are inadequate in ability to understand them)?

3. Write instructions for something you know how to do very well (knit a sock, change spark plugs, debug a program). Exchange instructions with your partner and critique each other's instructions.

4. Collect some editorials and/or letters to the editor, preferably ones that are addressed to a common issue. Identify the focus of each and analyze how it has been developed. Evaluate the effectiveness of each in attaining its purpose. Rewrite those that you believe can be improved upon.

5. Write a business letter to an insurance company reporting the theft of the contents of your automobile.

6. Take an assigned paper in some other course, or an unfamiliar topic you would like to know more about if you have no assigned paper, and formulate a focus for it. Describe the focus and how it would be developed.

7. Assemble a reference list for the paper in Exercise 4 above. Read two of the references and prepare a note card for each.

8. Start collecting some oral histories. Try to get several on the same topic so that you can compare responses with respect to their similarities and differences. Note that you need not choose an event in the distant past; for example, you might want to ask your friends what their high school was like or how Memorial Day is celebrated in their town. It would be very helpful to tape this so you could replay it and assess your own influence upon the history given by your informant.

9. Take a topic of interest to you and list at least three directing questions to be used in pursuing it in more detail. The topic chosen could be something quite technical (kinds of computer games and the sources of fascination of each; the apparent, sudden appearance of a new disease), a large social issue (abortion or capital punishment), or something quite frivolous (the vogue for ethnic foods, Cabbage Patch dolls, or Trivial Pursuit).

10. Generate an association network of your own using the diagram in Exercise 8 of Chapter 2 as a model. Does it provide an accurate and adequate model of your associations? Now that you have the network on paper, consider how you could increase your understanding of the subject (for example, by changing some connections of the network or adding others).

11. Detail some of your own organizing frameworks and how you use them; that is, become aware of your own favorite analogies or models and how

you use them to organize your own knowledge. Alternatively, you might take some field you know and identify the models and organizing frameworks used in it.

12. The game, Twenty Questions, is one in which good hierarchical classification pays off as may be seen by playing a few rounds in class. The rules are: (a) the leader announces a broad category, for example, an artist or a tool; (b) the players attempt to identify the answer by asking, at most, 20 questions, each of which can be answered only by "yes" or "no."

4

Detaching

In pursuit of the goal of meaning there are a number of basic contributory processes. Two of them, *encoding* and *organization,* have been considered in Chapter 2 and Chapter 3. To the extent that these processes are directly involved with symbolic activity and are intrinsic to thought, they are widely recognized and dealt with in many contexts (for example, courses in writing and rhetoric). The two processes to be considered in Chapter 4 and Chapter 5, *detaching* and *evaluation,* bear a less obvious but no less significant relation to the creation of meaning. That they are less frequently discussed in connection with thinking is perhaps attributable to their greater dependence upon self-awareness and self-direction, that is, upon style as contrasted with the skills aspect of thought. Detachment and evaluation are, in other words, essential ingredients of a reflective, thoughtful person.

Before going on to consider detachment specifically, it may be helpful to place it in the context of what you have already learned. The constraining effects of too literal an interpretation in problem solving (for example, in the problems in Box 1-1 as well as in the other exercises of Chapter 1), in interpretation of art or poetry, or in identification of intrinsic defining properties for classification (whether hierarchical, basic, or in defining concepts) have been demonstrated already. Related effects were encountered in the experiment in Box 2-6 and in other communication exercises of Chapter 3. The assumption that others, for example, the audience, think as you do—share your meanings, beliefs, and preferences—can pose an obstacle to communication. What all these instances have in common is a constraining effect that limits or precludes progress. The sources of that limiting effect lie, for the most part, in hasty, semiautomatic responses to a subset of contextual determinants. The effective thinker overcomes constrictions largely by preventing their occurrence in the first place. A major means of precluding constraint and promoting greater flexibility of thought is through *detachment* (a word that signifies removal without damage or destruction). This chapter will discuss three means of detaching: by overcoming impulse, by depersonalizing or unseating the self, and by freeing from context.

OVERCOMING IMPULSE

Everyone has encountered the injunction to "Look before you leap!" or the advice to count to ten as an antidote to losing your temper. Both bits of folkloric wisdom have a sound psychological basis. The immediate response is rarely the optimal one; often, it is inappropriate or, even, destructive. To the extent that the instigators of impulsive responding are powerful, impulses never can be completely controlled; but, as was noted in Chapter 1, some people are more prone to impulsiveness than others and all of us learn to control impulse as part of the process of growing up. Some major determinants of impulsiveness are largely situational while others seem to be emotionally mediated; both will be considered in this section.

Situational Impulsive Behavior.   Box 4-1 contains some excerpts from a student's journal documenting an instance of impulsive behavior. Each of us could supply additional examples from recent experiences. We all, on occasion, respond without thinking and, in retrospect, reproach ourselves for being so foolish, only to do something similar another time. Perhaps the best antidote is to become aware of the circumstances promoting impulsiveness and to acquire alternative ways of coping with them.

To some extent we are surrounded by deliberate incitement to impulsiveness. Every store with a checkout stand has a display of small, inexpensive non-essentials to tempt customers waiting in line; it is a rare person who never succumbs to them. Similarly, if you have ever watched a pitchman demonstrate household gadgets or grooming aids available at a fantastic price to the first few customers to come forward, you know how seductive incitements to impulse can be. Advertisers have devoted careful study to their creation. More subtle incitement abounds on television, radio, and a great variety of publications in what is presented as objective or, even, public service information. The section on stereotypes and propaganda in Chapter 2 provided some examples of this form of incitement. Perhaps the most frightening example of incitement to impulse is illustrated by newspaper accounts of audience vandalism or violence associated with athletic events or rock performances. Presumably when others are shouting and throwing pop bottles, it takes great control not to join them and genuine heroism to stand up and say "Stop this idiocy." The assumption is probably incorrect, in any event, there are too few direct tests of it.

The means for dealing with all these situations involve increased self-awareness for early identification of their existence and self-control in selecting alternative courses of action to block immediate impulsive responses. To promote

---

BOX 4-1

Some Examples of Impulsiveness

1. March 25.   My ID couldn't be found. Early this morning I went to the registrar and ordered a new ID. It cost me a $2 check. She gave me a temporary ID to use until the new one would be ready. She could give me no hint as to when I could expect it, but she believed it would take quite a while. We no longer have meal tickets. Instead our IDs are validated with a sticker displaying our meal ticket number. Thus when you lose your ID you also lose your meal ticket.

   By now it was nearing lunch time and I was getting hungry but I had no cash and therefore I could not purchase a new meal ticket. I headed toward the bookstore with a check I had written in hopes of obtaining enough money to buy a meal ticket. Unfortunately for me, the bookstore was not cashing any checks that day! Now what could I do? I decided to try the Rutgers bookstore. I hopped in my car and sped across town. At that time of the day, an empty parking space is a rarity. After about 15 minutes I finally managed to squeeze into a tiny space behind the student center. Then I remembered the only check I had with me was made out to the DC bookstore. I had used my blank check to pay the registrar that morning. I was really burned. Now I would have to go back to get a blank check!

   The next problem I faced was trying to enter the dorm parking lot. Some type of road construction was blocking the traffic. I finally eased my car among the various machines and found a parking space. After getting my checkbook I raced back to Rutgers. Now I faced another problem. The check cashier was not authorized to cash a check without a valid ID. I would have to have my temporary ID initialed by the store manager (all this I discovered after waiting ages in line). Naturally the manager was nowhere in sight. I had to wait while the cashier tried to find him. By this time I was practically on the verge of tears through sheer frustration. I

---

your own skill at identifying symptoms and causes of impulsiveness, list in your notebook (a) the kinds of occasions on which you succumb to impulse (for example, are you susceptible to group prompting and easily flustered?), and (b) your own personal signs of giving in to impulse (for example, poor management of time, wandering attention, excessive spending). By going over the lists in class you will probably find entries on the lists of other class members with which to augment your own list. As a result you should become more aware of the danger signs. What does one do about them? Taking a cue from the folklore at the start of this section, think of some ways to change the situation for yourself so that you will stop what you are doing and think about what you should do. It could

explained the problem to the manager and he was kind enough to okay my check.

To add an ironic note to the situation later that same day I was cursing the inconvenience I had caused by losing my stupid ID. I decided that maybe I hadn't lost it. I reviewed my method of search (see entry dated Mar. 20) and rechecked my steps. Step two (search coat pockets) had not been fully carried out. Wouldn't you know—my ID was hanging in my closet all the time! Now it was back to the registrar to try to cancel my order.

March 28.　After the fiasco with my ID I've decided that my real problem is disorganization and carelessness. 1. I must learn to think before rushing off to do something. 2. I should learn to replace objects when I'm finished using them. 3. I must overcome my impulsiveness and

>   (a) sit down when I feel the urge to rush off
>   (b) determine what exactly I want to accomplish
>   (c) plan my procedure carefully.

2. After leaving the basketball game at Monmouth College we noticed a pink Cadillac ahead of us and decided it must be _____ (a famous basketball player). My friend said "Let's follow him!" so we did. It was not easy because he was driving pretty fast and there was a lot of traffic. One time we almost lost him. Then there was another time when he went through a yellow light and we had to go through the red light not to lose him. We managed to keep following but then he turned onto the turnpike (a very limited access road with steep tolls) and we decided he must be going to New York and that was a lot out of our way so we turned off and went home instead. (From student journals, turned in over the years)

be something as simple as a self-instruction: "Stop!" "Think!" "Calm down!" "Cool it!" Or, it could be more specific self-advice, of the form: "What am I doing?" "Do I really need this?" "Look at all those crazies! I'm smarter than they!" Any of these devices could serve to detach you from the immediate context so that you may view it objectively and dispassionately and consider more desirable alternatives.

Emotion-Induced Impulses.　If someone shouts "Fire" or "Duck" there is a tendency for immediate compliance that is usually salutary. Some self-defending and life-preserving impulses are, in fact, "wired" into the nervous system in the form of defensive reflexes (startle, blink, fending off). In other instances, however, the results of impulsive or reflexive action can be destructive. Fear, for example, may lead to the blocking of overt behavior (as in the case of the rabbit who freezes in the middle of the road, or the common nightmare state of being unable to scream). For some animals freezing or death feigning is a common form of defense while others react with rage, flight, or frenetic activity. A deliberate choice between freezing or flight is not possible unless there is a pause for reflection prior to action. That pause can be achieved only by breaking the automatic link between emotional arousal and response or by blocking the emotional arousal that mediates automatic response.

Many students report fear, or its milder cousin, anxiety, to be crippling for them: for example, "I panic on exams." If that is, in fact, an accurate assessment (and in many instances it may be self-delusion) it suggests that fear blocks all reflection or constructive activity. The needed corrective is to eliminate fear by being equipped with a more effective means of coping. To the extent that anxiety is evoked by lack of preparation for a situation (that is, by perceived or anticipated helplessness or vulnerability), the general defense against it is adequate preparation. For example, many people who are anxious about getting lost in unfamiliar territory travel with maps or directions, others plan to orient themselves with respect to landmarks and seek specific directions when they are in the general vicinity. In preparation for some demanding test-like situation, such as an interview or a performance, most people find it useful to rehearse before the event until the required behavior is readily available and skillfully executed. In giving a performance of a play or a musical rendition, the required behavior is completely known in advance and can be rehearsed under conditions approximating those of the ultimate event (the dress rehearsal, for instance, provides the critical ingredient of a live audience).

What makes tests, or interviews, more difficult is that you do not know precisely what questions will be asked and, therefore, what responses should be forthcoming. It is not, however, difficult to imagine what kind of questions might be asked. In rehearsing for a test, therefore, the appropriate strategy is to prepare a varied list of test questions and to practice answering them. That strategy differs from the more usual student study method of reading material over and over (which could, conceivably, tie the information more tightly to the context in which it is encountered rather than repackaging it for greater availability in a variety of contexts). By way of contrast, inventing questions allows you to practice both the identification and evaluation of items of major importance, while answering the questions helps in organizing material and refining appropriate answers. Becoming prepared requires awareness of what will be needed and how it can be supplied.

On arrival at the test, it is always good practice to read the question carefully and rephrase it in your own words to clarify what is being asked. Some instructors deliberately phrase questions (or provide multiple choice alternatives) to trigger impulsive incorrect responding. It never hurts to look for a possible trap. After clarifying what is being sought, by checking with the instructor if necessary, you are ready to rehearse the answer. It is generally a good idea to outline the answer first to ensure that all the relevant points—and only the relevant ones—are raised in a coherent and organized fashion. In other words, plan ahead rather than learn what you know in the course of writing it out. Frequently a good outline is itself an adequate answer. As a first step towards consolidating this test-taking procedure into your repertoire you might go back to earlier chapters and construct a test of the material. Identify the major points, extract them from the context in which they were presented, devise additional examples and implications, and base your questions upon them. For example, as a test of your understanding of hierarchical classification, apply the concept to a specific instance or relate it to other concepts. This procedure is a more demanding test than reciting a definition. Give your test to other members of the class while you take theirs. In comparing each other's test items try to identify what makes a good question and to evaluate why most questions are not very good (too concrete or too specific).

The general procedure of rehearsal for anticipated contingencies, or even for unanticipated contingencies, is a good strategy for nonacademic situations as well as for academic ones. The test of a good driver, for example, is to be able to deal with unforeseen and dangerous emergencies. Practice under optimal conditions helps to consolidate the basic skills of steering, braking, estimating distances and stopping times to the point that they are effortless and habitual, but it does not necessarily prepare for unaccustomed conditions or emergencies. After braking on a deserted ice-glazed parking lot and practicing getting out of skids the driver is better prepared to know what the car does under those circumstances and to develop a repertoire for dealing with ice, snow, and slick surfaces that will preclude panic when these situations are encountered.

Before leaving the subject of emotionally mediated impulses, it is advisable to consider at least one other emotion. Anger is an emotion with which many persons have difficulty. It is an exceptional person who has not blurted out some hurtful statement in anger that he or she later regretted and longed to undo. The impulse to strike the child, kick the dog, curse the incompetent, is strong in all of us; rarely, if ever, is it an appropriate solution to the problem. The same is probably true of other strong emotions such as jealousy, greed, lust, and the chemically induced states produced by drugs and alcohol. All have the general property of (a) increasing the likelihood of impulsive behavior, and (b) decreasing the likelihood of self-awareness and prior reflection. All can be dealt with in the same manner as fear and anxiety by preventing strong emotional or chemical impairment and by having a rehearsed repertoire of coping techniques available. As an exercise for your notebook take an emotion that is destructive for you and identify the instigating circumstances, the symptoms of succumbing, and devise a coping repertoire for overcoming the disruptive effects of that emotion.

DEPERSONALIZING

One common meaning of the term "detachment" is "impersonal." That meaning is relevant to the suggestion that one of the most powerful obstacles to clear thinking and understanding is giving precedence to one's own predilections and points of view. To the extent that assertion is correct, a major avenue to clearer thinking lies in freeing oneself from the blinders of personal attitudes, values, and preferences not explicitly recognized as such. Another connotation of "impersonal" is "cold" or "unfeeling." That connotation is less relevant. The encouragement to detach is not intended to convey that all feelings and emotions must be banished. Far from it. Personal feelings and beliefs are an important part of life, but they are inappropriate as the exclusive determinants of one's behavior (as even small children quickly learn).

Unseating the Self.   Try asking your friends about a new film, record, or restaurant. It is quite likely that the reply will be "I liked it" or "I didn't like it," with varying degrees of conviction and elaboration. That is such a common response that most people are desensitized to the fact that it doesn't address the question posed. In asking about the film, record, or restaurant, you solicit a list of descriptive features about the plot, the acting, the sound quality, or the menu. Whether or not the friend liked it is really irrelevant except as a statement about the friend, or about your likely reaction if you and the friend have calibrated your respective tastes. Evaluating experience with respect to its acceptability or unacceptability to the experiencing individual is so common as to pass unnoticed; your personal evaluation is rarely of major interest to anyone else.

The young child or the untutored person is constrained by his or her own perspective and experience in manifest ways. A common laboratory task[1] for use with children, for example, is to present a scene containing several prominent features, such as a tree, building, mountain, cow, and ask the child for a description of the scene as it would appear to another observer, for example, a doll on the opposite side of the table. The task is illustrated in Box 4-2. Typically, the child describes what he or she sees. This is interpreted as evidence that the child is incapable of a perspective other than his own; that is, he or she assumes that all observers, wherever located, see exactly what he or she sees. Similarly, when the child is asked to imagine some unexperienced state of affairs, such as, if heaven has a flag and what it might look like, the answer is usually dictated by personal experience: "Yes. It is red, white, and blue." This kind of self-centered outlook is sometimes described as *egocentric,* a term with the added connotation of self-important or selfish which is less relevant to the present discussion. What is pertinent here is the implied assumption that what exists, or could exist, is isomorphic with your own experience. Other common terms for such a view are unsophisticated, naive, or ethnocentric. Some examples are given in Box 4-2; generate some additional ones in your notebook. As a more demanding illustration objectively consider some current issues such as abortion, free trade, trial

BOX 4-2

A. Examples of an Egocentric View

A. R. Luria interviewed residents of a collective in Soviet Central Asia. He told them to ask him three questions about what interests them. Here are some replies.

Kadyr, age 68, from remote mountain camp, illiterate.

Q: "What would you like to see—other countries, other cities—and what would you like to learn about them?"

A: "Probably there are interesting cities, as you say, but I don't know what's interesting about them. I know that I won't get to see them .... They took my horse away, and the road is long; I can't even imagine how I would get there."

Illi-Khodzh., age 22, from village of Sharmardan, slightly literate.

Q: "Ask me three questions, any you want."

A: "I'll give you one. 'Here I am now, but when I go to village X, they ask me, you were in Samarkand, what are the buses like there? Do they have hands and feet? How do they move?' I can't explain properly and I'm very embarrassed ... and then ... I don't know what to ask."

Siddakh, age 19, works on collective farm, two years in adult school.

Q: "Ask me any three questions."

A: "Well, what could I do to make our kolkhozniks (collective farmers) better people? How can we obtain bigger plants, or plant ones which will grow to be like big trees? And then I'm interested in how the world exists, where things come from, how the rich become rich and why the poor are poor."

Khushv, age 27, works on collective farm, two years of adult school.

Q: "Ask me three questions, any you like."

A: "I've never been anywhere or seen anything, so how could I have questions?"

Q: "But still, ask me whatever you like."

A: "Well, we asked the teacher how silk and velvet are produced ... he didn't answer, but it's something we're interested in."

"I don't know ... well, for instance, why is it wrong to slaughter sheep in the spring? Why cooperatives haven't yet been opened in the village, where they're very much needed!"

Aziz, age 36, organizer of Mikhnat farm, 2½ months in agronomy program.

Q: "Ask me three questions you would like to have answered."

A: "How can life be made better? Why is the life of a worker better than that of a peasant? How can I acquire knowledge more readily? Also, why are city workers more skilled than peasants?" (After Luria, 1976)

BOX 4-2 (cont.)

B. A Perspective-Taking Task

LOOK AT THIS PICTURE.

RITA

JOE

TIM

DICK

CLARA

DICK SEES THIS:

WHAT DOES JOE SEE?

A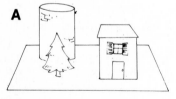

B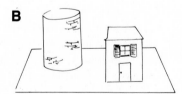

C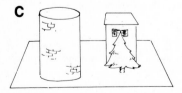

D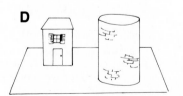

WHAT DOES TIM SEE?

WHAT DOES RITA SEE?

WHAT DOES CLARA SEE?

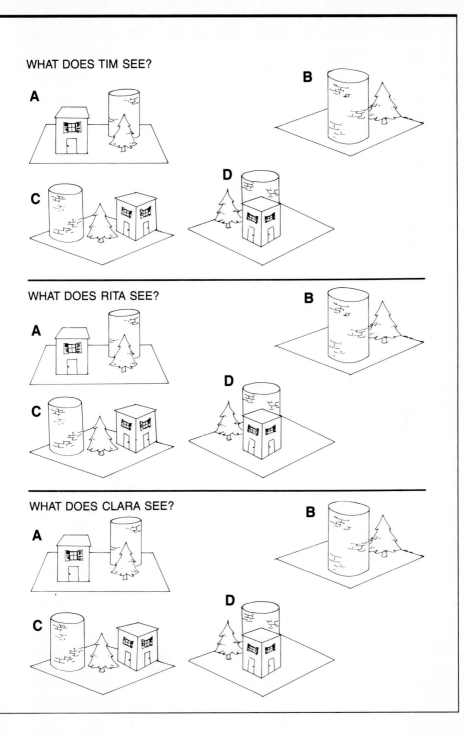

marriage, or closed shop, from the standpoint of advantages and disadvantages of the institution. Compare the "objective" lists you or your friends generate with your own personal view or that of your reference group.

Another example of egocentrism is the common tendency to interpret unfavorable evaluations of one's behavior or behavioral products as a personal attack or denigration of the self: for example, interpreting "That drawing is not a good likeness" or "The composition is not well balanced" as meaning "You are not an artist and never will be" or, even, "You are altogether worthless." Young children are especially prone to this sort of reaction to criticism, which further suggests that it is an immature reaction. Obviously, any accomplishment requiring skill or knowledge is rarely attained on the first try. Constructive criticism or, even, honest audience reaction is helpful in perfecting one's performance. Learning to accept and to utilize criticism in an objective manner is, therefore, a necessary accomplishment for any productive adult. List some examples of having interpreted comments personally in your notebook.

Although the transparent examples in Box 4-2 are rarely encountered among educated adolescents and adults, more subtle manifestations are still present, as you may have discovered from the last exercise. For example, most adolescents are intensely concerned with their personal appearance and assume that others are as keenly attuned to every aspect of it as they are.[2] To establish more realistic norms for what most people do and do not notice about the appearance of others you and your friends might try walking about in a variety of attires and conditions (for example, with Band-Aids of varying sizes covering different visible areas of anatomy). Then, an hour, a day, or a week after the encounter ask people to describe what you looked like. Presumably, in the course of devising test conditions, you will ask yourself what others are likely to notice. If so, one purpose of the exercise will already have been served: you are more aware that there are other possible views beside your own or, more generally, that you are not the canonical human being and that your views are not necessarily characteristic of others.

American society places a high valuation upon individual freedom. That value is not universally held in all societies. Many cultures place the needs of the collective above those of the individual.[3] Others prescribe roles determined by the age and sex of the individual. For example, the young person may be assumed to be inexperienced and inadequately prepared to make such major decisions as selection of a career or a mate or to manage resources on his own. Parents may be charged with the responsibility for those decisions. As one of your notebook exercises consider some of life's major decisions and list the person or institution charged with responsibility for those decisions in our culture (for example, declaring war, educational requirements, levying of taxes, zoning laws). You will find that some are legally prescribed whereas others are governed by informal traditions. As a final part of the exercise consider a decision such as choosing a mate from the standpoint of a culture with maximal individual freedom and a culture with minimal individual freedom. List the advantages and disadvantages of each approach, preferably in the form of a table so that they may be directly compared. The purpose of this exercise is to detach yourself from your own background and preferences and to view the issue impersonally. Try considering an alien position sympathetically in order to explore its ramifications on its own terms. Attaining that ability is one of the major goals of detachment and of becoming a clear, critical thinker.

Taking the Role of Another. One of your assignments in Chapter 2 was to notice how the skilled actor uses mannerisms and gestures to create a unique characterization and to attempt such portrayals yourself. In discussing their craft skilled actors indicate that they do not simply imitate actions but, rather, that they "get into their character" in the sense of trying to become that individual and to think as that individual would think. It is this assumption of a new persona that directs their portrayal on stage. Actors are by no means the only people who take the role of another in the course of their professional work; mediators, arbitrators, therapists, and teachers do so in the course of dealing with others. It is a necessary part of life. The purpose of this section is to make you more aware of the process.

If there was class discussion of the preceding assignment (or of earlier ones) you undoubtedly discovered that other members of the class fixed upon different features than you did or noticed some things that may not have occurred to you. One good technique for broadening your outlook and for generating new possibilities is to view an issue from someone else's perspective. That is also a good technique for becoming more open minded and considerate of the views of others. As a first step along that road, think about some issue from the viewpoint of a friend or relative (make sure you have not discussed the issue with them). Predict their likely view in detail and, after having recorded your predictions, discuss the issue with that person to test the accuracy of your predictions, preferably in a parallel column where you can tally their actual response in relation to your prediction to identify your hits and misses. Now, go over the places where you were wrong in your predictions and discuss them with your subject in more detail to help identify the source of your errors and to refine the model you used for generating predictions. You probably should repeat this exercise several times with a number of good friends before going on to the next assignment.

If you have developed some confidence in your skill at developing accurate models for assessing the thinking of close friends and relatives and of thinking as they would about a variety of issues (remember, it isn't a fair test if you have identical views) you are ready to take the next step of constructing models of unfamiliar persons such as casual or recent acquaintances. Again, record your predictions in advance and then go out to test them. A fringe benefit of this assignment can be getting to know people much better.

The final test of your abilities at taking the role of another person is to adopt the role of someone whose views are very different from, even antithetical to, your own. Your subject might be someone of the opposite sex or of a very different age, cultural background, or religious or political persuasion. It might even be someone you hate. In this instance a direct test of your model for prediction might be difficult or impossible, but you will have attained some measure of success if you find you can understand your subject in his or her own terms. You may have wondered, for example, how anyone could be a dentist, a parachute jumper, or a Ku Klux Klansman. What could have led them to their interest/belief? What satisfactions do they derive from it? What may have predisposed them to these interests? Writing up this assignment might very well take the form of a fictional biography, short story, play, or chapter of a novel. In other words, to complete it you will engage in the same sort of thinking as a professional writer. It is instructive to note that most writers start out by writing from their own immediate experience (in essence, objectifying their experience or detaching from self) before going on to create novel or composite characters.

Adjusting to the Views of Others.   Your assignments up to this point, however challenging or instructive they may have been, are academic in the sense that you have not had to do anything about your role enactment except to generate it. Role-playing is, however, widely used as a training technique in a great variety of contexts from marital counseling to arbitration to the playing of war games. To get some preliminary insight into these applications, you might begin by listening carefully to some arguments among friends or acquaintances as though you were a neutral observer simply recording the facts. What seems to be the source of the disagreement? What steps might be taken to reduce or resolve the conflict? What would serve to further escalate it? One question you should not be asking is who is right or wrong? Rather, view the conflict as an event to be understood in terms of its underlying dynamics. You may be able to test the adequacy of your analysis by stepping in to assume the role of peacemaker, but that is generally inadvisable.

As an additional means of testing your role-taking skills, notice occasions on which your behavior has led to misunderstanding or hurt feelings on the part of someone else. Analyze what you did to produce that effect and how you could prevent its recurrence. Where possible, test your analysis. You might even set yourself the task of brightening someone's day through some simple, thoughtful gesture after having first analyzed what type of gesture would produce such a response. In testing your predictions, record the results in order to understand the instances of inaccurate prediction so that you can correct them on subsequent retest.

As with earlier assignments a discussion of your findings with other class members should lead to broadened insights and to setting you on the path to formulating your own theory, to improving interpersonal relations generally, or to a more specific application of "How to Get Along with. . . ." The subject will be revisited when we discuss hypothesis testing and problem solving. To complete the discussion of detaching we turn now to detaching from context.

DETACHING FROM CONTEXT

With the very first problems of Chapter 1 you may have encountered the hazard of rigid thinking. This is a very common difficulty that arises because of semiautomatic habitual response patterns or other means of connecting response to a particular stimulus situation in terms of time, place, or specific features. I shall refer to all of these instances as context-tied thinking, a term which would encompass previous examples of impulsive and egocentric thought as well, but is used here to emphasize the external determinants. As will be shown in this section, context-tied thinking can often be efficient but it is inflexible. After considering some of the advantages and disadvantages of context constraints, I shall discuss how they arise and how they can be overcome.

The Pluses and Minuses of Situational Constraints.　All of us save time and reduce cognitive effort by creating habits such as daily routines and stereotyped patterns for dealing with habitual activities. Just how compelling those habits can be is illustrated by a change in the situation, such as, in driving a car with an automatic shift after becoming accustomed to a manual shift. There is unquestionable survival value for organisms that occupy a fixed territory in a predictable environment in adjusting behavior to that environment (for robins to seek worms after rain, or for rabbits to seek safety in bramble patches). Similarly, humans store information about where and when they are most likely to find a particular person or commodity: X goes for a walk after lunch; Y is stored in the dairy case. You were even exhorted in Chapter 2 to reduce demands upon memory by externalizing retrieval through systematic record keeping. A place for everything and everything in its place is an excellent maxim for keeping track of the impedimenta of daily existence be they keys, tools, letters, books, appointments, or whatever. The price paid for this convenience is the disruption that arises when something is not in its accustomed place.

An interesting example of situational constraint arises in classifying with respect to contextual features (see Chapter 2). They are rarely intrinsic or defining. One tends to identify people on first acquaintance with respect to where or with whom they were encountered (the person who was at Sally's house with John) or, even, what they were wearing or where they sat. That system may promote recognition when the original circumstances are reinstated but can lead to confusion when the person is encountered out of context (meeting one's dentist at a rock concert). Similar problems arise when information is classified with respect to contextual features. Knowing in what chapter of a particular text a topic is discussed is helpful when you want to review it at a later date but is not of much use on a test or in writing a paper in a different course where the subject would be highly relevant if it were retrievable (for example, using the economic principle of Gresham's law—bad money drives out good—as an analogy to account for neighborhood deterioration or the decline of courtesy). Another common description of this kind of situationally constrained thinking is literal thinking, as illustrated in Exercise 6 of Chapter 1. As noted in the discussion of a field-dependent cognitive style in Chapter 1, some people seem to be generally vulnerable to situational constraint.

At this point, it will be helpful for you to list some examples of context-tied thinking from your own experience and to consider them from the standpoint of how they arose as well as how they might be overcome. You might even try to develop a classification of the kinds of context-tied thinking.

Some Causes of Situational Constraint.   Situationally induced inflexibility, like impulsive, emotional, or egocentric thought, tends to be automatic rather than directed by prior reflection or planning. On the basis of that similarity, you would expect that it, too, should be overcome by detachment and the development of appropriate coping mechanisms. The analogy breaks down, however, with respect to ease of detection: that is, it is relatively easy to recognize when you are being impulsive or emotional and to become sufficiently sensitive to the symptoms and causes to deal with them. Although egocentrism and ethnocentrism are less readily detectible, it is possible to become more sensitive to tendencies towards them and to adjust your attitudes accordingly. In recent years there has been a significant societal change with respect to sexism, racism, and attitudes toward the aged or the handicapped. Regardless of room remaining for improvement, Americans are becoming more sensitive to others as a result of concerted programs of consciousness raising (promoting awareness and deliberate self-direction). But what kind of consciousness raising can be directed against situational inflexibility which is so much more varied in its manifestations and so specific in its origins? To the extent that instances of this class are a personal matter, each individual must identify instigating circumstances for himself or herself; to the extent that there are some universally common sources I shall try to suggest their nature. There seem, to me, to be two broad complexes of causal factors of situational inflexibility: (a) inadequate knowledge and experience or relative immaturity, and (b) inadequate analysis, attention, or encoding. In the second case, appropriate knowledge is potentially available but it is not retrieved and applied.[4]

Young children in the process of acquiring language are frequent victims of insufficient knowledge. Piaget cites the example of pointing out a snail to his child in the course of a walk. Farther along when they saw another snail the child announced, "There it is again." This observation suggests that for the child the word "snail" was interpreted as the name of a specific individual rather than of an extensive and varied class of organisms. An adult, on first encountering a new concept, or any other novelty, may be sufficiently sophisticated to appreciate that the name applied refers to a class rather than a particular instance but have no basis for identifying the defining feature(s) of the class or its realm of variation. For example, "Chinese food" might be equated to the chow mein occasionally served at the cafeteria or "detachment" might refer only to control of emotion and consideration for others rather than deliberate transcendence of immediate circumstances. All knowledge is limited in some sense. With advancing maturity we become (or should become) more conscious of the limits not only of personal knowledge but of human knowledge more generally. That heightened consciousness of the limits of knowledge leads inevitably to intellectual humility and open mindedness which is, if not the beginning of wisdom, at least an antidote to inflexibility. With respect to specific situational constraints arising from insufficient knowledge, one can always allow for the possibility of inadequate knowledge and develop a readiness to check the facts or seek additional information.

In the vast majority of cases of situational constraint, adequate information is potentially available but is not used effectively because of failures of attention, poor encoding, or inadequate analysis of relevant features of the situation. The discussion in Chapter 2 of the processes of attention, classification, and encoding is full of pertinent examples. In the nine dot problem of Box 1-1, for example, the figure of a square is so compelling that one does not attend to the surrounding space and consider the possibility of extending a line into it. Deciding whether to copy from a neighbor's paper (or to engage in any other infraction) may be more determined by the visibility of the paper, the absence of monitors, or ignorance of the answer than by principles of honesty. Objects encoded with respect to usual function, hammer, coffee cup, belt buckle, are less likely to be seen as useful for a nontraditional application, such as use as a paperweight. Classifying concepts and principles with respect to subject matter, physics, sociology, or economics makes them less available for application outside that realm. In all these examples selection of too limited a set of properties, or identifying them with a particular context, renders them unavailable in a different context. Such reasoning leads to a set of pigeonholes rather than to an interconnected network (remember Exercise 8 of Chapter 2 on hierarchical classifications). Awareness of the nature of the underlying processes of classification and encoding can lead to greater flexibility in dealing with their products. Other techniques are provided in the next section and in Chapter 12.

Promoting Flexibility.   To the extent that context-tied thinking results from a very narrow focus, the general method of detaching from situational constraints should lie in a deliberate attempt at broadening. Three techniques for broadening will be suggested here: *generalization, abstraction,* and *shifting from content to structure.* No one of them is cleanly independent of the others. While it is sometimes difficult in practice to differentiate generalization from abstraction they are, in principle, different processes as becomes clearer when their antonyms are considered: general-specific and abstract-concrete. Generalization involves expanding the scope of reference or number of exemplars encompassed at a given level of referential specificity whereas abstraction involves change in level. It is a useful habit in dealing with most material to consider how extensively it may be generalized or abstracted. That exercise helps to increase awareness of differentiating features. Proceeding in the opposite direction, to testing of general and abstract terms or assertions against specific concrete instances, is equally useful in promoting clearer understanding.

By way of example, statutes and regulations are stated—and are intended to be interpreted—quite generally. In considering their acceptability, therefore, it is necessary to determine if impermissible instances could arise within the stated limits. A recent New York City ordinance prohibiting the use of municipal funds for any project that discriminates against individuals on the grounds of sexual orientation is a case in point. Suppose that an individual were sexually attracted to children, would one want to employ such a person at a day-care center? Clearly not, although, if the decision were based solely upon sexual orientation, it would be in defiance of the law. That law is too general and, as evidenced by subsequent scandals at day-care centers, needs to be refined. Comparable thorny issues arise with respect to interpretation of first amendment rights of freedom of speech: are pornography, slander, sedition, or betrayal of state secrets permissible under the principle? At what point does freedom become license and an abuse of the principle? A similar process of refining should take place with subject matter concepts and principles, perhaps through a process of comparison with related concepts and principles (for example, what differentiates misperception from delusion from hallucination? mitosis from fission?). More techniques for analyzing concepts will be reviewed in Chapter 6.

Refining by broadening outward from presenting instances was discussed earlier, for example, determining whether "worm" refers to a particular creature, to all creatures exactly like it, to all little legless creatures, or all creepy crawlies. In attempting to generalize, differentiating features emerge. An analogous reasoning applies to abstraction. Consider the formula for computing the area of a rectangle, $A = hw$ where h = height and w = width. It may be generalized to all rectangles regardless of size or general proportions. Can it also be abstracted beyond a particular figure to squares, parallelograms, all quadrilaterals, or triangles?[5] Mathematical formulation is a very common means of abstraction used to transcend concrete properties (the treatment of the principle of diminishing returns in Chapter 2 and Gresham's law noted earlier provide examples). The equation $(a - b)^2 = a^2 - 2ab + b^2$ is not only general across all numerical quantities but it is also detached from any particular realm of application (numbers, units of distance, amounts of money, weights, areas).

As examples of verbal abstractions, the two legal principles discussed earlier, nondiscrimination on the grounds of sexual orientation and freedom of speech, are two general principles deriving from a more abstract belief in individual rights; the process by which clichés and stereotypes arise has been abstracted into a broader generalization about the hazard of focusing upon irrelevant features. Consideration of some common abstract nouns (love, awe, reciprocal) or verbs (clarify) should further illustrate the nature of abstraction. (Hint: all are relations not dependent upon concrete embodiments such as the nature of the love object or the means of clarification.) The systematic exercise of abstraction is an excellent corrective for unduly concrete thinking and the construction of concrete instances provides a "handle" for dealing with abstractions. Abstraction is also a useful vehicle for focus upon form (structure).

Form is never encountered in and of itself but always in some embodying content (a poem in iambic pentameter, a symphony in three movements, an *ad hominem* argument, an A-frame structure). For most purposes, the particular embodiment or content is the feature of major interest: the meaning of the poem or argument, or the comfort and convenience of the house. In those instances focus upon content is appropriate. But, in evaluating the adequacy of the argument as argument, the beauty of the poem as poetry, or the advantages of a particular construction as structure, focus upon content will not reveal formal inadequacies (you share the sentiments of the poem even though it doesn't scan). Many academic issues have to do with evaluation of form or structure rather than content. Students frequently have difficulty with these areas (logic, mathematics) largely because they cannot overcome focus upon content. For example, consider the following argument with respect to whether or not it is valid: "If lions are meeker than cats, and cats are meeker than rabbits, then lions are meeker than rabbits." That is a valid argument despite the fact that the component premises are empirically false. All arguments of the form $A\ r\ B, B\ r\ C,$ then $A\ r\ C$ (where r signifies any transitive relation, such as, greater or less than, is preferred to) are valid, because validity is determined by form rather than content. The matter of logic will be revisited in Chapter 7. As a final exercise, take some assignment in another course and consider the form (for example, a particular relation) independent of the content, perhaps by constructing instances of the same form but with different content.

SUMMARY

This chapter dealt with *detachment,* transcending the often compelling dictates of immediate circumstances by (a) becoming more aware of those circumstances and their effect, and (b) deliberately selecting a more appropriate alternative. Three manifestations of *context-tied behavior* were considered: impulse, self- or group-centeredness, and contextual constraint. All of them have in common the property of normally leading to semiautomatic and inflexible behavior (rigidity). Such behavior can frequently be characterized as immature. Examples and means of promoting greater flexibility were considered for each.

Impulsive behavior can be situationally triggered or emotionally mediated. In either case, flexibility can be promoted by imposing a pause for reflection and by having available a practiced repertoire for dealing with anticipated requirements. For example, in avoiding the panic of being unprepared for a test, an interview, a vacation, or deviation from accustomed routine and experience, you should anticipate possible outcomes and plan a means of dealing with them.

Egocentrism, and its more subtle cousin, *ethnocentrism,* can arise whenever you take a personal view of the situation. To the extent that the experiencer is always an individual and meaning is a personal construction, it is a very natural reaction, but it can be a constricting one. The means of overcoming it is a process of consciousness raising through which you (a) become aware that other individuals may have different views, (b) try to adopt the view of another for the purpose of understanding, and (c) try to broaden your own view to adjust to the views and needs of others.

External situational constraints are more varied in nature and harder to indentify. It was suggested that they arise because of (a) inadequate knowledge and experience or relative immaturity, or (b) inadequate attention, or faulty analysis/encoding so that potentially available knowledge is not applied. In principle, it is impossible to transcend the limits of personal knowledge, for this reason a certain amount of intellectual humility is always appropriate. In practice the second class of limitations is more common. The means of promoting flexibility recommended to deal with constraints were systematic procedures for testing and refining an interpretation through *generalization, abstraction,* and *attending to structure.*

EXERCISES

1. Write a paragraph on the value to the apprentice thinker of maintaining a journal in light of what you learned in this chapter.
2. Prepare a list of situations in which you habitually (a) panic, (b) become angry, (c) react uncritically, (d) react out of ignorance, or (e) react in response to any other state that is problematic for you. Devise a means of impulse blocking for the state(s) you selected or for preventing it from arising in the first place.
3. Collect some examples of egocentric thinking on your part or on the part of your acquaintances. How did they arise? How can they be combated?
4. Observe, or provoke, some reactions to criticism in yourself and your acquaintances. You might even try to vary systematically the form of the criticism to discover which forms lead to constructive responses and which lead to destructive ones.
5. Collect examples from your experience or reading of each of the following: (a) failures of attention, (b) poor classification, (c) poor encoding, and (d) inadequate knowledge. How do you differentiate among the four?
6. Describe some examples of context-tied behavior on the part of some person whose behavior is reported in the press or radio (for example, a public official) and try to diagnose the possible causes of that behavior.
7. Select some statements from the newspaper or from texts and tèst them for their generality by thinking up additional relevant instances and possible counterexamples. How would you test the same statements for their intended level of abstraction?
8. Look up some laws and regulations (for example, consult the constitution or bylaws of a group to which you belong; or some local, state, or federal

agency; or, even, a driver's manual). Try to generate some "test cases" for refining the interpretation of the law or regulation.

9. All of the following suggested examples for this exercise provide possible instances in which to focus upon form or structure rather than upon details of content. Do so for each as well as for a fifth example of your own devising: (a) the plot of a TV show, (b) the form of houses on a block, (c) the structure of a news report, and (d) the structure of a typical textbook chapter.

10. Describe heaven (or, if you prefer, hell). What does your description suggest about your personal value system?

11. Predict the behavior or attitudes of someone you know well in a situation or context you have not observed and then test the accuracy of your predictions (you might guess how each of your parents would respond to the question, "What qualities do you value most highly in a child?" or "What values are you trying to instill in your children?"). Test your predictions.

12. Read an ethnographic description[6] of a culture and try to imagine how someone of your sex, age, and station would be expected to act in that culture.

13. Imagine what it would be like to be very fat or very short, deaf, a new immigrant to a country where you do not speak the language, a person raised on a farm first arriving in a metropolis, or an aged person. How would the world look from that person's eyes? Try to get beyond the obvious to the small details of everyday life.

14. Assume that you are applying for a summer job. How would you prepare for the interview in light of the advice of this chapter? Be sure to consider the requirements of the job, your own skills and experience, and what the interviewer might be looking for. Outline your preparation. Note that this is not an academic exercise; most career counselors report that students do not prepare adequately for interviews.

· *5* ·

Judgment and Evaluation: Establishing Perspective and Priorities

Two roommates, one who knows a lot of girls and one who does not, are sitting and discussing possible blind dates for Saturday night. Of the three available possibilities one is a seven, the second a six, and the third a marginal four. The candidate for the blind date selects the best available prospect for the occasion while continuing to entertain dreams of being fixed up with a ten at some future time. I trust that the reader of this paragraph has no difficulty in understanding it although it involves a remarkable process worthy of additional comment: the fact that one can compare dissimilar commodities and evaluate each relative to the other and assign scale values to them. How is this accomplished? In comparing objects with respect to weight or length it is relatively simple to weigh each on a scale or to use a ruler. Not only are measurement scales available but exact reference units for the scale are maintained at the National Bureau of Standards. That is certainly not the case for assessing candidates for a blind date. Nevertheless, subjective scales are created and applied. Through this means consideration is given to what is important (or trivial), what is worthwhile (or frivolous), what is appropriate (or inappropriate), whether it is in good (or poor) taste, and so on. This process of evaluation is something we are all engaged in much of the time.

Evaluation is one of the most ubiquitous and absorbing activities of human existence. It cannot be ignored in any treatment of thinking; but, by the same token, it is impossible to treat it adequately within the confines of a chapter or of an encyclopedia. Over the centuries of human existence, philosophers, theologians, and serious thinkers in all realms have wrestled with questions of value concerning truth, justice, ethical conduct, or the goals of human existence. Satisfactory answers continue to elude us. This chapter has the far more modest goal of increasing the reader's awareness of the existence of profound questions and the need of explicit frameworks for addressing them. A deceptively simple paradigm will be introduced as a framework for describing the nature of the evaluative process and some examples of its application will be discussed.

THE NATURE OF EVALUATION

In everyday English the terms "judgment" and "evaluation" can refer both to a process and to its product. Both involve assessment relative to an implied scale. In judging, we assign a scale rating to an object, action, or event: too hot, too dark, guilty, adequate, working properly, and so on. Evaluations are judgments relative to a scale of value: good, desirable, beautiful, expensive, delicious, or other personal reactions, rather than intrinsic properties. To the extent that judgment is always involved and all assessments imply some subjective valuation, it is difficult in practice to differentiate judgment from evaluation. For this reason I shall use the terms more or less interchangeably, using judgment where assigning to categories is the major concern and evaluation where assigning values is more central. Both processes have three characteristics to be noted: they are inescapable, they are fallible (inherently subject to error), and they imply a criterion (some frame of reference). Because of these three defining characteristics, judgment and evaluation constitute different thinking processes than, for example, deductive reasoning or problem solving. It is, therefore, important to consider each of the defining characteristics in more detail.

Judgment Is Inescapable. Simple acts like throwing a ball or catching it, lifting an object, or turning onto a road require judgment. In the case of catching a ball, you estimate its trajectory and force in order to have your hand in position and appropriately braced for its impact. In turning into a road, you check for oncoming traffic, assess the speed of the traffic and whether there is an adequate amount of time to complete the turn in deciding whether to pull out or wait. These judgments are made so quickly and automatically that little thought appears to be involved; but they are, nevertheless, an important component of the skill. Much of the improvement with practice takes place in the judgment component of a skill. At a more conscious level, behavior is reviewed on a continuing basis as a guide to later action: What did he mean? Was my reply understood? Did it have the intended effect? Should I moderate my insistence?

The overall quality of an individual's judgment is, in fact, one of the common grounds upon which he or she is evaluated by others in assigning trust and responsibility. Every society has roles assigned to persons charged with the responsibility of making judgments and, ultimately, setting and upholding the values of the group. Typically those roles are assigned to persons who, by reasons of experience, knowledge, or wisdom, are best qualified to discharge them. Some of the more obvious examples in the political domain are incumbents of the judicial, legislative, and executive branches at all levels of government. Special interest groups also have their own panels of judges for sporting events, contests and competitions, submissions to professional journals, admission to societies, and awarding of prizes. Not only must judgments be made, but society also places a high value upon consistently judging well. Thus, it is important to attempt to characterize good judgment.

Judgment Is Fallible.   Perhaps one reason that good judgment is so highly prized is that the process of judgment is inherently subject to error. There is always a possibility of misjudgment. Everyone has experienced the fallibility of judgment, for example, in deciding whether something will match, or fit, or serve the purpose; in estimating time for task completion; or in forming first impressions. Common illusions, such as those of Box 5-1, provide additional evidence of tasks in which misjudgment is common.

To see why errors of judgment are unavoidable, let's consider another example of a perceptual judgment task, detecting a signal against background noise (the classic problem of signal detection).[1] Suppose you are taking a shower and hear what might be the telephone. Two judgments are possible: the phone is ringing (signal present) or it is not (only noise, signal absent). The structure of this judgment task is shown in Box 5-2. There are two possible correct judgments: judging the phone to be ringing when, in fact, it is or judging it not to be ringing when, in fact, it is not. Similarly, there are two possible errors: judging the phone to be ringing when it is not (a false alarm) or judging it to be not ringing when it is (a miss or failure or detection).

The signal detection analysis is applicable to nonperceptual judgment tasks as well. Consider hiring someone for a job. You can hire or not hire the individual; in either event, there is a possibility of error. Similarly, in making a purchase, accepting an invitation, or making any other decision, whichever choice is made (yes or no), there is the same possibility of error. For this reason, the matrix of Box 5-2 is presented as a prototype of all judgment tasks, as well as a justification for the assertion that judgment is inherently fallible. You will find additional applications of the matrix in Chapters 8 and 10. To become more familiar with it you should construct some additional examples of your own illustrating its application.

Judgment Implies a Criterion.   The third characteristic of the process of judgment is that it is made relative to a criterion. In the case of the telephone example above, the criterion is to a large extent a matter of sensory threshold— how loud the signal must be in order to be detected as a signal rather than as background noise. But the threshold is affected by other factors in addition to the sensitivity of hearing. It is likely to be higher when your attention is occupied or when the cost of error is high, as in tracking water for no purpose by racing

BOX 5-1

Some Judgment Tasks on which Error Is Common[2]

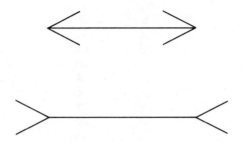

1. Compare line length. Is one longer than another or are they equal?

2. Compare the inscribed grey diamonds for relative brightness. Is one lighter than the other or are they equal?
3. Which of the pairs of events below is more likely to occur?
   (a) A massive flood somewhere in North America in 1988 in which 300 people drown.
   (b) An earthquake in California sometime in 1988 that causes a flood in which 300 people drown.
   (a) A 30% drop in U.S. oil consumption in 1988.
   (b) A sharp increase in oil prices and a 30% drop in U.S. oil consumption in 1988.

BOX 5-2

The Fate of Judgments

State of Reality

Judgment	Phone Ringing	Phone not Ringing
Phone Ringing	Hit	False Alarm
Phone not Ringing	Miss	Correct

For judgments where the state of reality is not knowable we might compare the judgment actually made to what an ideal ultimate judgment should have been.

Ideal Resolution

Choice	Do X	Do Y (Don't do X)
Do X	Correct	Error of Commission
Do Y (Don't do X)	Error of Omission	Correct

out of the shower for a false alarm; if, on the other hand, one is expecting an important phone call the threshold may be lowered. The role of additional subjective factors upon criterion setting is even more salient in the case of evaluation of a job applicant. If the need is pressing and little skill is required (for example, mowing the lawn) one does well to adopt a lax criterion and hire the first applicant capable of doing the job. If, on the other hand, there is a high cost associated with unsatisfactory performance or a high degree of expertise involved (as in fixing the car, a computer, or a partial dental plate) a stricter criterion is warranted. Problems of criterion setting in decision tasks will be considered in more detail in Chapter 10. At this point, however, it should be evident that there is some standard, a criterion, against which judgment is made. The nature of the criterion, as we shall see, varies depending upon the situation. In some instances, such as perceptual judgment, only a few factors are involved; in others there may be many. A more important consideration concerns the objectivity of the criterion.

In the case of the illusions in Box 5-1 it is possible to apply an objective scale as a basis for judgment: a ruler in the case of line lengths, or a screen to blot out the surrounding area when comparing the greys (or a calibrated brightness scale such as the Munsell scale or a light meter). In most cases, as in evaluating preferences, no such physical scale is available. There are, however, procedures that have been developed for the purpose of scaling nonphysical quantities such as intelligence, a great variety of other skills, and such human characteristics as prestige, attractiveness, poise, and beauty.[3] Some examples are shown in Box 5-3. They are presented by way of illustration of the importance attached to creating explicit criteria for evaluation that are, if not objective, at least consistent and systematic.

It should be clear why so much attention is directed to establishing criteria. Of the three characteristics of judgment presented earlier, criterion is the only one under the control of the judge. It is, therefore, the major controllable determinant of adequacy of judgment or evaluation and, by the same token, the major safeguard against error. For that reason it is important to consider the process of criterion setting, and of the creation of frameworks of judgment (such as perspectives and priorities) more generally. As a first step in this direction I shall consider some of the components of criteria and some grounds for their justification.

CONSIDERATIONS IN SETTING CRITERIA

As observed earlier, things are not intrinsically good, true, beautiful, important, or worthwhile. The assignment of such properties is the result of evaluation. The assignment of values is unavoidably made by an individual relative to a context of comparison. The removal of a gangrenous leg, for example, is a terrible thing relative to the pain induced (both immediately and in terms of later phantom leg pain) and the irreversible crippling that results. But, relative to the value of preserving life, it is usually judged to be necessary and, in that sense, good. The function of selecting a framework is to provide a fixed reference, or benchmark, that serves as an anchor for relating other considerations. The fixed reference so provided is better viewed as a domain rather than a point in the sense that there are a number of aspects to be taken into account. Let's consider a few of the major ones.

BOX 5-3

Psychological Scaling of Preference

Suppose the following nine items regularly appear as main courses in the dining hall. Three methods of scaling them for preference are given below: the method of paired-comparisons, rank order, rating.

The choices: Macaroni and cheese (A), Eggplant parmigiana (B), Baked halibut (C), Broccoli quiche (D), Mushroom tetrazini (E), Chili (F), Egg foo young (G), Liver and onions (H), Turkey and dressing (I)

Method of Paired Comparisons

All 36 possible pairs of choices are presented to subjects to indicate the preferred member of each pair. The resulting choices are tabulated in a 9×9 matrix showing the number of times each column entree was preferred to each row entry (ignoring comparison of item with itself; the diagonals of the matrix are blank). Compute a mean choice proportion for each column, M_p, by the formula

$$M_p = \frac{C + N/2}{nN}$$

Where: N = number of judges
C = total number of choices of entree
n = number of entrees, 9.

In the full application of the method, for which there are variants, the means are converted into standard measures which are then converted into scale values by setting the least preferred item to zero on the scale and adding successive differences. Procedures for that will not be elaborated here.

Rank Order Method

Each person ranks the nine choices from most preferred (9) to least preferred (1). A mean rank is then computed for the nine entrees. Once, again, there are additional procedures for converting mean ranks into scale scores but for present purposes comparison of mean ranks is adequate.

Rating Scale

How many steps of a rating scale are to be used is arbitrary, generally an odd number is used with the middle value used as a point of indifference. Thus, a five point rating scale for the entrees above might be:

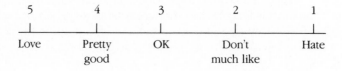

5	4	3	2	1
Love	Pretty good	OK	Don't much like	Hate

From the group ratings it is possible to compute a mean rating for each entree. As in the methods above, there are additional procedures for converting mean ratings into scale scores but, again, comparison of mean ratings suffices for present purposes.

If, as a class exercise, you compute a scale for the nine items above by each method you may well find that although all entrees receive a mean rating of three or less, it will nevertheless be the case that some are consistently preferred relative to the others by most persons, that is, scale value is a function of scaling method and, for the first two methods (if not the third as well) of the comparison set. Present day scaling methods are a good deal more sophisticated but, also, much too technical to be readily understood by the average person.

Semantic Differential Scale

As another example of a rating scale a semantic differential scale is given. Rate yourself and, for comparison, one other person (your best friend, a parent, President Reagan, whoever you choose). (After Osgood, 1962)

Bad	Good
Worthless	Valuable
Dirty	Clean
Insincere	Sincere
Foolish	Wise
Ignorant	Intelligent
Dangerous	Safe
Sad	Happy
Poor	Rich
Unpredictable	Predictable
Tense	Relaxed
Sick	Healthy
Weak	Strong
Delicate	Rugged
Passive	Active
Slow	Fast
Cold	Warm

Components of a Frame of Reference.   Four components will be considered here, some of which are not fully independent of the others. They are *time frame* (immediate or long range); *probable impact* (extent or ramification); *consistency* (the degree of coherence in relation to other frameworks); and *explicitness of formulation.*

Modern medical practice provides a wealth of examples of the effects of time frames. Many drugs that effect an immediate "cure" to the problem have been discovered to have serious long-range side effects: for example, birth control pills or the IUD; DES, originally used as a prevention of miscarriage; cortisone; or flu shots. Even aspirin can have later adverse consequences, for example, in producing Reye's syndrome in children. Yielding to the demands of the moment, as in terminating an act of terrorism or pacifying a child's temper tantrum, may produce immediate relief at the cost of increasing the likelihood of repetition in the future. Clearly, long-term considerations may lead to selection of a different criterion than short-term considerations.

With respect to probable impact, the burgeoning field of ecology provides some classic examples. When DDT was first developed it appeared it would prove possible to eradicate insect pests such as the mosquito that was the carrier of malaria. Later it was discovered that DDT accumulated not only in insects but also in other organisms, most notably birds, leading to thinning of egg shells which threatened the eradication of desirable species as well as insect pests. Now the insecticide that promised such beneficial miracles has been banned because its impact is much broader than intended. Similarly the importation of alien animals has upset the normal balance of nature with the result that new pests far worse than those they supplanted have become a problem: for example, the importation of rabbits into Australia, walking catfish into Florida, and starlings into the eastern U.S. Even television, which was hailed as a means of revolutionizing education, has turned out to have a broader and more mixed impact than originally foreseen. At this point, the probability of a broader impact has become so evident that it is commonly taken into account when determining criteria.

Consistency has to do with the coherence of criteria across realms of application. For some persons, the criteria for honesty, justice, consideration of others, to cite a few of many possible examples, appear to be narrowly formulated and situation specific. Honesty, for example, may have different criteria depending upon whether you are dealing with exams or financial matters among friends (vs business transactions), accurate reporting to parents (vs the IRS). The same is true with liberty, justice, or equity—the criteria may differ with respect to gender, race, age, or economic status or be more broadly defined independent of group differences. As a test of the coherence (consistency) of your own criterion of honesty, take the test in Box 5-4.

The degree of transsituational consistency in applying evaluative criteria is to some extent a function of the base of those criteria. Conceivably if one adopted a general principle transmitted by an authority such as parents, church, or other

---

BOX 5-4

A Test of Criterion Consistency: The Criterion of Honesty

Rate, on a five point scale, the likelihood of your doing each of the things described below. A rating of 1 = very likely to do; 2 = more likely than not; 3 = indifferent; 4 = unlikely to do; 5 = very unlikely to do. A high score indicates honesty.

1. Lying to a friend who has just bought a very expensive suit to wear at job interviews about how it looks. You think it ugly and unbecoming, but you know she can't return it.

2. Accumulating parking tickets when driving out of state. You assume that the police in these other states have no way of coming after you.

3. Using privileged information for personal profit. You overhear two men discussing a company takeover that will certainly shoot up the stock price of the company being taken over. Suppose, instead of overhearing this information you got it as part of your job as a financial reporter or as a worker in the company's accounting office.

4. Keeping a small gold ring that you find in the compartment of a box purchased at a flea market for $2. Suppose you had bought the box from an aged couple selling possessions to supplement their income rather than at a flea market.

5. Accepting the offer of a repair shop to include a number of dents that predate the accident in the accident damage estimate for the insurance company.

6. Padding a job resume you are preparing with assertions about course background that include courses you failed or dropped after the first week.

7. In pulling out of a very tight parking space you accidentally smash the headlight and dent the fender of the car in back. There is no one around so you drive off.

8. Accepting without question money you get from a teller machine that has read your check for $2.50 as a check for $250.

9. Lying to a police officer about having witnessed a crime that you actually did see in order to avoid all the time and nuisance of having to testify. Suppose (a) someone were seriously hurt or killed, and (b) that the perpetrator of this vicious crime will escape trial for lack of evidence.

10. Failing to report to the IRS your winnings in a big pool run by the employees in the company for which you work.

cultural institution and adhered to it unswervingly and unquestioningly (for example, don't ever lie, don't ever steal) there would be great consistency in the absence of much awareness or effort in the formulation of criteria. A more realistic scenario for most individuals, however, incorporates some value conflict. Most, if not all, social issues hinge upon value conflict. For example, Americans place a high value upon liberty and the rights of the individual to pursue his or her own goals free of institutional constraint. On the other hand, unselfish promotion of the welfare of society is also valued: we want to belong to the larger community and to contribute to advances that transcend the individual, mortal self. Conflicts between these two values arise constantly, both for the individual in the course of (a) daily living, for example, in choosing whether to devote a block of time to poll watching, visiting a friend, or working on a personal project, or choosing to spend a gift of money on a personal luxury or as a contribution to an emergency appeal for earthquake victims, or registering for military service, and (b) in setting rules for society, such as laws governing dress codes, pornography, or the accessibility of dangerous commodities such as alcohol, handguns, or drugs. Other value conflicts arise in promoting life vs death even when death would alleviate suffering (euthanasia), or honesty vs respect for the views of others. Supply other examples of value conflict from your own experience.

The recognition and reconciliation of value conflicts forces one to become more aware of values and the criteria upon which they are based. Many judgments derive from vague, unformalized impressions, feelings, or intuitions that may not even involve criteria. In defending the resulting judgment, however, grounds are invoked in support of your judgment. Why is it right (or wrong)? How is it preferable to other alternatives? How does it compare with other judgments in similar cases? Is it compatible with other values? In the course of answering such questions, you develop an aesthetic, a moral code, or philosophy of life. Thus, the dimension of explicitness also reflects the amount of conscious deliberation in arriving at the criterion. A consideration of the justification of criteria will be helpful at this point in clarifying the component of degree of explicitness of criteria.

How Are Criteria Justified?   Philosophers have long been concerned with either descriptive or prescriptive analyses of the basis of judgment, most prominently of ethical judgment, as well as aesthetics or epistemology. In this section I shall consider the grounds for justification of judgment along with examples from specific domains. It seems to me that there are three general grounds of justification that apply across domains. They are *personal/affective determinants, appeal to authority,* and informed conclusions systematically arrived at *(considered independent judgment)*. Each will be considered in turn.

1. Personal/affective determinants.   Many philosophers[4] conclude that judgments derive from individual preference. Common sense also generally aligns with that conclusion, for example, "Beauty is in the eye of the beholder," or "I don't know art but I know what I like" are two oft-heard dicta suggesting that there are no intrinsic criteria for aesthetic judgment but that each individual creates his or her own, mostly upon affective grounds. In the case of ethical judgment, there is often an additional influence upon the conclusion that there are no intrinsic criteria. In part, it derives from a wealth of ethnographic evidence, some of which you explored in the last chapter, indicating that social practices, such as education of the young, distribution of goods, funeral practices, and so on, vary widely among cultures. Of course, diversity among practices does not prove that underlying beliefs and criteria are substantially different, but it is so interpreted: for example, cremation, elaborate burial rituals, or even consumption of parts of the corpse, could all signify veneration of the departed. There is also psychological evidence that is interpretable as evidence against intrinsic criteria and for the role of personal preference. It ranges from the Freudian position that the determinant of many deep-seated beliefs is emotional rather than rational and influenced by very early experience, to behaviorist theories where the emphasis is upon the importance of past history of reinforcement.

Let's examine personal feelings as a basis of judgment. At first blush it may appear to be a defensible justification, especially for aesthetic judgments. That tastes differ is undeniable. We even say there is no accounting for tastes or that they cannot be disputed (*de gustibus non est disputandum*). But, if that were true, how could evaluations of good or poor taste ever arise? Those expressions surely suggest that some criterion other than the judge's own personal impression is evoked. On deeper scrutiny several difficulties of personal/affective criteria appear. For one thing, such criteria are not stable either in a given individual (consider your current taste in food, music, art, literature, clothing, or interior decor as compared with when you were a child) or in the social group (witness changes in fashion for all of the preceding examples as well as social norms for, for example, cohabitation of unmarried couples). Why should the pleasure-producing quality of a commodity or an experience change over time? Our immediate response is experience/education. But, adherence to a given affective criterion could preclude the possibility of any impact of education or experience; if you ate nothing but hamburgers or read nothing but adventure stories, how could taste be modified? From a practical standpoint, we know that values change with age and that some judgments can be accurately characterized as more (or less) mature than others. Maturity level will be considered at the end of this chapter.

Affect as a justification of evaluation is not readily communicated to others, or, even, to yourself. Nor is affective justification widely accepted as a sufficient justification: your feelings are rarely as compelling to others as they are to yourself. Reconstruct for yourself some recent instances of judgment of whether something was true, right, or important. Was it the case that you chose what you wanted/liked or were there instances in which you decided that something was true, right, or important despite the fact that it was not personally pleasing to you? A possible example could be foregoing a pleasurable activity to discharge an obligation. Even in the realm of aesthetics, personal/affective criteria can be seen to be a weak and unreliable basis for judgment. In the realm of ethics the conclusion is more evident.

2. Appeal to authority.   A major component of the education of every child is the learning of rules for personal conduct, for basic academic activities like reading and writing, and even for the playing of games. At first those rules are treated as inviolable and assumed to be promulgated by unquestioned authorities, such as parents, religious leaders, elected officials. The dicta of such authorities are accepted without question. Maturity brings a more sophisticated appreciation of the nature of rules, for example, a differentiation among laws and conventions, along with an appreciation of the somewhat arbitrary nature of collective agreement. Anyone can invent a new game or, for that matter, a system of jurisprudence, an economic system, a governmental structure, but the successful enactment of the invention requires that all participants be governed by the same set of rules. Where disagreement or uncertainty arises regarding interpretation of the rules an arbitrator must be consulted for clarification or revision: in the case of a game, a referee would decide, in the case of jurisprud-ence a judge would decide, and so on. The authority invoked is a person who, by virtue of position, training or experience is more knowledgeable than partic-ipants who consult him or her and, therefore, presumably more likely to produce an informed judgment.

Part of the process of socialization is learning the rules of the group and incorporating them into your own judgmental framework so that an external, all-knowing authority need not be invoked for each new circumstance of judg-ment because it has been internalized. Authorities, as knowledgeable members of the community, continue to play an important educational role. Consider, for example, the role of the critic in the realm of aesthetics. Critics, by virtue of their special training and broad experience as well as their skill in applying and communicating that knowledge, can heighten the reader's awareness and deepen understanding. To better appreciate that role, read several different reviews of a recently published book or a recent film (preferably one with which you are familiar), list the evaluative criteria employed by each critic, and how they are combined to reach an overall judgment. Compare the critics' evaluations with your own in terms of similarities and differences. Then, ask yourself if your own initial evaluation of the work changed as a result of this exercise. The foregoing exercise should be repeated in a different realm, preferably the realm of ethics. Take a recent event covered in the newspapers and, after establishing the facts of the event, read several editorial evaluations of it. What criteria did each com-mentator employ? Compare the editorial evaluations to your own; again, was your initial evaluation changed as a result of the exercise?

One probable result of these two exercises, along with the discovery that critics have more explicit criteria, is a discovery that authorities do not agree among themselves. How do you decide which, if any, critic has evaluated "correctly?" You could consult an authority's authority in a procedure analogous to going all the way up to the Supreme Court but, as that analogy suggests, there must be some end to the process of consulting ever higher authorities. If even authorities cannot agree, how do you ever decide what is good, true, just, worthwhile, or whatever? That is the fundamental question about the process of judgment regardless of the realm of application. As you might have predicted, there is no simple general answer to it but there are some relevant guidelines worthy of closer examination.

3. *Considered independent judgment.* That even authorities disagree should come as no surprise. Because of the nature of judgment, four classes of outcome are always possible: two of them correspond to correct judgments and two to error. Errors are identified in Box 5-2 as "Miss" and "False alarm"; in the case of ethical judgment they might better be called "Errors of omission"—failing to do what should have been done—and "Errors of commission"—doing something ill advised. Moreover, you also know that judgment always implies a criterion. Nothing is intrinsically good, true, right, just, beautiful, appropriate, or cheap; rather, it is judged so relative to a criterion. The crux of considered judgment must, therefore, lie in explicit justification in light of one's judgmental criterion. Several components are to be considered in the setting of criterion: time frame, probable impact, consistency, and explicitness were considered earlier; a fifth implied component should be added to them—purpose or intent of the actor. Those are the fundamental ingredients. Now they will be embodied in specific examples. Before going on to examples, however, it is worth noting that considered independent justification can, and often does, incorporate personal/affective evaluations and appeal to authority. Both are appropriate inasmuch as we live in a world with others and care about the judgments that are made.

Let's begin in the realm of aesthetics, playing critic for a work of art. Being critical does not mean finding fault but thoughtfully evaluating accomplishments as well as shortcomings. Whether you personally like it or not is not a generally useful criterion. The first two criterial components of time and impact lead into the future and the unknown. Whether a work will "stand the test of time" or have a major impact upon future artists are subjects of speculation. Those speculations are, however, worth making for purposes of providing a broader perspective—a very ambitious work warrants some respect by virtue of the fact that trivial undertakings are more readily attained than difficult ones. This description of broadened perspective has already taken into account the artist's purpose as an important consideration. As noted in Chapter 2, any work of art may be viewed as the solution of a problem the artist sets for himself or herself, generally to draw the attention of the audience to some heretofore neglected aspect of experience. The realization of that goal (and, even, the goal itself) is inevitably influenced by the customs and conventions of the culture and the era. Your first experience of Japanese No drama or of Chinese opera, for instance, can be unsettling because the conventions are so unfamiliar. Serious evaluation requires judging in light of the appropriate conventions rather than in light of your own. Detaching is appropriate.

Conventions of painting, for example, have changed considerably over the centuries. Early painters were concerned with conveying ideas, the myths and beliefs of their era, and frequently did so in a conventionalized manner. Egyptian, Assyrian, Medieval, and Oriental art provide good examples. With the Renaissance came a shift to themes of secular life and a more realistic depiction, along with the discovery of the rules of perspective. As those goals were attained, painters shifted to a depiction of the more fleeting and ephemeral (such as the treatment of light by the Impressionists), or emotion (such as horror by Münch, despair by Kollwitz), as well as social commentary (as in the work of Goya and Daumier). With the advent of photography direct depiction of reality declined in prominence as an artistic goal to be replaced by the increased prominence of abstraction. Comparable descriptions of historic changes can be made for literature and music.

Having placed a work in the perspective of its time and culture, we can assess how well the artist's intended purpose was achieved and evaluate it with respect to more specific technical criteria, such as composition and technical proficiency. A good work should be consistent across all applicable criteria; inadequacies of execution will doom a work regardless of other virtues. With that broadened perspective on setting and applying criteria you are in a position to undertake a classroom exercise in criticism of some work of art, literature, or music. To learn from each other's efforts all members of a group, assuming the class is broken into several groups, should choose the same work to enable comparison of similarities and differences among members with respect to choice of criteria and evaluations relative to them.

Ethical and moral judgments may be made with respect to a general issue or a specific act by a particular individual. Usually a general principle is involved, such as respect for life or for another's property. Discussion of issues such as abortion, euthanasia, or capital punishment hinges in part upon definition of a concept central to the principle, in this case, the definition of life as a sentient being. The issue of abortion includes considerations of time frame (the fetus as a potential person), quality of life (especially in the case of a deformed or defective fetus), probable impact (not only upon lives of other family members, especially the mother, but also on society if abortion becomes accepted), and consistency (of judgment about abortion with other judgments concerning life). The issue of euthanasia also hinges upon conscious awareness as a defining property of life. The resolution of that definitional issue has ramifications, by virtue of the consistency dimension, to other issues such as the taking of life of other species—the use of animals for research or for food. How far down the phylogenetic scale does consciousness extend? to insects? to plants? to viruses? Additional considerations arise when more than one life is at issue (as in the conduct of war, distributing limited resources in time of plague or famine, rescue in mass emergency). For a more searching examination of ethical and moral judgment, construct some ethical or moral dilemmas for class discussion in light of the criteria invoked and grounds of justification. To examine an instance where the intent of the accused (and, possibly, of the accuser as well) becomes an important criterial consideration you might review a current trial in your local paper.

THE EVOLUTION OF A JUDGMENTAL FRAMEWORK

The development of a judgmental framework is one of the major ongoing undertakings in the life of every individual. Psychologists have become interested in the developmental course of judgment and interesting work is beginning to accumulate.[5] Since the major focus of this research has been upon moral judgment, this concluding section will very briefly review some of the findings of two of the major investigators: Kohlberg and Gilligan. To provide a context for understanding their work consider the contents of Box 5-5.

Moral Dilemmas. Box 5-5 presents some everyday dilemmas of the sort that many of you may have encountered. Choice situations like those in Box 5-5 are called dilemmas because they involve selection among incompatible alternatives, each of which has a good justification, and whose denial would be a cause of concern. They are moral dilemmas because they involve personal and societal codes of what one ought to do. Take one or more of the examples given, preferably ones corresponding to some situation you have already encountered. Record in adjacent columns of your journal (a) what you actually did or would likely do in that situation, and (b) what you should do in that situation. Class discussion of the dilemmas would be useful as a demonstration of individual differences in dealing with them. You will undoubtedly encounter some considerations of which you have been unaware, as well as alternative criteria, and alternative weightings of the relevant considerations. Some answers may strike you as better than others even though, from a practical standpoint, they lead to identical choices and consequences. Three considerations that are likely to be prominent in discussion are: (a) the intent of the actor, (b) the consequences of the action, and (c) the laws or societal conventions being challenged or upheld. These three considerations are at the heart of all moral judgment. A fourth consideration, that has been repeatedly stressed in this chapter, is the choice of a judgmental criterion.

Kohlberg's Work on Moral Reasoning. The largest body of work on moral reasoning has been contributed by Lawrence Kohlberg, his collaborators, and his critics, as well. The procedure typically employed by them is to present a short vignette of a moral dilemma about which the subject is questioned and asked to defend his choices about what is right in the situation. Perhaps the best-

---

BOX 5-5

Everyday Moral Dilemmas

1. You share a small apartment with a roommate who is cheerful and pleasant but who is a slob about personal habits. Moreover, the roommate does not faithfully discharge his or her assigned share of household maintenance chores such as cleaning, shopping, or meal preparation. Previous appeals to the roomate's sense of fairness have been ineffective. What should you do?

2. On a mid-semester exam a friend asks to see your paper. You know that the friend has been having difficulty with the course and must get a grade of B or better in it in order to graduate. You personally have studied very hard for the exam. What should you do?

3. You are at a big beer party at which there is a lot of drinking. A group of party goers, all of whom have had too much to drink, decide to drive to a pizza parlor about ten miles away for one of its super specials. What should you do?

4. At this same party you overhear a conversation between an operator and a freshman girl from a small town who comes from a very conventional family and who you know has had no experience with fast-talking boys like this. He is inviting her to leave the party and come over to his place. You strongly suspect that he is going to take advantage of her naiveté and the fact that she is unaccustomed to drinking. What should you do?

5. At this same party there is a phone call from the people next door complaining irately about the noise and threatening to call the police. A group of attendees decide that they will fix the neighbors by getting a can of spray paint and writing "NERD" all over the front of their house. Should you join them or stop them?

6. You telephone a personnel manager regarding a well-paying position that you would like very much to get. The manager says that they will consider only applicants with prior computer experience and familiarity with several programs that he lists. You do not have the requisite experience. What should you do?

---

known dilemma is one in which a poor man, Heinz, whose wife is dying of cancer, is unable to afford the price of a costly drug treatment and considers stealing it from an intransigent druggist who is the exclusive supplier. Other dilemma vignettes involve such topics as (a) administering a lethal dose of pain killer to a patient dying in great pain in order to alleviate suffering, (b) the decision of an uninvolved observer as to whether to report an illegal act that only he observed, and (c) defying an unreasonable parental order. Evaluation of the judgments given and the justifications for them has led to the identification of three levels of justice reasoning, each of which has two stages. The stages are now used as a basis of evaluating responses. The levels and stages are shown in Box 5-6.

Some examples of the reasoning about justice of actions at each stage in response to the question "Should the judge punish Heinz if he steals the drug?" are given below:

Stage 2: The judge should be lenient because Heinz wanted to keep his wife alive.
Stage 3: The judge should be lenient because Heinz acted unselfishly in stealing the drug for his wife.
Stage 4: The judge should be lenient because s/he should recognize the extenuating or mitigating circumstances and be lenient within the parameters of the law.
Stage 4/5: The judge should be lenient because s/he can find a precedent or develop a rule of law that reflects *what is right* (Colby, Kohlberg, Gibbs, & Lieberman, 1983, p. 66).

The first justification is merely pragmatic, the second argues in terms of character and good motive. In the third, intention is dealt with within the framework of need for legal consistency. The fourth justification brings in the additional consideration that laws can be amended and interpreted in the interest of justice to maintain legal consistency. Evaluate each of the justifications in light of the earlier discussion of criteria, their components, and justification. You might also try to apply the scale to your own answers to the dilemmas of Box 5-5.

In a Different Voice.   Much of the work with the Kohlberg dilemmas and scales for interpreting responses to them is based upon the responses of male subjects. Carol Gilligan (1982), in using the methodology with women, found different responses emerging that would generally be scored lower on the Kohlberg scale although the reasoning behind them was often highly sophisticated. The "different voice" that she distinguished is characterized not by the gender of the subject but by the themes discussed. Those themes concern helping others and avoiding inflicting hurt as major goals rather than determination of justice. Another theme is the interdependence of people. The flavor of these themes can be seen in the context of a vignette, used by Gilligan and her coworkers, which concerns a badger who invited a porcupine to escape the winter cold in its burrow. When the grateful porcupine moved in the badger discovered the problems of living with a porcupine. What should it do? Most subjects agreed that the badger could not, in good conscience, go back upon its invitation and drive the porcupine out into the cold. Rather, it was necessary to arrive at an accommodation (such as covering the quills with a canvas) that would enable the porcupine to remain without harm to its host. The evaluative criterion underlying a response of this sort is concern for human welfare and for interpersonal accord rather than for maintaining standards of justice. That the two criteria are

BOX 5-6

Six Stages of Moral Judgment

	Content of Stage
Level and Stage	**What Is Right**
Level 1: Preconventional Stage 1. Heteronomous morality	To avoid breaking rules backed by punishment, obedience for its own sake, and avoiding physical damage to persons and property.
Stage 2. Individualism, instrumental purpose, and exchange	Following rules only when it is to someone's immediate interest; acting to meet one's own interests and needs and letting others do the same. Right is also what's fair, what's an equal change, a deal, an agreement.
Level 2: Conventional Stage 3. Mutual interpersonal expectations, relationships, and interpersonal conformity	Living up to what is expected by people close to you or what people generally expect of people in your role as son, brother, friend, and so on. "Being good" is important and means having good motives, showing concern about others. It also means keeping mutual relationships, such as trust, loyalty, respect, and gratitude.
Stage 4. Social system and conscience	Fulfilling the actual duties to which you have agreed. Laws are to be upheld except in extreme cases where they conflict with other fixed social duties. Right is also contributing to society, the group, or institution.
Level 3: Postconventional or principled Stage 5. Social contract or utility and individual rights	Being aware that people hold a variety of values and opinions, that most values and rules are relative to your group. These relative rules should usually be upheld, however, in the interest of impartiality and because they are the social contract. Some non-relative values and rights like life and liberty, however, must be upheld in any society and regardless of majority opinion.
Stage 6. Universal ethical principles	Following self-chosen ethical principles. Particular laws or social agreements are usually valid because they rest on such principles. When laws violate these principles, one acts in accordance with the principle. Principles are universal principles of justice: the equality of human rights and respect for the dignity of human beings as individual persons.

(After Kohlberg, 1976)

Content of Stage	
Reasons for Doing Right	**Sociomoral Perspective of Stage**
Avoidance of punishment and the superior power of authorities.	Egocentric point of view. Doesn't consider the interests of others or recognize that they differ from the actor's, doesn't relate two points of view. Actions are considered physically rather than in terms of psychological interests of others. Confusion of authority's perspective with one's own.
To serve one's own needs or interests in a world where you have to recognize that other people have their interests, too.	Concrete individualistic perspective. Aware that everybody has his own interests to pursue and these conflict, so that right is relative (in the concrete individualistic sense).
The need to be a good person in your own eyes and those of others. Your caring for others. Belief in the Golden Rule. Desire to maintain rules and authority which support stereotypical good behavior.	Perspective of the individual in relationships with other individuals. Aware of shared feelings, agreements, and expectations which take primacy over individual interests. Relates point of view through the concrete Golden Rule, putting yourself in the other guy's shoes. Does not yet consider generalized system perspective.
To keep the institution going as a whole, to avoid the breakdown in the system "if everyone did it," or the imperative of conscience to meet one's defined obligations.	Differentiates societal point of view from interpersonal agreement or motives. Takes the point of view of the system that defines roles and rules. Considers individual relations in terms of place in the system.
A sense of obligation to law because of one's social contract to make and abide by laws for the welfare of all and for the protection of all people's rights. A feeling of contractual commitment, freely entered upon, to family, friendship, trust and work obligations. Concern that laws and duties be based on rational calculation of overall utility, "the greatest good for the greatest number."	Prior-to-society perspective. Perspective of a rational individual aware of values and rights prior to social attachments and contracts. Integrates perspectives by formal mechanisms of agreement, contract, objective impartiality, and due process. Considers moral and legal points of view; recognizes that they sometimes conflict and finds it difficult to integrate them.
The belief as a rational person in the validity of universal moral principles, and a sense of personal commitment to them.	Perspective of a moral point of view from which social arrangements derive. Perspective is that of any rational individual recognizing the nature of morality or the fact that persons are ends in themselves and must be so treated.

by no means incompatible, however, is clearly indicated by the response of subjects to questioning about how else the situation might be viewed and resolved. In most cases whatever the first criterion had been, the alternative was readily available and adequately justified. The respondents appreciated that there was more than one way to view the situation, that alternative criteria were applicable, and that different resolutions were justifiably possible. The flexibility of thought reflected is, itself, evidence of a higher level of evaluative reasoning, a level generally called relativistic thinking.

From Absolutistic to Relativistic Thinking.   One conclusion to be drawn about moral reasoning is that it should not be approached within the framework of problem solving as exemplified by a mathematical problem. Rarely, if ever, is there a unique correct solution; rather, there are better or worse alternatives and each is so adjudged with respect to a particular criterion. Alternative criteria are also possible. Societies, and subgroups within a society, as you have seen in the previous chapter, differ in their preferred criteria.

The fact that alternative criteria justifiably may be invoked does not invalidate the existence of developmental levels in the quality of the evaluative reasoning or in their justification. Compare, for example, the pattern of justification (second column of Box 5-6) at Stages 1 and 6. Both contain aspects of appeal to authority and personal/affective justification; they differ with respect to the role of considered independent judgment. At the lowest level there is none. Authority is all-powerful and unquestioned; one obeys to avoid punishment and to obtain the rewards of compliance. This kind of thinking is often characterized as absolutistic thinking. Although it is most transparently present in the justifications offered by preschoolers, it is by no means absent in the thinking of adults. At Stage 6, on the other hand, although the authority of a universal moral principle is invoked, it is the principle rather than some all-powerful promulgator of it (mom, God, or the Pope) that serves the role of authority. Similarly, deep personal belief in terms of commitment to moral principles has been arrived at after considerable deliberation and weighing of alternatives. This form of deliberation has been characterized as relativistic thinking.

The course of personal growth from absolutistic to relativistic thinking in a group of Harvard students has been traced by William G. Perry, Jr. (1970, 1981) and his associates through interviews about college experiences and student reactions to them. They found that on arrival at college many students were confident of knowing how to succeed. There are right answers to everything that are known by the authorities, their teachers, whose role it is to impart answers to the students. The role for students is to work hard and follow instruction. Discussion with other students and their experience in classes begins to erode that security and to replace it with confusion, well represented by a student who complained, "In high school two and two was four; there's nothing to think out there. In here they try to make your mind work, and I didn't realize that until the end of the year." In response to a question about the elusiveness of answers, the student said, "Yeah, it wasn't in the *book*. And that's what confused me a lot. *Now* I know it isn't in the book for a purpose. We're supposed to think about it and come *up* with the answer!" In an attempt to maintain the belief in the existence of right answers, some students assume that such answers will eventually be known if they are not already known by someone. But, mounting evidence of disagreement among authorities undermines that belief. This realization leads to an unsettling confusion: Who does know? If no one knows, by what right do they judge?

There is, however, awareness that how an answer is defended is relevant. As one student put it, "Well—it's an opinion, but it's got to be an educated opinion. Have something behind it, not just a hearsay opinion. I mean, you can't form an opinion unless you have some knowledge behind it, I suppose." This level, which Perry refers to as multiplicity, is marked by an awareness that different views are possible and they must be considered. It leads to greater tolerance and appreciation of complexity but provides no path out of the complexity. Relativism differs from multiplicity by virtue of greater generality, an awareness that all thinking, not only for the self but also for those in authority, requires dealing with uncertainty and alternatives—thinking about one's own thinking. This realization is both liberating and frightening. Liberation arises from greater detachment and objectivity (an important side benefit of which is greater academic competence). The world becomes larger and richer, full of possibilities to explore, but the task of dealing with all this richness has a frightening aspect as well. How does one choose among alternatives? The problem is exacerbated by an appreciation of the limits of reason.

The answer to that deeply troubling question results from the realization that you have to assume the responsibility for directing your own life, that is, choose those aspects of life in which to invest your energies, care, and personal identity. It is this process of formulating and affirming your own values and forging a personal identity that Perry calls "Commitment." As one student described it, "There are all kinds of pulls, pressures and so forth . . . parents . . . this thing and that thing . . . but there comes a time when you just got to say, 'Well, . . . I've got a life to live . . . I want to live it this way, I welcome suggestions. I'll listen to them. But when I make up my mind, it's going to be me. I'll take the consequences.' " The realization must then be translated into actuality with choice of beliefs, a mate, a career, and a lifestyle. Having made successive commitments it is then necessary to balance them in a lifelong process of evaluation.

That is a very compressed summary of a long and difficult odyssey that everyone goes through in the course of personal growth and the forming of his or her own judgmental and evaluative framework. As someone at a relatively early stage of the process you might find it fun to go through the items in Box 5-7 for a rough assessment of your own position on the road from absolutism to relativism.

BOX 5-7

A Rating of Judgmental Framework

In each of the sets of three alternatives given below, select the one alternative that best corresponds to your own view.[6]

1. On the possibility of attaining a perfect society:
   (a) There can never be a perfect society because there is no consensus on what a perfect society would be. Different people have different conceptions of it, and there is merit to each conception but some are incompatible with others.
   (b) There can be a perfect society, at least in principle, because future technological and social developments should enable us to eliminate the major scourges of the past, such as starvation and disease.
   (c) There can never be a perfect society because every desirable feature also has its concomitant disadvantageous effects with the result that every change for the good leads to some undesirable consequence which, in turn, requires adjustment.
2. On looking for Mr. or Ms. Right:
   (a) There is a right person for everyone. Some people just belong together naturally because they have the same type of personality and tastes that make them compatible and congenial to each other.
   (b) There is no right person for anyone. Relationships form on the basis of existing circumstances and available individuals. It is up to them to work things out.
   (c) There is no right person for anyone. Every desirable characteristic has its undesirable aspects.

SUMMARY

This chapter dealt with the processes of *judgment* and *evaluation,* which are not cleanly differentiable, that share the property of assigning qualitative values on a subjective scale. Three characteristics of the process of judgment/evaluation were identified and illustrated: (a) the need to judge is ubiquitous and inescapable, (b) the process is inherently subject to error (two classes of error were identified), and (c) judgment always implies a criterion. Only the last characteristic is subject to control by the judge. Because of this fact, *criterion setting* is a major feature in the process of judging.

Four components of criteria were identified and illustrated: (a) *time frame,* whether immediate or long-range effects are considered; (b) *probable impact,* narrow or broad; (c) *consistency* with other criteria for related judgments; and (d) *explicitness* of the criterion (factors taken into account and related). As to

3. On the possibility of predicting the success of a marriage:
    (a) It is difficult to predict whether a marriage will last because many circumstances enter in, not all of which are predictable. However, commitment is a major factor. To the extent that it is present, other conditions are of lesser import.
    (b) It is possible to predict whether a marriage will last. Marriage involves finding the right person and treating him or her properly. If those conditions are met, there is no reason for failure.
    (c) It is not possible to predict whether a marriage will last. The future carries with it far too many circumstances beyond one's control to envision them or their possible effect.
4. On the sources of change:
    (a) Change is internally induced. It results from a change of outlook about things. No matter what happens in the world, it is possible to adjust one's outlook to cope with it.
    (b) Change is externally induced. It is for the most part forced upon one by such external circumstances as economic, social, and other conditions.
    (c) Change is induced by an interaction of internal changes in the individual and environmental changes as seen by the individual.
5. On the advisability of mandatory sentencing:
    (a) There should be tough, mandatory sentences for certain crimes that are destructive to the society and must be discouraged to promote the general welfare.
    (b) There should be no mandatory sentences for any crime. Every case is different and must be so evaluated.
    (c) Imposition of mandatory sentences is feasible but may pose additional problems. Strong deterrence is bought at the cost of greater flexibility of options.

justification of criteria three general bases were proposed: (a) *personal/affective considerations,* (b) *appeal to authority,* and (c) *considered independent judgment.* There are levels of each as was demonstrated in the concluding section on development of judgment.

Moral reasoning, as exemplified in reasoning about moral dilemmas, served as the example. After defining dilemmas and giving some illustrations, Kohlberg's work on reasoning about moral justice was described and the developmental stages presented. These specific stages are applicable to *reasoning about justice.* Gilligan maintains that they do not describe *reasoning about social harmony* very well. Her work was cited as evidence that alternative criteria can be applied.

The general course of development of evaluative reasoning was characterized in terms of a transition from *absolutistic* to *relativistic thinking.* Perry's work on intellectual growth was used as an illustration.

EXERCISES

1. Take at least one academic and one nonacademic example of a judgment you make frequently. Prepare a matrix for it, like that shown in Box 5-2, and state your criterion. In your description of the criterion give consideration of the four dimensions.
2. Prepare two scales for evaluation using the methods in Box 5-3. Your scale could rate relevance, attractiveness, preference (cafeteria food choices, friends, rock groups), prowess (of baseball, football, basketball, hockey teams), or overall effectiveness (of U.S. presidents), to suggest but a few topics. You will find that rank order and paired comparison scales become harder to apply as number of items included increases, but do at least one of them anyway. You might also want to construct two different scales for the same set of items to compare their relative positions on the two scales.
3. List some of your personal values and rank order them. You might also do this as a class project, for example, describe values of students at your institution or residents of your city, county, or state.

Are Your Values In Order?

A national sample of American adults was asked to rank these 18 values in order of importance. To compare your value system with that of the typical U.S. citizen, rank the values in order of their importance as guiding principles in your life, from most important (1) to least important (18). (After Ball-Rokeach, Rokeach, & Grube, 1984)

A Comfortable Life		A Comfortable Life
An Exciting Life		An Exciting Life
A Sense of Accomplishment		A Sense of Accomplishment
A World at Peace		A World at Peace
A World of Beauty		A World of Beauty
Equality		Equality
Family Security		Family Security
Freedom		Freedom
Happiness		Happiness
Inner Harmony		Inner Harmony
Mature Love		Mature Love
National Security		National Security
Pleasure		Pleasure
Salvation		Salvation
Self-Respect		Self-Respect
Social Recognition		Social Recognition
True Friendship		True Friendship
Wisdom		Wisdom

4. A values test that was printed in *Psychology Today* (1984, November) is given here. In the first column, enter your own rank orders going from 1 for most important to 18 for least important. Hint: sometimes it is easier to work from the extremes to the middle. In the second column give the class mean rank. The results obtained from a large sample can be found in the notes section.[7]

5. You may well have taken a preference test administered by a guidance counselor to help identify your career interest. If you have it, examine it for the values employed in the test. Many of these tests are based upon the Allport Vernon[8] scale of values that you might each take in class.

6. Construct some moral dilemmas of your own and administer them to the class. Try to evaluate the responses with respect to the Kohlberg stages in Box 5-6. You might also want to compare the dilemmas of other class members to determine what issues or values are commonly used and which are not. For the commonly posed dilemmas have a class discussion of the criterion to be employed. Can you arrive at a class consensus on it? There is a game, A Question of Scruples (1986) published by Milton Bradley that might be useful in answering this question.

7. Construct criteria for aesthetic judgment for specific domains, such as painting, sculpture, architecture, poetry, drama, film, dance, music, even mathematics. Apply them to at least three specific instances. As part of this exercise it would be instructive to consider alternative grounds for justification, such as personal feeling, rules from authorities such as critics or instructors in relevant courses, as well as independent considered judgments to see how your evaluation of the chosen examples differs depending upon the criterion selected. You might also consider returning to Exercises 2 and 3 of Chapter 2 for your choice of examples.

8. Although you have probably not yet had the experience of serving on a jury, you might anticipate that eventuality by taking a trial currently covered in the media and adopting the role of a juror in that trial; perhaps 12 members of the class could serve as a jury. Devise criteria for evaluating the evidence. If there is some current contest in progress one group might choose to constitute a panel for deciding it (for example, choice of a homecoming queen, assigning academy awards—Oscars—for this year's films, or awards for television programs). Try to come up with explicit criteria with which to justify your panel's selections.

9. Return to the previous exercise with a different framework, that is, the criteria you used undoubtedly reflected the values of your own culture. Consider what the criteria might be for a different culture (possibly one you viewed for Chapter 4). Formulate and apply criteria appropriate to that culture. An alternative might be to choose a different historical period (for example, the time of the American Revolution) and try to recapture the evaluative framework of that period.

10. As a group, identify a central ethical issue of our time. By way of perspective on why it is central for us, you might want to identify a central ethical issue for a different era or culture.

11. Take one of the issues identified in the preceding exercise and read the views of two authorities who take opposing views with respect to it. What is the basis of their disagreement? Could the differences be reconciled?
12. Why would anyone ever want to cheat or to plagiarize? Consider possible intents and criteria that might apply to them.
13. Why would anyone ever want to intimidate another anonymously, for example, through late night phone calls, written threats, or vandalism? In terms of the continuum from absolutistic to relativistic thinking where would you place such actions?

◆ Summary of Part 1 ◆

The major thread of Part 1 is enhancement of understanding by making experience meaningful. Attending, encoding, communicating, detaching, and evaluating are all processes that can be directed to the goal of understanding. Instead of reviewing each of those processes, five guidelines are offered which can be recalled easily. If you get into the habit of applying them, you should find that you are thinking differently than before you began.

Independence.   The effective thinker does not rely upon the vagaries of fortuitous circumstance or the prompting of others for investigation, inspiration, or direction of his or her thought. Rather, he or she is in charge of his or her own cognitive processes and directs them in a conscious and disciplined manner. Set your own goals, consider alternative means of attaining them, monitor your progress, and be ready to alter course as needed. In the course of time you should find thinking to be a more habitual and enjoyable activity.

Detachment.   Immediate personal reactions are a component of meaning but they should not be the exclusive constituent. Try to detach from your own emotions and preconceptions by deliberately adopting the role of another in order to assess the situation more fully and to arrive at alternative interpretations.

Transformation.   It is a poor practice to deal with information or ideas in a single unchanging form, generally, the form in which they were originally encountered. Information and ideas should be repackaged, transformed, and, even, played with. Express ideas in your own words, relate them to other ideas, consider them from alternative viewpoints, and look for implications. It is even useful to consider the consequences to be expected if an assumption were wrong or some alternative were correct. As you become more skillful at transformation, your thinking should become less literal and increase in both flexibility and creativity. The transformation of ideas should also assist in a more critical analysis of them, for example, through differentiation of intrinsic properties from more superficial ones, and in differentiating form from content.

Evaluation. Active transformation is necessary but not sufficient for effective thought. Some ways of stating an idea, organizing information, and so on, are better than others with respect to criteria of economy, elegance, clarity, generality, appropriateness, theoretical validity, or generation of implications. By becoming aware of these criteria and evaluating ideas with respect to them you become a more critical and more powerful thinker.

Organization. An organizing framework or perspective is necessary for effective communication, promoting understanding, utilizing knowledge, or any other enterprise requiring thought. The framework serves as an envelope or a scaffold for directing transformation and for setting evaluative criteria. It makes for more powerful thinking as well as for a broader utilization of knowledge.

2

The Tools of Thought

As every workman knows, having the right tool for the job contributes importantly to success. But good tools help only if used appropriately. A hammer is invaluable for driving nails or for removing them. It is useful, also, for providing extension or weight, as in propping open a door or holding up a window. It is worthless for applying paint. So, too, with the tools of thought: one must know not only how to use them but, also, when their use is called for. The chapters that follow are directed towards that goal. As an introduction to them, I shall remind you of what constitutes a tool of thought and present a classification scheme of types of thinking tasks as a basis for identifying appropriate tools.

You already have encountered some important tools and types of thinking. A tool of thought can be a concept, or a procedure, or even a specialized body of knowledge. The procedures of arithmetic, for example, are applicable to a great variety of quantities: money, length, liquid volume, weight, and so on. So, too, with the general concept of measurement or with some fundamental concepts of physics such as energy, inertia, and velocity. You can think much more precisely and analytically by applying these tools. Similarly, in the first part of this book you were introduced to a very powerful tool, classification, along with procedures to promote detachment, such as a shift of focus from content to form. You were introduced to some concepts such as meaning-making and encoding. Finally, you encountered a type of thinking, evaluation, and learned that a basic tool for evaluation is criterion setting. The ensuing chapters will deal with reasoning, problem solving, decision making, and creative thinking along with the tools appropriate to each. The types are summarized in the accompanying table.

Any classification scheme implies a theoretical basis. In the case of types of thinking there is no uniformly accepted theory of thinking upon which to base a classification scheme. Rather, the types arise from common usage and social consensus which rarely, if ever, make for consistency across classes in choice of

Summary Table Comparing Kinds of Thinking To Be Reviewed in Part 2

Type of Activity	Defining Properties
Evaluation	Assigning of value on some scale. Criterion central consideration.

Reasoning
I Deductive:
  A. Logical argument,
    mathematical proof
 	
  B. Other
	Conclusion based upon assertions. Argument structure determines cogency/validity. Premise truth determines soundness.

II Inductive:
  A. Explanation, theory,
    model
 	
  B. Hypothesis testing
	Relation among contributing variables expressed in equation or model.
	
	Prediction obtained by deducing consequences of model. Test emphasizes conditions for falsification of hypothesis.

Problem solving	Gap between start and goal state and constraints upon path to it. Allowed procedure rules and transformations generally specified.
Decision making	Alternatives must be evaluated on basis of likelihood and utility of alternative outcomes. Selection made with respect to criterion.
Creative thinking	Going beyond easy and obvious alternatives to generate novelty.

Nature of Solution	Likelihood of Error	Appropriate Tools
Rarely precise or unique.	Error inherent in process. Two kinds of error.	Explicit criterion setting, objectifying scale and its metric.
Conclusion uniquely determined by premises.	Can be error-free but there are many fallacies to avoid.	Schemes for describing and analyzing argument form. Inference rules and permissible transformations are explicitly formulated.
Conclusion likely, not certain.	Error possible.	
Set of possible solution constrained but not unique.	Error possible. No certainty attaches to conclusion.	Rules of theory construction, for example, consistency, generality, parsimony.
Hypothesis is rejected or it is not.	As in all evaluations, error inherent, takes one of two forms.	Procedures of experimentation, especially control. Statistical procedures.
Attainment of goal; may or may not be unique or, even, attainable.	Depends upon nature of problem. Some solutions can be error-free.	Schemes for representation of problem space. Procedures for solution planning, for example, information maximizing.
Many possible; which is optimal depends on selection criterion.	Always subject to error especially under conditions of risk and uncertainty.	Schemes for formalizing alternatives and outcomes. Calculus for assigning values to alternatives. Selection criteria.
Multiple possible solutions inherent in process.	Error not a relevant criterion.	Procedures for circumventing barriers and for generating many alternatives. Specific skills/knowledge.

defining properties, or for clarity of class boundaries. This problem is especially acute in the case of reasoning. Reasoning involves inference directed at a conclusion on the basis of presented evidence. There are, however, some important differences based upon the relation between conclusion and evidence and the form of inference required as a result. It is common practice to differentiate deductive from inductive inference: in the former the conclusion is dictated by the premises, in the latter it extrapolates beyond them. The first two chapters focus upon deduction within the context of assertions and arguments. Induction is covered within the framework of causal and probabilistic inference and procedures for model building and hypothesis testing. The justification for this extended treatment of reasoning relative to other categories of thinking is that evaluation of arguments and construction and testing of explanatory models constitute major continuing activities of adult existence. Responsible training in thinking should provide a foundation for them.

That is not to imply that problem solving, or decision making, for example, is any less important or ubiquitous than reasoning or, even, that it is meaningful to assume that pure unalloyed instances of a category arise. Most occasions of thinking require the exercise of several of the categories for successful resolution. The convenient fiction of independent classes is employed here in order to introduce the tools appropriate to each category (as well as the hazards of their misapplication) and to foster finer discrimination of task demands. There is no single all-purpose tool or procedure that applies for all the varieties of tasks requiring thought. The accompanying table gives a preliminary introduction to categories of thinking, their defining features, and dimensions of differentiation. At the completion of this section it should also serve as a useful summary that you may want to augment with your own notes.

Because of the variety of preparation among individual students, some may find the material of Part 2 to be difficult while others may find it superficial and simple. Probably no one will find it uniformly too difficult or too simple. I doubt that it is possible to attain a level that, like Baby Bear's bed, is just right for everyone.

CHAPTER

6

Evaluating Assertions

Much everyday reasoning takes the form of putting together evidence in a structure that leads inevitably to a conclusion. For example, detective stories lead to a conclusion on "whodunit" by gradually and indirectly presenting evidence concerning the likely culpability of all suspects. The reasoning involved may be formalized as a set of assertions, such as, "The niece had cause to kill the victim but she was out of town at the time the crime was committed. The sister had no access to a gun and no knowledge of how to use one. Killing with one well-aimed shot between the eyes requires great skill." The conclusion would be that one and only one person could have committed the crime. The conclusion and set of assertions leading to it are technically termed an *argument*. (Note that this differs from everyday usage in which the term "argument" refers to a disagreement among persons.) One criterion for a good argument is that the conclusion must follow from the evidence upon which it is based, that is, the assertions presented. A second criterion is that the assertions be true. This chapter will consider the evaluation of assertions and the individual statements which compose an argument. The next chapter will be devoted to an evaluation of arguments.

You already are acquainted with the process of evaluation and are aware of the importance of criteria in reducing error. The purpose of this chapter is to show that there are several different kinds of assertions. Each class of assertion has its appropriate evaluative criterion. Some tools for evaluating assertions will be presented.

CLASSIFYING ASSERTIONS

Consider the 20 assertions in Box 6-1. All are simple declarative sentences and appear to be legitimate assertions. You might even find yourself deciding that

135

BOX 6-1

Assertions for Testing

1. Homosexuality is an alternative life-style.
2. One's natural parent's parent is one's grandparent.
3. Fewer than 10% of all Americans own TV sets.
4. A thin turkey sandwich must be eaten with a knife and fork.
5. One need not be registered to vote in a local election.
6. Chocolate is delicious.
7. If God had meant us to fly he wouldn't have given us the railroad.
8. It is possible to spend all one's money and to save it, too.
9. Wednesday follows Tuesday.
10. Every woman has a navel.
11. The sun radiates heat.
12. Vehicles must keep to the right, except to pass.
13. Cleanliness is next to Godliness.
14. All the best writers are men.
15. Adam and Eve were the first human beings.
16. Love makes the world go round.
17. $6(2x + 3x) = 30x$.
18. Leaded gas costs more than unleaded gas.
19. A pound of bricks is heavier than a pound of feathers.
20. Blondes have more fun.

---

they are all facts; they are not. As you read them try to devise a classification system by which to group similar statements. Your natural reaction, doubtless, is, "Similar with respect to what?" One criterion might be acceptability; you will assent to some statements but have questions about others. You might also have an impression that they differ with respect to content or to purpose but you may have difficulty in stating the criterion of those judgments explicitly. Nevertheless, try to do so before reading on.

Let's start with Statement 10, which is a very sweeping generalization that every woman has a navel. Nevertheless, you are inclined to treat it as a fact and to accept it as true (even though conceivably there may be some woman somewhere who has had her navel surgically removed for some reason). The next statement, Statement 11, is of the same type; but, what about the first assertion, or Statements 6, 13, and 14? They propose an opinion which you may or may not share. The last statement would also seem to fall into that class but it is harder to evaluate because of its ambiguity (more fun than what?). Without proceeding on to each of the other statements, it appears evident that a classification system is needed. I shall offer one in the next section; you can then go back and try to apply it to the examples in Box 6-1. By way of introduction let's start with a smaller set of examples:

1. (a) The incidence of abortion is declining.
   (b) Abortion is murder.
2. (a) Girls seek eligible bachelors.
   (b) A bachelor is an unmarried man.
3. (a) There are two pieces of fruit in the refrigerator: an apple and a peach.
   (b) $1 + 1 = 2$
4. (a) Jacob saw angels ascending a ladder.
   (b) Nurses are angels of mercy.
5. (a) Eggs boiled in saltwater don't crack.
   (b) Water boils at 100° centigrade.

In each pair of assertions the same words appear but the statements to the left differ systematically from their counterpart to the right. I'll call the first group factual statements and the second group conceptual statements. Let's examine how they differ.

Factual vs Conceptual Statements.   All of the statements to the left share the property of asserting something about events; they deal with empirical matters and are properly tested against the evidence of experience. The nature of the relevant evidence may differ, as may the ultimate truth status of the assertion, but in principle all purport to convey information about observable events. The defining property of factual statements, then, is that they are assertions about the world that can be tested for truth or falsity against empirical evidence. Contrary to the everyday connotation of the term "fact" they need not be found true, but they must be testable for truth. This deviation from everyday usage may be confusing at first but should cause no serious difficulty: everyone has encountered purported facts that don't check out. They are classified as factual assertions nonetheless by virtue of being empirical and testable. In applying that criterion to the statements in the left column one can see that they all meet the criterion. The first statement will probably not be supported by appropriate statistical evidence (appropriately corrected for total number of pregnancies per time period), but it is a factual assertion nonetheless. Similarly, the statement about the contents of the refrigerator may or may not be correct, but again, it is a factual assertion. The assertions about girls, or about eggs, are not so readily tested, but reasonable evidence from large samples could certainly be obtained. That is, one could perform an experimental comparison of the incidence of cracking in two otherwise comparable samples of eggs, one boiled in salted and one in unsalted water. A similar comparison could be conducted for girls seeking eligible bachelors vs girls seeking married men. They, too, are factual assertions. For the remaining example, Jacob said he saw angels; whether he actually did so cannot be determined. That he asserted to have seen them is factual; he may, in fact, have been dreaming.

What about the statements to the right? What are the criteria for them? Here matters are more complicated. I will use the term conceptual to refer to any assertion that is not factual.[1] There is no single property common to all members of the class other than that they are not statements about empirical events and, therefore, are not properly tested for truth or falsity against observational evidence. Statements 2, 3, 5 (b) are assertions about the use of terms or symbols; they are definitional in intent. We would accept each as true, certainly, but they are "true" by definition rather than by the testing of evidence. Statement 2 tells how the word "bachelor" is to be used, Statement 3 is an arithmetic rule of symbol equivalence, and Statement 5 identifies the setting of a scale value on the centigrade scale (that is, the value of 100° is assigned to that temperature at which water boils and the value of 0° is assigned to the temperature at which it freezes). Statements 2 and 17 of Box 6-1 also fall into this category, so do 8 and 19 despite the fact that in the form in which they are stated, they are logical contradictions.

Statement 1(b) (like 1, 6, 7, 13, and 14 of Box 6-1) is a statement about opinions or values. Evaluation of statements of this form hinge upon definition of the central concept (such as, murder, life-style, delicious). Statement 4 is a metaphor (as is 16 in Box 6-1) and like all metaphors, is not intended to be taken literally but, rather, to invite comparison with respect to a relevant feature (compassion or motive force). Statements 4, 5, 9, and 12 of Box 6-1 are statements about conventions that are prescribed either informally or legally within a society. Here both 4 and 5 are stated in a way that does not accurately describe the convention whereas Statements 9 and 12 do. Note that an assertion about the convention is factual; for example, "The freeway speed limit, like other speed limits, is 55 mph" but an assertion of the convention "55 mph is the speed limit" is not.

The purpose of this exercise is to demonstrate that not all assertions are facts. In interpreting an assertion it is not sufficient to examine the meaning of its component words. You must ask what is being asserted. If the statement purports to convey information about real-world events and it is (at least in principle) verifiable as true or false, it is a factual statement; if it does not do so, then it is a conceptual statement. This distinction is similar to the differentiation of fact and opinion that you probably encountered earlier in your academic career. In this case, however, the class of conceptual statements includes statements (conventions) about the use of words or other symbols, other rules and conventions, metaphor, and statements of opinion, value and belief. The differences between factual and conceptual statements, along with subclasses and examples of each, are summarized in Box 6-2. As you have already discovered, the differentiation of factual and conceptual statements can be difficult but it is a differentiation that must be made because it determines what evaluative tools should be employed and what sort of evidence is pertinent (and, as will be seen in the next chapter, whether it may legitimately serve as a premise in a deductive argument). Additional exercises are given at the end of the chapter. Try them and bring to class your own examples of factual or conceptual statements which seem especially confusing. Opinion masquerading as fact is often especially troublesome to identify. You should also consider the possible consequences of misclassifying an assertion (treating opinions as fact) and of applying an inappropriate criterion to its evaluation.

Criteria for Evaluation.   The appropriate criterion for evaluating factual assertions is truth or falsity as determined by the proof or disproof of evidence. Just what sort of data are appropriate depends upon the nature of the assertion. As we have seen already, simple assertions (such as, it is snowing, John is sitting in the back, or there is a grease spot on your tie) are readily tested for truth or falsity. General assertions (such as, there is calcium loss with advancing age, women are shorter than men, or bananas turn brown in the refrigerator) require more elaborate testing (see the end of this chapter and Chapter 8). Predictions, of necessity, require appropriate time for testing (it will snow tomorrow, the national debt will exceed the gross national product in the year 2000). Despite these complications, it should be possible, in principle, to determine whether any factual assertion is or is not correct by looking at relevant evidence. Any other rejoinder is irrelevant. Factual matters are often beclouded by opinion in everyday life (for example, the candidate for the secretarial position may type 150 words per minute but hiring considerations may be contaminated by opinion, such as, "But I'm not sure I like him/her").

For conceptual assertions, on the other hand, truth/falsity is not the major criterion and, therefore, empirical evidence may be irrelevant or inconclusive. To conclude that the statement "Nurses are angels of mercy" is false because nurses don't have wings is irrelevant if not foolish. Metaphors cannot be true or false; they can only be apt or not. Mixed metaphors are often a source of amusement, for example, the second metaphor in Box 6-2. Similarly, definitional statements cannot be true or false in any meaningful sense but only adequate or inadequate. That evaluation can be reached only through a test of whether the definition applies where it should apply and does not apply where it should not. Definitions may fail the test of adequacy by being too broad—the definition of a charitable organization as an organization to serve a public purpose is too broad because it would include such public bodies as the police and the post office, which clearly are not charitable organizations. A definition may also be too narrow—the definition of caution as avoidance of risk of physical injury is too narrow because cautious people avoid material loss or psychological distress, as well as physical injury. My assertion that $2 + 2 = 4$ is not a fact, but a convention of our system of arithmetic, may be difficult for you to accept. We tend to use that statement as a model of fact. It is certainly true because it is true by definition. Whether or not that definition is adequate depends upon the coherence of the number system of which it is a component (that is, whether any

---

BOX 6-2

Comparison of Factual and Conceptual Statements

Statement Class

	Factual	Conceptual
Defining Property	Information purporting description of real world events or relations. Generally correct but may not always be so.	Essentially a default class of all statements that are not factual.
Means of Test	Compare to appropriate relevant data to test for truth or falsity.	Analysis of intended meaning and concept central to it.
Variants/Subclass	No generally accepted taxonomy. Statements may differ with respect to comprehensiveness (intended generality), time frame, completeness (whether all information is present or additional inference is invited).	May be statement of rule/definition for symbol equivalence, rule or convention of procedure, analogy, or statement of opinion/belief/value.
Examples	A. Generality variants. 1. Specific statement: It is getting dark. John is the boy in the blue shirt. This bread is stale. The meeting was held on Tuesday.	A. Symbol substitution rules/definitions: A widow is a woman whose husband has died. Stale means having lost freshness or interest. $\text{Tan } \theta = 1/\text{ctn } \theta = \sin \theta/\cos \theta$

	Statement Class	
	Factual	**Conceptual**
Examples (*continued*)	2. Limited general: The juniors in this class score higher on quizzes than do the sophomores. Siamese cats are often cross-eyed. Crimes of violence are increasing in the U.S.	B. Statements of rule or convention: No parking at any time. Passengers will please refrain from flushing toilets while the train is in the station. Convicted felons may not hold public office.
	3. General statements: Cigarette smoking is harmful to health. Front-wheel drive provides superior control. Sexual dimorphism exists among birds.	C. Metaphor. She has lost her marbles. The ship of state is sailing the wrong way down a one-way street. George Washington was the father of this country.
	B. Time variants. 1. Present or past: It rained yesterday. World War I ended with the armistice of November 11, 1918. 2. Predictions to the future: It will rain tomorrow. Population growth will outrun food supply.	D. Statements of opinion/belief/value: One picture is worth a thousand words. Sexual dimorphism serves an evolutionary function. The early bird gets the worm.

logical contradiction can be generated from the set of definitions and rules; if not, they are consistent and adequate).

Again, rules and conventions are matters of agreement, and, in some sense, arbitrary. They are properly evaluated with respect to a criterion of their likely consequences rather than whether they are true or false. While factual evidence might be relevant it is so only with respect to the criterion of consequences not in respect to its truth or falsity: for example, Sunday store hours might or might not increase sales, reduce traffic, or affect church attendance. Here the invocation of evidence is likely to arise not so much from evaluation of the rule, *per se,* as from additional assertions that arise in the course of reasoning about the rule. That is, assumptions, such as, "Allowing commercial zoning will increase traffic," or "Permitting smoking will cause air pollution," are factual assertions to which the criterion of truth/falsity apply, making the collection of evidence appropriate to the prediction. Evidence is irrelevant to the convention itself: for example, "Smoking prohibited" can only be observed or breached.

Comparable considerations arise in evaluating statements of opinion, belief, and value. In this case, a good term for the appropriate criterion is elusive. Sound/unsound comes close but poses problems to the extent that a criterion for the evaluation of arguments (as we shall see in the next chapter) is expressed in those terms. Tenable/untenable are more appropriate as a description of the appropriate evaluative criterion, although they are a bit too strong for the purpose. In any case, truth/falsity is not an appropriate criterion although, as was true of statements of conventions and rules, it can be applied to factual assertions generated in the course of evaluating opinions and beliefs. This is a subtle distinction that may be clarified by some examples. Phobias (irrational fear of specific animals, objects, or situations such as heights or crowding) are remediable to some extent by gradual exposure to the causal agent, as, for instance, giving a kitten to a cat-phobic child. Ethnic stereotypes provide another example. Prejudicial opinions are subject to modification through favorable experiences but it is not the experience *per se* that produces the change. Rather, the experience is effective to the extent that it leads to a change in the definition of the concept underlying that belief. For example, your belief that foreigners are ignorant would not necessarily be changed as a result of encounters with educated foreigners who could be dismissed as "the exceptions that prove the rule"— whatever that might mean. It would be changed only if such encounters led to a restructuring of concepts so that the class foreigner would no longer be defined by the property of ignorance (in which case they are connected by definition) but, rather, foreigner becomes a subset of the class human being, some of whom were born here and some not, where ignorance is not a defining property but an irrelevant feature associated with other life conditions, such as availability of education. As a result of such restructuring the belief that foreigners are ignorant is no longer tenable. To better understand this analysis you might apply it to some other belief, such as, what constitutes worthwhile activity, what is good

literature, and so on. If that assignment seems too formidable you might want
to postpone it until you have a helpful tool in hand, a technique for the clarification of concepts.

The Clarification of Concepts.   Wilson (1969) offers a number of useful
techniques for the clarification of concepts, six of which will be offered here.
To provide a consistent example for their application I shall take the concept of
"homeless" as it might arise in a belief statement: the homeless are a blot on
society, the homeless are the scum of the earth, or the homeless are the symptoms of a sick society. To evaluate whether or not the belief is tenable apply the
following steps:

1. *Isolating questions of concept.* In this case, I have already taken the step for
   you; the concept "homeless" is central to any belief about the homeless and
   it must be clarified before the tenability of the belief can be evaluated.
2. *Model cases.* A prototype (clear and unquestioned instance of the concept) is
   often useful as a starting point.[2] Many everyday concepts seem to be organized
   around focal instances: robin or sparrow as the prototypical bird; main course
   items as prototypical food. In the present instance of homelessness, perhaps
   an adult who has no immediate family, no fixed place of residence, and no
   stable source of support will serve as a model case.
3. *Contrary cases.* The bounds of the class are clarified by considering instances
   that clearly fall outside it: for example, bats or flying squirrels in the case of
   birds, chewing gum in the case of food, and so on. For the example of homelessness, perhaps someone who has wandered off and is temporarily lost
   (such as, a child or a confused, aged person) might qualify as an instance of
   a contrary case.
4. *Related cases.* Consideration of the concept of homelessness leads to related
   concepts such as poverty and social dislocation, for instance, alcoholics and
   noninstitutionalized psychotics, who may or may not be adjuged as examples
   of homelessness. There are also related concepts associated with availability
   and affordability of housing.
5. *Borderline cases.* One of the best ways to establish the bounds of a class is to
   examine borderline examples (for instance, water, condiments, food supplements, in the case of food). In establishing the bounds of homelessness, a
   person who has a home but chooses to leave it, such as a runaway, or someone
   that other group members cannot care for or do not want to care for (the
   seriously ill, abandoned infants, grown stepchildren) might serve as borderline instances.
6. *Invented cases.* Having established a clear focus and bounds of the conceptual
   class should help in identifying the defining properties of the class. A good
   test of their adequacy is the creation of invented instances or test cases that
   possess some but not all defining properties, or combinations of properties

not normally encountered. In defining food, for example, a delicious but totally noncaloric drink or a very nutritive but unappetizing substance are both questionable instances that force additional consideration of the properties of nutritional value and palatability. In defining homelessness, victims of massive infrequent catastrophes such as floods, fires, earthquakes, nuclear attacks, would all be possible instances to consider.

Have the results of this analysis of the concept "homeless" led to any modification of the belief statement you began with? If not, you may not have been sufficiently searching in your examination of the concept. A return to the exercise at the start of the section may help to reveal how the analysis of its central concept helps to clarify the tenability of statements of belief and opinion. As an additional test of your understanding of the techniques for analysis of concepts try analyzing some of the following statements: virtue is its own reward, all men are created equal, behavior that is totally predictable cannot be free, taxation is theft.

Evaluating Advertising. Advertising provides a good source of assertions requiring careful evaluation. Assertions of opinion often are presented as statements of fact where one is led to presume that they wouldn't say that if it were not true. In other instances, true but irrelevant assertions are offered to invite inference (the testimonial). A few current examples will be considered here; you can find many more in any publication or TV program.[3] You might, even, as a class project collect examples for analysis to see if you can devise a classification system (perhaps even a hierarchical one) of advertising techniques. Here are some instances to get you started:

"Wouldn't you really rather have a Buick?"

"You've come a long way, Baby!"

"Don't leave home without it."

"Fly the friendly skies."

"The quicker cleaner upper."

"Come to where the flavor is."

"Nine out of ten doctors recommend the pain relieving ingredient in. . . ."

"The right choice."

"The breakfast of champions."

"You deserve a break today."

"Ninety-nine and 44/100th percent pure!"

"Ring around the collar!"

"Aren't you glad you used. . . ?"

"Good to the last drop."

"We try harder."

If you try to apply the classification scheme proposed earlier, you will find few factual assertions, no doubt as a result of pressure for truth in advertising. Advertisers seem to be shifting to slogans that make assertions to which a criterion or truth/falsity does not apply. The slogan "Nine out of ten doctors recommend the pain relieving ingredient in . . ." is perhaps the most clearly factual assertion, but it is hedged. While it is probably true that most doctors do recommend aspirin for pain, brand is irrelevant. A comparable observation pertains to any soap; clean people do have less perspiration odor than people who have not bathed recently. Other slogans are simply too incomplete or vague to be classified, such as "99 44/100th percent pure" (pure what?). "It's the real thing" is a tautology (Coke is Coke). Still others invite filling in: "You've come a long way, Baby" suggests that many activities are now open to women, like smoking (and dying of lung cancer in greater numbers) implying that the former (smoking)—but not the latter (dying of lung cancer)—marks a woman as modern. A similar invited inference is made in "The breakfast of champions." Famous athletes eat this cereal and, if you eat this cereal, you too will be a champion. That, as it happens, is not a valid inference any more than most such invited inferences are valid. Many foods, for example, claim to contain a certain percentage of the daily requirement of some vitamin (a factual assertion) inviting the invalid inference that eating it will make you healthy (no more so than any other equally nutritious food will; and, of course, there is more to good health than diet alone).

This section has been concerned with evaluating assertions through identifying the purport of the assertion, applying the appropriate criterion, and gathering relevant information. As was suggested by a number of examples, however, rarely is one concerned with an isolated assertion. Commonly, a number of assertions are dealt with as part of a larger argument. In the remainder of this chapter I shall discuss methods for evaluating general factual assertions.

EVALUATING FACTUAL ASSERTIONS

All factual assertions should be subject to the test of truth or falsity in relation to experience, but the feasibility of testing can vary considerably, depending upon the nature of the assertion. Only specific assertions are subject to immediate direct test; generalizations and predictions, for example, require additional analysis to be rendered testable by prescribing appropriate test conditions. They are best treated as the conclusion of an inductive argument. As a first step toward testability, the meaning of the assertion should be precisely stated. Two means of increasing precision are discussed in the remainder of this chapter: (a) definition of connectives and quantifiers, and (b) characterization of populations on the basis of sample statistics. As we shall see, some assertions are so difficult or impossible to prove that the most direct and convincing means of testing them is to attempt to establish their falsity. Some of the logic of that strategy will be introduced here, the rest will be postponed for a full discussion of hypothesis testing in Chapter 9.

The Meaning of Logical Connectives: Truth Tables.   Factual assertions, or hypotheses as they are called in the case of experimental tests, are often stated in a standard form whose structure is characterized by specific terms called *connectives.* As the name implies, the function of a connective is to connect parts, symbolized by the letters p and q or their negation, $\bar{p}$ and $\bar{q}$, that serve as "place-holders" for an infinite variety of phrases that may be substituted for them. Some of the most common connectives are shown in Box 6-3. The table presented there is called a *truth table* because it gives the truth status of each assertion embodying the connective in relation to the truth status of the component terms, p, q, and their negations. There are only four possible combinations of components, as shown in the four rows of Box 6-3: pq, $p\bar{q}$, $\bar{p}q$, and $\bar{p}\bar{q}$. To get used to this convention, create some equivalents for p and q: "It rains," "I take the train," "It tastes good," "I eat it," and so on. For the first two suggested equivalents, "p and q" translates to "It rains and I take the train;" the implication, "If p then q" translates to "If it rains, then I take the train," and so on.

What should be readily apparent from the table is that for each possible combination of p and q, with respect to their truth status, there is a unique pattern of truth status for each assertion produced by the connective. For example, while "It rains and I take the train," p and q, can be true only if both p and q are simultaneously true, "If it rains, I take the train" can be true if pq, $\bar{p}q$, or $\bar{p}\bar{q}$ apply. That is, each of those states of affairs is compatible with the truth of the conditional assertion "If p then q." Observing $p\bar{q}$, on the other hand, falsifies the assertion "if p then q" (for example, if it rains and I don't take the train, then the assertion "If it rains, I take the train" is false). For conditional assertions, therefore, there is only one condition of falsification; thus, it is easier to disprove by looking for $p\bar{q}$ than it is to "prove" by observing all of the other three states of affairs. This strategy of assessing truth through falsification is an important strategy to which we will return often in ensuing chapters.

The Meaning of Logical Quantifiers.   The term *quantifier* refers to a word or phrase that answers the question, "How much?" There are four quantifiers whose meaning is established by logical convention: "All," "Some," "No," and "Some are Not." Their meaning is shown in Box 6-4 by means of Euler circle diagrams depicting the relation among sets (an alternative depiction is given in Box 7-4). All the possible relations between two classes, *A* and *B*, are illustrated at the top of Box 6-4. Those instances compatible with each of the quantifiers are illustrated. You should discover a number of things from examination of Box 6-4. One discovery is that the contradiction of "All *A* are *B*" is not "No *A* are *B*" but "Some *A* are not *B*." Similarly, "No *A* are *B*" is contradicted by "Some *A* are *B*." In logical terms, each member of the pair is the *complement* of the other. One important implication of this discovery is that to test sweeping generalizations like "All women are fickle," "All Christmas toys break in the first week," and "All birds fly," it is sufficient to find one contradictory instance. Finding an exception and therefore proving the assertion false is easier than testing its truth.

BOX 6-3

Summary of Truth Tables for Five Connectives

Status of Components		Conjunction "and"	Disjunction "or"		Implication "if"	Biconditional "if and only if"
p	q	$p \cdot q, p \cap q$	Exclusive $p \vee q$	Inclusive $p \vee q$	$p \supset q, p \rightarrow q$	$p \subseteq q, p \leftrightarrow q$
pq T	T	T	F	T	T	T
$p\bar{q}$ T	F	F	T	T	F	F
$\bar{p}q$ F	T	F	T	T	T	F
$\bar{p}\bar{q}$ F	F	F	F	F	T	T

The interpretation of truth tables. The components of an assertion are symbolized by p and q. They are "placeholders," which can be replaced by any phrase or assertion whatsoever: "It is cold," "It is wet," "John is a boy," and so on. The first two columns contain all the four possible combinations of components with respect to their truth or falsity. The remaining columns define five different connectives in terms of the truth or falsity of the assertion joining the specific combination of p, q, and their associated truth values by means of that connective. For example, consider the first connective, "and"; "p and q" is true *only* when *both* p and q are each true, otherwise it is false. Thus, the statement "It is cold and wet" is true only when both "It is cold" and "It is wet" are true. For the statement "It is cold or it is wet," on the other hand, the statement is true if "It is cold" *or* "It is wet," or both are true for the inclusive disjunction. An inclusive disjunction is false only when both components are false. For an exclusive disjunction, p or q will be false when both p and q are each false or when both p and q are true because it means one or the other, but not both. Now you can plug in some values for p and q and explore the use of the truth table for the remaining connectives.

A second important discovery is that conversion of "All A are B" to "All B are A" or "Some A are not B" to "Some B are not A" is incorrect; the two assertions are not equivalent as may be shown by diagramming. On the other hand, conversion of "Some A are B" to "Some B are A," or "No A are B" to "No B are A" is a correct inference. The ability to translate an assertion to an equivalent or to a contradictory form is often of value in testing the truth of an assertion or the validity of an argument.

BOX 6-4

**Euler Circle Representations of the Quantifiers
All, No, Some, Some are Not**

A. All Possible Relations Between Two Sets, *A* and *B*

A B	(A) B	(B) A	A (B	A B
1	2	3	4	5

B. The Quantifiers

A B	(A) B			A B
1	2			5
All *A* are *B*				No *A* are *B*

A B	(A) B	(B) A	A (B	(B) A	A (B	A B
1	2	3	4	3	4	5
Some *A* are *B*				Some *A* are not *B*		

As can be seen "All" and "Some are Not" are the complement or contradiction of each other as are "Some" and "No."

Other Quantifiers.   We have seen that whereas "All" and "No" have precise meanings, "Some" refers to a variable quantity of at least one and possibly all members of the class. What about other common language quantifiers like many, much, couple, few, rare, infrequent, lots, or little? To the extent that many quantifiers translate to "At least one but not all," they are a limited variant of "Some," but the imprecision can pose difficulties for testing assertions. On the other hand, that state of affairs characterizes many of the assertions to be tested for scientific or practical purposes. For example, the assertion that "Girls develop language earlier than boys" does not mean that this is true in every instance; rather, we know that the age at which children acquire speech varies widely, regardless of sex. There is no one number that can be assigned for a basis of comparison, which is also the case for product assertions like "Brand *X* towels last longer than brand *Y*." In each case, a generalization is made about a universe whose members cannot be exactly characterized with respect to the property in question. How are factual assertions to be evaluated under these conditions? The answer lies in the methods of descriptive statistics which will be addressed in the next section.

STATISTICAL CHARACTERIZATION OF EVIDENCE

Although the word "statistics" strikes fear in the hearts of many people, it is a subject of such great practical importance that no thinker can ignore it. This concluding section will, therefore, be devoted to some basic concepts of descriptive statistics: samples and populations, distributions, measures of central tendency, and measures of variation.

Samples and Populations. The term *population* refers to all the members of the group in question. A population can be anything you choose to identify as a population: all the members of your class, all students enrolled at a particular institution at a given time or over a specified time period, all the grains of sand on a beach or in the world, the production run of a particular commodity such as bolts or biscuits, and so on. The population in the first example is finite and countable, in the other examples it is still finite but larger. All the grains of sand in the world are to all intents and purposes an infinitely large population. A *sample* differs from the population in that it is a subset of the population selected for study purposes. From a practical standpoint it is much easier to obtain measures of size, preference, or whatever property is being studied from a sample than from a population. The property under study is called the dependent variable. There is nothing wrong with making inferences about a population value (technically known as a *parameter*) from sample measures (technically known as *statistics*) so long as the sample has two important properties: (a) it is large enough, and (b) it is representative.

The question, "How large is large enough?" can best be answered by, "Large enough to provide some idea of the form of the distribution and the variation within it." What those requirements entail will be discussed shortly. Let's consider the matter of representative. Statisticians use the term *unbiased* for this property. It means there are no grounds to believe that the sample statistic deviates systematically from the population parameter to be inferred from it. For example, if you wanted to poll voters in a town, it would not be advisable to draw your sample from all shoppers in the local supermarket at 10:30 a.m. That sample would probably overrepresent housewives and underrepresent men or employees in a 9-to-5 job. To the extent that housewives might vote differently from other segments of the population, they could constitute a biased sample of the residents of the town. Similarly, you would not want to take your sample from a meeting of the local Chamber of Commerce because in that case men, and especially businessmen, would be overrepresented in relation to other segments. You can, and should, come up with other examples to test your understanding of bias.

Two types of samples are accepted as representative: random samples and stratified samples. A *random sample* is one in which each member of the population has the same probability of appearing as every other member. Taking the first name on every tenth page of the telephone directory (to pursue the polling example above) would not provide a random sample because once the point of entry into the directory is chosen the first entry on every tenth page is certain to be selected and all other entries are certain to be omitted. The telephone directory is a poor listing of the population to begin with because it excludes all persons without a phone or with an unlisted number. It also includes institutions, agencies, and businesses that do not vote as individuals.

One model for a random sample is to put slips of paper, each containing the ID of a population member (in this example, the list of registered voters), into a large container and to draw n slips from it after shaking it well (where n = the size of the desired sample). That procedure satisfies the definition of randomness, and, thus, guards against bias. In a *stratified sample* one tries to ensure that various subsets of the population will appear with their population

---

BOX 6-5

Distribution Forms

Distributions may be symmetric or asymmetric, unimodal, bimodal, or, even, multimodal. The normal distribution is an idealized unimodal symmetric distribution for an infinitely large population whose properties have been extensively studied. It is widely used as a model for many phenomena. For some phenomena in which most values cluster around a low value mode, thus making large deviations possible only at the high end of the distribution, a positively skewed distribution provides a more accurate description. Some examples are reaction times or waiting times, and a variety of social phenomena such as annual income, family size, number of legal offenses, number of serious illnesses, and so on. A possible example of a negatively skewed distribution might be duration of pregnancy. When bimodal or multimodal distributions are encountered it is possible to suspect that they are the result of combining several different distributions; that is, that more than one phenomenon is reflected. For example, a bimodal distribution for life expectancy might suggest that two major causes of death were reflected: those affecting children and the hazards of normal aging that affected everyone who survived childhood. Rectangular distributions in which each outcome occurs with the same frequency as every other are rarely encountered and probably reflect artificial selection, for example, cookie varieties in a box of assorted cookies.

frequency: for example, age, sex, and income level of each group will be represented in the same proportions as they appear in the population. For polling, that is important; for some other estimates, where population members may reasonably be assumed to be homogeneous, it may not be, for example, when sampling color preference or number of cans of shoe polish purchased per annum.

Distributions. The property that is being measured (height, weight, intelligence, income, degree of party affiliation) is called the *dependent variable* because it varies. That is, the measure obtained for any given member of the population, or sample, is not constant. What is of interest, then, is determining how the value varies. One way of assessing variation is to plot a *frequency distribution* of obtained measures: that is, a plot of frequency of occurrence of each value. With only a small number of instances in the sample, the form of the resulting distribution is difficult to assess. As sample size increases, the form of the distribution approximates one of the forms shown in Box 6-5. Each of these forms tends to characterize some class of evidence. We will be concerned here only with the normal distribution, a statistical idealization that many measures reasonably

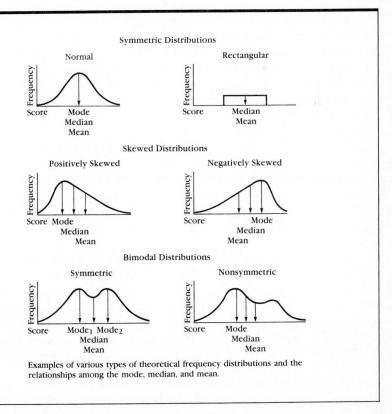

Examples of various types of theoretical frequency distributions and the relationships among the mode, median, and mean.

approximate: height, weight, age, IQ, shoe size, and so on. Some other variables are better characterized as skewed distributions: family income, consumption of alcohol or drugs, number of convictions, latencies and waiting times, and so on.

Measures of Central Tendency.   Because of the fact that measures of any dependent variable vary in a manner characterized by the form of the frequency distribution it should be clear that there is no single value, a constant, that characterizes each and every member of the sample. How then, can one arrive at a single value to characterize the sample? There are three choices available. (a) If the measures are reasonably well approximated by a normal distribution the *mean,* an arithmetic average is used. (b) Where the distribution is clearly skewed a more representative measure is provided by the *median:* the 50th percentile, that is, the value above and below which 50% of all measures fall. (c) For quick approximation a convenient measure is the *mode:* the measure that occurs most frequently. There is no assurance whatsoever that there will be a mode. For a normal distribution, these three values will coincide.

Measures of Variability.   The mean of a distribution of dependent variable measures generally provides the most representative measure for the population. It is the single measure that best characterizes its height, weight, and so on. In other words, if you had to make an educated guess about some population value, your best guess would be the mean. It is the guess most likely to be accurate more often than any other. But you know that your guess will be only the best approximation. It is wise to determine, in addition, how far off it is likely to be. The quantity that is used to provide an estimate of error is one that reflects variation of scores about the mean. Why a measure of variation should be chosen should be intuitively clear: the more that measures vary about the mean the larger will be the difference between your best guess and any obtained value. In other words, we do not expect a sample mean to reflect the population mean exactly; rather it should be a good approximation. How large a difference can be tolerated? By having some measure that reflects the magnitude of variation one can set bounds, that is, a range of values within which the best estimate is expected to fall a fixed proportion of the time. The value used for this purpose is the *standard deviation.* Its computational formula and other properties are shown in Box 6-6.

Because the standard deviation has these fixed properties (hence the name standard deviation), it can be used as a unit of measurement in the creation of a measurement scale (a scale of standard scores). You are probably more familiar with units such as inches, pounds, and centimeters. The standard deviation unit operates in the same way except that its scale is expressed with the mean as the origin or 0 point of the scale, and with plus or minus values indicating whether the standard score expressed on this scale falls above or below the mean.

The Uses of Statistics.   You probably have heard the expression, "There are liars, damned liars, and statisticians" and may believe that statistics are used to

BOX 6-6

The Standard Deviation as a Measure of Variability

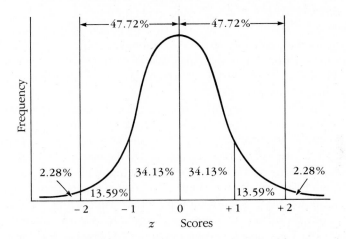

Normal curve: percent areas from the mean to specified z distances.

As an example of the use of standard deviation as a unit for interpreting variation of normally distributed measures about their mean, consider the Scholastic Aptitude Test (SAT), which is designed to have a mean of 500 and a standard deviation of 100. All scores should lie within the range ± 3 standard deviations from the mean, that is, $200 - 800$. A score of 600 is $+1$ standard deviation above the mean. Only $13.59\% + 2.28\% = 15.87\%$ of the scores are higher than 600 while $100 - 15.87 = 84.13\%$ of the scores fall below it. If you took the SAT you can interpret your score. The definitional and computational formulas for the standard deviation are:

$$s = \sqrt{\frac{\sum f(X - \overline{X})^2}{N - 1}} \qquad s = \sqrt{\frac{1}{N-1}\left[\sum fX^2 - \frac{(\sum fX)^2}{N}\right]}$$

$\qquad$ *Definition Formula* $\qquad\qquad$ *Computing Formula*

Where: s is standard deviation, f is the frequency, or number of cases, of each value of X, X is used as a placeholder for each obtained value of the dependent variable, $\overline{X}$ is the mean, N is the total number of measures, and Σ stands for the operation of adding, in this case, values of X each weighted by its frequency of occurrence.

confuse and to deceive. While that may sometimes be the case, it is more often the case, by far, that statistical tools are used to provide a measure of accuracy in a world of uncertainty where exactness is not possible. It is more often the case that the best one can provide is an estimate in projecting such quantities as annual income or expense for an individual or a group, rainfall, temperature, course grade, date of birth of an expected infant, or whatever. The estimate will not be exactly correct, but we would like to have enough information to be able to defend the estimate and to have some idea about possible magnitude of error. The methods of statistics are designed to answer such questions. They are powerful tools in dealing with a world of variation and uncertainty and one is well advised to learn to deal with them.

This brief introduction to some basic statistical concepts elaborated on the criterion for testing factual assertions. A specific factual assertion can be tested for truth directly; generalizations and predictions are subject to the same criterion but with a standard of correctness adjusted to the nature of the task. Factual assertions such as "The sun is out," "Henry is sitting in the second row," "The dog is barking," "The fire alarm is ringing" are either true or they are not true. For generalizations and predictions, on the other hand, we employ a weaker standard of truth: probably true where, ideally, we can assign a probability value to the likelihood. This subject will be pursued in Chapter 8. For the present, construct some examples of your own where statistical standards are appropriate in evaluating factual assertions: for example, in selecting tires or auto batteries, interpreting railroad schedules, and so on.

SUMMARY

This chapter dealt with evaluation of assertions or declarative statements. Not all statements are assertions: questions, commands, and expostulations don't count. Even in the subset of assertions, the members of the class are not equivalent in how they are to be interpreted. Two major categories of assertion were proposed: factual and conceptual. *Factual assertions* purport to provide some information about the real world. The criterion to be applied to them is whether they are true or false as determined by relevant evidence. Subclasses of factual assertions may be differentiated with respect to the nature of evidence required and the practicability of obtaining it. *Conceptual assertions* include all assertions that do not meet the definition of factual assertions. Included here are (a) rules and conventions for the substitution of symbols or words (basically, definitions), or for (b) prescribed procedures, and conduct, (c) metaphor, and (d) statements of opinion, value or belief. A criterion of truth or falsity is inappropriate for conceptual assertions. Definitions are evaluated with respect to adequacy, procedural rules are evaluated with respect to probable consequences, and metaphors are evaluated with respect to aptness. In all cases, factual evidence may be used but it does not provide a sufficient test of meeting the criterion.

Statements of opinion, belief, and value are perhaps the most problematic to assess. *Soundness* or tenability was proposed as a criterion for them. It was suggested that an appropriate criterion hinges upon the definition of a central concept and six procedures for the *clarification of concepts* were proposed: (a) isolating the concept, (b) finding a prototypical instance, (c) finding contrary instances, (d) finding related instances, (e) finding borderline instances, and (f) creating invented instances as a final test. The evaluation of advertising was considered as a practical example of the kinds of evaluation criteria to be applied.

The empirical truth or falsity of factual assertions is often not completely or directly testable. In those instances, some translation is needed to render the assertions testable. Two devices discussed were (a) use of relations among key terms, such as *connectives* and *quantifiers* to attain tests by falsification of a contradiction and (b) use of the procedures of descriptive statistics to base inferences about population properties upon sample statistics. A *sample* is a subset of a *population*. It should be representative of the population. *Random sampling* provides a safeguard against bias or systematic distortion in estimating population values from a sample.

The important descriptive properties of a population, and/or of the sample reflecting it, are (a) the form of the distribution, (b) a measure of central tendency (the mean is typically used for this purpose), and (c) the standard deviation as a measure of variability of values about the central tendency.

EXERCISES

1. Here are some more assertions to be evaluated. As in the case of the assertions of Box 6-1, decide (a) what kind of an assertion it is (factual, conceptual), (b) what criterion is appropriate to it (true, false, appropriate, adequate), and (c) its acceptability in relation to that criterion (yes, no, maybe).

	a	b	c
(a) John is brighter than Mary implies Mary is not as bright as John.			
(b) A napkin should be placed on the lap.			
(c) Creationism is the correct view of evolution.			
(d) Tallahassee is the capital of Florida.			
(e) War is good for a country.			
(f) Spare the rod and spoil the child.			
(g) Kissing is a sign of animosity.			
(h) Five is less than seven and less than two.			
(i) Reaganomics takes from the rich and gives to the poor.			
(j) A good name is worth more than gold.			
(k) Dogs lay eggs.			
(l) Burping is socially acceptable in our society.			
(m) A spinster is an unmarried woman.			
(n) Okra is the world's most popular vegetable.			

	a	b	c

(o) Since men are bigger than women men have bigger feet.
(p) A person is presumed innocent until proven guilty.
(q) The U.S. president serves for a term of six years.
(r) Blue is nicer than green.
(s) England is in central Asia.
(t) If all fathers are men then all men are fathers.
(u) $D = 2\pi r$.
(v) Human beings cannot live without oxygen.
(w) A photogram is a shadowy image produced without a camera by placing an object in direct contact with film.

2. Here are additional exercises. Take each assertion through the six-step procedure recommended to clarify concepts.
   (a) A good name is worth more than gold.
   (b) Pornography is misogyny.
   (c) The study of Latin trains the mind.
   (d) Fanatacism in the service of virtue is no vice.
   (e) The struggle for existence is a determinant of survival.
   (f) Liberal Democrats are liberal spenders. (This is tricky because the same word is used in two different senses. The shift in meaning can be the source of a fallacy of reasoning known as equivocation.)
3. What difference does it make how an assertion is classified? (You already may have asked this question yourself.) Devise some scenarios in which misclassification leads to error. Hint: problems are most likely to arise, as we shall see in the next chapter, in the course of reasoning and argument where, for example, belief statements cannot properly serve as premises although they are often presented as fact in real-life arguments. Find some examples in your reading where this is the case.
4. Return to Exercise 8 of Chapter 4 where you were asked to read the regulations of a group to which you belong and review that exercise in light of the discussion of criterion for rules and conventions presented here. You will probably also encounter some definitions as well. Can you refine your earlier answer in light of what you learned in this chapter?
5. Treat the class as a population from which to obtain some dependent variable measures for which you will get a group mean, standard deviation, and frequency distribution. Some measures you might use are: grade point average, number of mathematics courses taken, number of children in the family, number of years each member has resided in the county, amount of time spent on exercises for the preceding chapter, and so on. As a result of working

up several sets of such data you should get a better appreciation of differences in the form of the distribution for each, as well as differences in amount of variation in each distribution. Suppose that you wanted to use the class data as a sample from which to infer properties about the population of all students currently enrolled at your institution, how would your interpretation of the summary measures you obtained change? Your class is certainly not a random sample of the population, consider to what extent it might or might not be representative.

6. Find some examples in your reading of factual assertions that are supported by evidence. Evaluate the evidence in light of what you now know about statistical summarization of evidence. Hint: the example may well present some estimated values. Does it also indicate the size of the sample on which they are based? a description of how the sample was obtained? an estimate of error?

7. There are now so-called truth squads (as part of a program called Accuracy in Academia) sitting in on college classes throughout the country evaluating the "accuracy" of material presented by instructors. To what extent is it possible to do this? For a concrete example you might tape a lecture in some class you are taking and try to evaluate it as a truth squad member. You will then need to identify those assertions to which a criterion of accuracy is applicable and decide what sort of evidence is appropriate to them. It might also be interesting to do a tally of the proportion of factual and conceptual statements in the class and do a statistical summary of data collected for a number of different classes. How much variation is there in proportion of factual assertions? Is the proportion observed related to the nature of the subject matter? Are there instructor differences within a subject matter area?

· *7* ·

Evaluating Arguments

In everyday language we use the term "argument" to refer to a quarrel among individuals with respect to some issue. The same term is used in mathematics and in logic with a more restricted technical meaning assigned to it. In mathematics arguments are commonly called "proofs." No doubt you are familiar with proofs from geometry. As you may remember, you proved theorems and corollaries by making use of axioms, postulates, and definitions—you inferred a conclusion on the basis of more general principles and the conclusion you reached held without exception.

Logicians use the term *argument* to refer to a set of statements, or assertions, in the form of a *conclusion* and its supporting justifications; the justification statements are called *premises*. Arguments, in effect, formalize the result of a reasoning process in a conventional form. It is customary to distinguish two kinds of reasoning: deductive and inductive inference. In *deductive inference* one proceeds, as in a geometry proof, from general premises to a specific conclusion. A major evaluative criterion of deductive arguments concerns the validity of the argument, whether the conclusion necessarily follows from the premises. The criterion of validity depends solely upon the form of the argument, not its content. It is common, for this reason, to replace content terms with letters or other symbols to clarify the form of the argument and to prevent distraction by the meaning of its component assertions. To the extent that the conclusion of a valid deductive argument follows from the premises, it is inherent within them from the outset. The formal argument serves to demonstrate the logical necessity of the conclusion.

In *inductive reasoning,* on the other hand, content cannot be replaced by empty symbols, it is central to the argument. Moreover, because the conclusion is more general than the premises upon which it is based, no certainty is attached to the conclusion of an inductive argument. Rather, the conclusion is viewed as provisional subject to additional evidence. On the other hand, as shown in the last chapter, inductive conclusions can be conclusively shown to be false. Some examples of deductive and inductive arguments are shown in Box 7-1 along with a comparison of the two processes of reasoning.

This chapter will consider deductive arguments, tools for their evaluation and errors that may arise in dealing with deductive arguments. By way of introduction to the criteria for evaluating the soundness and validity of arguments, we will begin with the deductive arguments of formal logic and proceed to everyday arguments which arise more frequently, but lack the force of logical necessity that characterizes the deductions of formal logic.

CATEGORICAL AND CONDITIONAL SYLLOGISMS

The deductive arguments of formal logic are called *syllogisms*. There is a conventional form for their presentation. Each assertion of evidence, technically known as a premise, is stated on a separate line; the conclusion, preceded by $\therefore$, symbolizing "therefore," is given below the premises. By convention, the first premise is called the *major premise* and subsequent premises, of which there may be more than one, are called *minor premise(s)*. For example:

> All mammals suckle their young (major premise).
> All rats are mammals (minor premise).
> $\therefore$ All rats suckle their young (conclusion).

is an argument in the form of a categorical syllogism and it is a valid argument.

The reason that syllogisms are called formal arguments is that the validity of their conclusion depends solely upon the form of the argument. The conclusion of a valid argument necessarily follows. Logical necessity is a difficult concept to explain, but an easy one to recognize. Consider the linear syllogism: $A > B, B > C, \therefore A > C$. It must be the case that $A > C$; no other alternative conclusion is possible. It is logically necessary. This property of formal deductive arguments make them very compelling; for informal deductive arguments, the conviction of logical necessity does not hold.

The Criteria of Validity and Soundness. *Validity* is a property of arguments, not of individual statements; it concerns the relation among statements. An argument is valid if the conclusion necessarily follows from the premises; or, to put it another way, an argument is valid if it would be impossible for the conclusion to be false given that the premises are true. An additional convention is that the premises are assumed to be true for the purposes of testing the validity of a conclusion.

	BOX 7-1	

Comparison of Inductive and Deductive Reasoning

Feature in Question	Deductive	Inductive
Defining Property	The conclusion is tacitly contained in the premises; it would be self-contradictory to assert the premises but deny the conclusion.	Essentially a default class of arguments that are not deductive. Denial of conclusion does not lead to a contradiction of asserted premises.
Criterion for Acceptance of Argument	1. Validity. An argument is valid if the conclusion follows from the premises. 2. Soundness. All the premises of a valid argument must be true.	There is no accepted term but "reasonableness" comes close. The connection between premise and conclusion is not necessary, as in deduction, but it should be appropriate, likely, and compelling.
Means of Test	Test of validity is based on analysis of form of the argument.	Test of reasonableness of the conclusion is based upon analysis of the content of premises and conclusion. Are they correct? Is relation appropriate? Is conclusion more likely to be true than any equally detailed rival?[†]
Variants/ Subclass	Syllogism (complete or partial), conditional (if-then), and transitive reasoning. Mathematical proofs are also of the form of a deductive argument.	Generalization, inference of causal relations, analogical reasoning.

[†]I adopt here a criterion proposed by Swinburne. (1974)

Feature in Question	Deductive	Inductive
Examples	A. Syllogism: 　All A are B. 　C is A. 　∴　C is B. 　No A are B. 　C is A. 　∴　C is not B.	A. Generalization: 　A_1 is a B. 　A_2 is a B. 　. . . . . 　A_n is a B. 　∴　All A are B. 　A_1 is a B. 　A_2 is a B. 　A_3 is not a B. 　. . . . . 　$X\%$ of A are B. 　Also inference on basis of past experience, present experience, or sample to population.
	B. Conditional reasoning: 　If p then q. 　p. 　∴　q. 　If p then q. 　$\bar{q}$. 　∴　$\bar{p}$.	B. Causal reasoning: 　When I eat shellfish I get a rash. 　The rash does not occur under any other condition. 　∴　The rash is an allergic reaction to shellfish. (See Chapter 8 for an additional discussion of causal reasoning.)
	C. Linear ordering: 　$A > B, B > C, A > C$ 　or more generally, 　$A\ r\ B, B\ r\ C, ∴ A\ r\ C$ 　where r stands for any transitive relation.	C. Analogy: 　Members of class A have properties l, m, n. 　Members of class B have properties $l, m, n,$ and o. 　∴　Members of class A have property o as well.

Consider the next two syllogisms:

All rats are nocturnal.	All rats are cute.
All rats are mammals.	Wilbert is a rat.
∴ All mammals are nocturnal.	∴ Wilbert is cute.

You probably are unwilling to accept either argument and your reservations are well taken but the grounds for rejection differ. The first is an invalid argument: both premises are true, but the conclusion, which is false, does not follow from them (a tool for analysis of validity will be given shortly). The second is a valid argument: the conclusion follows from the premises but, convention or no, most people would object to the first premise. In that instance we encounter a second criterion, *soundness*. If an argument is invalid it may be rejected on that ground. If it is valid, then it must be tested for soundness. An argument is sound if and only if (a) it is valid and (b) its premises are true, otherwise it is unsound. The second syllogism is an unsound argument.

Truth and falsity were discussed in the preceding chapter where they were proposed as the proper criterion for evaluating factual assertions. It is still the case that truth or falsity are the property of statements, not of arguments. The truth of a premise statement is the basis for determining whether a valid argument is sound or unsound, the argument itself is not true or false.

Validity and Form.   As emphasized above, the form of the argument determines its validity. The three arguments considered to this point are instances of the categorical syllogism, an argument of the form:

Major Premise {
  (a) *Q* Middle term connective *Q* Predicate of conclusion *or*

  (b) *Q* Predicate of conclusion connective *Q* Middle term

Minor Premise {
  (a) *Q* Subject of conclusion connective *Q* Middle term *or*

  (b) *Q* Middle term connective *Q* Subject of conclusion

Conclusion: *Q* Subject of conclusion connective *Q* Predicate of conclusion

Where Q = Quantifier: All, Some, No, Some are Not

It is conventional to identify the three terms involved as *S* for subject of the conclusion sentence, *P* for the predicate of the conclusion, and *M* for the middle term that must appear in each of the premises but does not appear in the conclusion.

The three examples considered earlier have the structure shown below:

All *M* are *P*.	All *M* are *P*.	All *M* are *P*.
All *S* are *M*.	All *M* are *S*.	Some *S* are *M*.
∴ All *S* are *P*.	∴ All *S* are *P*.	∴ Some *S* are *P*.

where the specific content has been replaced by letters to emphasize the form of the argument. With four possible quantifiers (All, No, Some, Some are Not) and two possible term orders [(a), (b)] there are eight possible forms of the major premise and eight of the minor which, combined with four possible conclusion forms, yields a total of 256 possible syllogism forms. The great majority of the 256 forms are invalid. Fifteen valid forms are presented in Box 7-2 with letters substituting for the terms. Texts differ in their listing of valid syllogisms. All include the 15 in Box 7-2, some give up to 7 more (see Blumberg, 1976). You can replace *S, P,* and *M* in these valid forms with any content whatsoever and the argument must be valid although it need not be sound. You can readily demonstrate this by using a false premise such as, "All accountants are baritones" or "Some daisies are chipmunks." Thus, if an argument has one of these 15 valid forms it must be valid. It is, however, inconvenient either to memorize the 15 valid syllogism forms or to carry a list of them around at all times for handy reference. For that reason you will be introduced to the Venn diagram, which

---

BOX 7-2

Valid Forms of the Categorical Syllogism

All *M* are *P.*	No *M* are *P.*	All *M* are *P.*	No *M* are *P.*
All *S* are *M.*	All *S* are *M.*	Some *S* are *M.*	Some *S* are *M.*
∴ All *S* are *P.*	∴ No *S* are *P.*	∴ Some *S* are *P.*	∴ Some *S* are not *P.*
All *P* are *M.*	No *P* are *M.*	All *P* are *M.*	No *P* are *M.*
Some *S* are not *M.*	All *S* are *M.*	No *S* are *M.*	Some *S* are *M.*
∴ Some *S* are not *P.*	∴ No *S* are *P.*	∴ No *S* are *P.*	∴ Some *S* are not *P.*
Some *M* are not *P.*	Some *M* are *P.*	All *M* are *P.*	No *M* are *P.*
All *M* are *S.*	All *M* are *S.*	Some *M* are *S.*	Some *M* are *S.*
∴ Some *S* are not *P.*	∴ Some *S* are *P.*	∴ Some *S* are *P.*	∴ Some *S* are not *P.*
	Some *P* are *M.*	All *P* are *M.*	No *P* are *M.*
	All *M* are *S.*	No *M* are *S.*	Some *M* are *S.*
	∴ Some *S* are *P.*	∴ No *S* are *P.*	∴ Some *S* are not *P.*

The structure in each row is sometimes referred to as the figure of the syllogism. There are four figures distinguished by the arrangement of *S, M,* and *P* terms in the first two premises.

is a device for diagramming premises and arguments to determine validity. You were earlier introduced to Euler circles. They work well for individual assertions, but not as well for arguments.

Venn Diagrams. The *Venn diagram* represents an assertion in the form of overlapping circles. The assertion to be evaluated in an argument is the conclusion which may take one of four forms illustrated in Box 7-3A. *S* stands for the subject and *P* stands for the predicate of the conclusion. These forms embody the four logical quantifiers introduced in Box 6-4. Some possible wordings to correspond to the diagram are also provided below each diagram to illustrate how sentences not in the standard form may be transformed into it. All the premises as well as the conclusion of a categorical syllogism must be transformable into one of these standard forms. The convention of the Venn diagram is to shade all areas excluded by a categorical assertion about All or No. Thus, for "All *S* are *P*," there are no members of *S* that are not members of *P* and the nonoverlapping portion of the *S* circle is shaded to display this fact. In the case of "No *S* are *P*," on the other hand, it is the overlapping portion of the two circles that is shaded to show that this class has no members. This leaves the possibility there are members of *S* that are not members of *P* and members of *P* that are not members of *S*.

For assertions about "Some" the convention is to place an X in the area indicated to show that it contains at least one member. Thus, "Some *S* are *P*" is represented by an X in the overlap of the two circles to show there is at least one member of *S* that is also a member of *P*. "Some *S* are not *P*" is represented by an X in the nonoverlapping portion of *S*. Note that shading is inappropriate for assertions about "Some," although "Some" is never to be interpreted, as it often is in everyday usage, to mean "Some but not all." In logical convention the translation of "Some" is "Some and possibly all" (as in Box 6-4).

In applying the Venn diagrams to the evaluation of an argument the general procedure is to use three partially overlapping circles, one for each term of the argument, as shown in Box 7-3B. For each premise in turn, shading or entering of an X in the appropriate portion is done. Remember that when entering an X, no X can be entered if part of the relevant area is shaded. If there is more than one unshaded area, as in the second example of Box 7-3C, then the X could appropriately be entered in either and this is represented by an X in each, connected by dashed lines (it is called a floating X). To evaluate the validity of the argument from the resulting diagram, check whether the pattern for the relation of *S* and *P* circles is compatible with the appropriate conclusion form of Box 7-3A. The relevant portion for each example is indicated by a thicker outline in Box 7-3C. In the case of the first example, the conclusion is valid because the "All *S* are *P*" pattern results; that is, areas one and four are shaded. In the case of the second example, you might be tempted to conclude that the argument is valid because one leg of the floating X falls in area five. But, the floating X means there is at least one instance in either portion, areas two or five; one member might exist outside of the required area, but there is no guarantee that one also exists within it. Since the conclusion must follow from the premises, and it does not in this case, the argument is invalid. The third and fourth examples are easier to interpret: because part of the overlapping area is unshaded in the third example, we cannot conclude that "No *S* are *P*" (which would require shading of the entire overlap); and because there is an X in the outlined area for the fourth example, in area four, the conclusion that "Some *S* are not *P*" validly follows. The remaining examples are left for you to justify on your own.

Conditional Arguments. A conditional argument is one in which the major premise takes the form of a conditional assertion: if something (symbolized by *p*) then something else (symbolized by *q*). "If it doesn't rain then I'll do the laundry." "If you study hard then you will pass the exam." "If you develop a smoking habit then you'll regret it." Statements conveying the standard form may be expressed in variant modes: "You will pass the exam provided that you study." "You will pass the exam if you study." "You will pass unless you don't study." "Whenever you study you pass." "Given that you study you pass." "Studying is a sufficient condition of your passing." All of these translate to "If you study you will pass (the exam)." Note that there is a seemingly similar form that, in fact, differs in meaning, the biconditional, "You will pass if and only if you study." It is in essence two conditionals: "If you study you will pass and if you don't study you will not pass." The biconditional is introduced here only to point out that one common error is to interpret conditional sentences as biconditional sentences. The difference between them is perhaps best illustrated by displaying the conditions determining the truth and falsity of each form (see Box 6-3).

So far we have considered only a conditional assertion, which usually serves as the major premise of a conditional argument. For a conditional argument there also must be an additional premise and a conclusion. Four conditional arguments, two of them valid, and two invalid, are displayed in Box 7-4. The two valid argument forms that employ a conditional premise are "If *p* then *q*; *p*; therefore, *q*" and "If *p* then *q*; not *q*; therefore, not *p*." The first form is known as *modus ponens* or *asserting the antecedent* because its second premise asserts *p*, the antecedent clause of the conditional premise. A sample argument of this form is "If it rains, the game will be postponed; it is going to rain; therefore, the game will be postponed." The second form of valid conditional argument is called *modus tollens* or *denying the consequent* because its second premise, $\bar{q}$, denies the consequent clause of the conditional premise. An example of *modus tollens* using "If it rains the game will be postponed" continues with "the game will not be postponed; therefore, it will not rain." Invalid conditional arguments result from *asserting the consequent* and from *denying the antecedent*. An example of an argument that asserts the consequent is "If it rains, the game will be postponed; the game will be postponed; therefore, it will rain." An example of an argument that denies the antecedent is "If it rains, the game will be postponed;

BOX 7-3

Venn Diagrams for Testing the Validity of Syllogisms

A. The Four Possible Conclusion Statements and Alternative Wordings

All S are P

No S are P

Some S are P

Some S are not P

Tow away zone.	Patrons must wear shoes.	Some girls are pretty.	Not all doors will open.
All who park will be towed.	No barefooted person admitted.	Some girls are pretty creatures.	Some doors will not open.
If you park you will be towed.	No one without shoes admitted.	There are pretty girls.	It is not the case that all doors will open.
No parkers rest untowed.	None but the shod may enter.	Some pretty things are girls.	It is untrue that all doors will open.
Towed is he who parks.	It is untrue that shoeless persons are admitted.	Some creatures are both pretty and a girl.	
Untrue that it is safe to park here.		It is untrue that no girls are pretty.	
Only the parked are towed.			

B. The General Form of the Venn Diagram for Testing Syllogisms

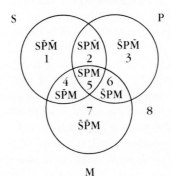

C. Venn Diagrams of Sample Syllogisms

| *a* | *b* | *c* | *d* |

All *M* are *P.*
All *S* are *M.*

∴ All *S* are *P.*
Valid

Some *M* are *P.*
All *S* are *M.*

∴ Some *S* are *P.*
Invalid

Some *M* are *P.*
No *S* are *M.*

∴ No *S* are *P.*
Invalid

No *P* are *M.*
Some *S* are *M.*

∴ Some *S* are not *P.*
Valid

| *a* | *b* | *c* | *d* |

All *P* are *M.*
No *S* are *M.*

∴ No *S* are *P.*
Valid

All *P* are *M.*
All *M* are *S.*

∴ All *S* are *P.*
Invalid

Some *M* are not *P.*
All *S* are *M.*

∴ Some *S* are *P.*
Invalid

All *P* are *M.*
No *M* are *S.*

∴ No *S* are *P.*
Valid

Diagram each of the examples above.
Practice generating examples by replacing *S, M,* and *P* with anything you choose.

it will not rain; therefore, the game will not be postponed." Or, translated into a justification, *p* is not the exclusive and invariant determinant of *q*. Additional examples are given in Box 7-4. Construct some examples of your own as well.

Before leaving the subject of conditional arguments, let's consider an assertion in conditional form that was encountered in the last chapter, "If God had meant for man to fly, He wouldn't have given us the railroad." One commonly encounters conditional arguments that are incomplete. In the example above, the assertion seems to have the force of an argument although one premise, or the conclusion, or even both, are unstated. If we complete the argument, "God has given us the railroad, therefore, He did not mean for man to fly," it has the

---

BOX 7-4

Four Conditional Arguments with Examples

Asserting the Antecedent *Modus Ponens*	**Denying the Consequent** *Modus Tollens*

If *p* then *q*.
p.
∴ *q.*

If it rains you'll get wet.
It is going to rain.
Therefore, you'll get wet.

If *p* then *q*.
q̄.
∴ *p̄.*

If we're in Paris it must be Tuesday.
It's not Tuesday.
Therefore, we are not in Paris.

These are both valid arguments.

Denying the Antecedent	**Asserting the Consequent**

If *p* then *q*.
p̄.
∴ *q̄.*

If it rains you'll get wet.
It doesn't rain.
Therefore, you won't get wet.

If *p* then *q*.
q.
∴ *p.*

If we're in Paris it must be Tuesday.
It is Tuesday.
Therefore, we must be in Paris.

These are both invalid arguments.

Construct some additional examples and try alternative wordings until you are convinced that the first two conditional arguments are always valid and the second two are always invalid.

form of denying the consequent. Here, you might note that, since the consequent was stated negatively—"He wouldn't have given us the railroad"—its denial is positive—"He gave us the railroad." A similar state of affairs appeared in the earlier example where the antecedent was stated negatively—"If it doesn't rain" (p)—so that its denial, $\bar{p}$, is "It rains," that is, "Not that it doesn't rain." In terms of form this looks like a valid argument, but it is patently preposterous. Can logic lead one astray like this? The answer is that not all valid arguments are sound. This is an instance of an unsound argument because the first premise is not true. It is not a factual statement (a member of the class of statements that are either true or false). The device that this example illustrates is commonly used as an ironic means of falsifying the antecedent: "If she is beautiful, I'm Miss America." "If the dark horse candidate wins, I'll eat my hat." "If that's sound reasoning, then $2 + 2 = 3$." Examples of this ironic usage are not hard to find; there is one in the exercises.

The Utility of Tools for Evaluating Deductive Arguments.   In this brief discussion, you have been introduced to some of the fundamental concepts of deductive reasoning and some of the tools for evaluating deductive arguments. There are many more.[1] The purpose of this introduction has been to make you aware that this is a large and active area of endeavor that has some practical applications. You should have learned the following:

1. The nature of an argument. An argument has a conclusion supported by premise statements.
2. The validity of an argument is determined by its form: whether the conclusion follows necessarily from its premises.
3. There are useful tools such as the use of Venn diagrams for assessing validity.
4. The soundness of a valid argument is determined by whether its premises are true.
5. There are many kinds of arguments. We have examined two: the categorical syllogism and the conditional syllogism. The categorical syllogism is the classical model that may have limited application but is nonetheless useful as an introduction to the concepts of validity and soundness. The conditional syllogism has an important role in scientific reasoning.

But, what about everyday arguments? Procedures to evaluate everyday arguments will be discussed in the next section.[2] You should be able to anticipate that their function must be the displaying of argument form to promote evaluation of the conclusion in relation to the supporting premises.

EVERYDAY ARGUMENTS

Scriven (1976) suggests a seven-step procedure for the evaluation of everyday arguments:

1. Clarification of meaning (of the argument and its components).
2. Identification of conclusions (stated and unstated).
3. Portrayal of structure.
4. Formulation of (unstated) assumptions (the "missing premises").
5. Criticism of the premises (given and "missing") and the inferences.
6. Introduction of other relevant arguments.
7. Overall evaluation of the argument in light of one through six.

Identification of Components. In evaluating an argument, or in present-ing one, the advice of Chapter 2 applies: effective encoding is directed by its purpose. The purpose of an argument is to support a conclusion; therefore, the conclusion should be stated explicitly, preferably at the outset of the argument. In formulating an argument, the intended conclusion should be stated at the outset so there is no problem in identifying it. In evaluating someone else's argument this is not often the case. There are, however, some clues to look for. Often a conclusion is signaled by words like: so, thus, therefore, obviously, consequently, hence, suggests, implies, or demonstrates. Some indicators of intended premises are: since, because, for, assuming that, in view of the fact that, or inasmuch as.

It is generally a good idea to check first to make sure that an argument is, in fact, being presented. People tend to run on in a manner that makes it difficult to identify premises and conclusions. As essential as a conclusion is to an argu-ment, it is not uncommon to find an argument in which the conclusion is unstated. In many such cases what we have is, effectively, simply a venting of spleen. Poorly written letters (for example, to the editor) fall into this category by providing a litany of grievances that could lead to the conclusion that the individual or institution being addressed is incompetent, stupid, or deliberately dishonest without stating that conclusion. While such letters may serve a cathartic role for the writer, they are not effective in remedying the situation. Similarly, premises may be omitted, perhaps because they are deemed too obvious to require stating. In those instances the additional premise must be supplied.

Portrayal of Structure. Although everyday arguments rarely have the stan-dard structure of a deductive syllogism, the same evaluative criterion applies: for an argument to be valid the supporting premises should lead to the conclu-sion. In the case of everyday arguments, there are frequently more than two premises and the supporting premises that are offered may be complexly related to the conclusion. One device proposed for displaying the structure of such arguments is the use of a *tree diagram*. Each of the component statements of the argument is first numbered so that the structure of the argument may be represented in the form of arrows connecting statement numbers to the conclu-sion (either stated or implied). Some tree diagrams are given in Box 7-5. The first example shows a good argument taken from a newspaper editorial in which three elaborated justifications are given in support of the conclusion. The second

---

BOX 7-5

Diagramming the Structure of Everyday Arguments

A. The proposed Delaware Expressway is an abomination that should not be built. At a minimum, it will cost 2 billion dollars, money that could be used for more pressing needs. So, even if it did no harm, it would still be a waste of scarce governmental resources. But there are stronger reasons for not building it: it will do serious economic damage to the city for it will remove valuable income producing land from the city's tax rolls. Furthermore, it will have a drastic effect on the health of the taxpayers of Philadelphia, because it will increase automobile traffic and consequently worsen the already bad pollution problems of Center City.

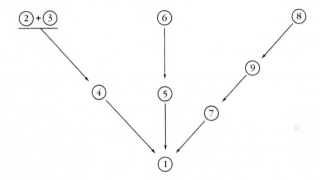

(1) [The proposed Delaware Expressway is an abomination that should not be built.] (2) [At a minimum, it will cost 2 billion dollars,] (3) [money that could be used for more pressing needs.] So, (4) [even if it did no harm it would still be a waste of scarce governmental resources.] But there are stronger reasons for not building it: (5) [it will do serious economic damage to the city,] for (6) [it will remove valuable income producing land from the city's tax rolls.] Furthermore, (7) [it will have a drastic effect on the health of the taxpayers of Philadelphia,] because (8) [it will increase automobile traffic] and consequently (9) [worsen the already bad pollution problems of Center City.] (After O'Connor, 1986)

B. The present system of financing political campaigns is far too costly because it makes it almost impossible for anyone who is not a millionaire or a friend (or employee) of millionaires to achieve high public office. This is why the alternative system, under which elections are publicly financed, ought to be adopted; but there is

---

BOX 7-5 *(con't)*

also the point that the public-financing system would help to democratize the process of choosing public officials by automatically involving every citizen in that process. It would certainly be desirable to free legislators as far as possible from dependence on particular economic interests, as well as to equalize the opportunities of candidates, for their merits ought to count more than their money in winning.

Original Argument	Revised Argument
(1) [The present system financing political campaigns is far too costly,] *because* (2) [(under the present system it is) almost impossible for anyone who is not a millionaire or a friend (or employee) of millionaires to achieve high public office.] *This is why* (3) [the alternative system, under which elections are publicly financed, ought to be adopted;] but there is also the point that (4) [the public-financing system would help to democratize the process of choosing public officials by automatically involving every citizen in the process.] (5) [It would certainly be desirable	(1) [It is time for us to adopt a system under which all elections are financed wholly by public funds]. There are at least four compelling reasons for this. First, [the present system of (2) unlimited private contributions is just too costly] for (3) [the system makes it almost impossible for anyone who is not a millionaire or a friend (or employee) of millionaires to achieve high public office.] Second, [it is highly (4) desirable to free legislators (as far as possible) from all dependence on particular economic interests.] Third, it (5) [is highly desirable to equalize the opportunities of candi-

---

example is more difficult to diagram. It was taken from a text by Beardsley (1975) who revised the argument (as shown to the right of the first) to conform to two rules of rhetoric that he proposed for the construction of forceful arguments. His first rule, *the rule of grouping,* is that all reasons for the same conclusion should be kept together and their similar logical status called to the reader's attention. The *rule of direction* recommends that the development of supporting assertions proceed linearly toward the conclusion to assist the reader in following the line of thought rather than placing upon the reader the burden of identifying and reassembling the justifications offered. Both rules make good sense although neither is logically mandated.

As should be evident from the two examples presented, analysis of the structure of an everyday argument can be difficult, especially as the argument becomes extended, but it is precisely on those occasions that one needs to become more analytic in assessing whether or not assertions are relevant to the argument and lead to a valid conclusion. With the technique for diagramming

to free legislators as far as possible from dependence on particular economic interests,] as well as (6) [(it would be desirable) to equalize the opportunities of candidates,] *for* (7) [their merits ought to count more than their money in elections.]

Assertion 5 is introduced a bit abruptly, without any indication of its relationship to what went before, but we can discern the most likely one. So the structure can be represented thus:

dates,] since their (6) [merits ought to count more than their money in elections.] And fourth, (7) [the public-financing system would help to democratize the process of choosing public officials by automatically involving every citizen in the process.] (After Beardsley, 1975)

If you renumber the statements in the order in which they now appear, the diagram of the written argument will look like this (and note that it is a good deal easier to construct):

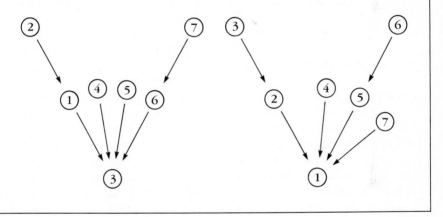

arguments in hand you can now turn to the arguments in the exercises. You should supplement them by collecting additional examples of your own to bring to class for analysis and discussion. It will be instructive to include among the examples at least one argument that you have constructed yourself (for example, an argument addressed to a parent or an academic advisor defending a selection of courses for the coming year, your choice of career, and so on). Class analysis of the adequacy of your argument can help you to become more persuasive in the future, by being more logical, not by being more intense.

Overall Evaluation of the Argument. As you are now well aware, validity is an important criterion which every argument must satisfy, but it is not the sole criterion; an argument must also be sound. In everyday argument that criterion is not easily satisfied, especially to the extent that beliefs and values are invoked, because they cannot directly be adjudged to be true or false. In other words, not only does evaluation of validity extend beyond the straightforward, relatively mechanical, techniques for evaluating syllogisms, but also, evaluation of the component premises may require more than the evaluation of factual assertions. Moreover, implicit premises or conclusions may have to be supplied and irrelevant assertions pruned away. Obviously, any comprehensive checklist for the evaluation of arguments would be so detailed and cumbersome as to limit its practical utility. As a guide through the thickets of evaluation of everyday arguments, I offer three informal criteria proposed by Johnson and Blair (in press), who suggest that any violation of their informal criteria is a fallacy. Fallacies will be discussed in more detail in the concluding section of this chapter.

The three informal criteria proposed by Johnson and Blair are relevance, sufficiency, and acceptability. Let's consider each along with the fallacy produced by violation of it.

1. *Relevance.*   A test of the relevance of any premise is whether or not it bears a logical connection to the conclusion as would be reflected by an arrow in the diagram analysis proposed earlier. If there is no connection we say that the conclusion does not follow—it is a *non sequitur.* In terms of our earlier discussion, an argument in which the conclusion does not follow from the premises is an invalid argument.

2. *Sufficiency.*   Do the premises furnish sufficient grounds for the conclusion given that they are relevant to it? In our legal system, for example, a person is presumed innocent until proven guilty. To support a conclusion that the defendant is guilty as charged, it is not sufficient to show that the defendant was at the scene of the crime or that the defendant had a motive or opportunity for commission of the crime. The criterion of sufficiency requires that all of these separate bits of evidence support the conclusion that the defendant and only the defendant must have committed the crime. Intuitions and partial truths based upon insufficient evidence may incline you to accept the conclusion but, in the absence of sufficient evidence, it is a hasty or ill-founded conclusion. The criterion of sufficiency, thus, does not correspond to either of the formal criteria of validity or soundness. In the case of the second argument of Box 7-5, for example, one could argue that the most compelling evidence of popular support for a candidate is voter readiness—to "put their money where their mouth is"—to the extent of providing either some minimal absolute amount in support of a candidate or some proportion of total campaign expenses. This additional proposed ground of sufficiency would require a change in the wording of the conclusion from "wholly supported by public funds" to "$x\%$ supported by public funds."

3. *Acceptability.*   This third criterion corresponds to the formal criterion of soundness and has to do with whether or not the supporting premises of a valid argument are true. If any premise is false the argument is, of course, unsound. It is harder to evaluate whether the premise is true in some cases. In the case of the fourth premise in the first argument in Box 7-5, or the third premise in the second, revised argument, while it might be too strong an

assertion to label either of them as "true," both would generally be accepted in the context of the total argument. Application of the third informal criterion of acceptability might, thus, lead to identification of what Johnson and Blair call "problematic premises."

ERRORS OF REASONING

There are many ways in which reasoning can go astray; logicians use the term "fallacy" to refer to any error of reasoning. In everyday usage we sometimes incorrectly use the term "fallacy" to refer to a mistaken belief (for example, that spinach is a good dietary source of iron, or that standing under a tree provides protection in a thunderstorm). Such erroneous beliefs are not included in the definition of the word by logicians; only errors of reasoning are included. Many fallacies have been identified. There is, unfortunately, no accepted classification of them. One group arises from violation of rules for valid arguments, for example, in conditional reasoning, asserting the consequent, or denying the antecedent. I shall not enumerate these errors, which are technically known as *formal fallacies*. That term derives from the Aristotelian classification of formal fallacies, fallacies of ambiguity, and fallacies of irrelevant evidence. Modern writers propose alternative classifications.[3] My purpose in discussing fallacies is to sensitize you to some of the more common sources of error to promote more critical analysis of arguments. To that end I shall use the labels *ambiguity* and *irrelevance*. I shall add a third source of error not usually identified in logic texts— *failure to appreciate that reasoning is called for*.

Failure to Appreciate that Reasoning is Called For.   The Russian psychologist A. R. Luria (1976) read to illiterate peasants of Soviet central Asia such syllogisms as: "In the far north all bears are white. Novaya Zemlya is in the far north. What color are the bears there?" He got such answers as "I don't know; each locality has its own animals." "We always speak only of what we see; we don't talk about what we haven't seen." "If a man was 60 or 80 years old and had seen a white bear and told about it, he could be believed; but I've never seen one and, hence, can't say." Other investigators present similar evidence that this form of reasoning is common among unschooled adults; it is a real phenomenon, but one that is open to a variety of explanations (for example, see Scribner, 1977). Luria's explanation is that his subjects failed to deal with the argument as a totality (and, thus, to see that the conclusion necessarily follows from the premises). Rather, they dealt with the component assertions in isolation, mostly the first and third. Since the first assertion is a factual statement, they, appropriately, sought relevant observational evidence.

Another possible example arises in a variety of conservation tasks used in the study of cognitive development (Piaget and Inhelder, 1969). In one form of the task, tinted water is poured into each of two identical containers until the child agrees that the levels are exactly equal in each container. The contents of one container are then poured into another container of a different shape (for example, a long narrow beaker) and the child is asked "Do we both still have the same amount to drink?" If the child approaches the task logically (as adults and older children do), it is obvious that the amount of liquid is unchanged by pouring into another container and that the correct answer is yes. Most young children, however, reply that now the tall container has more to drink than the comparison container (see Box 7-6). They appear to be approaching the task perceptually rather than logically.

Educated adults seem to be so prone to use of logical reasoning whenever possible that they are subject to inappropriate application of logic. A very compelling instance arises in the false conservation task[4] in which a loop of string is drawn taut around four equidistant pins to form a square, which is identified

---

BOX 7-6

Conservation Experiments

A. The Conservation of Liquid Quantity Experiment

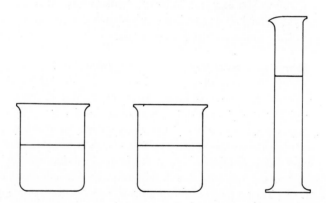

After establishing the equality of the first two containers liquid is poured from one of them into the third.

B. The False Conservation Experiment

Does a cow in field *a* have the same amount of grass to eat as a cow in field *b*? in field *c*? At first there is a tendency to treat this problem as the same as

as a meadow for grazing cows. The pins are then moved, still with the string taut around them, into a rectangular configuration and the subject is asked if the cows would have as much grass to eat in this field as the first. Many people agree that they do. With additional changes in the location of the pins to produce longer and narrower rectangles (approaching a straight line as a limit), they eventually recognize their error in treating perimeter, which does remain invariant, as equivalent to area, which is reduced.

Ambiguity.   Ambiguity refers to any unclarity of meaning. There are a number of possible sources of it. Sometimes ambiguity arises because there is more than one possible meaning of a word and the context does not provide a sufficient clue for which meaning is intended. Sometimes there is a shift in the meaning

the preceding conservation task until one realizes that it is the perimeter that remains the same, not area.

a

b

c

of a word during the course of an argument; this form of ambiguity is called *equivocation*. In still other instances, the sentence rather than a particular word in it is ambiguous; this form of ambiguity is called *amphiboly*. Another source of ambiguity is, of course, vagueness and imprecision of encoding, a problem to which you were alerted in Chapter 2. Some examples of ambiguity will be given here by way of illustration; it is a common source of error that can be avoided if you keep the purpose of the argument and its intended conclusion clearly in mind.

Some years ago it was common to encounter demonstrators chanting "End the war in Vietnam." Clearly, they were advocating termination of the war but there was ambiguity with respect to how the termination should be achieved: (a) through unconditional surrender by the enemy, or (b) by unilateral withdrawal. The two means are diametrically opposed; in this case, context made it clear that the second meaning of "end" was the course espoused.

A more serious source of ambiguity, equivocation, arises when the meaning of a word changes during the course of an argument. A contrived example using the word "end" is illustrated in the syllogism: "Happiness is the end of life; the end of life is death; therefore, death is happiness." In the first premise "end" means goal or purpose; in the second, it means termination. Another example of equivocation arose in Exercise 2F of Chapter 6: "Liberal Democrats are liberal spenders." The slogan for Bayer aspirin (see Chapter 6) also has a quality of equivocation in the shift from the ingredient, "Aspirin that doctors recommend," to a particular brand of the ingredient. Yet another possible instance arises in assertions such as "The Honda is a good car" where it is unclear whether reference is made to a class of all automobiles from that manufacturer or a particular member of it (as, for example, where someone with two cars is describing a good experience with one of them).

Amphiboly refers to ambiguity of a sentence: "They are eating apples," or "They are trotting horses" where it is unclear whether reference is made to an activity (eating or trotting) or to differentiation of a particular kind (of apple or horse).

The deliberate exploitation of vagueness to create an impression of prescience is commonly encountered in, for example, horoscopes, fortune cookies, or readings of tea leaves, in palmistry, or graphology. Such statements as "You will encounter difficulty," "Today is a good day for accomplishing things," "You have a talent," or "Beware of procrastination" are so general as to apply to anyone at any time. Very specific renderings of the same meaning, on the other hand, might seem ridiculous: "Your car won't start," "Straighten your sock drawer," "You can wiggle your ears," or "Phone your mother" are all too specific to appear oracular. This form of exploiting ambiguity is sufficiently common that examples are readily found and easily demonstrated. Demonstrate it for yourself by offering to tell fortunes for your friends and asking them to evaluate the accuracy of your predictions.

Fallacies of Irrelevance.   Many fallacies of irrelevance have been identified and given fancy Latin names; a few of the more common and serious examples will be illustrated here. The purpose of enumerating them is not to provide yet another list to be memorized but, rather, to alert you to the fact that irrelevant evidence is commonly invoked in argument, either deliberately or inadvertently, to influence acceptance of the conclusion. Frequently, the mechanism is one of appealing to emotion or existing predispositions rather than to logically developing the argument itself.

1. Ad hominem and tu quoque arguments.   The defining property of *ad hominem* arguments is a shift from the issue to the opponent. Children often engage in ad hominem argument: "You're a liar!" "You're another!" "So's your old man!" Often, but not exclusively, the intent is derogatory, as in offering (irrelevant) evidence that a witness has a criminal record (perhaps for theft or disorderly conduct) to impugn his or her truthfulness by casting doubt upon character. In political argument a particular view may be discounted as "party line" (usually when line is defined with respect to an altogether different issue) that is viewed as unacceptable by the group. For example, suggesting that concern for the environment is bleeding-heart liberalism (usually identified in terms of concern for society's underdogs) or pinko (soft on Communism). On occasion the *ad hominem* argument may be superficially sympathetic: "You are shaken by a harrowing experience," "You are not yourself," "You are innocent in the ways of the world." It may even be laudatory, as in extolling the speaker as a good father, a successful businessman, a churchgoer, or a pillar of society whose view on an unrelated matter must be correct by virtue of that standing. Instances of *ad hominem* argument are sufficiently common that you should have little difficulty in finding examples. Bear in mind, however, that the defining feature is not personal attack or innuendo *per se* but attack on a personal ground that is irrelevant to the issue at hand.

A related fallacy, *tu quoque,* impugns the arguer for not practicing what he or she preaches—"The pot calls the kettle black," "People who live in glass houses should not throw stones," "Let he who is without sin cast the first stone," and so on. Injunctions to a child to "keep your word" from a parent whose promises often go unfulfilled may lose force for that reason. Here, again, the soundness of an argument is not logically related to the speaker's personal observation of it: a smoker's argument for why smoking is injurious to one's health is probably identical to the nonsmoker's. That the argument is buttressed by the force of direct experience may, however, increase your acceptance of the speaker as "an authority."

2. Poisoning the well.   Poisoning the well refers to a technique that attempts to forestall disagreement altogether by making it uncomfortable or embarrassing to disagree. Whenever someone begins an argument with "Only a fool would suggest . . . ," "All right-thinking, red-blooded Americans believe . . . ," "It should be obvious to all . . . ," they are attempting to remove all grounds for questioning (or, in terms of the metaphor, trying to prevent dipping into the well). This device, too, is sufficiently common that you should be able to find examples of it.

3. Appeal to pity.   Appeal to pity exploits pathetic circumstances. An instance is provided by miscreants presented by their lawyer as helpless victims of society, or of cruel circumstances. While such appeals could provide mitigating considerations at the time of sentencing, they are irrelevant to the question of whether or not the defendant knowingly and deliberately committed the offense with which he or she is charged.

4. Emotional language.   As noted earlier in Chapter 4, emotional states are rarely conducive to considered judgment. We have all seen films in which a character delivers a rousing speech appealing to patriotism, righteous indignation, remorse, or some other emotion, in an effort to incite support for his cause. At that point the audience usually cheers but instructors of courses in thinking weep. By virtue of the nature of language, emotional coloration in an argument is often difficult to counter or to avoid. For this reason, techniques for neutral encoding and for focusing upon the structure of an argument (for example, the Venn diagram, tree diagrams, or substitution of content terms with letters) help to preclude emotional diversion. Whenever you feel swayed by an emotional argument, it would be beneficial to recall this advice.

5. Appeal to ignorance.   This fallacy is committed whenever someone argues that an argument is unsound because the premises have not been proven true or because they have not been shown to be false, that is, the evidence is unclear or unavailable. This form of reasoning is often invoked in defense of phenomena for which there is asserted to be no "scientific" explanation: UFOs, extraterrestrials, psychic phenomena, and so on. In some instances the grey area between ignorance (no relevant evidence either way) and absence of evidence, despite an extensive amount of research, can lead us to an erroneous conclusion. For example, if years of research on psychic phenomena yield no strong evidence of their existence, we are inclined to believe that they don't exist. As will be shown in the next chapter, failure to find a statistically significant difference between two or more conditions (in this example, between performance by psychics and what would be expected by chance) is never grounds for conclusion that there is no difference, even though the experiment may have been replicated many times under appropriate conditions with adequate controls. The absence of appropriate evidence (ignorance) is not grounds for a conclusion. In such cases one must accept uncertainty in order to avoid the fallacy of insufficient evidence.

6. *Appeal to Authority.*   In this fallacy the evidence for the argument is offered by a person of high status. If the "authority" is, in fact, an expert on the subject in question, it is reasonable to expect that the views offered are informed, and therefore, to be weighed seriously. The fallacy of appeal to authority arises when the authority is speaking outside his or her area of expertise, as, for example, when a Nobel laureate in science or literature speaks on behalf of some political issue outside his or her domain of expertise. More transparent examples arise in the case of the advertising testimonial where a popular sports or entertainment figure endorses a brand of cereal, clothing, and so on. Just because he or she alleges to do something—to eat Brand *X* cereal—is no reason that you should do so also. Certainly, it provides no evidence as to the merit of the product (the vitamin content or taste of the cereal).

Many of the fallacies of irrelevant evidence have been identified. It might be instructive to try to augment this partial list with analysis of faulty arguments you have encountered. The purpose of this section has been to demonstrate that in the evaluation of arguments, many arguments can be encountered in which the conclusion does not follow from the premises either because of defects in the structure of the argument or because of inadequacies of the evidence itself. The evaluation of arguments can be difficult, so much so that even experts will disagree. The best safeguard is to approach all attempts at persuasion critically by examining their structure to determine if the argument is valid and by evaluating the truth of the premise to see if it is sound.

A Final Caution.   In doing the exercises in this chapter you may encounter some difficulty, but you will doubtless appreciate that the criteria of validity and soundness, as well as the tools for analysis of arguments, should be applied in their solution. In addition you will encounter, outside of this class, assertions and arguments with great frequency and in many contexts. The material of this and preceding chapters is applicable there as well. In view of the extensive psychological literature[5] that most persons—even those with broad training in logic—do quite poorly on logical reasoning tasks presented out of context, it is perhaps timely to remind you again of Chapter 1. In becoming a serious thinker, in making sense of experience, you should strive to become more aware and deliberately directive of what you are doing and why you are doing it. In the search for general systematic procedures (which certainly include the tools being presented in this section) you should try applying them outside the confines of the classroom to make them a habitual part of your approach to everyday life.

SUMMARY

This chapter was concerned with the evaluation of arguments and sound reasoning. Two forms of reasoning were introduced: *deductive reasoning,* in which the conclusion is contained in its premises and, for this reason, leads to a necessary conclusion; and *inductive reasoning,* where there is no certainty attached to the conclusion.

Two models of deductive reasoning were described: the *categorical syllogism* and the *conditional syllogism,* in order to illustrate the criteria for evaluation of deductive arguments as well as some techniques for applying those criteria. The categorical syllogism asserts relations among classes; the conditional syllogism explores implications of a condition ("If p then q"). The form of a deductive argument consists of a conclusion and its supporting premises. There are two criteria for the evaluation of deductive arguments: *validity* and *soundness* which are applied in that order. The criterion of validity is satisfied if and only if the conclusion necessarily follows from its premises. Validity depends upon the form of the argument, not its content. The procedure of constructing Venn diagrams was introduced as a means of representing the structure of a categorical syllogism to assess its validity. In the case of the conditional syllogism, there are only two valid forms produced by *asserting the antecedent, p,* or *denying the consequent, $\bar{q}$.* Whether or not an argument meets the criterion of soundness is determined by the truth of the supporting premises; all of them must be true for a valid argument to be sound; an invalid argument can never be sound.

Everyday arguments also consist of a conclusion and the assertions supporting it, but the connection between them may not be logically necessary. The same criteria of formal reasoning should, however, apply along with a third possible criterion—*sufficiency.* Violation of any criterion leads to a *fallacy,* an error of reasoning. Some advice for the evaluation of everyday arguments proposed that the components of the argument be identified to promote evaluation of the structure of the argument as represented by a tree diagram showing how premises relate to the conclusion. Once the components and their structure are clear, it is possible to evaluate (a) whether the evidence is relevant to the conclusion, (b) whether it is sufficient to lead to the conclusion, and (c) whether the conclusion is acceptable on the basis of the supporting evidence. The chapter concluded with a consideration of some of the ways that reasoning can go astray: through *failure to appreciate that reasoning is called for,* through *ambiguity,* or through *fallacies of irrelevant evidence.* The chapter closed with a final reminder to guard against the failure to appreciate that reasoning is called for and to take seriously the lessons of Chapter 1 in applying your new tools to everyday experience as well as the exercises at the end of each chapter.

EXERCISES

1. Represent each of the statements below in the form of a Venn diagram (see Box 7-4A):
   (a) Absolutely no parking allowed.
   (b) The dodo is extinct.
   (c) Nearly all modern states have trouble with unemployment.
   (d) The easiest course is not always the most satisfying.

(e) Some problems are difficult.

(f) Some of the bills before the committee will not be acted upon.

(g) Nearly all disagreements are forgotten in the long run.

(h) All doors will not open at this station. Note that this is often announced by railroad conductors who don't mean it.

(i) Investments require reappraisal.

(j) Every human being wants love.

Hint: you need to translate each statement into classes representable by a pair of partially overlapping circles, for example, for question (b) the class of dodos and the class of living creatures. If you need help in solving a–j, see the notes section.[6]

2. Evaluate each of the syllogisms below for validity (write V or I in the first column) and for soundness (write S or U in the second column). Where a syllogism is invalid, or unsound, or both, give the reason for your decision. For help, see the notes.[7]

___ ___ (a) All rock fans are fanatics; some fanatics are unbalanced people; therefore, some unbalanced people are rock fans.

___ ___ (b) The dogs bark when there is someone outside; the dogs are barking; therefore, there must be someone outside.

___ ___ (c) If he liked the course he would turn in the assignments; he turned in the assignments; therefore, he liked the course.

___ ___ (d) No schoolteachers are wealthy; some wealthy people are yachtsmen; therefore, some school teachers are not yachtsmen.

___ ___ (e) If you brush with fluoridated toothpaste you won't get cavities; John doesn't brush with fluoridated toothpaste; therefore, he will get cavities.

___ ___ (f) Some cats are grey; all cats eat liver; therefore, some liver eaters are grey.

___ ___ (g) Senators are elected officials; some elected officials are not responsive to their constituents; therefore, some senators are not responsive to their constituents.

___ ___ (h) All liars get trapped eventually; all politicians are liars; therefore, all politicians get trapped eventually.

3. In recent hearings on preventing the spread of AIDS, it was proposed that clean needles be made available to all drug addicts. One response to this proposal was "If we are going to give clean needles to addicts, we should give binoculars to peeping Toms." Evaluate the argument. For help, see the notes.[8]

4. Here is an argument to be evaluated by going through the seven-step procedure recommended by Scriven. It is excerpted in part from a student newspaper. Do you find any fallacies in the argument? If you need help, see the notes.[9]

Punk, like the hippie's mendicant ethic, has become a product of Madison Avenue. Thus, most of the conceptions which the public holds of punk are absolutely wrong.

So maybe the word just shouldn't be used anymore; it has been so over-wrought that its [sic] lost its meaning. The "original punks" have all moved away from the ethic that sprung them forth onto the world, and many of them resemble the very rock stars they rebelled against more than anything else.

Punk has garnered an extremely negative connotation, thanks again to the media's one-sided interpretation of things (not that punk is purely positive—one need look no further than Sid Vicious). But for all world-hating nihilism and anti-institutional anarchism, punk aspired to an incredible aesthetic: the belief that almost anyone could be an artist. You no longer had to be a virtuoso to play music. In its return to roots (three-chord rock), it lashed back against the trend towards art rock and high-tech production that was overtaking the music industry. Ideally, punk took control of the finished product out of the hands of profit-minded, three-piece suit executives, and put it back into the hands of the artist.

So maybe this latest batch of "punk" bands shouldn't be called "punk" at all. A lot of them have progressed way beyond the three-chord idiom of '77 (and previous) punk; and they've also given the genre an amazing amount of variety and experimentation which was seriously lacking in the past. Another major difference is that most of these bands are American and not British. . . .

5. Evaluate each of the following from the standpoint of whether or not a fallacy is reflected and, if so, which one. For help, see the notes.[10]
   (a) Fluoride should be added to the local drinking water supply because fluoride has been endorsed as an effective antidote to dental decay by the American Dental Association.
   (b) American physicians believe that the insurance rates for medical malpractice have escalated dramatically because of the intrusion of lawyers.
   (c) "His lack of credibility should cause the charge to fall of its own weight," was the reply of former CIA director William Colby to a charge by Charles Colson that the CIA knew in advance about the Watergate break-in. Charles Colson was a White House aide at the time; he was also convicted for perjury.
   (d) Many homeless persons in New York City resist being taken to the shelters when the temperature is below freezing on the grounds that the shelters are unsafe and the treatment they receive there is insensitive and even hostile. What right have they to complain in view of their desperate living conditions out in the streets?
   (e) The following is part of a letter to the editor of the student newspaper about recent concern over asbestos removal. The first paragraph asserts that asbestos is a safe building material when properly maintained and that the cost of its removal is prohibitive. It concludes with the following:

There are other things in our lives that threaten us more than asbestos: smoking, chemical dumping and bad eating habits, just to name a few. These and many others kill more Americans than asbestosis. . . . These are all factors that the American public can control themselves. So why should we invest $50 million on a society that doesn't seem that concerned in preserving its life expectancy to begin with. Once America is able to reduce the other killers to the extent that asbestos is a major problem, then I think we will be able to address this problem with some credibility. The second I hear smokers or junk food junkies complaining about asbestos, you can be sure I will be there calling them hypocrites.

    (f) Being a good churchgoer makes one a good person. (Hint: try varying the argument by plugging in other terms for "churchgoer"—for example, clarinet player.)

6. Write the soundest, most clearly structured and convincing argument you can for some position you believe in. It is better, for this purpose, to take a small, manageable issue such as improving preregistration procedures for freshman registration, policy on incomplete grades, and so on. After having done this, do the same for the opposing point of view on the same issue. If you have done this exercise well, you should have a deeper understanding of the issue as well as an appreciation that in preparing an argument, it is useful to anticipate (and defuse, where possible) opposing positions.

7. Take one of the four figures of Box 7-3 and generate all 64 possible syllogisms of that figure. Select at random four of the forms generated and flesh them out by replacing S, P, M with meaningful content. Evaluate the validity of those four syllogisms through the use of Venn diagrams. For help, see the notes.[11]

8. Generate all 256 possible syllogisms. Although this may seem unduly tedious and time consuming, it is not all that bad if you use symbols, for example, "All S are M," and so on. It will acquaint you with creating tools for generating all possible arrangements, since it is clear that for 256 items you cannot proceed randomly but must create a scheme for organizing.

8

Foundations of Induction: Causation, Chance, and Information

The discussion of reasoning in the preceding chapters focused largely upon deduction. This chapter and the next will deal with how to construct and test inductive arguments. Inductive arguments do not have the clean, almost mechanical, structural simplicity of deductive arguments; they are harder to justify, and their conclusions lack the certainty of deductively attained conclusions. In fact, philosophers have grappled with the problems of inductive inference for centuries and continue to do so. Few, if any, agreed-upon principles have resulted. In fact, the systematic formulation of the three concepts central to empirical reasoning, which will be discussed in this chapter, is of very recent origin. The foundations of deduction, on the other hand, are far older and more secure.

Deductive arguments have a very reassuring quality. They are convincing because they carry the force of logical necessity. For instance, when confronted with a linear argument of the form $A > B$, and $B > C$, it is clear that it must necessarily be the case that $A > C$. This argument is true of all transitive relations and is inherent in the definition of transitivity. In that sense it may be said that we are discovering what is already known. Most deductive arguments are, however, less obvious in reaching conclusions inherent in their premises, largely because many of those premises involve the transformation of initial givens to equivalent forms or in light of basic rules and definitions. This is especially true of geometric or other mathematical proofs or of proofs in symbolic logic. Even informal arguments such as those constructed by prosecuting attorneys or mystery writers that build a converging net of circumstantial evidence carry conviction. We prefer logical arguments to empirical ones and we are right to do so because sense data and empirical evidence underlying inductive arguments are inherently subject to error. Things are sometimes not what they seem. That knowledge underlies our distinction between appearance and reality. We know that the magician did not really saw the woman in half, that the people reflected in the fun house mirror are not really wider than they are tall, or that pouring a quantity of water into a differently shaped container cannot change its amount. In all these instances, the force of logical necessity overrides the data of the senses or group consensus. Empirical truths, based as they are upon accumulated experience, lack the force of logical necessity. They are provisionally true until disconfirming evidence appears. They cannot be proven to be true.

What makes logical necessity so compelling? It seems to me that there are three related but differing components of logical necessity which, when treated as continua, lead to three concepts that underly modern experimentation: cause, chance, and information. To understand the reasoning behind that assertion, consider the following possible interpretations of logical necessity. (a) One and only one conclusion to the argument is possible; it is determined by the premises. (b) That conclusion follows with certainty; it is completely predictable. (c) Acceptance of the conclusion is accompanied by a feeling of certainty. Each of these interpretations leads to a pole at the opposite extreme from certainty. The three continua that arise are: (a) degree of determination of the outcome by its antecedents, (b) the probability of the outcome in relation to alternative outcomes, and (c) the amount of information associated with the outcome. The opposite pole from logical necessity for each of the continua are: (a) indeterminacy, many possible outcomes, (b) each of which is equally probable, with the result that one is (c) totally uncertain of the outcome. The three continua are shown in Box 8-1. The left line forms the basis for judgments about determination or causation, the middle line forms the basis for judgments about probability, and the bottom line forms the basis for judgments about amount of information.

I have differentiated these three continua because I believe they constitute the foundation of our understanding of empirical phenomena. I mean by that assertion that the process of constructing and evaluating inductive arguments about empirical phenomena may be viewed as locating them along the appropriate continuum. It is possible to achieve that end with much greater precision today because a metric for each of the continua is now available. The purpose of this chapter is to introduce you to each of the three continua and its metric as a background for the discussion of model building and hypothesis testing in Chapter 9.

CAUSATION AND DETERMINANTS

All of us use the word "cause" without scrutinizing its precise meaning. A resort to the dictionary reveals a number of meanings (my dictionary, *The American Heritage Dictionary*, lists seven). The synonyms *causation* and *determinant*

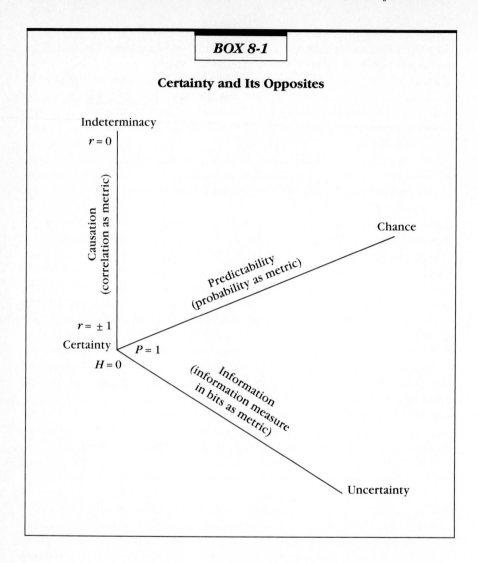

BOX 8-1

Certainty and Its Opposites

narrow the realm to the relation of cause and effect. The common sense construal of that relation assumes that (a) every effect has some enstating antecedent condition(s) that lead to it, that is, a cause; and (b) given a cause, its associated effect will follow. In essence, a simple mechanical analogue is invoked: press the cause button and out comes the effect in an invariant fashion. That model is too simplistic. As we shall see in this section, examination of the notion of cause and effect by philosophers has led to the conclusion that one cannot convincingly demonstrate causation. Partly in response to that finding current investigators couch explanations in terms of functional relations or of correlation rather than in terms of cause and effect.

Philosophical Consideration of the Meaning of Causation. What might it mean to state that *"A* causes *B"?* The answer *"B* follows *A"* is readily accepted but inadequate. Is *A* and only *A* required or are there additional or alternative antecedents? That question recognizes the possibility that many factors may operate in a complex fashion in the determination of *B,* as is clearly true when we substitute for *B,* "nutritional status of an individual," "economic condition of a country," or "occurrence of an event, such as a general strike or demonstration." For many events and conditions, it is not possible to identify either a single cause or a consistent pattern of contributory factors. Must *B* follow *A* invariably or only "more often than not?" For many phenomena we know that the relation of causation is not an invariant one. Exposure to an influenza virus need not be followed by developing symptoms of the disease. Appropriate conditions for the generation of a tornado may exist and prompt an alert without a tornado forming. Such relations are often described in probabilistic terms. How long an interval may intervene before the effect follows? Many effects are by no means immediate. We know, for example, that there is a gestation period for any organism during which it undergoes developmental transformations. Similarly, there is an incubation period for most diseases, in some cases many years. These three questions, and others that may have occurred to you, show that causation is not a simple obvious relation.

Philosophers[1] have grappled with the concept of causation since the time of Aristotle in an attempt to clarify its meaning and identify the conditions of its appropriate use. One of the most influential contributions was an observation by Hume in the mid-18th century that the relation of causation is not given in direct experience. One does not experience causation; nothing is inherently a cause or an effect. Rather, the ascription of causation is an *inference* made in the course of interpreting experience. To put it another way, causation is not in the world, we put it there in our search for understanding. The inference of causation takes the form of a conclusion of an inductive argument whose premises are descriptions of experience. No certainty can be attached to the conclusion.

To date, no one has successfully refuted Hume's reasoning although many have tried. One valiant attempt to spell out the conditions under which an inference about casuation is made and/or on the basis of which it may be justified was John Stuart Mill's five canons. They are summarized in Box 8-2. The first three canons seem especially reasonable and straightforward. If *B* invariably accompanies *A* (the method of agreement), or if *B* is invariably absent when *A* is absent (the method of difference), or if both apply (joint method of agreement and difference) and this is true of no other factor, then there is a relation between *A* and *B.* If, for example, influenza invariably occurs when an influenza virus is present in the blood stream, regardless of other prior conditions, we can infer that it causes influenza. Similarly, if milk doesn't curdle when bacteria are inactivated through pasteurization or irradiation but does otherwise, then curdling is attributed to the bacteria. The second example is an application of the third canon (which subsumes the first two and serves as a safeguard against errors that may result from exclusive application of them).

BOX 8-2

Mill's Canons of Inductive Inference

First Canon: Method of Agreement. If two or more instances of the phenomenon under investigation have only one circumstance in common, the circumstance in which alone all the instances agree is the cause of the given phenomenon.

Second Canon: Method of Difference. If an instance in which the phenomenon under investigation occurs and an instance in which it does not occur have every circumstance in common save one, that one occurring only in the former; the circumstance in which alone the two instances differ is the cause or an indispensable part of the cause of the phenomenon.

Third Canon: Joint Method of Agreement and Difference. If two or more instances in which the phenomenon occur have only one circumstance in common, while two or more instances in which it does not occur have nothing in common save the absence of that circumstance, the circumstance in which alone the two sets of instances differ is the cause or an indispensable part of the cause of the phenomenon.

Fourth Canon: Method of Residues. Subduct from any phenomenon such part as is known by previous inductions to be the effect of certain antecedents, and the residue of the phenomenon is the effect of the remaining antecedents.

Fifth Canon: Method of Concomitant Variations. Whatever phenomenon varies in any manner whenever another phenomenon varies in some particular manner is either a cause or an effect of that phenomenon or is connected with it through some fact of causation. (Note: a more modern statement of the canons with examples is given in Fearnside, 1980.)

While Mill's canons are useful as a checklist for systematic review of a putative cause, they are inadequate for initial identification of possible causes, and they provide no guarantee that a cause that passes the screening is, in fact, a cause of the phenomenon. Nor do they encompass the possibility of patterns of alternative factors operating in complex ways. Rather than expand upon the shortcomings of Mill's canons (Fearnside, 1980), however, I shall simply assert that they are inadequate to the task for which they were intended, urge you to examine them anyway because they are instructive, and proceed on to consider the description of functional relations as a more neutral and precise means of describing relations among factors. The great advantage of a statement of functional relations is that it provides as much information as a causal analysis without requiring the detailing of causal mechanisms (that is, explaining why the cause works as it does). This may appear to be making a virtue of ignorance, but it is very often a more realistic summary of current knowledge for conditions where predictive antecedents are known (for example, for earthquakes, inflation, unemployment, and so on) without being able to describe a causal mechanism. In still other cases, we may be sure that the predictive factors are not causal.

Functional Relations.   To provide a more flexible and general account of the relation among factors, the A and B of the preceding discussion, it is useful to view each factor as a quantity that may assume one of a range of values, that is, to treat it as a *variable* quantity. Hypothesized determining factors (the replacement for cause) are referred to as *independent variables* and their consequent effects as *dependent variables*. The relation between the two classes of variables may be expressed in the form of a *functional relation,* such as:

$$Y_i = f(c_{i1}x_{i1}, c_{i2}X_{i2}, \ldots \ldots c_{i(n-1)}X_{i(n-1)}, c_{in}X_{in}, a, b, d)$$

where Y_i represents the value of the dependent variable under a particular set of conditions, i; X_{ij} represents the value of the independent variable(s) with subscripts serving to name each of the possible antecedents: i indicates their value under condition i; $j = 1$ to n is an identifier; the c stands for coefficients whose value reflects the relative weighting of each independent variable; and other letters without subscripts identify other contributory factors whose value remains constant and independent of i. The letter f represents the form of the function.

The equation may look quite formidable but don't be put off by general notation. Each symbol is a *placeholder* for a specific quantity that may be substituted as dictated by a particular example. Let's say that a wrestler's weight is just a bit below the lower limit for his weight class and he does not want to be disqualified for the match at weighing-in time. In an attempt to raise his weight, Y, he may drink the requisite amount of water, X. The hypothesized relation between body weight and water consumption takes the form of a straight line and might be represented by:

$$Y = mX + b$$

where Y is body weight at weigh-in, X is amount of water ingested, b is body weight before ingesting the water, and m is the slope of the line relating body weight and water loading. Over a broad range of X values, it is unlikely the relation will be linear.

Describing the determinants of an effect in the form of a functional relation provides a number of advantages: (a) expressing the relation in mathematical/ graphical form clarifies the nature of the relation and (b) makes it possible to predict values of Y_i for any given value of X_i for purposes of experimental test. In addition, (c) alternative hypotheses may be similarly represented for purposes of identifying those conditions (values of X_i) that will provide the clearest test among alternative hypotheses. In the example of the wrestler, the question whether the function remains linear or levels off as amount of water increases can be tested by computing the function of Y for each hypothesized function form and selecting a value of X at which the two functions provide different predictions of Y. Finally, (d) the quantities of the functional relation are theoretically neutral. This means that the function may be used as an economical means of summarizing obtained evidence for which no adequate theory is available. It may, on the other hand, be coordinated to a theory that assigns meaning to quantities if circumstances warrant.

Three examples of reported functional relations are shown in Box 8-3. The first shows that the number of "waggles" per 15 seconds made by a forager bee on the wall of the hive declines exponentially as the distance of the food source from the hive decreases, that is, the bee waggles rapidly for nearby sources and much less so for distant ones. The second function relates relative frequency of use of various memorization strategies to grade level. The use of systematic grouping (into semantic or alphabetic categories) increases at the expense of simpler strategies such as repeating an item over and over. The third figure shows mean winter temperature (along with standard deviation) over an 89-year period. It shows that following a period of relatively stable winter temperatures, beginning in 1955, the temperature of the nine recent winters varied widely from above average warmth to extreme cold.

The three examples are alike in summarizing evidence of a clear relation in a detailed but economic manner. They differ with respect to amenability to a causal interpretation. For the bee data distance from hive to food source seems to be a clear determinant of number of waggles which, in turn, accurately convey distance information to recruit other foragers from the hive. We can devise several possible explanations for why that relation might obtain: for example, fatigue or forgetting increase with distance flown. In the case of the student memorizers, possible causal mechanisms may be hypothesized, but clearly grade level *per se* cannot be the determinant of strategy changes. Rather, grade level serves as a convenient index of other developmental changes that might be taking place, such as increase in experience with memorizing or increased familiarity with the demands of various kinds of material, the ability to shift from content to form, and so on. In the case of the winter temperature changes, calendar year is undoubtedly not the determinant of such changes. Here calendar year serves as a nominal variable, a convenient index of ongoing change rather than as a factor to which causal status might be assigned. A comparable state of affairs applies for newspaper charts of local mean daily temperatures, daily Dow-Jones averages, mean mortgage rate fluctuations, and so on.

These three examples are intended to provide some understanding of the use and interpretation of functional relations to help you appreciate why contemporary scientists describe phenomena in terms of contributory factors and functional relations rather than cause and effect. If you have not had much acquaintance with functional relations, it would be useful to assemble some additional examples of functional relations from newspapers, magazines, or text-books for added practice in their interpretation. You might even be inspired to collect and summarize some data of your own on the following: (a) time and/or amount of snacking in relation to what is on the TV screen (commercial or program); (b) weight change in relation to day of week (are weekends danger-ous?); or (c) duration of time spent viewing pictures of animals, infants, food, and so on, in relation to the age and sex of the viewer. As a result of that exercise, you should find that you have not only a better understanding of the phenomena, but, also, some idea as to possible determinants of it.

Correlation. Another widely used index of relation between two variables is the *correlation coefficient*. This is a statistical measure of the degree of relation between two variables expressed as a coefficient of correlation. The value of the coefficient ranges from -1.0 for a perfect negative relation to $+1.0$ for a perfect positive relation. A value of 0 indicates that there is no relation between the two variables—that they are uncorrelated. Intermediate values indicate lesser degrees of connection. Scatterplots illustrating these values are given in Box 8-4A. A *scatterplot* is obtained by getting two measures (one of A and one of B—or X and Y as they are more typically symbolized) for each individual in the sample and plotting the resulting individual scores. To make the illustrations more mean-ingful for yourself, you might assign labels to the X and Y axes. Some possible labels, for example, might be X = number of pretzels consumed and Y = weight change for the first plot; X = yearly income and Y = value of house for the second; X = average annual rainfall and Y = marital satisfaction for the third.

The correlation coefficient[2] (and there are a number of them, all designed to yield values on a scale of ± 1) is widely used in the social and behavioral sciences to determine possible relations, such as determinants of intelligence, marital satisfaction, yearly income, gross national product, and so on. In those examples direct experimentation is obviously impossible; instead, one must assemble information based upon the instances that naturally arise, and try to infer from them what variables, or factors, might be correlated with the depen-dent variable in question. As was true of the interpretation of functional relations, the finding of a statistically significant correlation is not to be interpreted as evidence that Y is caused by X. In some instances it might, in fact, be the case that X causes Y, or that Y causes X, since there is no basis for distinguishing one variable as a dependent and the other as an independent variable; both are dependent variables (this will become clearer after experimentation has been discussed). A correlation between income and education, for instance, would generally be interpreted to show that education increases income potential, but it is also true that higher income increases the availability of education. In other instances it would seem more likely that the covariation of X and Y is to be attributed to the effect upon each of a third variable, Z. For example, although height and weight tend to be positively correlated, especially in childhood, it is

BOX 8-3

Some Examples of Functional Relations

A. Forager Bees Communicate Distance

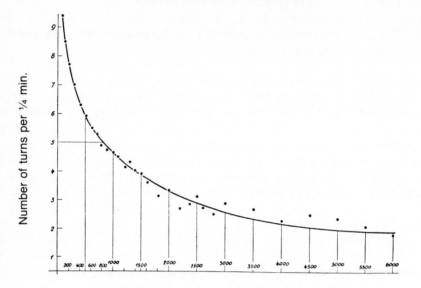

The distance of the feeding place in meters

A1. Number of dance turns by bee as a function of distance to food source. Data based on 3,885 observations for distance from 100–6,000 meters. (After Von Frisch, 1950)

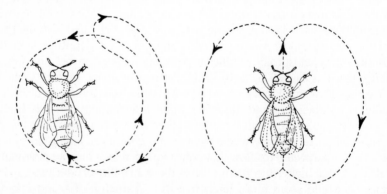

A2. Round dance (left) and wagging dance (right) of the bee.

B. Age Changes in the Use of Mnemonic Strategies in List Learning of Words and of Pictures.

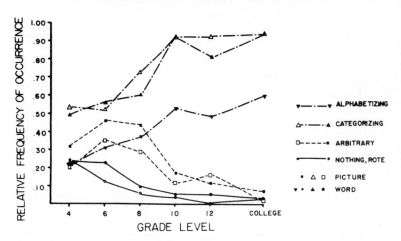

Rote memorization and forming of arbitrary groups declines among higher grades while placing in alphabetical order or forming meaningful categories increases. (After Neimark, 1975)

C. Variation of Mean Winter Temperature of the 48 States Over an 89-Year Period

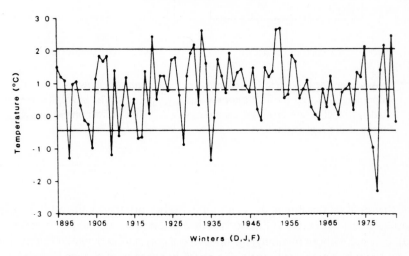

Here year is a nominal independent variable rather than a direct causal one. (After Karl, Livezey, & Epstein, 1984)

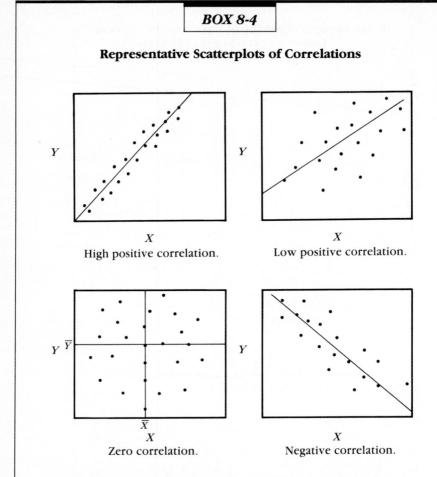

BOX 8-4

Representative Scatterplots of Correlations

High positive correlation.

Low positive correlation.

Zero correlation.

Negative correlation.

A. A scatterplot is obtained by plotting each data entry to show its *X* and *Y* value and depicting the relation of *X* and *Y* graphically. The examples are made up to illustrate expected configurations. The line shown on each scatterplot is the regression line.

clear that neither variable is the cause of the other but that both result from an ongoing growth process. A final possibility is that the obtained correlation is fortuitous and without meaning; the apocryphal correlation between Dutch birth rate and number of nesting storks is a possible instance of chance correlation.

One might assume that adventitious correlations are unlikely events, but that is not the case. A good demonstration of this derives from B. F. Skinner's (1953)

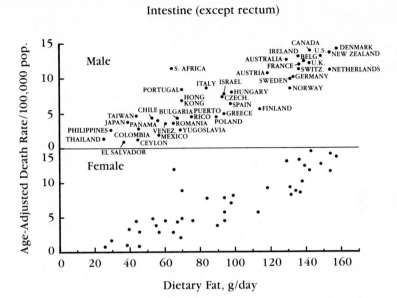

Intestine (except rectum)

B. The plot shows some actual data reflecting a high positive correlation between per capita consumption of fat and age-adjusted mortality from cancer of the intestine (not including rectal cancer). (After Carroll & Khor, 1975)

$$r = \Sigma Z_x Z_y / N - 1 \text{ where } Z_x = (X - \bar{X})/s_x$$

or,

$$r = \frac{\Sigma(X - \bar{X})(Y - \bar{Y})}{\sqrt{\Sigma(X - \bar{X})^2 \Sigma(Y - \bar{Y})^2}} = \frac{N\Sigma XY - \Sigma X \Sigma Y}{\sqrt{[N\Sigma X^2 - (\Sigma X)^2][N\Sigma Y^2 - (\Sigma Y)^2]}}$$

C. Some useful computational formulas for the Pearson product-moment correlation coefficient, r.

demonstration of superstitious behavior. He presented water to a thirsty pigeon at irregular intervals according to a predetermined schedule which was in no way related to the pigeon's behavior. After a period of this treatment, he returned to find each pigeon engaged in some atypical behavior, such as stretching its neck or cocking its head (no two pigeons displayed the same unusual behavior). His explanation for the phenomenon was that whatever behavior the pigeon was engaged in at the time water was presented was reinforced and its likelihood of recurring increased. As a result, the pigeons developed a new behavior pattern suggesting they "thought the behavior produced water" whereas there was no causal relation whatsoever. Through a similar mechanism we acquire belief in the efficacy of "lucky" items of clothing, special rituals, lucky numbers, and so on, that, in the absence of controlled testing, would reveal them to be the product of chance correlation.

If a correlation coefficient is to be interpreted so tenuously, one might question why anyone goes to the bother of computing it. One use was noted earlier, it is the only means of demonstrating a relation where experimentation is not possible. A second advantage is that, although it does not demonstrate causation, it does provide a basis for prediction. That use is made in, for example, the creation of screening or selection tests such as the SAT. Using scatterplots as in Box 8-4A we could determine the best-fitting straight line through the obtained points (it is known as a *regression line*) and use that function to predict values of Y from values of X. This usage illustrates a geometric interpretation of the correlation coefficient as the slope of the best-fitting regression line relating X and Y. What such a regression line would look like for the first and last scatterplot is pretty obvious; it would have a slope coefficient of 1. The slope approaches a horizontal line as the correlation decreases for a correlation of zero. Since there is no relation between X and Y, the best prediction of Y that we could make based on a knowledge of X is $\overline{Y}$, is the mean Y value. But, that is the best prediction that we could make of Y in the absence of any information about X, or any other variable. In other words, knowledge of X contributes nothing by way of improvement of prediction relative to what would be predicted in its absence. Another way of describing that state of affairs is to say that Y is independent of X. For a high positive or negative correlation, on the other hand, prediction improves considerably relative to what would be predicted in the absence of information, as is clear from comparing the regression line to a horizontal line at $\overline{Y}$. This illustrates another means of interpreting a correlation coefficient, that is, in terms of degree of improvement in prediction (a value given by r^2, where r is the correlation coefficient). A final use for the correlation is in providing an index of reliability of measurement, a subject to be treated in the next chapter.

To increase your understanding of correlation, find some examples in your own reading of the use of correlational evidence. Where a specific value of a correlation coefficient is cited, it is obvious that you are dealing with correlational evidence. Often, however, a relation is asserted without information about how it was obtained. In those cases try to guess how an asserted relation was determined. This exercise will help you become more critical in evaluating evidence. Whenever there is data consisting of two measures (one of X and one of Y) for each member of the sample, it is reasonable to assume that correlation is the index of relation between the two measures. If the term "correlation" is used without any evidence of computation of a coefficient value, then only a speculated covariation of two factors is involved.

The Current Status of "Causation." Should the word "cause" be removed from the language? Not at all. What I have tried to show is that a simple deterministic model of cause and effect or exclusive reliance upon criteria such as Mill's canons, especially the first canon, is inadequate to the needs of modern science. I have suggested that any assertions of causation can be viewed as the conclusion of an inductive argument, the evidence for which can be summarized as a statement of functional relations. Even in the three illustrative functions considered, however, it was clear that some functions are much more conducive to causal interpretation than others. The basis for a causal interpretation is, and must be, a theory detailing the causal mechanisms underlying the obtained function. In the case of the honeybee's code for distance, for example, it might be that after a long flight the forager is too tired to waggle energetically, or that it has forgotten how good the nectar tasted and waggles with reduced enthusiasm.[3] There are other possible mechanisms, all of which could lead to testable predictions. As we shall see in the next chapter, a major role of theory is to promote the hypothecation of causal mechanisms. The value of stating hypothesized relations in terms of contributory variables and the function describing their effect is that one is led to (a) identify contributory variables, and (b) describe the form of the function describing their effect (in mathematical form if possible). Causation is alive and well, but belief in strict determination of all effects is not.

PROBABILITY AND CHANCE

At the opposite pole from complete determination of effect is indeterminacy, or chance. But how should chance be characterized? You may have answered that question, "In terms of probability, of course." The answer is so obvious that one may not appreciate the fact that modern probability theory[4] is a relatively recent mathematical discipline generally dated to the work of Kolmogorov in 1933. I shall be concerned here not with computation of probability, which is dealt with in the Appendix on Probability. Rather, I will discuss the role of probability concepts in inductive inference: as a metric for indeterminacy, as a basis for a model with which to evaluate determinacy, and as a source of predicted values.

A Metric for Indeterminacy. When someone is asked if he or she will do something and responds with "Probably," we presume that there is a likelihood less than certainty but greater than never that the task will be done. Even common parlance treats probability as a scalable continuum with clear limits of $p = 1.0$ corresponding to certainty and $p = 0$ corresponding to never. But, how do we assign numerical values to the intermediate points of the continuum? The subjective continuum reflected in statements like "I'll probably go away for the weekend" or "It is unlikely that I'll take the car" is not amenable to quantification. A more promising lead arose from a consideration of games of chance where gamblers wanted a systematic basis for wagering. It led naturally to a *relative frequency definition of probability,* that is, a ratio of the number of favorable outcomes to all possible outcomes. In tossing a coin, there are only two possible outcomes to a toss: heads or tails. Thus, the likelihood of a head is $p(H) = \frac{1}{2} = p(T) = \frac{1}{2}$. Similarly, for the roll of a die there are six faces, the probability for any one of which is $p = \frac{1}{6}$; for the drawing of a card from a deck of 52 cards, the probability is $p = \frac{1}{52}$ for any particular card. In the case of cards, there are other means of partitioning the set of possible outcomes. We can assign the probability of a particular color, $p(\text{Red}) = \frac{26}{52} = \frac{1}{2}$; of a particular suit, $p(\text{Club}) = \frac{13}{52} = \frac{1}{4}$; or of a particular value, $p(7) = \frac{4}{52} = \frac{1}{13}$.

It would seem relatively straightforward to generalize a relative frequency definition beyond the realm of games of chance. For example, what is the probability that any individual picked at random was born on January 31? Since there are 365 days in the year, it would seem that the answer should be $p(\text{Jan. }31) = \frac{1}{365}$. But, what about leap year? And, more importantly, what about an implicit assumption that all birthdays are equally likely? There is evidence that more babies are born in the spring than in the winter, and there is even evidence of specific events, such as the great New York City power blackout, as being especially conducive to increasing the number of conceptions and consequent births nine months later. How do we deal with those complications? The answer in this case is straightforward, at least in principle: we take a large sample, or some existing pool of data, such as all recorded births in a large city over a period of time, or all the conscripts in a country with required military service, and for that entire population of N items, count the number of births, n_i, on each day of the year. That would give a probability for each day of the year, $p_i = n_i/N$, and allow for the outcome of unequal probabilities over days.

This example introduces some eventualities worthy of additional comment. First, it suggests that there are alternative means of computing a relative frequency and that they don't necessarily lead to the same estimate. That was true even in the earlier examples; for example, in computing the probability of drawing a red card, we might have reasoned that there are two colors, red and black, and obtained $p(\text{Red}) = \frac{1}{2}$ directly. We could have done the same for the probability of a particular suit or a particular value. Clearly, applying the definition of probability to computation requires careful attention. A more subtle consideration is that in the birthday example, actual data were proposed as a basis for determining relative frequencies; that is, there is a difference between gathering *observed frequencies, n_i,* and computing on the basis of *a priori considerations* for which all possible events are treated as equiprobable. Finally, to the extent that observed frequency values are estimates based upon a sample, there is a margin of error associated with them, that is, repeated sample estimates will vary somewhat, yielding a distribution of sample values.

Use of Models of Chance as a Basis for Inference of Determinacy.

It may have occurred to you, in the course of considering the birthday probability example, to speculate about possible values that might have been obtained. Suppose, for example, that in a population of 10,000 school children only 12 were born on January 14, whereas 55 were born on August 31. That might suggest not only that all dates are not equiprobable as birthdays, but, also, that something systematic might be going on to make January 14 so unlikely and August 31 so popular. To generate a hypothesis, you might even start counting backwards on your fingers for a date of conception. Before you do that, however, let's pause to state, explicitly and systematically, the inferential process upon which you have embarked. It goes something like this: (a) If all days were equally likely as birth-days—or, to state it more precisely, if date of birth were a random event—then for any given day, d_i, the probability of being born on that day is $p_i = \frac{1}{365}$. (b) On the average, 27.4 children in a sample of 10,000 should have been born on each day. (c) The observed frequency for August 31, however, is double the expected frequency, whereas the observed frequency for January 14 is less than half the expected frequency.[5] What we have just done is to compare observed frequencies to expected frequencies derived from an assumption of equiprob-able events (chance). (The next section will take up computation of expected values in greater detail.) The discrepancy between observed and expected values then led to a speculation that some non-chance or deterministic process was going on. In other words, although we had no idea about the determination of birthdate—what might cause some birthdates to be more popular than others—we inferred some deterministic process on the basis of evidence not in accord with expectation based on chance. That is a somewhat indirect basis for inferring determination—dividing options into two complementary sets, determined or chance, and concluding that the denial of one corresponds to the assertion of the other—but it is a process that goes on all the time in hypothesis testing by means of statistical inference. As a result, we can add rejection of a hypothesis of indeterminacy to our list of bases for inferring determination (cause), along with functional relations and correlation. More will be said on the procedure of testing hypotheses through falsification of a negatively stated assumption in the next chapter, but first let's consider the use of models of chance a bit more.

Suppose that your parent, on seeing your grade on a true-false test, berates you for such a low grade and asserts that it shows you don't know anything. You, on the other hand, insist that the grade, in fact, proves that you do know some-thing. If the grade were 100 (N out of N questions correct), or if it were 0, there would be no ground for argument. What is needed is a basis for generating a value to be expected on the basis of knowing nothing, and showing that it does not square with your grade. An alternative strategy of asserting a less than perfect knowledge, on the other hand, would lead to too many values to test (assume you knew $\frac{2}{3}$ of the material, or $\frac{3}{4}$, or $\frac{7}{10}$, or whatever). There is no ground for selecting a specific value. This being a true-false exam the likelihood of getting any item on it correct by chance is $p = \frac{1}{2}$. In effect, you could imagine answering each question by flipping a coin. That would yield a model[6] of a mindless respondent (chance) against which to compare your performance.

You might assume that for a true-false test of N items, the number correct on the basis of chance would be $\frac{N}{2}$. That, on average, is what we would expect over a series of trials. On any given trial, however, the obtained value might well differ. To pursue the model of flipping a coin, if everyone in the class each flipped a coin ten times and you compared the number of heads, it would not be the case that every class member would obtain exactly five heads. Some might get more than five heads, some would get fewer, and large deviations from five would occur less often than small ones. If for each possible outcome on the X axis you plotted on the Y axis how frequently it arose, you would obtain a frequency distribution like that shown in Box 8-5, the binomial distribution; but, depending upon class size the sample might be too small to yield a good approximation. By consulting the right-hand column showing the probability of getting r heads in n tosses, which for this example translates to r correct in n questions, you can see that the probability of getting nine or more correct by chance is indeed low. On the other hand, the probability of getting exactly six out of ten items correct is a little better than one in five—not at all unlikely. The probability of getting six or more items correct is the sum of the probabilities of six, seven, eight, nine, or ten, correct $p = {}^{386}\!/_{1024} = .377$ or better than one out of three (see the Appendix on Probability). That outcome is so compatible with chance occurrence that you could not argue from it that you really knew something. Where the cutoff should fall depends upon your criterion for "beyond the realm of chance." Five times out of 100 on the basis of chance is a criterion that is commonly employed; eight or more items correct is just a bit more frequent than that criterion. As you can see, defending the assertion that chance cannot account for your performance requires a fairly high standard of performance for a short test.

If you have never been exposed to computation of probability values this may seem an overwhelming introduction. At this point, you should be less concerned with how the numbers were arrived at than with the general form of the reasoning in using a model of chance as a basis for comparison in evaluating observed evidence to decide whether some non-chance, systematic process is operating. More examples of this form of reasoning will be encountered in the next chapter.

Computation of Expected Values.   In the preceding examples probability considerations were used to arrive at predictions of values expected on the basis of chance against which to compare observed values. That general procedure is so useful, and so widely employed, that it is advisable to consider it in more detail. Any variable, by definition, may take on any of a range of values. How do we select one from among that range as the best single value to use for prediction to future events or as a best representation in characterizing the distribution of values obtained for that variable? The desired quantity is called an *expected value* and is defined as the sum of the possible outcome values, o_i, each weighted by its probability of occurrence, p_i. In notation, $EV = \Sigma_i p_i o_i$. As an illustration, let's use the preceding example of a ten item true-false test, how many items would you expect to get correct if you answered each question by flipping a coin? The

---

BOX 8-5

The Binomial Distribution

The binomial distribution is generated from $(p + q)^n$ where p is the probability of one event (heads, female, yes) and $q = 1 - p$ is the probability of the other (tails, male, no); n is the number of events. For instance, in tossing one coin, $p = .5, q = .5, n = 1, (p + q)^1 = (p + q)$. With two coins $(p + q)^2 = p^2 + 2pq + q^2$ reflects all possible outcomes: (a) 2 heads can occur in only one way with a probability $p^2 = .25$; (b) there are two outcomes corresponding to one head and one tail (HT or TH), and their probability is $2pq = .5$; (c) two tails whose probability is $q^2 = .25$. The probabilities of these three outcomes sum to 1. For three coins $(p + q)^3 = p^3 + 3p^2q + 3pq^2 + p^3$ the outcomes are (a) three heads with a probability $p^3 = .125$; (b) two heads and a tail (HTH, HHT, THH) with a probability $3p^2q = .375$; (c) one head and two tails (HTT, THT, TTH) with a probability $3pq^2 = .375$; or (d) three tails with a probability $q^3 = .125$. You can do $n = 4$ and $n = 5$ for yourself.

As should be evident, the expansion of $(p + q)^n$ has a predictable form:

$$(p + q)^n = p^n + np^{n-1}q + \frac{n(n - 1)}{1 \times 2} p^{n-2}q^2 +$$

$$\frac{n(n - 1)(n - 2)}{1 \times 2 \times 3} p^{n-3}q^3 + \dots + q^n$$

While that formula may look formidable, the orderliness of it should be apparent; any term of the binomial expansion may be written $C_r^n p^r q^{n-r} = \frac{n!}{r!(n - r)!} p^r q^{n-r}$. While your reaction to that assertion may be that it is no simplification at all, a little calm scrutiny should convince you that with each successive term n decreases by 1 while r increases by 1 to $(n - 1)$. C_r^n gives the value of the coefficient. It equals $\frac{n!}{r!(n - r)!}$, in which the new symbol, $!$, stands for factorial, that is, a product of decreasing values of the initial quantity; for example, $n \times n - 1 \times n - 2 \times \dots \times n - (n - 2) \times 1$. A handy device for obtaining these coefficients is Pascal's triangle, shown for $n = 1 - 10$. The number in any row is the sum of the two numbers to the left and right on the row above. The sum of coefficient values for any value of n is equal to 2^n; since $\frac{1}{2}^n$ is the likelihood of each identifiably different outcome of n events, it yields the denominator to be used in computing probabilities for equivalent outcomes ($n - r$ heads and r tails). Play with it until you see how it works. In effect, I am instructing you to apply Goldberg's law, which states "If you play with something long enough you'll break it." It is a very useful principle to apply whenever you encounter something that you don't understand.

BOX 8-5 *cont.*

A. Pascal's Triangle

n

0									1								
1								1		1							
2							1		2		1						
3						1		3		3		1					
4					1		4		6		4		1				
5				1		5		10		10		5		1			
6			1		6		15		20		15		6		1		
7		1		7		21		35		35		21		7		1	
8	1		8		28		56		70		56		28		8		1
9	1	9		36		84		126		126		84		36		9	1
10	1	10	45		120		210		252		210		120		45	10	1

B. The Probability of *r* Heads in *n* Coin Tosses

No. of heads	Probability
10	1/1,024
9	10/1,024
8	45/1,024
7	120/1,024
6	210/1,024
5	252/1,024
4	210/1,024
3	120/1,024
2	45/1,024
1	10/1,024
0	1/1,024

I have gone into detail on binomial distribution because it is a useful model for any situation in which there are two mutually exclusive and exhaustive events with probabilities p and $q = (1 - p)$ respectively (and where it is not necessary that $p = q = \frac{1}{2}$). For instance, in rolling one die you might want to use the outcome 2 vs any other outcome. There $p = \frac{1}{6}$ and $q = \frac{5}{6}$. This model may be applied for such situations as predicting how many true-false items in a test of n items would be correctly answered by chance (for example, by a student who flipped a coin to answer each question). Think of some other possible applications of the binomial distribution model.

possible outcomes range from 0 to 10 items correct. The probability of obtaining exactly r out of n items correct may be obtained from Box 8-5B. Using that information to weight each outcome we obtain:

$$EV = \frac{1}{1024}(0) + \frac{10}{1024}(1) + \frac{45}{1024}(2) + \frac{120}{1024}(3) + \frac{210}{1024}(4) +$$
$$\frac{252}{1024}(5) + \frac{210}{1024}(6) + \frac{120}{1024}(7) + \frac{45}{1024}(8) + \frac{10}{1024}(9) +$$
$$\frac{1}{1024}(10) = \frac{5120}{1024} = 5.$$

That quantity is the mean and you probably arrived at the value far more directly by multiplying the number of test items, n, by the probability of getting any one of them correct, p, thus correctly employing the formula for the mean of a binomial distribution, $EV = np$, on largely intuitive grounds. Some additional examples of computation of expected values will be encountered in the discussion of decision making in Chapter 11.

What is so wonderful about an expected value and where would you want to use it? An expected value is used wherever you want an exact prediction for experimental test of a theory, or for purposes of planning, or for evaluating obtained evidence. For example, what is the payload weight of a 727 passenger plane? The answer is an expected value based upon the number of passengers and crew and their average weight, plus the average number of items of luggage and their average weight. To interpret a score on a test, a blood pressure reading, a cholesterol level, or to evaluate the cost of a house, a car, a mortgage, it is important to have an expected value, an average, against which to compare it. For *distributions* of values or scores that could be treated as outcomes of a random process, the mean of the distribution of scores serves this purpose.

INFORMATION AND UNCERTAINTY

We live in a world in which the term "information" is used with great frequency, with the result that every reader knows what the word means. Can some item of information, call it info$_i$, be more informative than another item of information, info$_j$? That may be a question that you have not considered before, but you will probably agree that the answer is yes even if you cannot concoct an example. A possible example is "Chicago is in Illinois" to be compared to "The population of Chicago is 3,005,072." To the extent that everyone knows that Chicago is in Illinois, the first sentence is not informative at all. The statement about the population of Chicago, on the other hand, probably does increase your knowledge. You would agree that it is more informative than the first statement. Just how informative is it? That is a puzzling question because it implies that we can measure information and assign a value to it. That may seem to be an impossible thing to do but the very fact of your being able to compare statements and to order them with respect to informativeness suggests that there is a continuum. Moreover, your evaluation of the statement that Chicago is in Illinois strongly suggests that zero is an appropriate origin for the scale, that is, the smallest possible amount of information is no information at all. So far so good. What about the upper limit of the scale? Our intuition is that it could be quite high, but the value to be assigned is problematic. What about a unit of measurement for the scale? That may strike you as a mind-boggling question; let's pursue it.

Consider the popular toddler's game "Which hand?". Knowing which hand contains the surprise would certainly constitute information. Let's say that you guess that the surprise is in the left hand and that that hand is duly opened, palms up. Regardless of what you see when the left hand is opened, you know the answer: if a surprise, then the surprise was in the left hand; if nothing, then you know that the surprise is in the right hand (assuming that this is a fair game and that there really is a surprise in one hand). Now, suppose you are playing "Which hand?" with an octopus or with a centipede. You would agree that playing with an octopus requires more information than playing with a person, and that playing with a centipede requires more information than playing with an octopus. In other words, the more alternatives you have the more uncertain you are in selecting one from among them (note that the alternatives are equally likely in this example). That obvious observation suggests that information should be defined in terms of *reduction of uncertainty*. The more alternatives there are the greater the uncertainty. Moreover, for any given number of alternatives, uncertainty is greatest where the alternatives are equiprobable. In the game of "Which hand?" for example, if the octopus had some injured and bandaged tentacles, it could be assumed that they would be less likely to be used, thus, effectively, reducing the number of alternatives and the resulting uncertainty. Similarly, if you play "Which hand?" with someone who has a long history of preferring the right hand, you would do better to guess right; again, uncertainty is reduced by the unequal probability of alternatives. Or, to view the assertion that uncertainty is greatest with equiprobable alternatives within another framework, a pure chance situation is characterized by equiprobable alternatives. There is more uncertainty associated with chance outcomes than with determined ones; where the outcome is completely determined, there is no uncertainty at all.

By associating the amount of information with uncertainty reduction rather than with the meaning of the message—which is the common sense coordination for information—it becomes possible to quantify the amount of information and to assign values for messages differing considerably in their content. The unit of information measurement is the *bit,* a contraction of *binary digit.* It describes the reduction in uncertainty resulting from halving the alternatives. In playing "Which hand?" with a person, one bit of information is required for solution; in playing with a centipede, one bit of information is obtained by learning whether the surprise is on its right. An additional 5.64 bits are required to identify which of the 50 right feet holds the surprise. In playing "Which hand?" with an octopus, 3 bits of information are required, one to identify a set of four tentacles, the second to narrow that set down to the appropriate pair, and the third to identify the member of the pair containing the surprise. Thus, information is measured on a logarithmic scale to the base two. In selecting one from among n equally likely alternatives the amount of information required is $H = \log_2 N$ (where H is characteristically used to represent the amount of uncertainty in bits).[7]

An understanding of the concept of uncertainty and its means of measurement is central to an appreciation of information-maximizing strategies in diagnostic problem solving (see Chapter 10). Without uncertainty, that is, more than one alternative to consider, there can be no information. If you are certain, as has already been noted, there is nothing to be learned. Where certainty is the result of a prior process of information gathering, it may be treated as a goal and an appropriate stopping point. Often, however, the absence of uncertainty results from inadequate awareness that there are alternatives and that certainty is unwarranted. In that case a belief that you already know forecloses the option of becoming informed. The conclusion of this argument should be obvious: be open and alert to alternatives. Token alternatives will not adequately serve the purpose since uncertainty is maximized when alternatives are equally likely.

SUMMARY

This chapter began with a consideration of *certainty* and its opposite. There are three possible interpretations of the opposite of certainty, each of which leads to a concept that is important in inductive reasoning. The dimension of *determinacy-indeterminacy* leads to a consideration of causation; *predictability-unpredictability* leads to a consideration of probability and chance; and *certainty-uncertainty* leads to information.

The terms "cause" and "effect" of everyday usage connote a simpler and more determined relation than is found in real-world phenomena. Contemporary workers have replaced the problematic terms "cause" and "effect" with more precise and more neutral descriptions in terms of *functional relations* among classes of variables. The phenomenon under investigation is referred to as the *dependent variable,* while the factors presumed to influence its manner and frequency of occurrence are called *independent variables.* The nature of the relation between the two classes of variables is expressed in terms of a *function*—that can be expressed, where possible, in the form of a mathematical equation. In other instances, especially those where it is unclear whether a causal interpretation may ever be placed upon the relation, a *correlation coefficient* may be used to summarize the degree of relation between two variables. Another usage of the correlation coefficient is in predicting future states of affairs.

Probability was defined as a quantity ranging in value between the limits $p = 0$ and $p = 1.0$. The quantity is expressed as a relative frequency of the number of outcome events falling in a defined class to all possible outcomes. The probability values assigned to each outcome class sum to unity. Three applications of probability measures were discussed:

1. The use of probability as a measure of outcome likelihood in situations of uncertainty or indeterminacy.
2. The use of models of chance as a basis for inferring systematic effects/determination. The reasoning upon which this usage is based is that rejection of the assumption of chance or random determination implies acceptance of non-chance or causal determination.
3. The assigning of expected values. The expected value to be assigned to an outcome was defined as the sum of all possible outcome values, each weighted by its probability of occurrence. For any random event its expected value constitutes the best single prediction of the value of that event.

Information was defined as *reduction in uncertainty*. It was shown that uncertainty can be measured on a logarithmic scale to the base two, the unit of which is the *bit*. Uncertainty increases with the number of alternatives and is greatest where the alternatives are equally likely, that is, under *conditions of chance*.

EXERCISES

1. In each of the examples below indicate the cause or causes and the basis of their identification. Which, if any, of Mill's canons applies to your identification process for each cause? If you need help, see the notes.[8]
    (a) A light bulb burning out (this generally happens when it is turned on).
    (b) The souring of milk.
    (c) Rain (or snow).
    (d) A poor grade on an exam.
    (e) The usual response to an item in Box 5-1.
2. Subject one of your own clear examples of causation to the class for criticism.
3. To better understand correlation, collect some bivariate data (two measures for each member of the sample) on anything of interest to you and prepare a scatterplot of it. Since computer programs for correlation are commonly available, you might even want to compute the correlation coefficient. Some possible problems to tackle include: expensive clothing has more pockets; duration of precipitation and predicted precipitation probability (that is, does it rain longer when the prediction probability is higher?); distance from front of classroom and final grade; weight and rated attractiveness (do separately for males and for females); number of pages of assigned reading and amount of time spent on assignment.
4. Some of the examples above could also be used as a basis for determining possible functional relations. As above, take some phenomena for which you believe there is a functional relation, collect the data, plot and interpret it. As an alternative, you may want to use examples from published material.
5. For the array of letters given here compute the required probability values

assuming that a sample of one letter is randomly drawn. If you need help, see the notes section.[9]

AAAAAAAAAAAAAAAABBBBBCCCCCCDDDDEEEEE
FFFFFGGGHHHHHHHIIIIIIIIJJJJKKKKKKKLLLLLLLL

(a) The probability of a D
(b) The probability of an L
(c) The probability of an A or a G
(d) The probability of a letter falling at H or beyond in the alphabet.

6. Suppose that for the letter set in Exercise 5, you mixed the letters in a hat and sampled one letter, then returned it and sampled again. This process is called *sampling with replacement.* What is the probability of drawing the following? (If you need help, see the notes.[10])

(a) Two As.
(b) An A and any letter besides an A (A and $\overline{A}$).
(c) An L and a D.

7. Assume a game in which one letter is drawn from the letter distribution in Exercise 5 and you must guess what it is. What should be your strategy? (Help is provided in the notes.[11])

8. For each of the pairs below, what is the more informative in terms of uncertainty reduction? (See the notes section for help.[12])

(a) The flip of a coin or the roll of a die.
(b) The draw of a card from a regular deck or the roll of a die.
(c) The announcement of Miss America (out of 50 contestants) or the draw of one from 50 cards.
(d) A correlation of +.83 or a correlation of −.57.

9. In rolling a die ten times, an odd number comes up seven times and an even one three. Is that a fair die? Detail the basis for your conclusion including the criterion for your judgment. Suppose that an affirmative action company hired seven women and three men. What would be your speculation about whether or not they discriminate? (See the notes for help in answering this problem.[13])

10. Although Mill's canons do not provide a satisfactory solution to identifying the cause of such events as wars, inflation, changes in public attitudes toward poverty, old people, and so on, they are useful in pinpointing the defining properties on a concept. Return to Exercise 2 of Chapter 6 and use Mill's canons for some of the examples to which you earlier applied Wilson's procedure for the clarification of concepts. To what extent do the two procedures overlap and to what extent do they supplement each other?

11. On the basis of data shown for six children who studied incidence of colds (as indicated by hanky to nose) in relation to items of diet, what interpretations might be made? List all possible interpretations of the data (for help, see the notes[14]). You will be asked as an exercise in the next chapter to design an experiment for eliminating some of the possible interpretations. (After Kuhn, 1986)

12. To explore the differentiation of appearance and reality a bit more, list some examples of your own and indicate how you know which aspect is appearance and which is reality. For starters, consider the daily rising and setting of the sun.

• *9* •

Model Building and Hypothesis Testing

$\mathbf{M}$aking sense of one's experience and organizing knowledge frequently takes the form of constructing and testing what might be described as theories. It is such a common and important part of everyday thought as to warrant closer scrutiny to which this chapter is devoted. As an example of the general process, consider the following two examples. You notice that in the course of his nightly walk your dog stops at specific spots and sniffs them intently. What meaning can be assigned to this behavior? At the outset you probably make two assumptions: (a) the behavior is lawful, that it can be described in terms of some explanatory principles, and (b) it is purposeful, serving some useful role in the life of the dog. A possible justification for both assumptions is the consistency of the behavior. The sniffing suggests that there is an odor at the spots investigated that may or may not be apparent to a human. If you have read that animals mark territories as a signal to other animals you might hypothesize that the presumed odor to which your dog is reacting is the territory marking of another animal. How would you go about testing the hypothesis? Consider a second example. You throw a ball straight up into the air and it comes down. How do you describe the determinants of its trajectory? Are they the same as would apply in throwing the ball straight ahead? Was its motion uniform throughout its path? Was your explanation affected by what you may have learned in a physics course? These examples are samples from a variety of similar instances so frequent and so common as to be taken for granted.

How should theories be constructed and tested? There is an extensive amount of literature on this subject. A major purpose of this chapter is to introduce you to some of the concepts and rules proposed in that literature to help you think like a good scientist. There is another, more recent and less extensive literature describing what people (including professional scientists) actually do in developing and testing theories. That evidence shows the process to be error-prone in systematic ways, some of which are described as *confirmation bias.* The average person is too willing to accept a theory, too uncritical in the testing of it (by seeking confirmatory rather than disconfirmatory evidence), and too loathe to abandon the theory in view of accumulating evidence that it is inadequate or incorrect. As an antidote to those natural tendencies, this chapter will focus upon *normative* rules for what one should do in reasoning about evidence rather than *descriptive* accounts of what people do in practice. To differentiate formal theory for any specific discipline from informal "theories" developed by an individual, I shall use the term *model* with qualification to refer to the latter.

THEORIES AND MODELS

Theory.   The word "theory" is used in everyday parlance more or less synonymously with "speculation" as in "It's my theory that the X are not to be trusted." There is often the additional implication that the speculation is baseless or frivolous: "It's ok in theory, but . . . ." Those everyday connotations are not central to theory in the more technical sense. The term *theory* is used to describe an organized body of principles and assumptions that account for a set of phenomena along with the rules for its application. Most theories attempt to account for the mechanisms underlying observed regularities: for example, not only the fact that repetition of material to be learned promotes its retention but also why it does so, for example, through strengthening traces or associations among elements. In other words, theories attempt not only to describe recurrent regularities but also to account for the conditions under which they do or do not occur. Often there are contending theories providing different accounts for the same set of phenomena: for example, wave and particle theories of light or other energy.

A good theory serves two very important functions. The first is that it *summarizes a great deal of knowledge economically,* that is, by means of a limited set of general principles. To return to the first example as to why your dog sniffs specific areas, to apply one theory only to your dog, a second only to the neighbor's dog, and so on, would be of little, if any, value. A satisfactory theory should account for the behavior of all dogs, and quite possibly, for other animals as well. A theory of territoriality does that. It does so through the fact that, in order to maintain a territory, there must be some way for the animal to designate it as his or her territory in a manner that is recognizable to other animals.

A second requirement of a theory is that it *lead to specific, testable predictions.* The predictions take the form of conclusions deduced from the principles of the theory expressed in the form of a conditional assertion: if p then q (where p specifies conditions of test and q observed consequences). It should be impossible to deduce contradictory conclusions from the same assumptions or for the same conditions. This is a requirement for *coherence* or *internal consistency*. *Ad hoc* explanations or informal theories consisting of a collection of limited principles frequently do not meet the criterion of internal consistency. Another requirement of the predictions is that they be sufficiently specific to be *capable of disproof.* Why should one want to prove a theory wrong? First, because if it is wrong one would want to know that in order to modify and correct it. Second, although repeated confirmation of theoretically derived predictions may strengthen one's confidence in a theory, they can never prove it to be correct. On the other hand, a theory can be disproved by nonconfirming evidence because of the logic of testing conditional implications.[1] One should, therefore, be leary of theories that can, generally after the fact, account for any possible outcome with the same set of principles.

Models.   An important component of many theories is a model of the phenomena to be explained. A model, as we have seen in Chapter 2, is basically a representational device. Sometimes representation may be of form or structure, as in scale models of vehicles, buildings; of relations among functional components as in a blueprint or flowchart; or of idealized qualities, as in a model student, fashion model, or model apartment. The latter feature, *idealization*, is a common one in the sense that central features are emphasized while peripheral ones are omitted (as in assuming free fall in a vacuum or movement on a frictionless plane). Whatever the particular form of the representation, its intended function is as a conceptual tool for understanding the workings of the system in question. The helix model of the DNA molecule or atomic models of chemical elements are examples of models as are star charts and planetaria.

   Structural and mechanical models provide a more or less direct representation of a system. A more abstract means of summarizing and representing is provided by expressing the workings of a system in terms of a *set of equations.* This medium is widely used in the physical sciences but has been less readily applicable in the social sciences. The advantage of so neutrally expressed a model is that it is less likely to suggest extraneous and, possibly inappropriate, applications. The potential for error in the use of models can be high as will become clear in the consideration of specific classes of models.

   1. Mental models. The summary that every individual makes of his or her own knowledge often takes the form of an informal theory, a set of principles summarizing observed regularities. The principles, like the principles of formal theories, may invoke unobservable forces or states that have the status of a concept. Unlike the forces of the formal theories, however, the forces are rarely sufficiently well defined[2] that anyone can identify the conditions under which they are appropriately invoked. Moreover, informal theories lack the power and the internal consistency required of formal theories. In order to differentiate formal theories from informal, individual theories, it has become common to refer to the latter as *mental models.*

Some examples of mental models are theories you may have to predict the behavior of friends and family members, of traffic patterns, procedures of maintaining good health, and so on. In some instances, such as the last example of the previous sentence, the mental model may incorporate parts of formal theory, such as theories of nutrition or of exercise physiology. In many instances a mental model may exist alongside a formal theory acquired through instruction or observation. An example of such coexistence is the explanation tribal members may offer regarding natural phenomena, such as thunder, in terms of action of a particular god, while at the same time invoking naturalistic explanations about cloud formation based on observation (for example, see Dart & Pradhan, 1967). Similarly, many persons account for the second introductory example of throwing a ball straight up in terms of two reciprocal forces: one, imparted by the throw, that accounts for the movement upward that dissipates with distance; the second, gravity, accounting for the downward motion. The same example is accounted for in Newtonian physics by the operation of only one force: gravity. Even students of physics, however, may offer a two-force explanation. A third instance arises, as we saw in the first chapter, in describing water level in a tilted vessel.

The systematic study of mental models is of recent origin[3] but consistent evidence about the properties of mental models is already emerging. We know that the construction of mental models begins quite early; preschoolers propose models. As suggested by the few examples just noted, mental models lack the properties required of formal theories, such as internal consistency or parsimony. *Parsimony* refers to accounting for many observations with a few general principles; for instance, throwing a ball horizontally or downward may be described differently in a mental model than tossing it up. Furthermore, as we shall see shortly, people do not test their mental models systematically or critically; nor do they reject or revise when evidence indicates that they should.

2. *Analogical models.* Analogy is based upon similarity with respect to some property or relation: such as North is to South as East is to West; Lamb:sheep::fawn:deer; soft:marshmallow::hard:rock. In each example you should be able to identify the basis of the analogy. You might even construct some analogies of your own. Reasoning by analogy is based upon an implicit conditional premise: if two phenomena are alike in n respects they should be alike in some additional respects as well. Where the implicit conditional premise is true we may validly and profitably go on to use the model of a well-known system as the basis for exploration of a lesser-known system. It is a very common tendency to do so; analogy is perhaps the major source of models.

The history of Western thought is full of examples. Newtonian mechanics helped not only to organize thought about physical phenomena, but it was also used as a framework for viewing physiological, psychological, and social problems as well. When the body, or its component parts, is viewed as a machine, important implications follow from the analogical model. If, for example, the heart is a pump then it must have pump features such as valves to regulate the flow of blood, a mechanism to regulate the cycle, and so on. Moreover, as with other machines, it should be possible to replace parts: for example, to install new valves or a new pacemaker or even the entire unit. Such analogical models have led to important developments in medicine, including a deeper understanding of where the analogy breaks down as in rejection of transplanted hearts and other organs, awareness of the defects of mechanical hearts stemming from the dissimilarity of blood to water, and awareness that many other organs, such as the brain, are not simple machines.

Some analogies rest upon so limited a number of similarities as to be better described as metaphors: "the body politic" suggests an analogy of society to an organism as, for instance, being composed of related parts such as a nervous system, skeleton, muscles, digestive system, and being subject to disease and other malfunctions. Clearly, in trying to spell out the basis of similarity, the analogy becomes more tenuous. One such analogical model is the sleeping beauty model for the role of the egg in the process of fertilization in Box 9-1. In order to avoid the pitfalls of inappropriate analogy it is always a good idea to scrutinize the similarities upon which it is based and decide if they are, in fact, central to the particular application.[4]

3. Statistical models. For a great many phenomena it is difficult, if not impossible, to provide a simple representation of them. One widely used class of model for dealing with phenomena that may assume a range of values (variables) is to make use of a statistical model appropriate for that particular form of distribution. You have already encountered the use of a statistical model in the previous chapter where the binomial distribution was used to provide a basis for discussing performance on a true-false exam. A binomial distribution applies wherever there are two mutually exclusive and exhaustive events each of which occurs with relative frequencies of p and $q = 1 - p$ respectively (and there is no requirement that $p = q$, although it is assumed in many applications). The classical application of this model is for coin tossing, a game of chance. Other applications include sex distributions (male vs female for birth rate, employment, longevity); voting behavior (Republican vs Democrat, yea or nay on a referendum); choice; and so on. For large numbers of events this distribution is well approximated by the normal distribution, which is the preferred model for most applications.

Consider the following questions. What is normal body temperature? pulse rate? blood pressure? cholesterol level? How large a deviation from it is cause for alarm? What is the modal age of speaking? walking? onset of puberty? What is the composition of the average American family? What is the normal duration of periods of unemployment? What is normal life expectancy? How does it differ among nations? Questions of this sort are commonly raised and have an important role in evaluation and planning (for example, in setting insurance rates, budgeting governmental assistance programs, or medical diagnosis). In answering

BOX 9-1

Analysis of an Analogical Model

Sleeping Beauty Reread

Sleeping Beauty, *engraving after Gustav Doré*

KNOWING WHAT WE DO NOW of the egg's enterprise during fertilization, it is amusing to reread the tale of Sleeping Beauty. Though the story served until recently as a metaphor for the egg's passivity, read another way it seems to have anticipated—by some happy coincidence—something of the egg's real energy.

Once upon a time, the Grimm brothers wrote, a princess fell into a magic sleep in her castle's tower, and a thick hedge of thorns grew about the place. "From time to time many kings' sons came and tried to force their way through the hedge; but . . . the thorns held fast together like strong hands, and the young men were caught by them, and not being able to get free, there died a lamentable death."

At last, a luckier prince heard rumors of the enchanted princess: "When the prince drew near the hedge of thorns, it was changed into a hedge of beautiful large flowers, which parted and bent aside to let him pass, and then closed behind him in a thick hedge." He found everyone asleep in the castle: from king to cook, all were frozen immobile, and even the kitchen fire was asleep beneath the meat. The prince made for the tower, climbed a winding staircase, and kissed the sleeping princess. The instant their lips met, she awoke, and the castle burst back into business: "The horses in the yard got up and shook themselves, the hounds sprang up and wagged their tails," and "the kitchen fire leapt up and blazed." The prince and princess, of course, were married and lived happily ever after.

With poetic license, it is easy to see in the hedge of thorns the formidable barriers of the electric and physical blocks, which prevent more than one sperm from fertilizing the egg. The hedge of flowers welcomes the prince rather the way the egg's surface receives the successful sperm. The castle's magic sleep is like that of the egg (which can lie dormant for decades). And the striking way the castle leaps from sleep to hubbub is paralleled in the transformation of the egg, whose metabolic fires leap up and blaze at its fateful meeting with the sperm.

The article, from which this excerpt was taken, notes that in earlier theories of the process of fertilization, no role was assigned to the egg and the sperm was largely held responsible for the entire process. The authors speculate that one reason this inaccurate view persisted may be its conformity to existing stereotypes of female passivity and male assertiveness, drawing an analogy between germ cells and the organisms producing them. (After Schatten & Schatten, 1983)

these questions we seek a model of how things are or how we normally expect them to be. These models are statistical in nature. You have been introduced to their basic ingredients in Chapter 6. In essence, the core requirements for a statistical model are (a) some best estimate value with which to characterize the population (the technical term for which is population parameter); (b) a measure of expected variation about that value; and (c) an estimate of the likelihood of occurrence associated with variations of any given magnitude. The normal distribution is widely used as a model for many purposes. Some examples are presented in Box 9-2. Before going on to see how these models are used, it is worth noting that each of us constructs statistical models all the time, for example, in deciding when late or overdue implies the event will not happen, in assessing the seriousness of malfunctions, and so on. List some of your own statistical models as, for example, for your normal weight, time to allow in studying for an exam, or for waiting for a friend. Attempt to be as specific as possible about all the properties of the distribution.

BOX 9-2

Examples of Statistical Models

A. Distribution of Stanford-Binet IQ Scores for the Original Standardization Group

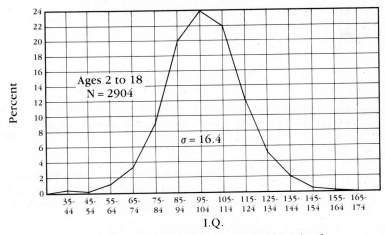

Distributions of Composite L–M I.Q.'s of
Standardization Group

The mean is 100 and the standard deviation is 16.4. (After Terman & Merrill, 1937)

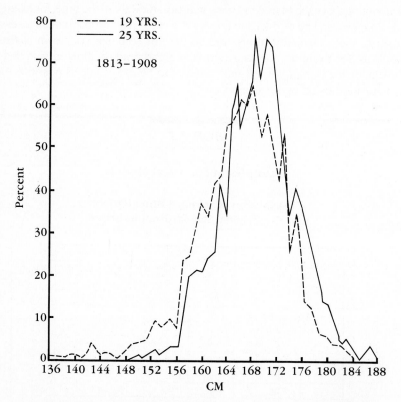

BOX 9-2 *(cont.)*

**B. Distribution of Standing Height in Centimeters
for Dutch Army Conscripts at Age 19 and at Age 25
(Measured between the Years 1813 and 1908)**

Legend:
- - - - - 19 YRS.
———— 25 YRS.

1813–1908

Y-axis: Percent (0 to 80)
X-axis: CM (136 to 188)

It appears that the men continued to grow between these ages. (After Roche, A. F. [Ed.] Secular Trends in Human Growth, Maturation, and Development. *Monographs of the Society for Research in Child Development, 44* [3-4] No. 93, p. 23.)

C. Height in Centimeters for Youths Aged 12–17
by Age, Race and Sex

Age, race, and sex	n	N	$\bar{X}$	s	$s_{\bar{x}}$	5th	10th	25th	50th	75th	90th	95th
						Percentile — Height in Centimeters						

Age, race, and sex	n	N	$\bar{X}$	s	$s_{\bar{x}}$	5th	10th	25th	50th	75th	90th	95th
WHITE												
Male												
12 years---	540	1,746	152.3	8.40	0.48	138.6	141.2	146.8	152.5	157.4	162.7	165.9
13 years---	542	1,728	159.9	9.11	0.49	145.4	148.3	153.5	159.4	166.2	172.6	174.7
14 years---	527	1,685	166.9	8.70	0.53	152.2	154.9	161.0	168.2	173.3	177.0	179.7
15 years---	525	1,646	171.6	7.23	0.35	158.5	161.8	167.1	172.3	176.1	180.5	183.1
16 years---	496	1,594	174.4	6.94	0.37	163.2	165.7	170.3	174.3	178.8	183.4	185.8
17 years---	417	1,527	175.7	6.99	0.42	162.8	167.1	171.2	175.9	180.2	184.4	187.3
Female												
12 years---	455	1,684	155.0	7.43	0.34	141.5	145.2	150.7	155.2	159.9	164.2	167.2
13 years---	490	1,667	158.7	7.02	0.34	146.6	149.4	154.1	158.9	163.4	167.7	170.1
14 years---	484	1,632	161.4	6.25	0.35	151.1	153.7	153.7	161.1	165.4	169.5	171.5
15 years---	425	1,594	162.4	6.98	0.53	151.3	153.1	157.5	162.6	167.3	170.7	173.0
16 years---	441	1,542	162.8	6.41	0.38	151.6	154.4	158.6	163.3	166.6	171.0	173.1
17 years---	393	1,501	163.0	6.32	0.32	152.6	155.1	158.3	163.1	167.3	171.2	172.9
NEGRO												
Male												
12 years---	101	280	152.1	6.87	0.92	140.6	143.2	146.8	152.6	156.6	161.4	164.1
13 years---	80	262	159.7	9.29	1.00	143.5	147.5	153.5	160.9	165.6	173.1	174.4
14 years---	88	256	165.7	8.62	0.92	152.0	154.5	158.7	166.1	171.1	177.9	180.0
15 years---	84	240	170.4	7.81	0.85	156.7	160.9	165.5	168.9	176.0	179.8	182.7
16 years---	57	231	174.0	6.80	1.26	162.1	163.1	170.1	174.5	178.6	181.7	183.0
17 years---	69	225	174.5	7.01	0.68	162.4	165.8	169.6	174.2	179.9	183.3	186.8
Female												
12 years---	88	271	156.5	6.59	0.51	145.5	148.6	152.6	155.9	161.3	163.8	168.5
13 years---	91	275	159.0	6.55	0.66	147.9	150.2	154.6	159.5	164.1	166.6	169.5
14 years---	101	265	161.5	5.69	0.66	151.7	153.5	157.4	162.1	166.0	168.6	169.8
15 years---	73	235	161.7	6.16	0.71	153.0	154.0	157.4	161.5	165.4	170.1	173.3
16 years---	93	242	161.9	6.51	0.90	151.4	153.2	157.6	161.7	166.6	169.9	173.3
17 years---	74	236	162.7	6.61	0.50	151.3	152.6	158.3	164.1	168.1	169.9	173.5

Note: n = sample size, N = estimated number of youths in population in thousands; $\bar{X}$ = mean; s = standard deviation; $s_{\bar{x}}$ = standard error of the mean. Data are for the United States 1966–1970. (*Vital and Health Statistics*, Series 11 No. 126, August 1973. DHEW publication No. [HRA] 74-1608, 16.)

In interpreting models based upon the normal distribution, we expect most events to be like most events—that the mean or expected value is the best single predictor—but deviations from the mean are also to be expected. How large must a deviation be to be interpreted as "abnormal"? The beauty of models deriving from the normal distribution is that there is a unit for interpreting variation, the *standard deviation,* and the relative frequency of deviations in terms of standard deviation units is tabled.[5] As a convenient rule of thumb, about 2/3 of all measures fall within one standard deviation on either side of the mean; 1/3 above and 1/3 below the mean. Thus, for the distribution of scores on the Stanford-Binet, 2/3 of the population are expected to have IQs in the range of 84–116. About 95% of all measures fall within two standard deviations of the mean; again, half above the mean and half below it. Thus, IQ scores lower than 68 or higher than 132 would be expected in only about 2½ cases out of 100 in each direction. Deviations of three standard deviations or more from the mean in either direction are expected in less than 2½ cases per thousand. For the 1937 IQ distribution, this corresponds to IQs lower than 42 or higher than 148. How large a deviation is significant is a somewhat arbitrary decision. Statisticians use the convention that deviations that would occur only 5 out of 100 times or less by chance are significant.[6] Unfortunately, many published norms do not provide the standard deviation along with the mean (the height/weight norms provide a common example) so there is no basis for assigning likelihood to deviations. This information is, however, always useful in interpreting any specific value, such as yearly income, life expectancy, or height, in relation to norms.

Not all populations are well represented by a normal distribution. Many social phenomena, such as yearly income, family size, recorded offenses, are better represented by a skewed distribution. Consider, for example, the number of recorded criminal charges per individual over a fixed time interval. A population frequency distribution of criminal charges would yield a positively skewed distribution with the bulk of the values close to zero, reflecting the law-abiding majority, and a long tail at the positive end reflecting a few habitual criminals. For such distributions the *median* (the score above and below which 50% of all scores fall) provides a better estimate. From a practical standpoint, it is advisable to be on guard against mean values for distributions that are likely to be skewed. If, for instance, it is argued that teachers are well paid and that the mean teacher's salary in a community is $30,000, you should question whether that average includes a few high-paid administrators and ask for the median as well. If it is well below the mean, you are dealing with a skewed distribution.

EXPERIMENTATION AND HYPOTHESIS TESTING

A model, or a theory incorporating a model, as we have seen serves two very important functions: the first is to summarize existing knowledge economically in terms of a minimum number of assumptions or principles; the second is to provide a means of expanding knowledge through the generation of testable hypotheses. A hypothesis is a prediction stated as exactly as possible in the form of a conditional assertion. For example, suppose there is smoke or steam billowing from below your car. One possible explanation might be an overheated radiator. If it were an overheated radiator, then the temperature gauge would indicate overheating, the smoke would be coming from the radiator area of the hood, and so on. A conditional formulation of the hypothesis indicates conditions for testing. If the conditions do not obtain then the hypothesis may be rejected; if they do, it is tenable and more exacting tests should follow. Another hypothesis may be that water has splashed on the catalytic converter. If that were the case, then there should be no steam in dry weather, and smoking should cease when all the water has been converted to steam and dissipated. As should be clear from these examples, hypothesis testing takes the form of generating a conditional assertion relating the antecedent and consequent conditions.

The rationale of testing a conditional, as we saw in Chapter 6, is that there is one condition that falsifies a conditional statement: nonoccurrence of the consequent in the presence of the antecedent condition. While the occurrence of any other conditions may be compatible with the statement and make for a valid argument, it does not prove the initial assumption to be true. Thus, in testing a hypothesis we want to set up conditions to discover if it is false. The best means of attaining such conditions is through experimentation.

Hypotheses. The illustrative example of the preceding introduction to hypotheses dealt with alternative hypotheses for a particular event—a smoking automobile. In everyday life we formulate hypotheses about particular events; in most sciences, on the other hand, hypotheses deal with general classes of events. The form of the hypothesis and its level of specificity will naturally, differ with the discipline and the directing theory or model. In the discussion of experimentation which follows the general form of the hypothesis appropriate to the example concerns *whether an independent variable has an effect at all.* For practical considerations or in the early stages of investigation, identification of relevant independent variables (hypothesized antecedents) is a common starting point: Is a new seed variety more disease resistant than the standard variety? Is a drug effective? Does a new production method reduce production time/costs? Is a new text more comprehensible? These, and questions like them, ask whether some modification makes a difference. They are, for the most part, straightforward empirical questions, although the hypothesis that a given factor should have an effect may be, and often is, derived from a theory.

At more advanced stages of theoretical development hypotheses are likely to be directed toward more specific assumptions about the nature of the effect: for example, how does test score relate to amount of study time? How does reading speed relate to size of print? How does rate of plant growth relate to temperature? How does egg production relate to feed composition? As the form of the question suggests, here interest is in the form of the function relating the independent and dependent variables. The hypothesis will be more specific when a theory predicts the nature of the effect of an independent variable (for example, that the form of the function should be linear, or exponential, that there should be an inflection point in the function at a particular value, and so on). Where alternative theories are available, a test of them is obtained by devising conditions under which a different outcome value, or function form, is predicted by each in order to determine which best describes the data.

The Nature of Experimentation.   As would be expected from the foregoing discussion, an experiment must provide antecedent conditions, an independent variable or variables in which to observe a consequent (the dependent variable). You have encountered these terms in the discussion of functional relations. In addition, there must be adequate *control* to ensure that the results are unambiguously interpretable. For "adequate control" three conditions must be satisfied: (a) the independent variable can be systematically varied while other conditions are maintained constant; (b) there is a basis for comparison with which to assess the effect of the independent variable(s); and (c) other possible explanations and/or sources of error must be ruled out. The means of satisfying these requirements may vary depending upon the nature of the experiment.

Let's consider an example. Suppose a vaccine to protect against the common cold is developed and we want to test its effectiveness. Giving the vaccine to one person and observing whether or not that person comes down with a cold is clearly not an adequate test for several reasons. For one thing, an effective vaccine should work for all people (a population) and we know that people vary in many respects—of most immediate relevance, their susceptibility to colds. Thus, we would want to give the vaccine to a representative sample of people. If the vaccine were to be administered to a representative sample, we would confidently expect that some of them would not come down with a cold but some probably would. How could these results be interpreted? Clearly, it could not be interpreted without a basis of comparison. We would need a control group, which would not get the vaccine so that a reliable estimate of the likelihood of catching cold in the absence of vaccine "protection" could be computed. While the function of the control group in providing a basis of comparison is fairly obvious, the significance of "reliable estimate" should not be overlooked. We will return to the issue of reliability after completing the discussion of control.

Another function of the control group is to rule out alternative explanations and possible sources of error. Just by virtue of having been innoculated with a putative cold preventive, the members of the experimental group might acquire a confidence that would lead them to neglect their usual safeguards against catching a cold. That could work against the hypothesis. In other circumstances, knowing that one is a member of an experimental group might have the opposite effect of biasing results in favor of the hypothesis. Thus, it is highly desirable to treat both groups as identically as possible; for example, by giving all members of both groups an injection—one, of carrier solution (for the control group) and the other, of carrier plus vaccine (for the experimental group). It is also a good idea if both the subjects and those administering the injection and recording the data are ignorant as to the group assignment of each participant. There are additional safeguards to be observed. We would not want to run one group in the summer and the other in the winter when colds are more likely. The groups should not differ with respect to overall health status, frequency of exposure to colds, and so on. In other words, we would need to control other contributory factors to ensure the comparability of the two groups (it usually is not possible to control at the level of the individual group member).

To use another example, suppose you were comparing two (or more) types of cinder block for their ability to withstand compression by placing samples of each in a press. After the block is placed in the press, pressure is increased in graded amounts until the block starts to crumble; the pressure is recorded at that point. In this case the types of blocks (independent variable) are compared to each other with respect to crumble pressure (dependent variable). Which block group is viewed as the control group is arbitrary (except if one is an existing standard and the other is asserted to be improved in some way). Again, size and shape of the blocks in the two groups should be comparable as should be treatment during testing. As an exercise, outline necessary control considerations for comparing methods of freezer storage, study techniques, sewing sleeves, housebreaking puppies, or some other comparison of your own devising to broaden your understanding of the nature of experimentation.

Experiments to evaluate the nature of an effect, or the form of the function describing it, must have several levels of the independent variable varied systematically. For the cold vaccine example, dose level might well be varied to determine if there is a maximally effective dose. A very low volume of killed virus may be ineffective, a very high volume might be no more effective than lower volumes or might even have harmful side effects. In assessing hypotheses about the form of a functional relation, the number of independent variable groups and their specific magnitude will be directed by the hypothesis in question. For example, in assessing the effect of study time on test scores if you compared a group investing three hours of study time and a group investing eight hours to a zero-study control group, the resulting data for only three points (zero, three, eight hours) could show whether there is an increase in test scores but would provide an inadequate basis for differentiating a linear increase from an exponential one—that is, an increase that showed decreasing improvement and gradual leveling off with additional increases in study time (see Box 9-3). More points along the independent variable continuum are required to determine the form of the relation. Where effects at some particular value are predicted (for example, effects upon plant growth of temperatures below 40° or above 80°), then a narrow range of values around those specific points is desirable. Each discipline has its own experimental methods, traditional research designs, and characteristic modes of formulating hypotheses; this brief introduction cannot attempt to deal with them. If, however, you are taking one or more science courses, try to characterize

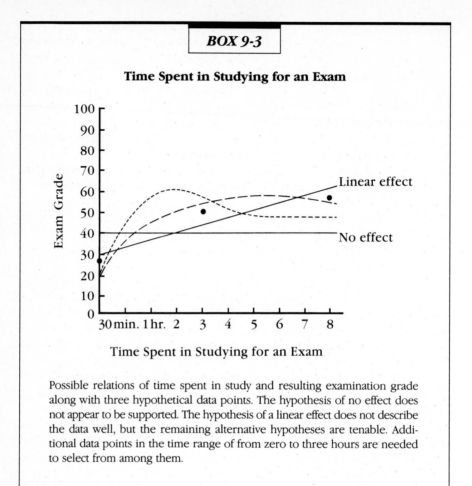

BOX 9-3

Time Spent in Studying for an Exam

Time Spent in Studying for an Exam

Possible relations of time spent in study and resulting examination grade along with three hypothetical data points. The hypothesis of no effect does not appear to be supported. The hypothesis of a linear effect does not describe the data well, but the remaining alternative hypotheses are tenable. Additional data points in the time range of from zero to three hours are needed to select from among them.

(a) the level of hypotheses examined (identifying variables vs assessing the nature of their effect), (b) typical experimental procedures employed, and (c) kinds of control employed.

Reliability. As you are now well aware, all judgments are subject to error. The same is true of measurements. For example, if you have a bathroom scale you know from experience that you can weigh yourself several times repeatedly and come up with a slightly different weight each time. Which is your true weight? Possibly none of the readings; the usual bathroom scale is not a precision instrument. This observation applies to many measurement instruments, such as, sphygmomanometers, electrocardiographs, commercial scales, achievement tests, and so on. No measurement is free of error. The consistency with which repeated measures yield the same value is called the *reliability* of the measure. To ensure that a reliable estimate has been obtained (as in the example of the preceding section where an estimate of the likelihood of catching cold was at issue), several estimates based on repeated measurements are needed to yield a distribution providing some measure of variability among estimates. The smaller the standard deviation of the distribution of estimate values, the more reliable is the estimate. The standard deviation of a distribution of estimates is known as the *standard error*.[7] Estimates are sometimes reported with their standard error: for example, poll results may indicate that 27% of the respondents ± 2% are in favor. Although indexes of reliability are not reported as often as we might wish, it is advisable to be aware that a single measure is always to be interpreted with caution and that reliability (or reproducibility) of results is always a source of concern.

The Logic of Hypothesis Testing.   The results of an experiment are used to judge the tenability of the initial hypothesis. That judgment, like all judgments, is subject to error and requires a criterion. Is there a general, all-purpose criterion to serve the purpose? There is, and the general rationale of the procedures embodying it is illustrated in Box 9-4, whose similarity to Box 5-2 should be immediately apparent. It illustrates the use of a criterion of *statistical hypothesis testing*. The statistical hypothesis differs from the experimental hypothesis. They differ in form in a way that might at first seem perverse; a statistical hypothesis is tested first and, on the basis of results from it, the experimental hypothesis is then evaluated. The logic, in each case, is related to the logic of testing a conditional assertion.

If the independent variable has an effect, then there should be a difference between the experimental and control groups; for example, if the cold vaccine is effective, there should be fewer colds on the average among experimental group members than among members of the control group. But how large must the difference be to demonstrate an effect? It will certainly not be the case that all of the control group members have a cold and that none of the experimental group members do. Such results would be readily interpretable but not representative of more usual experimental results. There is generally no basis for predicting the exact magnitude of the difference required and any other criterion would be arbitrary. The solution is to form a statistical hypothesis, called the *null hypothesis*,[8] that there is no difference between the experimental and control groups and, therefore, that the observed difference between the two groups is of no greater magnitude than would be expected on the basis of normal variation and error of measurement. There are many statistical tests of the null hypothesis; in essence, they evaluate observed group differences in relation to expected error variation. For each test a frequency table of outcome values of the statistical test is consulted in evaluating the results of the statistical test of the null hypothesis. The distributions resemble those in Box 6-5 but are specific to the test in question. The tabled distributions enable one to evaluate how likely it would be to observe a difference between groups as large as, or larger than, the observed difference by chance if there really were no difference. The

BOX 9-4

Testing the Null Hypothesis

Decision Made	True State of the World	
	H_0 is True	H_0 is False
Accept H_0	Correct Decision $p = (1 - \alpha)$	Error, Type II $p = (\beta)$
Reject H_0	Error, Type I $p = (\alpha)$	Correct Decision $p = (1 - \beta)$

A. The decision matrix for testing a null hypothesis, H_0, and the consequences of accepting or rejecting it (note the similarity to the signal detection matrix of Box 5-2). Once again, there are two possible correct decisions: accepting the null hypothesis of no difference between experimental and control groups when it is true, and rejecting it when it is false. There are also two possible errors: rejecting the null hypothesis when it is, in fact, true, which is called a Type I error, or failing to reject a false H_0, which is called a Type II error. The probability of a Type I error, α, is determined by the confidence level criterion selected. The probability of a Type II error, β, is a function of α and also of what is called the power of the test used.

Experimental Decision	True State of Affairs	
	IV Has Effect	IV Doesn't Have Effect
IV Has Effect	Correct	Erroneous Causal Assumption
IV Has No Effect	Erroneous Rejection	Correct

B. The experimental hypothesis and possible consequences of accepting or rejecting it. The decision here is contingent upon the outcome of the test of the statistical hypothesis, H_0. If the statistical hypothesis is rejected, the experimental hypothesis is tenable that the independent variable has an effect.

reasoning is similar to that employed in the previous chapter to decide how many true-false items should be correctly answered as evidence that you knew the material. To ensure that the magnitude of the observed difference is sufficiently large that it could not be attributed to chance variation, a decision criterion, called a *confidence level,* is set such that if the obtained value of the test equals or exceeds it, then the null hypothesis is rejected. That is, we conclude that so unlikely a difference could not be a chance occurrence and, therefore, the null hypothesis is wrong. If the obtained test value is less than the critical value, we do not reject the null hypothesis which, as a conditional statement, cannot be proved. The criterial value typically chosen is one with a chance probability of 5 out of 100, the .05 level; for a more stringent test, the .01 level may be used. An example of evaluating experimental evidence is given in Box 9-5.

Thus, in order to test an experimental hypothesis that some independent variable has an effect, one disproves a statistical hypothesis that it has no effect. While this may seem unduly indirect, it is an inevitable consequence of the logic of testing a hypothesis, or any other conditional assertion: that is, that one cannot ever prove a hypothesis but only disprove it. Therefore, one states a statistical hypothesis, the null hypothesis, whose disproof shows the experimental hypothesis of an independent variable to be tenable. If the statistical hypothesis cannot be rejected, then we are inclined to reject the experimental hypothesis that a real difference exists. Whatever conclusion is reached, there is a possibility of error to which some probability value can be attached. As you have been cautioned repeatedly, there is no certainty attached to the conclusions of inductive reasoning.

Hypothesis Testing in Everyday Life.   Given this brief, general introduction to hypothesis testing, to what use can the concepts and tools be put? Certainly they can help you evaluate experimental evidence a bit more critically. You are now aware of such questions as, Are the reported differences statistically significant (that is, at what level of confidence is the null hypothesis rejected)? Was the experiment adequately controlled? Are the measures reliable? What is normal variation in this situation? They are questions worth raising. For example, the next time a physician tells you that your weight, pulse, blood pressure, or some other indicator is "not normal" you need not be intimidated but can ask about the reliability of the measure, the form of its distribution, and the range of variation (and, perhaps, discover that many physicians are less aware of these issues than you are). You may also be less likely to be impressed with newspaper accounts of dramatic new discoveries. And you may find that some of these concepts and tools are applicable to everyday experiences although there are also limitations of which you should be aware.

Adopting the role of an empirical scientist as a framework for confronting the problems of everyday life can have some desirable consequences. First, it

---

BOX 9-5

Possible Experimental Outcomes and Their Interpretation

A young member of the Lykus tribe questioned the tribe's prevailing spirit possession theory of disease and managed to convince the tribal ethics committee to permit an experimental test of the theory despite their objection to the propriety of wanton cursing of innocent people. All members of the tribe were assigned randomly to one of two groups: an experimental group, whose members were subjected to a curse of disease spirits, and a control group, which was not cursed. Each of these two groups was divided into an additional two groups, one of which was informed that a curse had been placed upon it and the other, which was not. The interesting feature of this design is that it allows for the role of an additional factor, knowledge of the curse, as a contributor to or moderator of the effect of the curse itself. The effect of the curse was measured in terms of how many times the experimental participants visited the offices of the Witch Doctors over a six-week period. At least one complaint visit was taken as evidence of disease. A nurse receptionist/fee collector recorded the number of tribe members making at least one visit (duplicates were not counted) over a six-week period. Neither she nor any of the Witch Doctors knew the group assignment of any tribe member, or, even, the existence of an experiment.

The matrices show the experimental design of the experiment, A, and B, the expected outcome for a null hypothesis in which there is a .40 base rate probability of a complaint visit over a six-week period. The remaining six matrices show some possible experimental outcomes and the interpretation to be placed upon each. There are, of course, many more possible outcomes. This sample illustrates some noteworthy features. The effect of the curse can be evaluated by comparing the marginal total of the curse column to the no curse column; the effect of knowledge of the curse, by comparing the marginal total of the two rows. Matrix C shows an outcome in which curse alone is effective (it is in accord with the spirit possession theory); in matrix D, knowledge alone is effective (not in accord with the spirit possession theory). Matrix E shows a state of affairs in which neither factor has an effect but, as is shown by comparing diagonal sums, they interact such that one or the other but not both (the exclusive or) has an effect. The presence of an interaction is indicated by unequal diagonal sums; interactions may take many forms as shown in G and H where there is intensification of factor effects with combination in G, and cancellation, in H. In F there is no interaction, both curse and knowledge have an effect and those effects operate independently. Decide which outcomes are compatible with the theory and what modification is required by those which disconfirm the simple spirit possession theory of disease.

Treatment	Curse	No Curse
Informed	25	25
Not Informed	25	25

	Curse	No Curse	Effect of Information
Treatment			
Informed	10	10	20
Not Informed	10	10	20
Effect of Curse	20	20	40

A. Design of the experiment in which 25 individuals are assigned to each of four treatment conditions.

B. Expected outcome under null hypotheses. Cell entries are number of members of each group visiting the witch doctor.

Possible Experimental Outcomes and Their Interpretation.

Cell entry shows number of members of each experimental group visiting the witch doctor. Note that for all possible outcomes the overall relative frequency of illness is $p(\text{ill}) = .40$.

	Curse	No Curse	Effect of Information
Treatment			
Informed	15	5	20
Not Informed	15	5	20
Effect of Curse	30	10	40

	Curse	No Curse	Effect of Information
Treatment			
Informed	15	15	30
Not Informed	5	5	10
Effect of Curse	20	20	40

C. Only curse is effective: more cursed than uncursed individuals visit the witch doctor.

D. Only knowledge is effective: more informed than uninformed individuals visit the witch doctor.

BOX 9-5 *cont.*

Treatment	Curse	No Curse	Effect of Information
Informed	5	15	20
Not Informed	15	5	20
Effect of Curse	20	20	40

E. Neither variable consistently effective; only one or the other has an effect. There is a cancellation (interaction) for both present or both absent.

Treatment	Curse	No Curse	Effect of Information
Informed	15	10	25
Not Informed	10	5	15
Effect of Curse	25	15	40

F. Curse and knowledge are each independently effective: more cursed and more informed individuals visit witch doctor.

Treatment	Curse	No Curse	Effect of Information
Informed	20	5	25
Not Informed	10	5	15
Effect of Curse	30	10	40

G. Each variable effective alone but there is an interaction as well such that effect is intensified in combination.

Treatment	Curse	No Curse	Effect of Information
Informed	10	15	25
Not Informed	10	5	15
Effect of Curse	20	20	40

H. Information has an effect but only where no curse has been given.

---

helps promote detachment from the situation in order to examine it more objectively. Second, it provides "handles" for becoming more aware and directive. For example, to the extent that we develop informal explanatory models for a variety of events (for example, why people act as they do, how to succeed in a given enterprise or operate within a system), it helps to formulate the model more explicitly in order to identify its assumptions and to test their adequacy. The resulting evidence may lead to a revision of your model. Note, however, that revision will be indicated only to the extent that you can generate hypotheses capable of disproof. As a test of the adequacy of this framework consider some situation you deal with regularly and in which you have evolved some understanding. Formulate that understanding explicitly in terms of relevant factors and the nature of their effect and try to generate some hypotheses from it to test. Some possible candidates for exploration are your informal theories for dealing with specific friends, for coping with difficult situations, for organizing daily activities, for producing superior performance on the tennis court or in the kitchen.

If you have taken the suggested exercise seriously, you should have become more aware of some important differences between the laboratory and everyday life. In trying to design an experiment, for example, you may have become aware of the difficulty of establishing appropriate controls. In trying a new diet or a new exercise regimen, for instance, you can keep a daily record of your weight for a two-week interval while you are on it and for a two-week interval during which you revert to normal practice (remember, you need a control group as a basis of comparison). For other attempts at experimentation, you may find it hard to vary only the independent variable while keeping other conditions constant or to establish an appropriate control condition. Another difference between the laboratory and everyday life that should become more evident concerns the purpose of the enterprise. In the laboratory the goal is understanding and knowledge; in life the goal is often immediate results. To take a trivial example, if you think you have the secret of perfect sponge cake you would be loathe to test your hypothesis by enstating conditions to disprove it, and risking a rotten cake by omitting a special ingredient or procedure. Similarly with other possible examples, we keep doing what has worked in the past, although some features of the process may have no effect, without risking the kind of test that could demonstrate whether our informal theory is, in fact, adequate. As a final illustration of the conflict between understanding and results, consider the following example from my own experience. On awakening during the night with a terrible itching behind the ear drum, I generate four explanatory hypotheses: a developing case of swimmer's ear, an allergy, or a sinus condition, the last two of which may have been aggravated by the damp night air. As a very uncomfortable sample ($n = 1$), I might cover all bases by closing the window, taking an antihistamine, putting drops in my ear and a decongestant spray in my nose and crawling back into bed. Any one of those remedies singly or in combination (or perhaps none of them if it is a temporary self-limiting condition) may work. Should the problem arise in the future, however, I will have no more precise understanding of it as a result of my poor procedure of dealing with four hypotheses simultaneously without adequate controls for any of them. Knowledge has its costs.

Everyman as Scientist. The focus of this chapter has been a normative one—explaining how to proceed in formulating and testing hypotheses. Since the nature of the process is such that it is inherently subject to error, you are well advised to safeguard against error as much as possible; that is, to emulate the inductive reasoning of a good scientist. I remind you that this is not mere fussy academic advice. To the extent that much of the process of acquiring and applying knowledge–whatever that knowledge may concern—takes the form of developing informal theories or mental models, everyone is confronted with the task of acting like a scientist much of the time. Moreover, to the extent that your goal as a thinker is to become aware and directive of your thought processes, it is important to become a sophisticated hypothesis tester.

To what extent does the average person act as a model scientist? Before answering this question, you might note that we are comparing the behavior of the average person with the model scientist in testing hypotheses. Do they differ? They do. The nature of the deviations are systematic and will be characterized here briefly.[9]

1. *Assembling evidence.* People, even sophisticated college students, when confronted with a conditional statement and required to test it, have a propensity to look for confirmatory instances rather than to seek disconfirming instances. Because this is a very consistent finding, it is therefore, worth repeatedly reminding yourself to look for conditions under which the hypothesis can be shown to be wrong, if it is. Although superstitious behavior was introduced as a laboratory curiosity, there is a tendency to treat fortuitous correlation as cause and to assume that something that accompanied an early success is a necessary ingredient of it. The correlate therefore gets repeated and becomes part of a practiced repertoire. Skill, attained in that fashion is a matter of technique, if not habit, rather than understanding. To understand what some hypothesized factor contributes, see what happens when it is omitted.

2. *Identifying and controlling variables.* When asked to identify the variable responsible for an effect, such as the period of a pendulum, the bending of a rod, or a chemical reaction, people do not use adequate controls. They do not vary one potential variable at a time in a systematic fashion, keeping all else constant to provide evidence that the specific factor, and only that factor, is operating. There is less evidence on the appreciation of control as reflected in providing a basis of comparison; but, since that is a common criticism in the work of professional scientists, it is unlikely that the average person adequately appreciates the need for a baseline or a zero amount control group. There is also probably inadequate appreciation of the need for assessing reliability of measurement.

3. *Interpreting results.* Here, as might be expected from the preceding points, there is a tendency to interpret evidence as supporting the hypothesis, and the theory that led to it, although as you are now abundantly aware, one cannot prove a hypothesis or a theory. Here a confirmatory bias may take the form of (a) overvaluing positive evidence and ignoring negative evidence, (b) judging evidence to be more confirmatory than it is, and (c) failing to look first for disconfirmation. There is also a tendency to cling to a hypothesis in the face of disconfirming evidence, even to the extent of failing to recognize a superior alternative hypothesis. There seems to be an unwillingness to reject a hypothesis, as though even a poor theory were better than none. In actuality, however, that is never the choice. There are always alternative hypotheses, and theories should be modifiable. Finally, to the extent that there is evidence on this point, it appears that scientists are as prone to confirmatory interpretations as nonscientists.

SUMMARY

Making sense of experience and organizing knowledge often take the form of building informal theories and of testing hypotheses deduced from them. How one should go about this process differs from how people generally go about it. *Formal theory* serves to summarize existing knowledge in an economical and internally consistent fashion as well as to generate new testable assertions. Informal theories or *mental models* lack one or more of these properties. Two classes of model were discussed, *analogical models* and *statistical models.*

Theories and models are used to generate hypotheses. *Hypotheses* are *conditional assertions.* One can disprove a hypothesis, but one cannot prove it to be true. Two general kinds of hypotheses were considered: *identification of variables* and hypotheses about the *nature of their effect.* Where possible, hypotheses are tested by means of an experiment. A defining feature of experimentation is control. *Control* serves to provide an adequate basis of comparison and to ensure that other possible explanations and/or sources of error are ruled out. An additional consideration is *reliability of estimates of dependent variable values.*

In order to test an experimental hypothesis that the independent variable has an effect, one tests a statistical hypothesis, the *null hypothesis,* that the effect is no greater than would be expected on the basis of random variation. If the value obtained on the statistical test exceeds a criterion value, one rejects the null hypothesis and, by so doing, indirectly demonstrates the tenability of the experimental hypothesis. Failure to reject the null hypothesis implies rejection of the experimental hypothesis.

A concluding section on hypothesis testing in everyday life focused upon two differences between laboratory conditions and everyday life: the difficulty of attaining adequate control and a shift in the ultimate goal. The goal of laboratory research is the refinement of knowledge; the practical goal is achieving results. Pursuit of practical goals can lead to inadequate hypothesis testing. Evidence concerning the behavior of average people, and even scientists, on hypothesis testing tasks shows a *confirmatory bias* as reflected in (a) collection of confirmatory rather than disconfirmatory evidence; (b) inadequate use of control in testing one variable at a time, while holding all else constant; and (c) a tendency to interpret evidence as more confirmatory than it is and to cling to a defective hypothesis.

EXERCISES

1. We frequently hear something described as "the exception that proves the rule." What might that assertion mean? For each possible meaning, is it true?
2. Continuing from your evaluation of the diet and colds data given in Exercise 11 of Chapter 8, design an experiment to determine the causal role of the foods that seem to be associated with the incidence of colds. One possibility to be considered that you might have noted earlier is that there is a synergistic relation between apples and french fries such that one intensifies the mephitic effect of the other (that is, their effects are not independent of each other).
3. As a topic for class discussion propose a theory that you regard to be a good theory and justify your belief. As a contrast, identify a theory that you consider to be poor and indicate why you believe it is poor. Are there any proposed examples upon which all members of the class agreed at the end of the discussion?
4. For a simple experiment that you can conduct in class, determine the effect of variation in the recommended amount of hot and cold water upon the resultant quality of gelatin dessert. You could also do this experiment with temperature as the independent variable but that requires a reliable thermometer.
5. In a very widely studied experimental task subjects are told that a set of cards is so constituted that every card has a letter on one side and a number on the other. The task is to test the proposition that if there is an E on one side there is a 7 on the other. Four cards are displayed for test purposes: E, K, 7, 2. Which of the four cards should be turned over? Why? (For help, see the notes.[10])

   Construct another task that has exactly the same form (testing a conditional assertion) but different content and see how performance is affected by the content change. Some sample statements, to get you started, might be: if there is a snow storm, then school will be closed; if you exceed the speed limit, you will get a ticket; if you run in the hall, a monitor will stop you. You might also profitably explore counterfactual conditionals—if it is orange then it is a fish—or some more arbitrary relations, such as are illustrated in the four card problem. For each of your variant tests the material should be presented on four cards: p, $\bar{p}$, q, $\bar{q}$.
6. Complete the following exercises on models:
   (a) Find five examples of the use of an analogical model (either explicit or

implicit). State the model and evaluate its appropriateness. (Hint: disease analogies are very common as are adversarial models for determination of fact, or for the relation among parties, such as, management and labor in a labor dispute or husband and wife in a marital dispute. Contest models are implied where people are labeled "winner" or "loser".)

    (b) Find examples of statistical and structural models.

7. Criticize each of the experiments below and, where needed, redesign it to more adequately satisfy the requirements of a good experiment. (For help, consult the notes.[11])

    (a) A recently reported study (*New York Times,* Dec. 18, 1985) in Canada reports that consistent moderate beer drinkers, as a group, are healthier than wine drinkers, hard liquor drinkers, or the general population.

    (b) A study, comparing the number of deaths listed each day on the obituary page of the newspaper between cities of varying size, reported more deaths in larger cities and concluded that urban life is more stressful.

    (c) A group of sophomores at a large university were compared with respect to semester grade point average and self-rated overall satisfaction with college in relation to whether they were housed in the dormitory with one, two, or three roommates. It was found that people in triples were the least satisfied.

8. Take some question of interest to you and design an experiment to answer it. Be sure to state your hypothesis, your independent and dependent variables, and the kinds of control employed. Also consider possible outcomes of the experiment and how they might be interpreted. A possible candidate for this exercise might be your explanation of why the dog regularly stops at specific places during his nightly walk.

9. Consider the following use of a statistical model (for help, see the notes[12]).

    (a) How might you define poverty for a community in which the average yearly income is $19,436 and the standard deviation is $2,224?

    (b) In a shipment of 200 bags of apples labeled 3 lb net wt, the average bag weight is 3½ lbs, with a standard deviation of 2 oz. Are the bags accurately labeled?

    (c) The work force of a company that advertises itself to be an equal opportunity employer is composed of 20 women and 18 men. Is the advertisement correct? Would your conclusion change if you knew that the composition among hourly workers was 18 women and 12 men whereas the composition among administrative employees was 2 women and 6 men?

10. Four mental model problems follow. If you need help solving the problems, see the notes.[13]

    (a) You have two Lincoln head pennies, one atop the other with the face upright on each. Imagine rolling the top coin around the circumference of the lower until it is directly below it. Will the Lincoln head of the coin that moved be upside down and facing left or right side up and facing right, or something else?

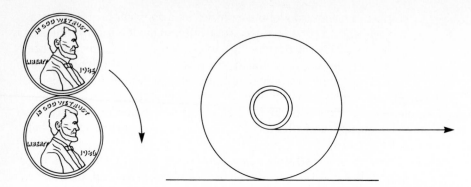

(b) Imagine pulling the string of a yo-yo to the right. In which direction does the yo-yo roll? Why? These two problems have been taken from diSessa (1983). The chapter by McCloskey on naive theories of motion in the same volume contains additional good examples, two of which are given below.

(c) A plane is flying at a constant altitude and speed in the direction shown. A metal ball is released; the plane continues in the same direction, speed, altitude. Draw the path the ball will follow from release to impact on ground, disregarding wind. Also show where the plane will be when the ball hits the ground.

(d) A metal ball is rolling along a frictionless cliff, as shown, at 50 mph. It goes over the edge. Draw its path, ignoring wind. Is this the same problem as the airplane problem?

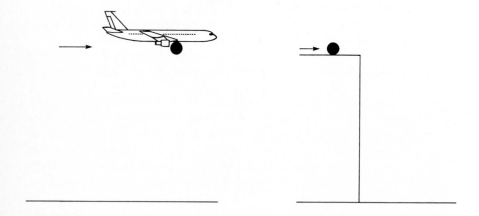

· *10* ·

Problem Solving

Your first introduction to this book included the problems of Box 1-1 followed shortly by Polya's advice on problem solving. In this chapter, the process of problem solving will, at last, be considered in greater depth. As you might expect, Polya's advice will play an important role, but before considering it, the defining properties of problem solving will be identified and classes of problems will be proposed. As will be seen repeatedly, a major step toward problem solving is a good formulation of the problem. Often the road to a good problem statement and the subsequent plan for solution is paved by a transformation of the original statement. At this point you are well practiced in looking for alternatives. That orientation is appropriate in all stages of problem solving: finding and formulating the problem, considering possible routes to solution, testing and revising them, checking the solution to see if it satisfies the requirements and if there are alternative solutions, and augmenting understanding in light of what was learned.

DEFINITION AND TAXONOMY

What Is a Problem?   Although your first reaction may be that this is a rhetorical question that need not be answered on the grounds that you recognize a problem when it is encountered, understanding of the general structure of a problem helps in finding its solution. Many definitions of the word "problem" have been proposed. Although they differ in wording, there is general agreement on the defining ingredients of a problem. A common ingredient for all definitions is the presence of a gap, a discrepancy between the existing state of affairs, the starting state, and where one wishes to be, the goal state. Moreover, that gap is one that is not readily and directly bridged. If, for example, your leg itches and you can scratch it there is no problem; if the leg is in a plaster cast, however, you have a problem. That consideration suggests an additional defining property of problems, the existence of barriers and constraints upon the course of bridging the gap. Those defining properties are represented in the general scheme of problem solving in Box 10-1. This particular pictorial scheme suggests an analogy of problem solving to finding a detour around a barrier, an early association in the study of problem solving that should not be taken too literally. The set of all possible paths to the goal, the s_i, or solutions, of Box 10-1 are called the *problem space*. In some applications a finer differentiation of solution components is made into *actions* or operations allowable under the rules and *states* resulting from their application. For this form of characterization a representation of the problem space takes the form of a *state-action tree*.[1] An example of a state-action tree for tossing a coin *n* times (a problem considered and represented in Chapter 8) is shown in Box 10-2. For any specific problem, it is often

---

BOX 10-1

A General Scheme of Problem Solving

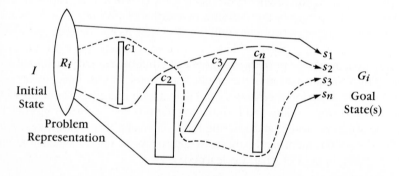

Legend: I represents the initial state. R_i, the representation of the problem, is shown as a lens to emphasize its importance in directing the solution process. It is subscripted to indicate that alternative problem representations are always possible. The c_i represent barriers and constraints that must be observed in attaining a solution. The s_i represent solution paths or strategies. They, too, are subscripted to allow for the more usual circumstance of more than one possible solution. G_i represents goal state. Again, a subscript is used to show that alternative goals are possible in some problems. For any given problem it is usually possible to create this type of depiction, called a problem space, capturing the ingredients of the specific problem.

BOX 10-2

A State-Action Tree for Coin Tossing

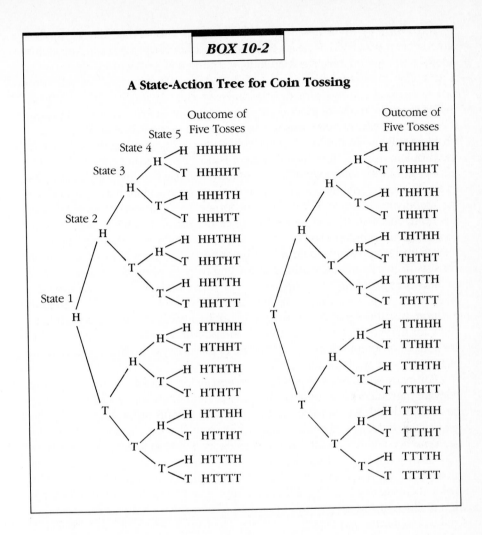

possible to draw a scheme representing the defining conditions of that particular problem. We will encounter such schemes of problem spaces in the ensuing pages. They are very helpful in clarifying the structure of the problem and in suggesting solutions. Represent a problem in this manner whenever possible.

There is an additional possible assumption that seems to be inherent in most definitions of a problem although it is rarely stated. That is an assumption that a solution exists, at least in principle, and that there is a means of attaining it. Often, for example, people create pseudoproblems for themselves by setting unrealistic goals; for example, for possessions well beyond one's means or unrealistic time frames for completing certain assignments. The creation of such pseudoproblems will be taken up in the discussion of problem formulation.

A Taxonomy of Problems.   A major first step toward problem solving has already been proposed, a clear representation of the structure of the problem. Another bit of good advice is to identify the particular problem as a member of a class of problems for which there is a solution procedure and apply the solution procedure to it. You have already had some experience with that general strategy in, for example, translating deductive arguments into standard form to evaluate them more easily. Another lesson learned in that context is also applicable to problem solving: do not focus exclusively upon content but identify the form of the problem as well. Unfortunately, there is no agreed-upon general taxonomy of problem forms (although in a narrower domain such as integral calculus, for example, there certainly are several procedures for integration as well as bases for identifying which one will be appropriate to a particular problem). The taxonomy that I shall propose derives from the problem scheme presented in Box 10-1. The simplest class of problems is one in which all the ingredients of the scheme are present and known at the outset with the result that the solution consists primarily in restructuring according to prescribed procedures. I shall call this class *problems of restructuring.* For such problems it is customarily the case that there is only one possible solution, in which case it is called a *unique solution*; but, there may be alternative solutions as well. It is always advisable to allow for that possibility. The problems and puzzles widely encountered in discussions of problem solving are members of this class, as are many problems in mathematics or symbolic logic.

For many other kinds of problems, adequate information concerning all the relevant ingredients is not known in advance, and additional information must be collected with which to refine the problem, identify constraints, clarify the goal state, or narrow down the realm of potential solution paths. *Diagnostic problems* are familiar members of this category. For diagnostic problems there may or may not be a unique solution. Again, it is generally wise to assume that more than one solution exists. To the extent that additional information is a major requisite of all such problems, an important tool in their solution is adoption of efficient and economical information-gathering techniques that are often called *information-maximizing strategies.* Mechanics, repairpersons, physicians, remedial specialists, and counselors are confronted with problems of this sort.

A third class of problems, to be discussed in the next section, consists of unstructured problems with multiple possible solutions and/or goals. Most real-world problems are of this sort. In dealing with them, one must first identify possible alternative problem formulations and courses of action and then proceed to evaluate them in relation to appropriate criteria in order to select a course to be adopted. Some members of this problem class could also be included in the category of decision making which will be discussed in the next chapter.

This is a very broad classification scheme designed to impress upon you the fact that there is no one uniform model of problem solving and no set of procedures that applies to all problems. Within whatever realm most of your problem-solving activity occurs, it will be helpful for you to classify the kinds of problems you encounter and the solutions that apply for each.[2] The discussion that follows should assist in this process by elaborating upon three problem classes identified above and some solution tools appropriate to each class.

RESTRUCTURING SELF-CONTAINED PROBLEMS

Many puzzles and problems may be characterized as exercises in restructuring of presented information in the sense that (a) the form of the desired goal is specified, (b) the starting state is given, (c) the allowable transformations are clearly stated, and (d) one has only to apply them to generate the solution. In principle, problems of this form could be solved ultimately by trial and error alone; in practice that is usually a tedious and unsatisfying approach. Some form of conceptual machine for economically cranking out a solution is desirable. Special devices for producing a solution are often called *heuristics*. One of the best-known examples of restructuring is Wertheimer's (1959) example of a little girl confronted with the task of computing the area of a parallelogram. She asked for a pair of scissors and proceeded to cut perpendicular to the troublesome, projecting side. The excised triangle was then rotated and placed at the opposite end (see Box 10-3) to create a neat rectangle, thereby transforming the novel problem to a familiar one for which she had a solution. Some additional examples of problems of restructuring are given in Box 10-3.

Consider the second problem, a code task similar to the one encountered in Box 1-1. Each letter must be replaced by a digit unique to the letter; when the substitution is correctly made, the solution has the form of a correct arithmetic sum. The first step in efficiently solving such problems is to find a good starting point. The best start is at a *point of maximum constraint,* that is, a point where the number of alternatives that can be considered is very limited. That is a good heuristic for many problems. For instance, what car to buy is constrained by how much money is available, the intended use of the vehicle, and so on. In the cryptarithmetic example, four + five = nine, it is clear that $r + e = e$ is the most constrained sum because in order for a number, n, plus some other number, m, to equal the original number, n, the second number must be zero. Therefore, $r = 0$ and the remaining nine possible digits are to be assigned to the remaining letters. At first blush, it would appear that the identical constraint appears in $o + i = i$. But, it cannot be the case that $o = 0$ because 0 has already been assigned to r. In this case, if the preceding sum ($u + v = n$) exceeded 10, then if $o = 9$, the constraint would be satisfied and as a result, one would be carried to $f + f = n$. Therefore, n must be an odd number. Nine has already been assigned, one is impossible, so there are only three possibilities to consider: three, five, and seven. From here you should be able to complete the solution. Note that there is not a unique solution to this problem but a number of possible solutions. See if you can find all of them through a more efficient procedure than trial and error. Having solved that problem continue on to the others shown. Solutions are given in the notes.[3]

BOX 10-3

Some Problems Involving Information Restructuring

A. The Parallelogram Problem

 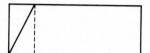

B. Cryptarithmetic or Code Tasks

		P E T E
		A T E
F OUR	CR OS S	AL L
+ F I VE	+ ROA DS	THE
N I NE	DAN GE R	TRI P E

C. Anagram Problems

LAIDISOUNS, MESRTICMY, RIDACOTINY

D. Matchstick Poblems

(1) Given six matchsticks arrange them to form equilateral triangles, one stick on a side.

(2) Convert the five square configuration below into a four square configuration by moving three match sticks.

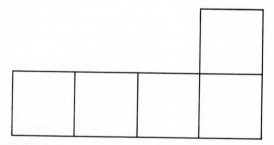

E. Tangrams

A tangram is a puzzle consisting of seven flat geometrical segments which can be arranged in a multitude of ways. The legendary invention of this puzzle is credited to an unknown Chinese man who accidentally broke a tile and then discovered that he could entertain himself by forming the pieces into the silhouettes of different objects.

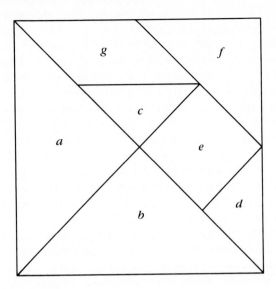

Directions:

Cut the tangram along the lines. Without overlapping the pieces, arrange them to make the shapes below. You may even want to invent your own designs.

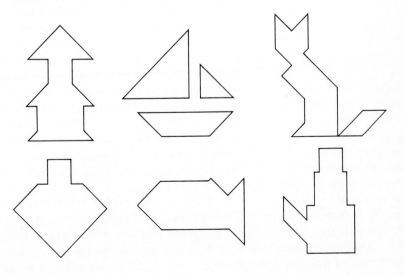

In anagram problems and other tasks requiring variation of the material presented, all the ingredients are there but in an improper arrangement. This description also applies to puzzles such as tangrams that require construction of new patterns from a set of forms, or, even, to jigsaw puzzles. As you probably know from past experience with jigsaw puzzles, there is a general strategy for dealing with them that might be considered a way of working from maximal to minimal constraint: you start with pieces sharing common colors or patterns, and it is not a bad idea to start from a corner or edge. With anagrams the parts that "go together" or points of maximum constraint are defined by our knowledge of conditional probabilities (the likelihood of one letter following another) of various letter combinations in the English language: for example, q is almost always followed by u; p is never followed by q, and so on. That aid can also be a hindrance, however, when the anagram is presented with letters in a frequent order that does not apply to the particular word. The frequency of the answer word in English also seems to play a role: common words are more easily solved.[4] Sentences in which the words are in scrambled order might be another example of this class of problems in which application of the constraint rule leads to finding the verb and working from it.

Matchstick problems[5] are a type of restructuring puzzle in which the number of squares (or other configuration) is to be changed by adding or removing matches. The guiding principle in dealing with them is to appreciate the reduction in number of matches needed through the use of shared sides. For example, to construct four isolated squares of one matchstick on a side, 16 matchsticks are required; by putting the four together in an encompassing square of two matchsticks on a side, four matchsticks can be eliminated and only 12 used. Reasoning of this sort helps in solving the problems in Box 10-4.

A widely studied class of problems of restructuring is one in which elements must be shifted by a constrained process. The Missionaries and Cannibals[6] (or Hobbits and Orcs) problem is a common example as is the Tower of Hanoi problem,[7] both of which are shown in Box 10-4. In the first problem three missionaries and three cannibals are on a small island about to be engulfed by a monsoon and must get to the mainland. They have a boat that will carry only two people at a time. The constraint is that you must never let the cannibals outnumber the missionaries because they might eat them. In the Tower of Hanoi problem, a stack of disks must be moved from one peg to another observing three constraints: (a) only one disk at a time may be moved, (b) the top disk on a peg must be moved before the lower ones, and (c) a larger disk may not be placed atop a smaller one. With two, three, or even four disks to be moved, it is not a difficult problem but as the number of disks increases, the required moves increase exponentially ($2^n - 1$); moreover, the strategy for an even number of disks differs from that for an odd number. Such problems require a plan rather than trial and error. A state-action tree for this problem is illustrated in Box 10-4. It is a good means of expressing the solution plan. Another feature of solutions to problems of this sort is that it helps to break the problem into a series of subgoals and proceed through them. These classic problems do not provide a very close analogue to the routing and sequencing problems of everyday life, such as organizing errands for minimal time and travel, routing a mail carrier or traveling salesman, and so on. They will be considered later as problems with multiple solutions.

Another puzzle class that looks complicated but yields readily to the appropriate tool might be described as *assemblage problems*. An example of some assemblage problems, along with the general form of their solution, is shown in Box 10-5. The solution form is known as a *Latin square*; it and its extended variant, the Graeco-Latin square, is used as a technique for generating constrained combinations (Fisher, 1951). You encountered an assemblage problem earlier in Exercise 8A of Chapter 1. In this problem category, the use of a matrix representation for summarizing and ordering the use of constraints materially promotes solution.

One conclusion that you should have reached in the course of doing the problems presented is that solution of this class of problems is substantially advanced by a few general tools, including: (a) a good representation of the problem space, such as a state-action tree or matrix, and (b) a strategy of working from maximum to minimum constraint. Those strategies also apply to problems encountered in studying mathematics and the physical sciences. As a final test of your increased sophistication in dealing with restructuring of self-contained problems, you might try to invent some new puzzles. Don't introduce variations on the problems covered here but try to employ the general form with new content.

Breaking Interfering Sets. One of the chief obstacles in successfully solving restructuring problems is to overcome strong interference with appropriate restructuring from what used to be described as a set, functional fixity,[8] or even ingrained habit, but is now more likely to be attributed to poor initial problem representation. You first encountered some problems of this type in Box 1-1, and should now be more sophisticated about avoiding the traps they set. Some additional problems are given in Box 10-6. The source of interference for each problem is identified, following the statement of the problem. You might want to test your understanding by trying to anticipate that discussion.

One general means of combating problems of interference from prior habits is to seek a *neutral representation* of the problem. For example, consider the problem: A man bought 100 shares of XYZ Co. at $40 a share and sold it two months later for $55 a share. Since it continued to rise, he bought it back at $60 and later sold it for $80. How much money did he make altogether? Note that the problem is identical to one in which he bought XYZ for $40 and sold it for $55 and then bought ABC for $60 and sold it for $80 but that the second problem is trivially simple. Let's do another old chestnut. A man climbs a mountain in the course of a day, camps overnight at the summit, and returns by the same route the following day. He wonders if there is one point on his return route that is

BOX 10-4

Problem Space for Two Sequential Transformation Restructuring Problems

A. State Space for the Missionaries and Cannibals Problem

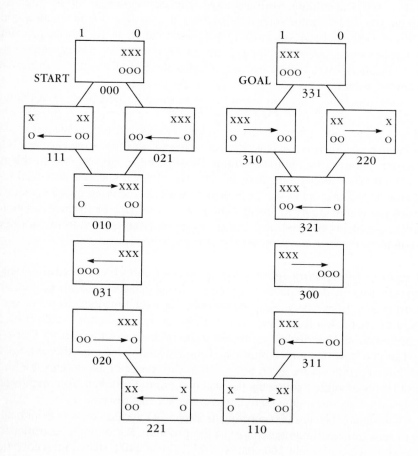

The three digit code below each state indicates the number of missionaries on the starting side, the number of cannibals on the starting side, and the location of the boat. Missionaries are indicated by an X, cannibals by a O, boat location by the head of the arrow, island by 0, and mainland by 1.

B. State Space (or State-Action Tree) for a Three Disk Tower of Hanoi Problem

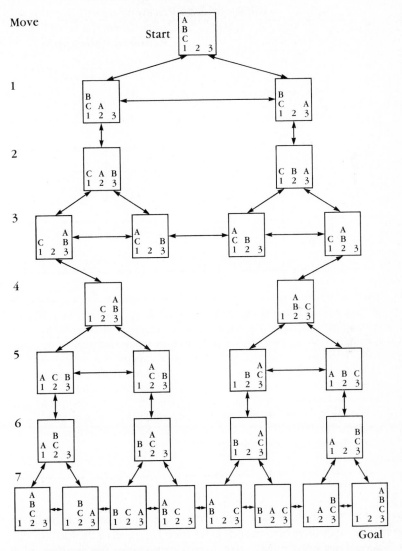

The pegs are represented by the numbers 1, 2, 3; disks in order of increasing size, by the letters A, B, C; states by squares and actions leading from one state to another by arrows. Note that each of the 27 possible states of the problem is distinguishably different from every other state.

BOX 10-5

The Latin Square and Its Application to Assemblage Problems

B. Graeco-Latin Square

A_{d2}	B_{c1}	C_{a3}	D_{b4}
D_{c3}	A_{d4}	B_{b2}	C_{a1}
C_{b1}	D_{a2}	A_{c4}	B_{d3}
B_{a4}	C_{b3}	D_{d1}	A_{c2}

A. Latin Square

B1	A3	C2
A2	C1	B3
C3	B2	A1

The Latin square is an arrangement in which each letter appears exactly once in each row and each column, always in a different position. In a Graeco-Latin square the same constraint applies to other symbols along with the constraint that any pair, triplet, and so on of symbols appears only once. Fisher advocated this device for the design of experiments in fields such as agriculture where many independent variables are dealt with in a single experiment and employing all possible combinations of them is impractical. The same constraints apply in commonly encountered puzzles involving n individuals no two of whom have the same birth place, occupation, place of residence, and so on. For this reason, entering the given information into an $n \times n$ square is a useful solution tool.

---

traversed at exactly the same clock time on the return as it was on the ascent. The answer, regardless of variations in his speed of travel or the locus or duration of occasional rest stops, must be that there is such a point. Proving that conclusion is trivially simple when the problem is recast in terms of two individuals, one ascending and one descending on the same day; there must be a point at which their paths cross. Now that the point has been made with relatively simple examples, consider how the same state of affairs may have arisen in your own experience; for example, in casting about for some person to fill a particular role did you overlook a good, likely candidate because you had pigeonholed him in some other role? Other instances arise when a replacement part or a usual ingredient is unavailable and a substitute must be found. In such instances, it helps to label what is sought in terms of its function, rather than its particular identity.

Perhaps the most frustrating illustration of the difficulty of overcoming a set arises when you have tried a potential solution, discovered that it was inadequate, but could not come up with an alternative. This state of affairs commonly arises in dealing with practical problems with multiple solutions such as writing a letter or paper, trying to smooth a sticky social situation, and so on. One useful escape device on such occasions is to leave the problem and turn to something altogether different, preferably a physical, mechanical, undemanding activity such as running, swimming, pulling weeds, or chopping wood. An alternative solution path sometimes appears at such times. This process has been called *incubation,* a term that names, rather than explains, the phenomenon.

PROBLEMS REQUIRING ADDITIONAL INFORMATION AND STRUCTURE

The problem types to be discussed here partially overlap the problems of decision making, which will be discussed in the next chapter. They differ in that the emphasis here is upon gathering and evaluating information without regard to the considerations of risk and utility. It is, perhaps, an arbitrary distinction, but efficient information gathering merits consideration in its own right.

Going Beyond the Information Given.[9]   The problems of real life are rarely self-contained and/or uniquely solved. One common recurrent problem involves selecting among nonequivalent alternatives when confronted with the need to choose a dinner entree, an article of clothing, a car, or a career. To reach a good decision in such cases, it is often necessary to obtain additional information upon which to base the decision. The procedures for combining obtained information in reaching an optimal decision will be discussed in Chapter 11. What will be considered here is efficiency in gathering information. For the purpose of discussion, let's consider the process of diagnostic problem solving. In a diagnostic problem, the determinant of some problematic state of affairs is to be identified and corrected. The problem could be malfunctioning equipment, malfunctioning physiology, or malfunctioning social relations; the general form of the problem is the same in each case. To the extent that it is a question of identifying cause, considerations of proper testing of conditional assertions and maintaining adequate control that were discussed earlier apply here as well.

The formal structure of the diagnostic problem is illustrated by the laboratory analogue[10] in Box 10-7. First, there is a *presenting state* of affairs, a TV set with no picture, a car that won't start, or in the illustration of Box 10-7, a board with all the shutters closed and no elements revealed. In each instance there are

---

BOX 10-6

Some Classic Problems of Breaking Set

O X X 0 X X 0 X X X X X 0 X X 0 X X 0 X X

1. Imagine that the letters above are beads on a string; your task is to regularize the pattern without unstringing, restringing, or breaking the thread (Bulbrook, 1932). This can be solved by violating the implicit assumption that no bead is to be destroyed; for example, it can be solved by breaking and removing 3 of the center X beads.

2. A person goes to the river with three jars having the ounce capacities listed. How can he get the desired amount of water?

There are 3 jars	A	B	C	Desired Amount
	17	7	4	2
	22	9	3	7
	30	19	3	5
	20	7	5	3
	28	7	5	11
	17	7	3	4

These are the Luchins water jar problems, the first five of which can be solved by a formula of $A - B - 2C$. Typically after people discover this solution they continue to use it although the last problem may be solved more directly by $B - C$.

3. Two strings hang from the ceiling in a large, bare room. The strings are too far apart to allow you to seize one while holding the other (that is, tie them directly). How can the task be accomplished when there is nothing else in the room but a book of matches, a small screwdriver, and a few pieces of cotton?

The typical approach here is to think of lengthening (either ones reach, for example, with a coat hanger, or the strings), but that is not possible. The solution is to attach a weight to one of the strings and to set it swinging like a pendulum so that you can reach it as it swings close. The only object adequate to create a pendulum is the screwdriver which, because you think of it as a tool for driving screws (or prying off lids) is not readily conceived as a pendulum bob.

4. Create a candle holder so that you can place and light the candle. Available for the purpose are a candle, a box of wood table matches, and a box of thumbtacks. The difficulty here is to create a holder. Although the matchbox will serve admirably for the purpose it tends not to be thought of because it is seen as a container of matches. The usual solution sought is

to have the solver remove the matches, fasten the candle to the top of the box with melted wax, fasten the inside of the box to the wall with thumb-tacks, and slide the outerbox—with candle attached—over it. Voilà!

5. The most prolific early deviser of problems was Duncker (1945), some of whose problems are given below.
   (a) The X-ray problem: How can you apply X-rays, high intensities of which destroy normal tissue, to destroy a stomach cancer?
   (b) The 13 problem: why are all six-place numbers of the form 276,276, 591,591, or, more generally, $n_i n_j n_k, n_i n_j n_k$ divisible by 13?

   For the X-ray problem, people tend to impose the unnecessary constraint of only a single source of rays. One satisfactory solution is obtained by having several sources, no one of which emits rays intense enough to destroy normal tissue, and focusing all of them upon the tumor, which can be destroyed by their combined intensities.

   For the 13 problem, most people tend to divide all the possible numbers by 13, to apply the customary habit for division. Calling attention to the comma, or reminding the subject of the principle of a common divisor is not of much help, whereas the suggestion that 1,001 is a common divisor does help. Can you see why it should? Having seen it, can you find another number or numbers that all such six-digit strings should also be divisible by?

6. Now that you are used to looking for the immediate tendency that inter-feres with reaching a solution, here is an old unicursal puzzle from 1897 to solve. Trace it without taking your pencil from the paper or retracing any line.

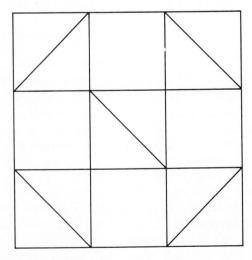

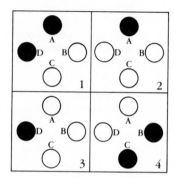

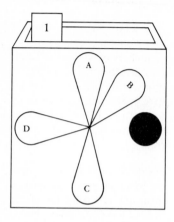

BOX 10-7

Some Diagnostic Problems

A. Schematic of problem board with four shutters (Shutter B open) and an answer sheet with four patterns of four binary elements each. (Since the circle at B is black, only Pattern 4 can be the right answer. In this instance gambling is rewarded.)

B. The schematic in A displays the basic structure of the task: One of n patterns is concealed in a board with a shutter over each circle. Given

only a finite number of *possible solutions* or possible causes of the state of affairs, and they can be enumerated at the outset; for the illustration in Box 10-7, the possible solutions are the presented array. These possible solutions may serve as hypotheses for testing. For instance, reasons why the car won't start may include a dead battery, wet spark plugs, poor connection in the starter, and automatic choke problems. You then proceed to gather information with which to eliminate inappropriate alternatives in a procedure of hypothesis testing of the sort considered in Chapter 9. Tests differ with respect to cost in time and money, risk, and the likelihood of leading to a solution. The effect of those additional complications will not be considered here. As an example, in the case of a TV with no picture, checking whether it is plugged in, whether it is turned on, and whether there is power, are all such simple tests that they could be

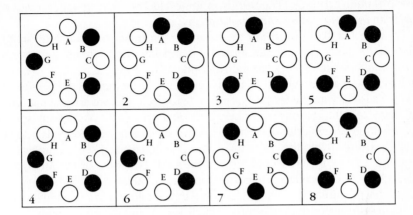

that one of the eight patterns above is concealed, map out a strategy to identify it with a minimum number of shutter openings.

C. Here is another task with the same structure. Suppose I have a cup containing eight marbles: four red, two blue, one green, and one white, your job is to determine the color of a marble drawn randomly by asking a series of questions about the color that can be answered with yes or no (is it color R, B, G, W?) using one color on each question. It can always be solved in three questions; but, depending upon the correspondence of your guess and the color drawn, it might actually be solved in one or two questions. Draw a tree diagram (state-space) model of the strategy for this task and see if you can determine why 1.75 questions will be required on the average. The answer can be found in the notes section.[11] (After Rubinstein & Pfeiffer, 1980)

conducted first even though they may be unlikely to solve the problem. One way of quantifying various information-getting procedures for purposes of comparing their effectiveness is in terms of expected informational outcome (see Chapter 8). The optimal information-gathering procedure is one that maximizes expected informational outcome.

In the illustrative example in Box 10-7 possible information-getting moves, shutter openings, differ only with respect to their expected informational outcome (that is, there is no associated differential cost or difficulty). Opening shutters B or C, for instance, are unique diagnostics for pattern four, but if pattern four is not the answer then three possibilities remain to be considered. Opening shutter B after having tried C, or vice versa, yields no information at all. Opening shutter A or D, on the other hand, will eliminate half the possible answers, regardless of what is found. A choice of both of them will guarantee an answer in two shutter openings. The use of an information-gathering approach of this sort is an *information-maximizing strategy.*

A more familiar example of the use of an information-maximizing strategy arises in the game Twenty Questions. In that game, the goal is to arrive at the correct answer (known only to the respondent) by asking at most 20 questions each of which can be answered only by yes or no. The winner is the person who gets the answer with the fewest questions. If, for example, we are playing "guess the state," all 20 questions could be wasted in a procedure of guessing specific states without finding the correct one. A more efficient procedure is a logical procedure—to divide the alternatives into two equal-sized sets by alphabet or geography. Does it start with a letter from A–M? Is it west of the Mississippi? Through such a procedure the correct one of the 50 states could be identified in 6 or fewer questions. The general strategy for information maximizing is to partition the universe into two equally likely sets: A, and its complement, $\bar{A}$. Such a strategy is sometimes called a *split half strategy.* In view of the fact that uncertainty is greatest when alternatives are equally likely, it should be clear that forming complementary sets of equally likely alternatives is maximally informative because it results in the greatest reduction in uncertainty (see Chapter 8). A medical application of an information-maximizing strategy for the diagnosis of acute chest pain is given in Box 11-5.

As might be expected, people are not very efficient information processors.[12] They tend to gather too much information and to gather useless information, such as information that confirms a preexisting hypothesis or information that verifies an established solution. Errors of this sort suggest that information may provide reassurance as well as edification. If so, errors of gathering redundant information may not be the result of inadequate processing. A more serious error is failure to identify all the alternatives with the result that one may fail to attain a solution or prematurely fix upon an inferior or inadequate solution. In recent years computer diagnostic programs have been devised; they often do as well as, or better than, trained human diagnosticians.

A final example of going beyond the information given concerns extrapolation and interpolation based upon existing evidence as, for example, predicting some future state of a set of values on the basis of current information. Tests of functional relations are often of this form. For example, if the function (see Box 8-7) relating study time to obtained grade appears to be leveling off at three hours, extrapolation of the function would lead to a prediction that five hours of study would produce no significant improvement in grade. In evaluating any function, it is always a good strategy to ask how it will behave at limiting values (for example 0 and ∞).

Problems with Multiple Solutions. As suggested earlier, most meaningful problems encountered are problems with many possible solutions. In fact, seeking a unique solution might interfere with an expeditious solution of the problem. Thus, if papers are blowing off your desk and scattering about, putting them in a drawer, putting a weight on top of them, or closing the window, all constitute acceptable solutions to the problem. That example is transparent and trivial. That people do not appreciate the possibility of multiple solutions is, however, easily demonstrated, for example, by asking a young person "What do you want to be when you are older?" The answer is usually quite specific, suggesting that the individual has divided the universe of possible careers into the occupation in question and everything else without first generating an array of acceptable alternatives; in effect, foreclosing one of the most important decisions of his or her life. A superior approach would be a strategy of working from constraints in a 20-question-like procedure: for example, what is clearly ruled out? In this example, of course, additional information would also be helpful.

One obvious conclusion from this simple preliminary discussion of problems with multiple solutions is that one should never settle on the first solution that comes to mind; but, rather, generate and compare additional possible solutions from the standpoint of a variety of criteria. This might seem, at first glance, to be exhortation to obsessive deliberation for no practical purpose. To see why it is not, let's consider two of the many classes of problems with multiple solutions: resource allocation and instituting change.

1. Resource allocation. Problems of resource allocation, where the resource may be time, energy, affection, money, or whatever else, are ubiquitous: for example, stocking a tool chest, a refrigerator, or a travel wardrobe. What makes resource allocation problems difficult is that (a) resources are limited, as a result of which allocation to one need entails denial of another, and (b) any allocation plan has consequences for the future. While these two considerations might not be too pressing in planning the weekly food budget, they assume greater importance when planning institutional, business, or governmental budgets, in the accumulation of inventories, and so on. Another class of resource allocation problems has to do with routing problems ranging from sequential ordering of daily chores to routing of deliveries, or of service or sales personnel by large industries. In view of the many factors to be taken into account, the number of possible solutions to be generated, and the variety of criteria that can be applied in selecting a solution, it is not surprising that computers are increasingly employed to deal with allocation and routing problems. In their absence a need arises for a technique to simplify the problem. Tools for simplification will be discussed in the next section.

2. Instituting change. Problems of instituting change may take a variety of forms from augmenting storage space, or remediation of personal inadequacies, to decreasing conflicts among individuals or nations, urban redevelopment, and so on. As was true for problems of resource allocation, despite great variety among instances in complexity and potential impact, there are some common structural similarities. Whether the problem is trivial or profound, the first step takes the form of identifying key features—causes of the problem and candidates for change. The next step involves planning of change. The important new ingredient here is *anticipation of consequences* because one inescapable result of change is that each potential solution introduces a new set of problems. To support this assertion, let's look at some examples of social change. The rise of the automobile, for example, led to greater ease of travel, to the building of roads, to the movement of people and industry away from the cities with consequent urban decay, increase in the importance of oil, decline of the railroads, separation of the wage earner from the family, and so on. A comparable litany of consequences could be enumerated for many less profound changes, for example, in construction techniques, modes of dress, and so on. The relevance of this feature for problem solving is in highlighting the importance of anticipating potential consequences and their impact in planning a solution. In many instances, the anticipation of consequences may require a more advanced level of knowledge than is currently available. In these instances, also, there may be a number of potential criteria for evaluating possible solutions. Conceivably, no solution will be adjudged best with respect to all criteria. Although dealing with problems of this magnitude far exceeds the scope of this chapter, some tools for simpler problems are clearly applicable, such as working out from greatest constraints, efficient information gathering, and so on.

In ranging so broadly over the realm of problems, from relatively trivial puzzles for diversion to some of the profound problems of our time, I have tried to emphasize the importance of reducing the enormous variety of problems to manageable size by identifying problem classes on the basis of problem structure and applicable solution procedures. The solution procedures have been slighted in this discussion. I will consider them in the next section within the framework of the stages of the solution process.

STAGES OF THE SOLUTION PROCESS

Analysis of the stages of problem solving has, for some reason, been a continuing popular activity. Many analyses have been offered,[13] most of them quite similar to the Polya analysis with which you are already familiar. I will offer an analysis that adds an additional step at each end of the Polya sequence. I offer it not as the definitive analysis, or in the belief that an analysis into stages offers any special contribution to the understanding of problem solving, but by way of providing a useful heuristic—a checklist of considerations to assist you through the problem solving process. The five stages of the process are problem finding, stating the problem, planning a solution, executing the plan, evaluating the solution, and consolidating gains. Let's consider each in turn.

Problem Finding.   Your first reaction may be, "Why go looking for problems? They find me soon enough." While it is true that many problems are thrust upon us by others and by outside circumstances, these are not the exclusive source of problems, nor should they be. Some of the most interesting and absorbing problems are challenges we set for ourselves. One reason for emphasizing the importance of problem finding is because of its central role in one's attitude as a thinker. There can be no problem solving without a problem; there can be no thinking without something to think about; there can be no ongoing learning for someone who already knows all there is to know. The hazards of unwarranted certainty (Chapter 8), of untested assumptions (Chapter 9), and of incompletely elaborated alternatives or unanticipated consequences have already been noted. An openness to doubt and discrepancy and a readiness to raise additional questions or withhold conclusion are good safeguards against those hazards. Problem finding, as will be seen in Chapter 12, is also a wellspring of creativity.

Instances of problem finding abound. They are the sort of thing that inspire people to smite their brow and exclaim, "Why didn't I think of that!" One of the most frequently cited examples is the story of Sir Alexander Fleming and the discovery of penicillin. He noticed that some of his bacterial culture plates had developed mold and that the cultures in those plates had died. Colleagues assured him that mold was a fairly common problem, the implication being he should throw out the moldy cultures and start over. Instead, he asked himself why mold should so invariably kill bacteria, thereby appreciating the more general importance of an antibacterial agent. The rest, as they say, is history.

How does one go about finding problems? The most general answer to that question is to allow uncertainty to arise: by questioning assumptions, habitual modes of behavior, initial perceptions, cherished beliefs—in short, by openness to alternatives. There are many good problems waiting to be found.

Stating the Problem.   A major step in the solution of any problem is to state the problem well. What constitutes a good problem statement? A good statement of the problem identifies all the relevant ingredients as well as whatever may be missing and should be supplied. Depending upon the specifics of the problem at issue, you need to specify (a) the initial state (the symptom, the givens, what's wrong), (b) the goal state and criterion for its solution or conditions for stopping, and (c) what is available and/or constraint imposing in the process of going from the initial to the goal state (available data, allowed operations, evaluation of their adequacy). Having attained an adequate statement of the problem one is in a better position to classify the nature of the problem and possible avenues of its solution.

Poor problem solvers hasten through this stage or omit it altogether, to their ultimate regret. For example, many students when faced with a "word problem" may free associate to salient words and procedures dictated by them with the result that they solve some other problem if they attain a solution at all. You have all been cautioned to "read the problem carefully." A popular current translation of that good advice is "achieve an accurate problem representation," that is, identify the key ingredients and the form of their relation in order to classify the kind of problem you are dealing with. Earlier in this chapter you encountered several problems whose reformulation hastened their solution, such as those in Box 10-6 or the area of a parallelogram. You were also warned that "interfering set" might better be described as poor problem representation and urged to detach from the immediate phrasing to find a more neutral means of problem encoding. Obtaining a good problem representation is probably the most important step for problem solving. It should lead to a plan for the solution.

With respect to the problems of real life, a clear statement of the problem is often elusive and problems are capable of alternative representations. A simple example of this state of affairs arises in the common battle between parents and adolescents over the untidy bedroom. A quick and obvious representation would treat the messy room as the initial state and a neat room as the goal. That, however, is a superficial and temporary rendering. A longer range goal from the parents' point of view might be expressed in terms of habits and values, for example, instilling valuation of orderliness and self-discipline in maintaining it as the goal state. For the child, on the other hand, the goal might be keeping peace with the parents, perhaps as a subgoal to some other goal such as working to a reward. ("If you get me a . . . I promise to clean my room.") Here the same objective start and goal state are subject to different characterizations that would lead to different solution paths.

In the example above, the goal state was more subject to alternative characterization than the initial state. That is not always the case. In therapy, for example, a very common outcome is a discovery by the patient that the problem to be dealt with is not the initial presenting problem but something quite different. Newlywed couples, for example, often find holiday times and deciding whose family to spend them with to be occasions for dispute. The immediate occasion of disagreement in this instance might be where to go; but, when viewed in the context of other occasions of disagreement, a more comprehensive problem of establishing a new identity as a couple and satisfactory loosening of parental demands upon each member as a child may emerge. Another common example involves bringing in a child for problem behavior which later turns out to be the child's response to parental conflict. Another common occasion of problem clarification in counseling involves the setting of unrealistic goals, often couched in such terms as "I must have . . .," "I can't live without . . .," and so on. In many instances the stated goal state is, in fact, an inaccurate representation or a surrogate for a different goal.[14]

Real-life problems in arriving at a clear statement of the problems are not exclusively associated with, or antecedents of, therapy, they arise all the time in many contexts. A common symptom of that state of affairs is the recognition that something is wrong—that involved parties are unhappy or in disagreement, and, perhaps, that positions have become rigidly defined as a result of the state of affairs (see Fisher, 1983). On these occasions of disharmony in work or social contexts, the person who comes up with an incisive description of the problem is often hailed for his or her superior wisdom. It is also often the case that identification of acceptable solution paths follows more or less directly from a correct analysis of the problem. Time devoted to a clear statement of the problem is never time wasted.

Planning a Solution.   The value of planning (for example, in outlining a communication, or in scheduling activities) is surely familiar. A solution plan, like other plans, identifies possible avenues to a solution and anticipates their associated requirements and consequences in order to evaluate and select from among them the most appropriate according to the selection criterion. As was true for stating the problem, rarely if ever is there only one possible solution path; rather, the number and complexity of alternative solutions will vary with the particular problem. There is, however, one tool that is invariably helpful at this step: displaying all the alternatives. You have already encountered some graphic means such as state-action trees for graphic representation of the problem space (see Boxes 10-2 and 10-4). For a well-formulated problem, such devices can lead directly to a solution. In poorly formulated problems, a good display of all alternative solution paths can clarify the structure of the problem and lead to a revised representation of the problem. It also guarantees that an optimal solution will not be overlooked.

Although exhaustive enumeration of all possible alternative solution paths is a procedure that will always work in principle, it may be tedious and time consuming to apply in practice. There are a number of devices for simplifying the process of generating and evaluating alternative solutions, some of which are described here.

One efficient device for pruning state-action trees is to classify some of the nodes and branches into *equivalent classes*. For example, in exhaustive enumeration of the coin toss problem of Box 10-2, you soon notice that it is a symmetric tree in which, for example, 3H 1T is functionally equivalent to 1H 3T so that you need expand only half of the tree with the result that you automatically have its mirror image by simply reversing H and T.

Another device for simplifying a problem for purposes of solution planning is to *break it down into component problems* to be solved in sequence. The attainment of long-range life goals clearly proceeds in this fashion. In becoming a surgeon, the subgoals of undergraduate school, medical school, internship, and residency must be attained in order to establish a practice. At a much simpler level, even word problems profit from this approach. John sells apples at the market. In the first three hours he made $6 selling them at 15¢ each. After that he cut the price to 10¢ and sold twice as many apples. How much did he earn that day? One subgoal is to compute how many apples he sold; to determine that you need to know how many he sold in the morning, x, in order to compute how many he sold later, $2x$ to obtain the total receipt of $14.

Two less organized and riskier means of breaking the problem down are *hill-climbing* and *means-end analysis*; both proceed by reducing the distance between your present state and the goal. Of the two processes, means-end analysis is the more powerful. Hill-climbing is so named because in getting about unfamiliar terrain, attaining a higher vantage point provides a broader view of the immediate surroundings. We use hill-climbing automatically in such tasks as adjusting the TV picture or tuning the radio (if it gets better keep going, if worse, back up), or in retrieving a trapped kitten (proceed in the direction in which the meowing gets louder). The strategy in hill-climbing is to do whatever decreases the distance to the goal. In some cases this process can lead to a dead end.

Means-ends analysis proceeds in three steps: (a) list all the differences between the current state and the goal (for example, a table you bought for your typewriter is too low and too narrow and the color is wrong); (b) find an operator to reduce the difference (putting a small rug under the table will raise the height, putting a larger piece of wood on top can change both height and depth); and (c) compare conditions for applying the operator with the current state in order to find a difference (by putting the typewriter on the table and trying to type you discovered that the typewriter projects out too far and is too low for comfortable typing). For the examples given, both hill-climbing and means-ends analysis are adequate strategies for solving the problem. There is, however, no guarantee that this will always be the case. Where there is a detour, literal or figurative, these methods may not lead to success.

One common strategy with which you are probably familiar is *working backwards.* You most likely have applied it in a math course by looking up the answer in the back of the book and determining how it was arrived at. Formal proofs, as in geometry, constitute another example of types of problems that readily yield to working backwards. Another variant of working backwards as applied to real-world problems is to analyze the goal in detail and to proceed backwards in terms of the constraints imposed by the analysis (as contrasted with proceeding from the constraints of the immediate start situation). For example, one good procedure in evaluating possible career choices is to get temporary jobs that will enable you to sample as many features of the goal state as possible to see if you like it—working at a newspaper to evaluate journalism or at a hospital to see if you like medicine.

Another strategy, touched on in Chapters 6 and 7, is the use of *contradiction.* In other words, assume that what you are to prove is untrue and show that the assumption leads to a contradiction. In a multiple-choice test this might take the form of showing that some alternatives cannot be correct which leads to identifying the most appropriate answer through a process of elimination. Or, in evaluating arguments, assume that the conclusion is false. Would a false conclusion be possible given the supporting premises offered? It should not be if the argument is sound.

One of the most powerful strategies of all in formulating a solution plan is to identify the present problem as an instance of a class of problems, preferably a class for which you have a solution (as, for example, the area of the parallelogram problem). Good formal instruction always attempts to lead the student in this direction by emphasizing the defining features of the problem class and by reminding the student that specific problems are particular examples of a larger class. The device of requiring the student to devise his or her own examples is another procedure to induce identification of defining features of the class, as is looking for an appropriate model and conceptual tools. You should develop a general orientation so that (a) you can express the problem in an alternative, more neutral form to better emphasize its basic structure, and (b) you can ask yourself if you have encountered a problem of that form before. If the problem is not like one encountered before, ask yourself if it is similar to one of past experience and, if so, can it be altered to fit the model of the similar problem? By focusing upon a problem class, in contrast to the details of a specific problem, you increase the likelihood of finding a solution and expanding your understanding, while at the same time avoiding the hazards of an interfering set or fixing upon an unsatisfactory solution. Polya's suggestions in Box 1-3 are as good a summary of the strategy of placing the problem in the context of a class of similar problems as you are likely to find. Go back and review it. You might also return to Box 10-3 to see how all the problems of a subclass are related and how all the subclasses are similar with respect to a general strategy for restructuring. You might also review Chapter 2 to see how attention and encoding apply in problem representation and solution planning.

Executing the Plan, Evaluating the Solution, and Consolidating Gains. Most discussions of the problem solving process give little space to the final stages, thereby implying that they are more automatic or of lesser importance. Because that is definitely not the case, a few words are in order about each of the final stages.

For a carefully considered and appropriate solution plan, execution may run off smoothly and effortlessly. More often it is the case that one or more hitches are encountered in translating the plan into action. The first check, of course, is to determine if the plan was executed properly: Is there a mistake in addition? Did I skip a step? If the plan was executed as stated, then the problem is in the plan and it is necessary to go back and revise it. There is often a great deal of shifting back and forth from execution to planning as anyone who has ever written a computer program or a term paper is all too well aware. Debugging and revision are important parts of the problem-solving process as well.

Once a solution has been attained it is not the end of the process. It is always a good idea to check the solution to determine if it is, in fact, a solution that satisfies all the criteria for solution. Here a combination of the methods of contradiction and working backwards may help in evaluation. Given a solution, is it a unique solution or are there other possible solutions some of which may be more satisfactory? As emphasized earlier, for many problems there are likely to be a number of solutions available. Terminating the process with the first solution obtained may yield a less satisfactory solution (as anyone who has accepted a substitute in place of a particular commodity may have discovered). For example, in the typewriter table problem discussed in means-ends analysis, raising the legs may make it more difficult to solve the problem of narrowness because the table extension must be at the same level as the existing top.

Finally, having obtained a solution and determined that it is not just satisfactory but, even, optimal it is a very good idea to go back and consider the problem from the standpoint of augmenting or revising your classification of problem types and solution strategies. In order to convert success into understanding, it helps to revise your framework in light of experience with the completed problem. Possibly you can refine the conceptual tools that led to a solution or, even, improve and expand your model for the general problem class. Thus, you discover again, the lessons of Chapter 1: there is a difference between success and understanding. Success is resolution of the immediate problem. Understanding of how success was attained and its generality to related problems can promote future success on similar problems if your tools and the classification of them are revised accordingly. The journal entry of the impulsive student in Box 4-1 is a good example of how deliberate scrutiny of present success can promote understanding as well as the likelihood of future successes.

SUMMARY

A problem was defined as a situation in which there is a discrepancy between present state and desired goal and where there are constraints upon the routes to solution. A taxonomy of classes of problems based upon the form of the problem was proposed and some classic problems were presented in the context of it. The taxonomy consisted of (a) *self-contained problems of restructuring* or transforming presented material (tangrams, anagrams, codes and other such puzzles); (b) *problems requiring additional information* (diagnosis or extrapolation problems that generally involve hypothesis testing); and (c) *problems with multiple solutions.* One suggested tool for all these problems (but especially the first class) is identification of constraints and a process of starting with maximally constrained components and working outward to lesser constraints.

Some more general suggestions for effective problem solving were offered within the context of a six-step systematic procedure for problem solving:

1. Problem finding is a process of identifying problems and understanding why they are problems. It can promote creativity as well as detachment.
2. Stating the problem well is a crucial step in identifying and relating all the relevant elements (and in avoiding becoming bogged down in irrelevancies).
3. Planning a solution is not a unitary stage in the sense that it may necessitate revision, not only of the initial plan, but of the problem representation as well. Planning generally involves outlining possible solutions and intervening states, identifying equivalent classes and identification of components and subgoals. Some additional useful tools for planning include *hill-climbing, means-ends analysis, working backwards,* and *contradiction.*

4. Executing the plan. Here, too, difficulties may arise that necessitate a return to an earlier stage.
5. Evaluating the solution is necessary to determine that the solution satisfies the criteria and that it is optimal, if not unique.
6. Consolidation of gains is a final step in understanding the successful solution in relation to existing knowledge in order to refine your knowledge as well as your armamentarium of solution tools.

EXERCISES

1. Because word problems tend to be more difficult for most students, several are given below. For each one, instead of just racing off to solve it, go systematically through the six steps described at the end of the summary section. You will see that, for most of the problems, representation is an important stage and that there are alternative representations. Write down the alternative representations before proceeding. Answers are given in the notes if you need help solving the problems.[15]
   (a) The sum of the ages of a husband and wife is 98 years. He is twice as old as she was when he was the age she is today. What are their ages? (After Rubinstein & Pfeiffer, 1980).
   (b) A group of children returning from their Halloween trick-or-treating assemble to count their goodies. Mary has three times as many pieces of candy as do Nora and Aaron together. Dan has twice as many pieces as Bob. Mary has 1½ times as many pieces as Dan. Aaron and Dan together have as many pieces as Nora has, plus twice the number Bob has. Altogether, Bob, Dan, Mary, Nora, and Aaron have 28 pieces of candy. How many pieces of candy does each child have?
   (c) Dick who is 5 foot 4 inches tall is 6 inches taller than one of two boys, Tom and Harry, and 2 inches taller than the other. Harry is taller than Tom. What are the heights of Tom and Harry?
   (d) Five boys (Jack, Dick, Tom, Bob, John) go to five different schools in the same town: North, South, East, West and Central. To which school does each boy go?
   Tom has never been inside Central.
   Jack does not go to North, South, or Central.
   Bob does not go to North or Central.
   Dick goes to West.
   (e) There are 3 boxes and inside each of them are two smaller boxes, each of which contains 4 even smaller boxes. How many boxes are there altogether?
2. Here are some anagrams to unscramble. If you need help, see the notes.[16]
   (a) F R O G I L Y
   (b) S H I R T O C

(c) I F E P A G R U T R

(d) T I E T I N S T U

(e) I N L O A N A T

(f) Take a nice long word of which you create several alternative anagrams to give to your friends and determine their order of difficulty. On the basis of the evidence you collect formulate a hypothesis to account for your results and test it with a new anagram set developed for that purpose.

3. Take some problem of a recent experience that was difficult for you to solve and analyze the source of your difficulty. Now, in light of this chapter, go through it systematically in order to profit from your experience and see if there is, perhaps, an even better solution (or representation, or plan) than the one you came up with originally.

4. Find the pattern in each of the series below in order to supply the missing item. For help, see the notes.[17]

(a) 47 44 37 41 38 __ 35 32 25 29

(b) 15AA 20BB 22CD 27DG 29EK ____ ____

(c) 6 18 9 8 24 12 11 33 __

(d) 2 4 3 5 4 6 5 _

(e) D W E V F U G T _ _ I R

(f) Once again, create some series completion problems of your own with which to test some hypotheses about what makes a series problem difficult. You might want to try some series created by transforming geometric figures. Into what category of the taxonomy proposed in this chapter do series completion problems fall?

5. Devise a plan for testing, in the minimum number of weighings on a pan balance, two dozen coins to determine which one of them is short weighted. Suppose, instead, that you knew only that one was lighter or heavier, but not which. How would that change your plan? (For help, see the notes.[18])

6. Take a problem, preferably a genuine personal problem, that has been bothering you and to which you do not yet have a solution. Apply the methods outlined in this chapter. If it has more than one solution, try to generate all the possible solutions and evaluate them with respect to a criterion to determine which solution would be the best. Note that there might be alternative criteria that you could use; if so, work your problem for each of them.

7. I proposed a classification scheme for problems that is only one of many possible such schemes. For another taxonomy couched in software terms, see Lenat (1984, September). Consider the kinds of problems that you frequently encounter and create a classification scheme to encompass them. On what basis are you classifying? Structure of problem? content? solution tool? If you are taking one or more courses in which you do problems as a regular assignment, you might want to construct a scheme for each course and compare schemes across courses. You might also compare it to a classification you come up with for work-related problems, problems in getting along with roommates, or some other domain of interest to you. Is there

any domain for which the six-step systematic procedure outlined in this chapter is not helpful?

8. Historically, earlier theoretical discussions of the problem-solving process included a stage of incubation (that is, a time during which one did not address the problem). Many anecdotes by famous people on solving important problems have suggested that a period of incubation is helpful. Consider why this may be the case. List as many alternative hypotheses as you can generate. You might also consider how those hypotheses could be tested as well as whether some of them have implications for a deliberate tool to employ (that is, an alternative means of achieving the same effect as incubation).

9. Is there some class of problem that is especially difficult for you? If so, try to determine the source(s) of difficulty and devise a procedure for eliminating or reducing it. Alternatively, you might want to consider a class of problems that you are very good at. Outline what you do that might account for your skill and consider how other kinds of problems could be related to this class at which you excel.

10. Summarize the problem taxonomy presented in this chapter in the form of a table or of a hierarchy or tree-structure. Are there any problem forms omitted? As one way of answering that problem take all possible combinations of problem conditions, such as unique vs multiple solution or requisite information supplied vs unsupplied. For each cell of the resulting matrix provide (a) an example of a problem of that class and (b) a solution tool for that class. This taxonomy is based upon problem form. Was that the basis for the classes you created in answer to Exercise 7?

11. Express some general solution tools, or strategies, as a computer program, or generate a state space for a four-disk Tower of Hanoi problem.

12. Create some examples of your own, preferably instances you experienced, of poorly formulated problems where the major obstacle to a solution was getting a good representation of the problem. Can you distill from that experience some rules for devising a good problem representation?

· *11* ·

Decision and Choice

The topic of decision and choice is in many respects a special case of problem solving and is to be dealt with by the procedures for problem solving. The topic is treated separately in order to emphasize a distinguishing feature—that there rarely is a unique or even ideal solution. More often there are many alternative courses of action, each with its associated assets and liabilities. In this respect, decision making is a judgment task and criterion is an important ingredient. One of the crucial features of decision making is the need to avoid hasty decisions in order to identify all the alternatives and their associated assets and liabilities. To this end, techniques for adequate formulation and representation of the problem become especially important. As might be expected from the similarity to judgment, a matrix relating alternatives and states of the world is a useful representational tool.

"Decisions! Decisions!" is the punch line of a great many jokes, all of which derive from the difficulty many people have in making decisions. There are so many alternatives, so many possible criteria for evaluating them, that it never is the case that, from among the many alternatives, one clearly stands out as best. Part of the difficulty in choosing is an awareness that choosing A with all its advantages and disadvantages also means foregoing B with its different set of advantages and disadvantages. We can't, as all of us have been told repeatedly, have our cake and eat it, too. If ever there was a need for a conceptual machine that could generate an answer at the turn of a crank, that need arises in the area of decision and choice. There are, you may be relieved to know, models and machines for decision making; but you should be forewarned that, although decision making has been an active theoretical area for many years, its products are not altogether satisfactory in application. In part the dissatisfaction results from the need for simplifying underlying assumptions that are not supported by the evidence of experience. Dissatisfaction also arises from failure of the theories to capture some of the dimensions that are so troubling in real life. With that precaution we now look at some practical devices for decision making before addressing its theoretical treatments.

SOME SIMPLE HEURISTICS

The Balance Sheet.   A well-known procedure for dealing with a two-choice, yes or no situation was described by Benjamin Franklin in a letter to Joseph Priestley in 1772.[1] The method, which he called "moral algebra," consists in dividing a sheet of paper lengthwise, labeling one half *pro* and the other half *con*. Over a period of time you list all the assets and liabilities you can think of. In deciding you eliminate a factor in one column by one or more in the opposite column that exactly counterbalance it. The side left with the greater weight wins. The method has some desirable properties: it assembles all the considerations systematically and attempts at a rational procedure to evaluate them. For important decisions like buying a new car, taking a year off from college, marrying a particular individual, the decision should not be made impulsively. But there are also some severe limitations. One limitation is that only two alternatives can be considered; often the choice involves more than two alternatives. A second limitation is nicely illustrated by a story told me by a New York colleague about a job offer from a university in another city. He followed Benjamin Franklin's method. Under *pro* he wrote "It's not NY" and, under *con* he wrote "It's not NY," then he threw away the paper. Clearly, those two identical arguments could have been detailed and would translate differently: lower costs, less hectic pace, less danger vs fewer cultural activities, loss of old friends, and so on. Nevertheless, it illustrates the problem of dealing with incommensurables. One answer to this problem is to devise a common metric.

The Choice Matrix.   This method reduces the alternatives to be considered and the bases for their evaluation to an orderly array such as is shown in Box 11-1. Suppose you are choosing a vacation site, a house or apartment, a graduate school, or a new car. Let's use the new car example for which yearly information is readily available. You decide what kind of car you want (a four-door sedan, a convertible, a van, a subcompact) and then see what is available in that category. Among the factors you might want to consider are price, repair record, quality of ride, safety features, gas mileage, and room. These factors constitute the rows, the available alternatives the columns, resulting in a matrix.

Now, what do you put in the matrix? As a first approximation you might decide whether each car is acceptable with respect to each factor and enter $+$ if it is or enter $-$ if it is not. On the basis of the resulting matrix of $+$ and $-$ entries you can rule out the alternative(s) with the most minus ratings (although you should note that doing so assumes equal importance of each of the row factors—a consideration to which we'll return). In comparing the columns with

---

BOX 11-1

Two Hypothetical Decision Matrices for Choice of a Two-Door Compact Under $9,000

Factor	GM	Ford	Nissan	Toyota
Cost	+	+	+	+
Crash Protection	+			+
Engine Size	+	+		
Brakes	+	+	+	+
Handling	+		+	+
Room	+	−		+
Gauges	−		+	+
Fuel Economy	−		+	
Reliability	−		+	+

A. A matrix of + and − where + means better than average and − means worse; blank means average or no information available.

Factor	GM	Ford	Nissan	Toyota	Weighting
Cost	2	4	8	6	8
Crash Protection	8	5	5	7	2
Engine Size	5	7	5	5	4
Brakes	6	8	9	9	4
Handling	7	4	7	7	6
Room	7	4	7	9	3
Gauges	0	3	9	7	2
Fuel Economy	4	7	9	7	7
Reliability	2	5	9	9	8
Mean	4.56	5.22	7.56	7.33	
Weighted Mean	4.16	5.30	7.86	6.95	
Standard Dev.	2.74 (2.30)	1.72 (1.53)	1.67 (1.39)	1.41 (1.10)	

B. A matrix (hypothetical) of weightings on a ten-point scale and subjective weighting of importance of each factor in the decision. Simple means, weighted means, and standard deviations for (weighted) and unweighted ratings are also provided.

each other, wherever one column is at least as good as the other on all bases of evaluation and is better on at least one, then that column dominates its comparison which may be eliminated as a result. Some columns may be eliminated but you may be left with a number of others that are not directly comparable. What do you do then? Even counting the total number of pluses and choosing the car with the most may not be completely satisfactory because not all bases for evaluation are equally important and "acceptable" or "unacceptable" is a coarse rating.

A more discriminating procedure might be to assign a rating on a scale of zero (the worst) to ten (the greatest) to each car on each evaluative point. Now you have a matrix of numbers. Can those numbers be reduced to one value for each car? If you remember the statistical models of Chapter 8 you know that a mean is the best single value with which to characterize a distribution. Since the divisor is the same for all cars a simple sum will do. On the basis of these mean ratings you now have a basis for selecting a first choice, a second choice, and so on. You could also compute a standard deviation to evaluate how consistently the mean rating is approximated by each of the bases for evaluation. In other words, a car with a large standard deviation is high on some factors and low on others; a car with a low standard deviation is more consistent in rating on each of the component factors.

In the event that the resulting values do not seem completely satisfactory, there is still a more refined procedure available, one which does not give equal weighting to all judgmental factors, as did the previous methods, but assigns them weightings in accordance to their importance for you. Suppose, for example, that cost is a major consideration and roominess a minor one; perhaps cost is three times as important as room and repair record is twice as important as room. You would assign a weighting to each row factor, multiply the ranking assigned on each factor by its appropriate weight and compute a new weighted mean for each car. That weighted mean is the best single value you can obtain to characterize a choice (or, more generally, any variable). Admittedly, it took some time and effort to arrive at these numbers, but that is usually quite trivial in relation to the importance of the choice to be made. Moreover, the resulting clarification has led to a more refined analysis of the alternatives, one that may lead to a different choice than the cruder procedures considered earlier.

The apparent precision of the method is in part illusory, however, when the nature of the metric used is considered: the ratings are arbitrary values on a scale that may not even have equal intervals (that is, psychologically, the scale difference between ratings one through three may be greater than the scale difference between ratings four through six although arithmetically they are equivalent); the weightings are equally subjective/arbitrary. As we shall see shortly, this problem of lack of an objective basis for assigning numbers is one that plagues the field of decision theory, but it is inherent to the nature of the phenomena dealt with and, therefore, an irresolvable problem. In some instances, as for example, in deciding upon a value to bid on a house, you might want to assign dollar values to each of the evaluative factors you consider: How much is a big backyard with a flat sunny area for a garden worth? an extra bath? an attached garage? a beautiful shade tree? Again, you arrive at a figure with a defensible rationale behind it, but how do you measure in dollars the pleasure of sitting under a big tree on a sunny afternoon?

The difficulty encountered here is one of treating subjective or psychological scales as equivalent to more familiar objective scales, such as those for length, weight, time. The problem of scaling such seemingly imponderable quantities is one which has generated a lot of technical literature.[2] Suffice it to say that there are procedures for creating measuring scales. Some of the simpler techniques have been used in the examples above, for example, rank ordering or rating which you first encountered in Chapter 5. They are useful in rendering a problem amenable to conceptual machinery available for that class of problem. You may, however, be a bit more cautious in interpreting the exact numerical value of the solution in view of the nature of the scale on which it was obtained. One way to deal with this problem is to make several decision matrices: for example, one with the maximum ratings you could possibly assign to each car on each factor and a second with the minimal ratings you could assign. You might also want to try several different weightings of factor importance on these matrices. If the outcome of the new matrices yields the same decision, you can feel more confident about your decision. If the outcome changes, you might want to do a more careful comparison among the top contenders. To familiarize yourself with the process of constructing a matrix and assigning values for ratings and weightings, you should practice with some choices of interest to you, perhaps something so trivial as selecting a brand of cereal or something so important as selecting a graduate school or a career.

Perhaps the last exercise has left you with the impression that the available conceptual machinery for choice is cumbersome and time consuming. The methods for choice outlined are designed to yield an optimal choice with respect to a variety of criteria. In some instances where (a) the number of alternatives is very large and (b) the need for optimal choice is not so pressing (as, perhaps, in choosing a temporary employee, or selecting a relatively inexpensive product for some need), it is adequate merely to find an alternative that meets your needs. In those instances the method of *satisficing* is sufficient (see Hayes, 1981). To apply that method a minimal acceptable value of rating on each of the dimensions of judgment is set and the first alternative that satisfies all of them is selected. Any column with all +s in Box 11-1, for example, would suffice.

DECISION MAKING UNDER CONDITIONS OF RISK AND UNCERTAINTY

Making a choice where relevant information is available is relatively simple in comparison to those situations in which there is inherent uncertainty or substantial costs of making a poor decision, or where a course of action must be planned in which the choice of later steps is contingent upon the outcome of earlier ones and where the outcome cannot be known in advance. To choose a simple example, you are planning a trip with an itinerary of places to visit and a schedule of activities for each place. The activities contemplated are often constrained in the sense that they are available only on certain days and hours or they require other conditions for optimal enjoyment (no crowding or traffic, good weather). Under those conditions additional quantities must be included in the decision computations: for uncertainty, the probability of each of a number of possible states (for example, of good weather or poor weather) and for risk, the costs or rewards associated with each possible state or outcome. Much of the conceptual machinery derives from models for games of chance where probabilities and outcome values can be assigned; technically, this is referred to as conditions of *risk*. In real-life applications those values cannot be known but must be estimated, often with little ground for estimation. The term *uncertainty* characterizes situations where exact probability values cannot be assigned to alternative outcomes. Nevertheless, it is helpful to examine procedures for the laboratory analogue of games of chance to see how the procedures operate.

Maximizing Expected Value.   Suppose you are rolling a pair of fair dice and can win $1 each time you correctly predict the sum of the two faces. What number should you choose? Box 11-2 shows all possible outcomes of a roll of two dice. Clearly, two or 12 are the least likely outcomes since there is only one way out of 36 that each can occur; seven, on the other hand, is the most likely outcome since there are six different ways it can occur. Of all the 11 possible outcomes, since seven is the most likely over a long number of plays, you stand to win the most by betting seven every time.

Suppose that the person with whom you are playing is too smart to offer you the chance to win $1 at no cost to you and says that it will cost you 20¢ every time the number you bet fails to appear. Should you play that game? To answer this question you might want to make use of what you learned about problem solving and represent the problem space. For this problem a simple decision tree will serve. There are only two possible outcomes: you win $1 or you lose 20¢. The probability of winning is the relative frequency with which the number you bet appears: for seven, for example, it is six out of 36 or $p = \frac{1}{6}$; the probability of losing is $q = (1 - p) = \frac{5}{6}$. From that information how do you assign a single number to the bet? The answer is to compute an expected value by multiplying each outcome by its probability. The computation of expected value was introduced in Chapter 8.

$$EV = p\,(\text{winnings}) + q\,(\text{loss}) = \frac{1}{6}(\$1) + \frac{5}{6}(-20\text{¢}) = 0$$

Should you choose to bet seven each time over a long number of plays you stand to win nothing and neither does your opponent. It is a fair game. If, on

---

BOX 11-2

A Model for the Dice Game

Die II	Die I					
	1	2	3	4	5	6
1	2	3	4	5	6	7
2	3	4	5	6	7	8
3	4	5	6	7	8	9
4	5	6	7	8	9	10
5	6	7	8	9	10	11
6	7	8	9	10	11	12

All possible outcomes of a roll of two dice. Assuming they are fair each of the 36 cells is equally likely, $p = \frac{1}{36}$. The relative frequency of each total is:

$$2, p(2) = \frac{1}{36} \qquad 12, p(12) = \frac{1}{36}$$
$$3, p(3) = \frac{2}{36} \qquad 11, p(11) = \frac{2}{36}$$
$$4, p(4) = \frac{3}{36} \qquad 10, p(10) = \frac{3}{36}$$
$$5, p(5) = \frac{4}{36} \qquad 9, p(9) = \frac{4}{36}$$
$$6, p(6) = \frac{5}{36} \qquad 8, p(8) = \frac{5}{36}$$
$$7, p(7) = \frac{6}{36}$$

To compute the Expected Value (EV) of any given bet on an outcome o_i, where W = winning and C = cost of the wager:

$$EV(o_i) = p(o_i)(W) + (1 - p(o_i))(-C)$$

---

the other hand, you bet any other number then you stand to lose: for example, 10¢ per play if you bet ten or four. Compute an expected value for the other bets to see how much you would lose. As an additional test of your command of the model for this game, compute what you would be willing to pay (risk) on the alternative bets in a fair game.[3]

Criteria for Decision Under Uncertainty.   In decision making under conditions of risk, you should construct a matrix which relates possible alternative choices and states of the world in order to evaluate outcomes. An expected value is obtained by weighting the gain or loss associated with each outcome by its likelihood of occurrence. A good criterion for selecting among alternatives is to maximize the expected value. In decision making under uncertainty as, for instance, in investing in the stock market, planning a vacation, or a career, this simple model is not directly applicable. Here, because possible gains or losses frequently cannot be measured, it is traditional to speak of the *utility* of possible outcomes: a subjective measure of the state of satisfaction associated with each outcome. The value assigned to utilities may be positive or negative relative to whether they fall above or below some point of indifference, for instance, how much you believe you would enjoy becoming a physician, an architect, or a plumber. Several decision criteria are possible[4] because the likelihood associated with various states of nature cannot be known (for example, the demand for various occupations or the hazards associated with each). Two extreme decision criteria and two intermediate ones are presented in Box 11-3. The maximin criterion focuses upon the worst possible outcome associated with each choice and selects the least terrible from among them. The maximax criterion, by contrast, focuses upon the best possible outcome for each alternative and chooses the best among them. The remaining criteria take both extremes into account.

The Maximin Criterion. This is a conservative criterion for guarding against the worst possible outcome. In earlier writings it was called *minimax* to indicate that one minimizes maximum loss. As an example of it, suppose that having bought the new car, you considered saving the cost of insurance and that you live in a state permitting that option. The expected values for the two options between which you must decide are shown in Box 11-3 with the probability of an accident indicated by p and the probability that the accident is limited to vehicular damage represented by r. What values are to be assigned to p and r? Now you understand what is meant by decision under uncertainty. You might assume that had an individual been driving for a long time, the relative frequency of accidents could be taken as a basis for estimating p, but clearly there is no guarantee to even the safest driver in the world that he or she will not be involved in a very serious accident. How then can expected values be computed? Instead of resorting to arbitrary values—or to a range of them to yield a family of *EV* estimates—the very useful strategy of setting bounds on the function by computing its minimal and maximal values can be adopted. The minimal cost clearly occurs when $p = 0$, no accident of any sort occurs. In that case you would have no expense if you had not invested in insurance or only the cost of the policy if you had. If, on the other hand, you had an accident then your maximum expense with insurance would be the cost of the policy, plus the cost of whatever deductible you had selected, whereas your maximum cost without insurance coverage could run into thousands of dollars. Even though the probability of astronomical expense might be very low, it is always greater than zero under conditions of uncertainty. Where great risks are possible, therefore, it makes sense to guard against them by a choice of a maximin decision rule. Insurance companies exist because of prudent application of the maximin criterion. Some other occasions

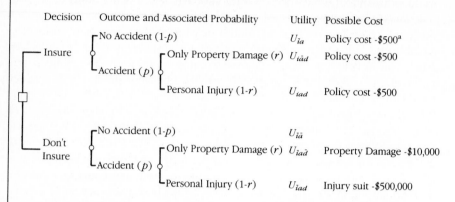

BOX 11-3

Comparison of Criteria for an Auto Insurance Decision

Decision	Outcome and Associated Probability	Utility	Possible Cost
Insure	No Accident (1-p)	$U_{i\bar{a}}$	Policy cost -$500[a]
	Accident (p) — Only Property Damage (r)	$U_{i\hat{a}\bar{d}}$	Policy cost -$500
	Accident (p) — Personal Injury (1-r)	U_{iad}	Policy cost -$500
Don't Insure	No Accident (1-p)	$U_{\bar{i}\bar{a}}$	
	Accident (p) — Only Property Damage (r)	$U_{\bar{i}a\bar{d}}$	Property Damage -$10,000
	Accident (p) — Personal Injury (1-r)	$U_{\bar{i}ad}$	Injury suit -$500,000

A. A decision tree for insuring or not insuring a vehicle with some possible associated costs. [a] is the minimal loss, [b] the maximum gain. In the case of a decision to insure, the same value is associated with each possible outcome. Insuring leads to the lowest maximum loss whereas not insuring leads to the highest maximum gain (0 in this example).

$$EV_{ins.} = (1 - p)U_{i\bar{a}} + p(r U_{ia\bar{d}} + (1 - r)U_{iad})$$
$$EV_{no\ ins.} = (1 - p)U_{\bar{i}\bar{a}} + p(r U_{\bar{i}a\bar{d}} + (1 - r)U_{\bar{i}ad})$$

Where: p is the probability of an accident
r is the probability that only property damage occurs
u_{ijk} is the associated utility

of applying that rule might involve avoiding high, wet, open areas in a thunderstorm; avoiding raw shellfish from waters where there is pollution; or avoiding cigarettes, alcohol, and other addictive substances. Given the last example, you might begin to suspect that adherence to a maximin criterion substantially reduces the excitement of living.

The Maximax Criterion. For adherents of excitement the *maximax* decision rule is a natural choice. It, too, requires computation of maximum and minimum values for each course of action and then choosing the one with the *maximum possible gain.* An obvious example of the use of this decision rule arises in playing the lottery. In the New York State lottery, for example, the player selects six numbers each of which may be any number between 1–44. The probability of selecting all six numbers is $p = (1/(^{44}\!/_6))$ (where the denominator

In subscripts: $i = i$ for insurance; $\bar{i}$ no insurance
$j = a$ for accident; $\bar{a}$ no accident
$k = d$ for personal injury, $\bar{d}$ for no personal injury

The expected value for each decision is shown on the facing page. The value of p for which the two expected values are equal would define a point of indifference.

Payoff Matrix

	No Accident	Damage to Property	Personal Injury	Max.	Min.
Insure	− $500	− $500	− $500	− $500	− $500[a]
Don't	0	− $10,000	− $500,000	0[b]	− $500,000

Regret Matrix

	No Accident	Property	Personal	Max Regret
Insure	500	0	0	500
Don't	0	$9,500	$499,500	$499,500

B. Above are payoff and regret matrixes on the basis of which decisions could be made. Regret is defined by the difference between the particular value and the maximum in that column. In the above payoff matrix, [a] shows the minimum loss and [b] the maximum gain. This regret matrix measures regret directly in dollars, which is not the usual procedure.

is the number of ways of selecting a specific six from 44 numbers), about one in seven million. If the ticket cost $1 and the jackpot is less than seven million dollars then, by expected value standards, it is not a fair game and you ought not to throw your money away on a lotto ticket. Nevertheless, in comparison to the no-play alternative for which $EV(\text{max}) = EV(\text{min}) = 0$, the prospect of an $EV(\text{max})$ of even a million or less against an $EV(\text{min}) = -\$1$ frequently leads to defiance of the odds. Daredevils who risk their lives for fame and fortune, or heroic persons who defy great dangers, may be characterized as applying the maximax rule.

Other Criteria. Is there no happy medium between the anxious dullness of maximin and the risky thrills of maximax? Of course there is. One general but arbitrary solution, the *Hurwicz strategy* (Hurwicz, 1953), is shown in Box 11-4.

BOX 11-4

Payoff and Regret Matrixes for Purchase of a Winter Coat

Let's consider another problem to illustrate decision criteria. Suppose you are buying a winter coat and are considering three quite different alternatives that are about equivalent in initial cost. The options are (a) a traditional wool coat, (b) a down coat, or (c) a vinyl coat. Each has its advantages for a particular kind of weather. The features of winter weather that enter into this decision are windy, wet, and warm spells. The payoff matrix and regret matrix for this decision might have subjective values as shown below. The best choice in each criterion column is indicated by an asterisk.

Payoff Matrix

	Windy	Wet	Warm	Max.	Min.	Hurwicz Strategy[†]
Wool	8	2	1	8	1*	5.2
Down	10	2	−2	10	−2	5.2
Vinyl	12	5	−4	12*	−4	5.6*

Regret Matrix[††]

	Windy	Wet	Warm	Max. Regret
Wool	4	3	0	4
Down	2	3	3	3*
Vinyl	0	0	5	5

[†]The utility values computed for the Hurwicz strategy with $w = .6$ are obtained as follows:

$$EV_{wool} = .6(8) + .4(1) = 5.2$$
$$EV_{vinyl} = .6(12) + .4(-4) = 5.6$$

[††]The utility values in the initial payoff values are arbitrary. The regret matrix values are obtained by getting the difference between a given cell entry and the maximum of the column. For the first column, $4 = 12 - 8$, $2 = 12 - 10$, $0 = 12 - 12$. In the third column the highest utility is $+1$.

It assigns a weighting factor, w, between 0 and 1.0 to the maximum for each alternative and its complement, $(1 - w)$, to the minimum for each alternative: at $w = 0$ the Hurwicz strategy reduces to the maximin rule whereas at $w = 1.0$ it reduces to the maximax rule. A sample computation is shown in Box 11-4. A more intuitively appealing rule is the rule of *minimizing maximum regret* (see Hayes, 1981).

One of the most difficult aspects of decision making lies in the fact that there is no control group for oneself. There is no way of knowing what might have happened had another alternative been chosen. The discrepancy between the best of what might have been and the actual outcome provides a natural basis for defining a new psychological quantity, *regret.* Assuming that you could quantify regret, and why not since we have already talked about quantifying utility and other intangibles in arriving at a decision, a criterion aimed at minimizing maximum regret seems reasonable to consider. To apply the minimizing of maximum regret decision rule a regret matrix is generated by computing regret for each possible outcome, where regret is defined as the difference between the outcome you actually got and the maximum value you could have gotten had you chosen a different alternative. The option that yields the *lowest row maximum* on the regret matrix is the option that satisfies the minimax regret rule. Application of the minimax regret rule and comparison of the alternative decision rules is illustrated in Box 11-4.

Cost Benefit Analysis.   Another possible criterion for choice among alternative courses of action is the one first described, maximizing expected value. That criterion, under conditions of risk, uncertainty, and difficulty in estimating values to be fed into the equation, is embodied in a procedure called *cost benefit analysis.* As in computation of an expected value, all possible alternative courses of action and their possible outcomes are listed and both a probability and a utility value assigned to each outcome. Desirable outcomes with positive utilities are labeled *benefits* while undesirable outcomes, including the cost of producing a positive outcome, are labeled *costs.* The best choice, in principle, is the alternative that produces the greatest benefit at the lowest cost. That is so self-evident and obvious it seems pretentious to assign it a fancy name. The reason for considering cost benefit analysis is to emphasize that, although the model is straightforward, its application is not. In real life it is often difficult to envision all the alternatives that need to be considered, to assign probabilities to them, and to measure costs and benefits accurately. Case histories in support of potential problems are abundantly available. Some may recall the swine flu epidemic scare of 1976. President Ford had to decide whether to initiate a costly mass inoculation program to prevent what might have been an even more costly loss (in terms of human lives and productivity time lost to illness) in the event there was an epidemic. He chose the inoculation program (essentially a maximin solution). It turned out to be a poor solution because the epidemic never materialized and because the inoculations had some grave, unanticipated side effects such as Guillain-Barré syndrome. Another example can be found in cities which have chosen to specialize in gambling as a local industry but have encountered unanticipated costs and problems as a result.

DEALING WITH COMPLICATIONS

Given the difficulties in applying cost benefit analyses, are we to conclude that the benefit of such analysis is not worth the cost in time and effort plus the risk of error? Or are there some ways to hedge our "expected value" bets? In answer to the second question, there are two procedures for dealing with some of the weaknesses of the system: decision trees and sensitivity analysis.

Decision Trees.   One hazard already noted is incomplete analysis of alternative courses of action and their possible outcomes. Another, not mentioned, is recognition of dependencies among outcomes, that is, that some outcomes are contingent upon others. An excellent device for representing such states of affairs is the *decision tree,* an example of which is shown in Box 11-5. That the example is drawn from medicine is not accidental, for this form of analysis is increasingly recommended in medicine as a basis for treatment decisions. The decision rule described uses a threshold value (see Pauker and Kassirer, 1980), or indifference point, p_O, at which the expected values of treatment and no treatment are equal, that is, at p_O EV(treat) = EV(no treat). Thus, if the probability that some medical condition requiring treatment, p_a, exceeds the threshold value ($p_a > p_O$), treatment is recommended. The value of p_O may also be expressed as the ratio of cost of treatment to cost plus benefit. These equations are also given in Box 11-5.

The theoretical rationale of Box 11-5 might appear a bit daunting. How can appropriate probability values be assigned to each of the branches? Since probability is typically defined in terms of relative frequency of occurrence it is, in principle, possible to assign values. In fact, the theoretical decision tree provides a good framework for empirical research. The product of one such study is shown in Box 11-6. Here the decision tree is presented in the form of a flow diagram that starts at the top with a patient appearing in the emergency room and filters down through a sequence of binary tests to identify the likely presence or absence of myocardial infarction (MI).[5] The data on which the tree is based were collected at Yale-New Haven Hospital in 1977. A prospective study done with 468 patients at two Boston hospitals in 1980–1981 showed the decision tree to be as accurate as physicians' judgments. When the tree was used in conjunction with physicians' judgments, specificity of diagnosis improved significantly. The finding that a decision procedure formalized for computer application does as well as or better than human judgment is not unusual. These models utilize what is useful in the human procedure while filtering out all the sources of random

---

BOX 11-5

A Decision Tree and Expected Values for Treatment vs No Treatment

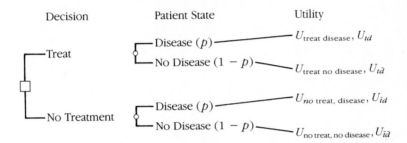

The decision tree shows two therapeutic choices for patients who either have or do not have a given disease. The square node is a decision point; the circular nodes denote a chance happening.

The expected value, *EV*, of each course of action:

$$EV_{\text{treat}} = (p)U_{td} + (1 - p)U_{t\bar{d}}$$
$$EV_{\text{no treat}} = (p)U_{\bar{t}d} + (1 - p)U_{\bar{t}\bar{d}}$$

One should choose the course of action with the higher expected value. Where the expected values of treatment and no treatment are equal, an indifference point, or threshold, exists. Using the *EV* equations above to solve for the value of p_0 where:

$$EV_{\text{treat}} = EV_{\text{no treat}}, pU_{td} + (1 - p)U_{t\bar{d}} = pU_{\bar{t}d} + (1 - p)U_{\bar{t}\bar{d}} \text{ yields}$$
$$p_0 = U_{\bar{t}\bar{d}} - U_{t\bar{d}}/(U_{td} - U_{\bar{t}d} + U_{\bar{t}\bar{d}} - U_{t\bar{d}})$$

This threshold value can also be defined in terms of costs and benefits of treating the disease as:

$$p_0 = C/(B + C) \quad \text{where} \quad B = U_{td} - U_{\bar{t}d} \text{ and } C = U_{\bar{t}\bar{d}} - U_{t\bar{d}}$$

(After Pauker & Kassirer, 1975)

---

variation to which a human is subject, such as how much time is available for the task, competing time demands, preceding cases judged, and so on. The clear implication of these findings is that it is useful to formalize decision and choice procedures for repeated decisions, especially when establishing cutoff values for eliminating unlikely alternatives from further consideration. One example is processing applications for admission to academic institutions.[6]

BOX 11-6

Computer-Derived Decision Tree for the Classification of Patients with Acute Chest Pain

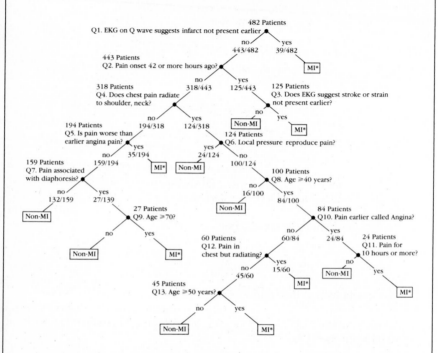

Computer-Derived Decision Tree for the Classification of Patients with Acute Chest Pain. Each of the 14 letters (A through N) identifies a terminal branch of the tree. For any given patient, start with the first question regarding ST-segment elevation and then trace the patient through the relevant subsequent questions until a terminal branch is reached. In the Yale–New Haven Hospital sample, seven terminal branches (C, D, H, I, K, M, and N) contained all 60 patients with acute myocardial infarction as well as 28 patients with unstable angina and 43 patients with other ultimate diagnoses. ER denotes emergency room, EKG—electrocardiogram, and MI—myocardial infarction. (After Goldman *et al.*, 1982)

While you may never be confronted with repeated decisions such as selecting candidates or making diagnoses and thus, in no position to complete a decision tree to the detail of Box 11-6, the decision tree is still a useful device. It serves to emphasize the importance of foreseeing a sequence of actions and allowing for contingencies associated with each. It is also advisable in developing a plan to include tests of its adequacy so that you can recognize when a plan is not working in time to revise it or drop it in favor of another alternative. To better appreciate these possibilities, set up a decision tree for some project such as a camping trip allowing for contingencies such as poor weather or mosquito invasions, along with the means of confronting these contingencies.

Sensitivity Analysis.   If you did the above exercise you may have discovered that after having completed the tree, you found many branches leading to regret or even to a decision to abandon the plan. Should that deter you from starting in the first place? Obviously, the answer depends in large part on the probabilities of the undesirable contingencies and the costs associated with them, none of which can be known in advance. A good procedure for dealing with these questions is *sensitivity analysis* (see Anderson, 1980). It is accomplished by setting a range of values: the maximum and minimum probability values and maximum and minimum utilities associated with each outcome, and computing *EV*s over the ranges of values thus produced. If the plan and decision outcomes are not affected by the range of variations, that is if the same conclusion is reached over a wide range of values, you can choose it with confidence; if not, you may need more information to narrow the range of possible values, or, possibly, more branches to the decision tree.

This general procedure of plugging in maximum and minimum values to determine limits, or a range within which expected values will fall, has been invoked several times in this chapter as well as in the last one. It is a useful tool for exploring the behavior of any model or any mathematical function. If you are now taking a course or dealing with some enterprise that exposes you to mathematical equations, try it and see how it enhances your understanding of the system described by the equation.

PROBLEMS OF APPLYING DECISION MODELS

Difficulties in applying conceptual machinery for decision making have been touched upon throughout the chapter. It is time to examine them in more detail. To the extent that the models identify component processes, such as elaborating alternatives, foreseeing contingencies, evaluating costs and benefits, and assessing probabilities, they do help to make a complex process more systematic. Difficulties arise in assigning values and applying equations. Although complete, accurate information on probabilities and utilities as well as perfect rationality in setting the decision criterion can be assumed in principle, in practice that is almost never the case. Now, however, perhaps you can better appreciate the task of those in government and business responsible for planning. They must anticipate possible future developments, such as wars, economic depressions, floods, droughts, population declines, blackouts, inflation, change in immigration patterns, and new modes of transport and develop means of dealing with them within the constraints of a limited resource pool. It is understandable why large sums of money are invested in getting information (from census data to CIA reports) on which to base estimates. But, it is the nature of uncertainty and risk that they cannot be eliminated or even estimated accurately. The average person has limited information sources at best. What to do? The advice in the remainder of this chapter takes the form of warning you about some of the decision errors to which even experts seem prone in order that you may guard against them.

There is extensive and interesting literature[7] on the systematic errors made in evaluating utilities and assessing probabilities. Only a few of the hazards of assigning probabilities will be considered here. For the most part, people—even trained statisticians—do poorly at the task of estimating probability. Errors can be attributed to (a) poor models of chance phenomena (hence, the earlier emphasis on the importance of learning some probability and statistics), (b) biasing of estimates by immediate conditions, and (c) failure to adjust estimates in light of later evidence.

Inadequate Models of Chance.   Consider the outcome of ten successive tosses of a coin, where p(heads) $= p$(tails) $= .50$. Which of the two outcomes below is more likely to be observed?

H   H   H   H   H   H   H   H   H   H

H   H   T   T   T   H   T   H   H   T

If you thought that the second sequence was more likely than the first you are not alone, but you and everyone else are wrong. While it is certainly true that the likelihood of observing five heads and five tails in any order greatly exceeds the likelihood of ten heads, which can be realized in only one order (see Box 8-6 or 9-6), that was not the question. The probability of any unique sequence of 10 tosses is $(\frac{1}{2})^{10} = \frac{1}{1024}$, and the first sequence has the same probability as the second, or any other sequence of the 1024 possible sequences. Most persons dispute the inescapable truth of that statement on grounds of "the law of averages" or what is known as the *gambler's fallacy*. It is a belief that where alternative outcomes with independent probability ($p = 1 - q$) can occur, after each successive outcome of one the other becomes more likely. For example, after a week of cloudy days the sun must come out, or after five girls have been born to a pair of parents the sixth child must be a boy. For *independent probabilities* the probabilities remain the same however long the string. For nonindependent or *contingent probabilities* the prediction should go in the opposite direction: for example, another cloudy day is more likely than a sunny one given a continuing weather system, or another girl is more likely given the same parents and the father's probabilities of contributing an X chromosome. (The Appendix on Probability discusses independent vs contingent probabilities.)

Another common error is insensitivity to base rate information (see Tversky and Kahneman, 1974). Suppose a friend phones to ask your identification of an itchy rash. It could be a contact dermatitis, such as poison ivy or poison oak, food allergy, or anthrax. In the absence of any other information, you should not pursue the third possibility because its relative frequency of occurrence is much lower than that of the other two. Nevertheless many people automatically assume the worst possible diagnosis.

Some additional errors that an understanding of statistics should help to combat are (a) a tendency to predict greater consistency than is in fact consonant with what we know about normal variability and (b) a tendency to generalize on the basis of very small and/or unrepresentative samples: for example, the Republicans are sure to win the election, everyone on my block is voting Republican. (The discussion of sampling in Chapter 6 defined "representative.")

Biasing of Estimation by Immediate Circumstances. One form of biasing is called *availability bias* (see Tversky and Kahneman, 1974). The term refers to a tendency to assign higher probabilities to events that come quickly to mind—possibly because they are more dramatic or are widely covered in the press—than to less colorful events. For example, it has been shown that people tend to overestimate the incidence of cancer, motor vehicle accidents, or nuclear explosions as a cause of death while underestimating the incidence of more commonplace conditions, such as emphysema or diabetes. Estimates also seem to be affected by the recency of occurrence and press coverage of the event in quesiton, for example, estimates of the likelihood of an air crash or grizzley bear attack increase after an incident has been reported.

Another source of bias has been called *anchoring bias* (see Tversky & Kahneman, 1974). The term refers to a well-substantiated tendency for an initial estimate to influence subsequent revisions of it. For example, if you were asked about some state of affairs on which accurate information is available but unknown to you, such as the number of Asian immigrants per year entering the U.S., the number of murders per year in Peoria, the incidence of triplet births, if your initial estimate errs in one direction or another (too high or too low) subsequent corrections will continue to err in the same direction. In fact, even when people are asked to estimate a value range in which the true value has a 98% probability of falling, their range includes the true value only 25–40% of the time. Thus, given any bias, such as an availability bias, it is unlikely to be adequately corrected due to anchoring bias. The moral of this evidence is to beware of overconfidence in judgments derived from ignorance (a warning given earlier in Chapter 7).

Inadequate Correction of Estimates. In constructing a probability model in the absence of any information, we often assume independent probabilities and take the relative frequency of occurrence in the population as a best estimate of the probability of the event. For instance, since the incidence of Tay-Sachs disease in the U.S. is low, we would assign a low probability of Tay-Sachs to any newborn. But there is information that incidence of this disease is much greater in Jews of Eastern European origin than in the population at large. Thus, given that one or both parents are Eastern European Jews or have an ancestor who is, conditional probabilities derived from the relative frequency of Tay-Sachs births in that particular population provide a more accurate estimate. The prediction can be further refined by use of genetic screening or from information that the parents have produced a Tay-Sachs child in the past. Given that one child has been born with the disease, it is possible to revise the prior probability estimate through the use of Bayes' theorem.[8] Because the use of Bayes' theorem is a difficult and confusing subject, it will not be treated here except to note that people do not revise prior estimates nearly as much as they should. In the case of this example, the birth of one Tay-Sachs child makes it certain that one or both parents has the genes for the disease. Thus, the likelihood of a second child with the same disease is high.

The use of Bayes' theorem is common in industrial applications, such as inferring whether the shipment is defective from observing the incidence of damaged parts in a sample drawn from a large order of parts. By adjusting the prior probability estimate after each successive part is sampled, probability estimates on which to base a decision about accepting or rejecting the shipment stabilize quickly (see Bross, 1953). Use in everyday life, on the other hand, is almost nonexistent. Evidence of our inadequate adjustment of estimates in light of incoming data, coupled with anchoring bias, suggests that we cling to erroneous or inaccurate judgments far more than we should.[9] We have seen in the last chapter that inflexible thinking makes problem solving more difficult, now we have seen that it makes for poor decisions, and, in the next chapter, we will see that it is inimical to creativity.

SUMMARY

This chapter dealt with decision and choice, processes shown to be related to both problem solving and to judgment and evaluation. The defining feature of decision situations is the need to select one from among a number of alternative courses of action, each of which has associated costs, benefits, and utility to the decision maker. Although choice of a course of action is under the control of the decision maker, possible states of the world that will influence costs and benefits are not. Decision where some probability value can be assigned to outcomes and utilities, as in games of chance, is called *decision under risk*; decision where probability values cannot be assigned accurately is called *decision under uncertainty*.

As a preliminary introduction to the nature of decision making, some simple heuristic tools for identifying alternatives, outcomes, and utilities were described. One of the simplest is the *balance sheet* in which advantages and disadvantages are listed in vertical columns and the factor(s) in one column that exactly balance factor(s) in the second are crossed off. Choice is determined by the column having the greater final weight. A second device is to prepare a *choice matrix* which can encompass a greater variety of alternative choices and bases for selection among them. Several means of assigning utility values to the cells of the matrix were considered. The simplest is to assign + or − for acceptable or unacceptable. A finer comparison is obtained by assigning ratings on a 1 to n scale. This will provide a mean rating for each alternative. A third method weights each rating by the importance of the factor in question. This method leads to *weighted mean* ratings. Assignment of other possible weightings to see if they affect the final decision can also be explored.

Explicit criteria for decision under risk and uncertainty were described. For decision making under risk *maximizing expected value* is a good criterion to adopt. For decision making under uncertainty four alternative criteria were described. The *maximin* criterion focuses upon the worst possible outcome associated with each choice and chooses the least terrible from among them. The *maximax* criterion focuses upon the best possible outcome associated with each choice and selects the best from among them. The remaining criteria use more information. The *Hurwicz strategy* assigns an arbitrary weighting, w, to the best and $(1 - w)$ to the worst possible outcome associated with each alternative and provides expected values from which to select the maximum. The fourth alternative creates a new quantity, *regret,* which is the difference between the best possible outcome for each alternative and the obtained outcome. The selection criterion is to minimize maximum regret. A final possible method is *cost benefit analysis.*

Two additional methods were described: decision trees and sensitivity analysis. The use of *decision trees* in medical diagnosis illustrates one practical application of this tool. *Sensitivity analysis* is a useful tool for pruning decision trees by assessing the difference among alternative courses of action over a range of values.

The chapter concluded with an identification of some common sources of error in decision making. These were discussed under the rubrics of inadequate models of chance, sources of bias in estimates, and inadequate correction of estimates.

Although a great deal of material was covered the central lesson to be derived is that there are many alternatives in making decisions. Tools for systematically identifying and evaluating them as well as an explicit criterion for selecting from among them are needed. Because of inescapable risk or uncertainty, there is often no one best alternative, but an informed decision is usually better than an impulsive one.

EXERCISES

1. Take some decision you frequently confront, for example, going home for the weekend vs staying at school to study or allocating limited time among a number of competing demands upon it. Apply several of the methods described in this chapter to its resolution, such as use of a balance sheet or decision

tree or the assigning of various means of rating utility. Does each method lead to the same decision? What are the strengths and weaknesses of each method for your purposes?

2. Take some important decision that you are faced with or can foresee arising and, as in the first exercise, apply several of the methods described in this chapter to its resolution. At the very least, this exercise should help clarify the factors involved in the decision and the alternatives available to you as well as your own utilities. It might also lead you to develop your own classification of which kinds of decision situations are most amenable to which techniques.

3. Take the decision you used for the first or second exercise and add considerations of risk or uncertainty to it (for example, the likelihood of a pop quiz for the study example). Apply each of the decision criteria proposed: maximin, maximax, and so on.

4. To the extent that you have applied explicit decision criteria in the past try to characterize them. Do you tend consistently to apply one of the decision criteria described in this chapter or does your choice of criterion vary with the situation? Are there additional criteria not described that have some merit and should be added, for example, doing what is easiest at the time—maximin for effort? Can you identify classes of decision situations for which one criterion is preferable to others?

5. Find in the newspaper some account of a recent decision made by someone in authority, for example, retaliation to an act of terrorism, the jury verdict in a trial, a change in existing law for the minimum drinking age, and reconstruct a decision analysis that might have led to it (that is, apply one of the decision methods described in this chapter). Was it a good decision or, in light of your analysis, are there better alternatives that should have been selected? What decision criterion appears to have been applied in this case?

6. Take some existing game of chance or invent a new one and construct a model for it like the one for betting on rolls of a pair of dice in Box 11-2. On the basis of it, identify some fair game bets.

7. Find in your reading or your own experiences some instances of the kinds of errors and biases described at the end of the chapter: for example, a drop in the volume of air traffic following a crash or a hijacking as a possible instance of availability bias. Is there one or more of these errors to which you are particularly subject? How might you guard against it?

8. Assume that you are the leader of a boy scout or girl scout troop that is about to embark on a group project, such as a cookie sale in support of some charitable effort. How could you teach your troop members to be informed decision makers?

9. Consider first impressions of acquaintances, or the procedure of labeling elementary school children as "slow learners" from the standpoint of anchoring bias and problems of inadequate correction. Does the model have implications for those sorts of situations? Is it appropriate?

· *12* ·

Creativity and Imagination

You no doubt had little difficulty in the previous material in accepting the view that you can master more efficient procedures for reasoning, for forming and testing hypotheses, for solving problems and reaching decisions; but, for creativity? The presence of a question suggests some preconception that creativity is a special gift with which one is born rather than a dimension of thought present in everyone. To convince yourself that creativity, at some level of the definition, is a universal human dimension you need only watch an infant of 12 to 18 months for a few hours. There is steady activity, exploration, variation, provoking of novelty and attempt to comprehend it. On the other hand, there is little stereotyped repetition of mastered schemes or direct imitation. One could properly characterize this as creative activity in the sense that the child is creating his or her understanding of his or her own world through provoked interaction with it. It is also true, on the other hand, that all infants go through this stage of development in highly similar ways so that there is little that is original or of lasting social value in any individual child's behavior. To the extent that originality and value are part of the criteria of creativity, as they are for most applications of the term to adult behavior, we would deny creativity in the infant; to the extent that creativity is a dimension of greater freedom and variation possible in all behavior, it is attainable to an infant. Given the acceptance of levels in definition of the term creativity, it should be clear that everyone is capable of creativity at some level and, quite possibly, of raising the level as well. With that introduction we are now faced with the need to consider varying approaches to and criteria for creativity.

APPROACHES TO CREATIVITY

Creativity in the Narrow Sense.   Psychologists, especially those who have attempted to develop "objective" measures of creativity, tend to equate it with divergent thinking.[1] Divergent thinking is directed toward the creation of many alternatives (diversity) in contrast to convergent thinking, which is directed to fixing upon a unique solution. The tests of creativity dictated by a divergent thinking definition ask, for example, for a listing of uses for some homely object such as a brick or an egg carton. The creative person is one who comes up with a number of unusual uses where unusual is defined in terms of low relative frequency of occurrence in some normative population. (There is, for example, nothing particularly creative about such suggested uses for a brick as to build a house, a wall, or a garage.) There is no requirement with respect to the quality of the unusual uses; they could be totally bizarre or psychotic. Implicit in the selection of such measures is emphasis upon the fluency of thought, the absence of constraint by convention or context, or, in the language of Chapter 4, the ability to detach. A correlated connotation is one of playfulness (see Kogan, 1983) and delight in the creation of novelty.

Narrow definitions of creativity often tend to be tied to the context of problem solving as do many of the suggested methods of promoting creativity which will be reviewed shortly. In effect, narrow definitions focus upon fluency in a relatively constrained situation where the problem is posed along with some implied constraints on what is acceptable as a solution. Some examples of the kinds of problems posed are given in Box 12-1. Responses to questions of this sort are relatively small scale and self-contained in contrast to the kind of thinking that occurs when one creates a problem or devises a creative undertaking of some scope, such as writing an opera.

Creativity in the Broad Sense.   Creativity in a broader sense is generally defined with respect to at least two criteria: *originality* and *quality*. There is often a third criterion for *sustained production of superior achievement*: that is, it is not a rare and unrepeated occurrence. When creativity is defined in this manner the focus tends to shift to the talented and creative person and his or her personal characteristics and developmental history rather than to a particular class of behavior (divergent thinking) and the factors that tend to promote it.

There have been several studies of gifted individuals and of high achievers within particular areas of specialization.[2] There are also a number of prospective studies of adolescents who show precocious talent in some area (generally mathematics) or high scores on a test of creativity.[3] All of the data so assembled are flawed by some inescapable problems of interpretation: the groups are not randomly selected, often there is no counterpart control group, and the data are correlational in nature (where measures entering the correlation are often of unknown reliability and validity). Because of these flaws generalizations which can be drawn from consistent relations that do emerge should be interpreted

BOX 12-1

Tests of Divergent Thinking

Guilford's structure of the intellect model is itself an instance of morphological analysis (see Box 12-4) consisting of all possible combinations of five types of *operation* (evaluation, convergent production, divergent production, memory, and cognition), six *products* (units, classes, relations, systems, transformations, and implications) and four kinds of *content* (figural, symbolic, semantic, and behavioral). Thus, the product of products and content yields 24 forms of divergent thinking. (After Guilford, 1967, and Hendricks, Guilford, & Hoepfner, 1969) Some forms of thinking include the following:

Consequences. What would be the results if people no longer needed or wanted sleep?

Unusual uses. List as many uses as you can for a brick.
This is scored for fluency (total number) and flexibility (no. of categories).

Sentence construction. Fill in the blanks with words to make a sentence:
F_____ _____ N_____ _____

Multiple grouping. Arrange the following words into several different meaningful groups: (a) arrow, (b) bee, (c) crocodile, (d) fish, (e) kite, (f) sailboat, (g) sparrow.

Multiple emotional expressions. Write a list of things a person might say when frustrated.

Possible jobs. Write the different jobs, occupations, or kinds of people that might be indicated by the light bulb emblem.

Alternate picture meanings. List many different things that a person might say if s/he felt as does the person shown in the picture.

with caution. For example, although there do seem to be consistent characteristics of architects, scientists, and writers, who are acknowledged by their peers to be creative, it is also possible that these individuals have achieved prominence in contrast to possibly equally creative unknowns. Thus, their characteristics are those of successful, creative persons and one cannot tell which characteristics are associated with success and which with creativity or, even, whether that is a meaningful distinction. With respect to correlational evidence, you are already well aware that correlation is not to be interpreted as causation. Given these precautionary hedges, we now can examine the characteristics of creative individuals.

One of the major potential correlates of creativity to be examined is intelligence as measured on a standard test like the Stanford-Binet or some measure of academic achievement like the Scholastic Aptitude Test, SAT V and Q. Studies that take a large sample of adolescents or young adults (college students), on whom there are both intelligence/achievement and creativity measures, report no significant positive correlation between them.[4] It is to be noted, however, that here we are dealing with creativity in the narrow sense and among groups possessing above average intelligence. These conditions would tend to minimize evidence of correlation. An interesting early historical attempt (see Cox, 1926) at assigning IQ estimates to 300 geniuses born between 1450 and 1850 on the basis of evidence concerning their early mental development comes up with estimates that range widely from normal to highly exceptional (IQ = 200) but with a low positive correlation of IQ and eminence. Studies of achievers rated by peers as creative find them to be of above average intelligence but not more so than their less creative peers (see Barron, 1969). The general conclusion that seems warranted by the existing evidence is that a certain minimum level of intelligence is probably required for achievement. What that minimum is depends to some extent on the field. Beyond that level, creativity bears little correlation to intelligence.

Two major contributing factors to creative attainment that cannot be separated from each other are knowledge/skill and hard work. With respect to hard work, biographies of creative individuals almost uniformly reveal that the creative person devotes a great deal of time on a continuing basis to his or her professional activities, frequently setting aside a block of time each day for creative efforts and protecting it from interference or distraction. In other words, creativity is serious, steady, and sustained work viewed by creative persons as the most important and rewarding aspect of their lives. There is a powerful and continuing commitment to it. With respect to the high level of skill and knowledge, which is deepened and strengthened over the course of the individual's career, there is less objective evidence as to the particular level of proficiency needed, although the notion of a creative writer, artist, composer, or scientist who is not totally proficient in his or her craft is almost a logical contradiction. Hayes (1981) has plotted number of recordings of a composer's work as a function of the number of years into his or her career at the time of the composition of the work. The results suggest that composers need about ten years of work at their craft before really excelling (if one assumes that works of which many recordings are made are more highly esteemed than those which are recorded little or at all). Although many creative individuals begin their careers very early,[5] professional maturation is not a matter of personal maturity as is shown by comparing composers who started early with those who began later in life. Even geniuses need an apprenticeship/maturation period to develop their creativity.

Many of the more recent studies of creative achievers have examined personality characteristics and developmental background. The personality characteristics associated with creativity vary somewhat, depending upon the field in question, but there seem to be some similarities across fields. A summary of 13 personality characteristics of productive scientists is shown in Box 12-2, along with a description of young art students. Prominent among the characteristics of creative persons are independence (intellectual and social), detachment, devotion to intellectual pursuits, and a drive to seek challenges. You might want to review the biographies of some of your own intellectual heroes to see to what extent these characteristics apply. Whether personality traits of independence and self-confidence are prerequisite for creativity, or develop and strengthen during the course of creative work, are questions that cannot be answered on the basis of existing evidence.[6]

Creativity in the Broad Sense as Process.   Creativity in the broad sense has been identified in terms of characteristics of creative persons, a procedure whose inherent circularity leaves much to be desired. Although there has been less effort at characterizing the process independent of its practitioners, it seems to me to be readily feasible on the basis of current evidence. Creativity in the broad sense is first and foremost intellectual activity of a very high order. It is high order not only in the sense of being abstract, but also in the sense of being extended over time and topic, requiring overall organization to bring to fruition projects of some magnitude. What I am suggesting is that creativity may accurately be treated as higher order problem solving in the sense that the creative individual poses himself or herself problems and challenges, the solution of which constitute the creative work. Duchamp (see Chapter 2) set himself the task of depicting an action sequence through time and three-dimensional space on a flat, two-dimensional surface in his painting *Nude Descending a Staircase.* Inventors are perhaps the most transparent example of this process, but it is equally descriptive of artists, writers, scientists, and statesmen. The process also has been described as *problem finding* (which was discussed in Chapter 10), an evocative description of the higher-level aspects of this form of problem solving (for an example see Getzels, 1979). Creativity is not a process of solving externally imposed problems but of actively seeking and creating the challenges themselves: recognizing, for example, as did McLuhan (1964) that in considering the possible future impact of technological advances such as television, social critics were far too superficial in their analyses, failing to appreciate that a new mode of communication and thought had come into being. To better appreciate the proposed definition consider some of what you regard to be outstanding creative works (in art, literature, science, or religion) and identify the challenge being addressed as well as the means applied to its solution. It is a good idea to include

---

BOX 12-2

Personality Characteristics of Creative Persons

A. Personality Characteristics of Productive Scientists

1. A high degree of autonomy, self-sufficiency, self-direction
2. A preference for mental manipulations involving things rather than people: a somewhat distant or detached attitude in interpersonal relations, and a preference for intellectually challenging situations rather than socially challenging ones.
3. High ego strength and emotional stability.
4. A liking for method, precision, exactness.
5. A preference for such defense mechanisms as repression and isolation in dealing with affect and instinctual energies.
6. A high degree of personal dominance but a dislike of personally toned controversy.
7. A high degree of control of impulse, amounting almost to over-control: relatively little talkativeness, gregariousness, impulsiveness.
8. A liking for abstract thinking, with considerable tolerance of cognitive ambiguity.
9. Marked independence of judgment, rejection of group pressures toward conformity in thinking.
10. Superior general intelligence.
11. An early, very broad interest in intellectual activities.
12. A drive toward comprehensiveness and elegance in explanation.
13. A special interest in the kind of "wagering" which involves pitting oneself against uncertain circumstances in which one's own effort can be the deciding factor. (After Taylor & Barron, 1963)

B. Personality Characteristics of Innovators in Business Management in Ireland

This group of leading Irish managers, taken as a whole, is impressively stable, intelligent, and socially effective. The managers, though open to innovation, do give the impression of being rather content with their lot; as a group they would not like to be original at the expense of being controversial, as they indicated in a Q sort designed to elicit their impressions of "the ideal manager" (Barron and Egan, 1968). But the more original among them have much more of an edge to their personalities. They see themselves and are seen by others as daring, tough, cynical, assertive, power-oriented, and unconcerned about their "popularity" or their obedience to conventional demands. At times they create an impression verging on willfulness and acerbity, though not in petty ways; they have a strong sense of destiny, independence of judgment, and cognitive flexibility and inquiringness. There is an odd combination of masculinity and sense of the poetic in them. Their vision is of conquest, mastery, personal dominance, command. (After Barron, 1969)

C. Personality Characteristics of Student Artists at the College of San Francisco Art Institute as Based Upon Results from a Variety of Personality Tests Administered to 88 Male and 65 Female Students

In personality, the students are notably independent and unconventional, vivid in gesture and expression, rather complex psychodynamically but with an emphasis upon openness, spontaneity, and whimsicality rather than neurotic complicatedness. They are very much like other artists—including musicians and writers—in their interest patterns and in their aesthetic preferences.

Their pattern of interests is appropriate to some extent to any profession calling for intellectual creativity. The distinction between profession and vocation does seem apt, however; these students most strongly *value* art and the independent way of life, and this has determined their vocational choice.

In brief, they choose to do what they value most, and this itself sets them apart from many apparently better adjusted people who are doing what they would rather not. (After Barron, 1972)

D. Personality Characteristics of Female Dancers Reflected in Responses to a 300 Adjective Check List Administered to 26 Women in the Boston Area and 15 at Mills College

Perhaps the best way to begin to describe the female dancers is to characterize them as women with a lot of "steam." Active, energetic, emotional, and excitable, they would tend to react strongly and deeply to their environment and to themselves. This energy has a certain driving quality to it; they describe themselves as determined, ambitious, and capable, and need to succeed in their chosen field. Their goals, however, are not the usual and cannot be pursued within the normal channels of endeavor. Individualistic, original, and independent, they tend to be headstrong and follow their own lead in developing themselves. Their development, however, is most likely construed by them in highly personal terms: There is a serious side to them—sincere, thoughtful, and reflective—and they have a thirst for experience that is perhaps related to a need for meaning in their existence. In pursuit of goals and self, they are adaptable, changeable, and adventurous; far-ranging in interests;

BOX 12-2 *cont.*

and versatile in applying themselves. Individualism is tempered by an appreciation of the most basic social virtues: they describe themselves also as considerate, reasonable, civilized, responsible, and tolerant. Their femininity would be more of the generous, affectionate, understanding, and appreciative type, rather than the more conservative, submissive, deferring, and passive feminine nature. Their openness to themselves and their feelings, however, includes also an awareness of discord and anxiety. Nonetheless, they have considerable ability to use their dissatisfactions in creative ways, describing themselves as idealistic, imaginative, sensitive, and artistic. (After Barron, 1972)

E. Personality Characteristics of Women Mathematicians

(a) Rebellious independence, narcissism, introversion, and a rejection of outside influence; (b) strong symbolic interests, and a marked ability to find self-expression and self-gratification in directed research activity; (c) flexibility, or lack of constriction, both in general attitudes and in mathematical work. (After Helson, 1971)

These are a sampling of the descriptions of personality characteristics of creative people in various areas of endeavor. As you can see, there are some similarities (for example, all are flexible and independent) as well as differences among groups. It is worth adding that these are normative descriptions; there are variations among the individuals within a group, as well.

---

at least one realm requiring much technical motor skill (artistic, dramatic, musical, or athletic) to appreciate the intellectual activity directing that overt behavior. For example, tennis champions report the importance of intellectual preparation for superior performance.

Now that you have a deeper appreciation of what creativity is, you are in a better position to consider whether it is possible to increase creativity not only in the narrow sense and within more circumscribed contexts but in the broad sense as well. A great variety of techniques have been proposed, some of which are outlined in the following section; references to others are included in chapter notes.

FOSTERING CREATIVITY IN THE NARROW SENSE

As one might logically expect, where creativity is defined in terms of divergent thinking, procedures to promote heavy production of alternatives are proposed; where creativity is defined in terms of breaking free of barriers and constraints, procedures addressed to those goals are proposed. Since there is a degree of similarity among methods they will not be exhaustively covered.

Brainstorming and Its Kin. *Brainstorming*, the oldest and best-known technique for promoting fluency, was developed as a group problem-solving technique for an advertising agency and has been widely used and studied since.[7] It works. The basic rationale is that there should be two stages in idea production: first ideas must be generated (this includes fact finding and idea finding) and then they may be evaluated. Brainstorming is a technique for the first phase and its success is asserted to depend upon deferral of judgment (a judgmental attitude is assumed to inhibit idea production). There are four rules for the process: (a) all ideas are acceptable, (b) criticism and evaluation are not allowed, (c) quantity is desired, and (d) ideas may be generated by any association to, combination of, or revision of earlier ideas. The connection suggested earlier, of a relaxed, uncritical, even playful or fanciful attitude and ideational fluency is invoked in the four rules of brainstorming. Although it was formulated as a group method, clearly it is also applicable on an individual basis.

A more structured technique for withholding critical judgment and increasing fluency is the *PMI procedure* of de Bono (1984) in which, for consecutive brief periods, you list all the positive (P) features of an idea, then all the minuses (M), and then other interesting (I) features and aspects. To see how the PMI procedure works, apply it to some possible procedural revisions (for example, doing away with fares on short downtown loop bus rides, eliminating all special income tax deductions, using paper plates in all restaurants, dispensing beverages in plastic bags).

A wealth of variations on brainstorming have appeared, usually with more focus upon what is to be varied or how one goes about generating alternatives. One simple variation is the generation of an *attribute list* which, as the name implies, is a listing of all attributes of the object or concept in question. For example, to deal with the unusual uses of a brick test, you might list all the attributes of a brick that you can think of and then go through them, singly and in combination, to generate possible unusual uses.[8] The rationale here is that by listing attributes one breaks the barrier of initial, strong associations to brick (weight or shape) and allows weaker, but possibly useful associations, such as heat retention or possibility of variation of surface texture, to arise. To the extent that a problem may arise because an immediate response is incorrect, looking for weaker members of a response hierarchy is always a good procedure for finding possible solutions. (Maltzman, Belloni, and Fishbein, 1964.)

In a method called *synectics* (see Gordon, 1961), deferral of judgment is again enforced and explicit generation of analogy is employed as a device to make the strange familiar (put a new problem in the context of a familiar one) and to make the familiar strange. Some possible examples might be to analogize tires to shoes, or vice versa, insurance to maintenance or replacement cost, traffic flow to Brownian motion, and so on. Problem solving under this method proceeds in three stages: (a) in the first, a group definition of the problem is reached;

(b) in the second, focus is shifted away from the problem *per se* to a search for useful analogies from, for example, biology, personal experience, fantasy, or alternative means of encoding; and (c) in the third, these analogies are then evaluated and applied to the problem solution.

Other procedures such as the *K–J method,* the *method of morphological forced connections* and *morphological analysis* (see Hogarth, 1980) are all, in essence, tools for generating combinations of alternatives which are then evaluated as possible solutions for some initial problem. In morphological analysis, for example, one takes parameters of the problem at issue, generates alternatives for each, and then generates all possible combinations of alternatives by constructing a matrix for examination and evaluation. The method of morphological forced combination samples alternatives, and the K–J method assembles them randomly by writing each parameter alternative on a card and shuffling cards. To illustrate, suppose you wanted to design a good cheap shoe. Some parameters to consider are the material used for the sole, the material used for the upper part, and the means of joining them. Sole alternatives are rubber, crepe, wood, leather, or a synthetic; upper alternatives are leather, a synthetic, or a fabric; uniting methods include glue, stitching, nails, or heat fusion. Applications of the two morphological analysis variants are shown in Box 12-3.

To get a deeper understanding of these methods of generating multiple alternatives, you might want to apply each to some problem of your own devising (for example, designing a better egg carton), or perhaps several different kinds of problems, to better appreciate the strengths and weaknesses of each method. Additional examples are included in the exercises at the end of the chapter.

Checklist Methods.   The *checklist,* as the name implies, is a series of considerations, checks, or tests, to ensure that nothing important is overlooked and that everything relevant is covered. The Polya procedure for problem solving (Chapter 1) might be considered a checklist—a simple and very general one— in contrast to some of the more limited purpose checklists, shown in Box 12-4.

Osborn (1957), the father of brainstorming, is also responsible for the first checklist shown. As is evident, it is simply a list of nine questions that can be raised with respect to any possible task in the hope of generating some possible solutions for consideration. It is a mechanical and probably tedious method to apply, but it certainly should help prevent fixing upon too narrow and inadequate a set of alternatives, or being blind to some overlooked considerations or contingencies. More to the point, anyone who develops the habit of employing a checklist, of whatever sort, is developing a useful general orientation to problem solving: to avoid fixing upon the first solution that comes to mind but, instead, to generate a variety of additional alternatives, some of which may be unusual or even bizarre, in order to increase the likelihood of an optimal or original solution.

BOX 12-3

Morphological Means of Combining Attributes

A. The Method of Morphological Forced Connections and an Example of Its Use to Invent a Pen

It begins with existing attributes (here, of a ballpoint pen), lists possible alternates for each, and then tries combinations of the alternates as indicated.

ATTRIBUTES:

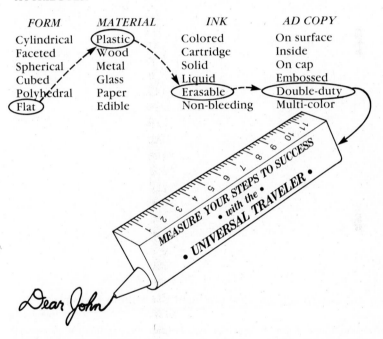

FORM	*MATERIAL*	*INK*	*AD COPY*
Cylindrical	Plastic	Colored	On surface
Faceted	Wood	Cartridge	Inside
Spherical	Metal	Solid	On cap
Cubed	Glass	Liquid	Embossed
Polyhedral	Paper	Erasable	Double-duty
Flat	Edible	Non-bleeding	Multi-color

(Reproduced with permission from *The Universal Traveler* by Don Koberg and Jim Bagnall. Copyright © 1981 by William Kaufmann, Inc., Los Altos, CA 94022. All rights reserved.)

B. The Zwicky Procedure of Morphological Analysis

In this example the object is to design a new concept in personal transportation. Three factors—motive power, medium of operation, and type of pas-

BOX 12-3 *cont.*

senger support (with 8 values of the first two factors and 5 of the third) are shown as a cube, each cell of which represents a unique combination and a potential solution.

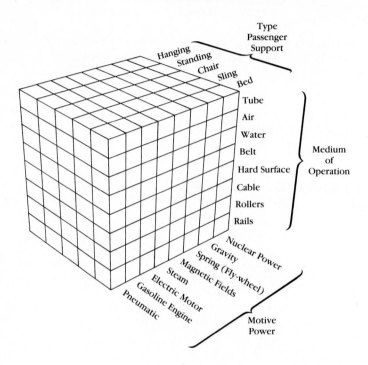

C. "How to Join the Intelligentsia without Trying"

An interesting version of morphological combination techniques appeared in a *New York Times* editorial by D. D'Souza, titled "How to Join the Intelligentsia without Trying." It suggests that one select a word from each of the following three columns to describe an interaction, whether it be societal, international, economic, or other. The result is a description conforming to the latest "in" language. (After D'Souza, 1986)

Column A	Column B	Column C
Profound	Interpersonal	Awareness
Diverse	Emotional	Oneness
Genuine	Dialectical	Relationship
Subjective	Harmonious	Network
Complex	Communal	Response
Sophisticated	Open	Linkage
Realistic	Humane	Consensus
Meaningful	Interactive	Context
Mutual	Collective	Dialogue
Objective	Societal	Forum

D. Demonstrating that One Is Really With It

Now that you understand the spirit of this technique for generating alternatives, apply your understanding by creating your own device, somewhat comparable to D'Souza's, for demonstrating that you have a grasp of the lingo of whatever group you choose to do this for (hackers, jocks, and so on).

BOX 12-4

A Sampling of Checklists for Promoting Fluency

A. Arnold's Version of Osborn's Checklist

Checklist for New Ideas

Put to other uses?
New ways to use as is? Other uses if modified?

Adapt?
What else is like this? What other idea does this suggest? Does past offer a parallel? What could I copy? Whom could I emulate?

Modify?
New twist? Change meaning, color, motion, sound, odor, form, shape? Other changes?

Magnify?
What to add? More time? Greater frequency? Stronger? Higher? Longer? Thicker? Extra value? Plus ingredient? Duplicate? Multiply? Exaggerate?

Minify?
What to subtract? Smaller? Condensed? Miniature? Lower? Shorter? Lighter? Omit? Streamline? Split up? Understate?

Substitute?
Who else instead? What else instead? Other ingredient? Other material? Other process? Other power? Other place? Other approach? Other tone of voice?

Rearrange?
Interchange components? Other pattern? Other layout? Other sequence? Transpose cause and effect? Change pace? Change schedule?

Reverse?
Transpose positive and negative? How about opposites? Turn it backward? Turn it upside down? Reverse roles? Change shoes? Turn tables? Turn other cheek?

Combine?
How about a blend, an alloy, an assortment, an ensemble? Combine units? Combine purposes? Combine appeals? Combine ideas? (After Adams, 1986)

B. List of Manipulative Verbs Proposed by Koberg and Bagnall

These are actions one might take to transform an object or situation. They suggest that the reader supply five more verbs.

Multiply	Distort	Fluff-up	Extrude
Divide	Rotate	By-pass	Repel

Eliminate	Flatten	Add	Protect
Subdue	Squeeze	Subtract	Segregate
Invert	Complement	Lighten	Integrate
Separate	Submerge	Repeat	Symbolize
Transpose	Freeze	Thicken	Abstract
Unify	Soften	Stretch	Dissect, etc.

(Reproduced, with permission, from *The Universal Traveler* by Don Koberg and Jim Bagnall. Copyright © 1981 by William Kaufmann, Inc., Los Altos, CA 94022. All rights reserved.)

C. Crovitz's List of Relational Words

To be applied in "Take one thing _____ another thing," for example as applied to Duncker's X-ray problem, "Take rays through the esophagus," "Take tissue off the tumor," etc. (After Crovitz, 1967)

about	at	for	of	round	to
across	because	from	off	still	under
after	before	if	on	so	up
against	between	in	opposite	then	when
among	but	near	or	though	where
and	by	not	out	through	while
as	down	now	over	till	with

D. Anderson's Techniques for Stimulating Creativity

A. Vary the stimuli about you in order to vary your thoughts.
1. Observe carefully.
2. Use checklists.
3. Rearrange the elements of the problem.
4. Discuss the problem with someone else.
5. Take a break.
B. Vary the way in which you represent the problem in order to vary your thoughts.
1. Abstract coding
Represent the problem in terms of abstract codes, attempting to state it in verbal or mathematical symbols or analyzing it into attributes and recombining the attributes.
2. Concrete coding
Represent the problem in terms of concrete codes, translating it into actions, pictures, or analogies. (After Anderson, 1980)

BOX 12-4 *cont.*

E. Adams's Bug List of Things that "Bug" Him

TV dinners
buying a car
relatives
paperless toilets
men's fashions
rotten oranges
hair curlers in bed
hypodermic needles
   for shots
sweet potatoes
cleaning the oven
no urinals in home
   bathrooms
bumper stickers that
   cannot be removed
broken shoelaces
ID cards that don't do
   the job
pictures that don't
   hang straight
ice cubes that are
   cloudy
glary paper
swing-out garage doors
dripping faucets
doors that swell and
   stick in damp
   weather
newspaper ink that
   rubs off
bikes parked in wrong
   place
lousy books
blunt pencils
burnt out light bulbs
panty hose
thermodynamics
dirty aquariums
noisy clocks

plastic flowers
instant breakfast
buttons which must be
   sewn
hangnails
small, yapping dogs
waste of throw-away
   cans
soft ice cream
crooked cue sticks
prize shows on TV
static charges—car,
   blankets, etc.
ditches for pipe that
   are dug too large
bathtubs
cigarettes
balls which have to be
   pumped up
changing from reg. to
   sunglasses
reading road map
   while driving
wobbly tables and
   chairs
big bunches of keys
shoe heels that wear
   out
campers that you can't
   see around
corks that break off in
   wine bottles
soap dishes that you
   can't get the soap
   out of
vending machines that
   take your money
   with no return
buzzing of electric
   shavers

pushbutton water taps
Presto logs
one sock
stamps that don't stick
chairs that won't slide
   on the floor
banana slugs
trying to get change
   out of pockets
red tape
smelly exhaust
high tuition
writing letters
strip mining
dull knives
conversion of farmland
   into homes
chlorine in swimming
   pools
polishing shoes
broken spokes
stripped threads
cold tea
X-rated moves that
   shouldn't be X-rated
bras
mowing lawns
locating books in
   library
miniature poodles
parents' deciding a
   kid's career
solicitors—telephone
   and door-to-door
typewriter keys
   sticking
shock absorbers that
   don't work
shaving

(After Adams, 1986)

The next two checklists in Box 12-4 include a list of verbs describing various possible transformations and a list of prepositions describing relations. Use of such lists is another device, similar to attribute lists and generation of all possible combinations, to promote consideration of novel transformations upon or relations among elements of the problem. They, too, are promoters of fluency and removers of blocks. The final entries in Box 12-5 are more broadly applicable and place more demand upon the resources of the would-be creator. The "Bug List" is one example of a list that might be generated given the assignment to list things that "bug" you. Anyone who wants to create, for example, a worthwhile invention might start from such a list as a source for areas in need of improvement and, therefore, areas where innovation is likely to be welcomed and rewarded. Most of us use something like a bug list every time we make out a schedule or a budget, that is, we start by listing what must be included or attended to, possibly in order of importance, before considering assignment of time (money) to each. The final example to be discussed is a brief, sensible, listing of general procedures to promote fluent production of alternatives and removal of blocks to imagination.

Removal of Blocks.   Earlier treatments of problem solving, especially Gestalt approaches, tended to emphasize the interfering effect of prior sets (such as those illustrated in Box 1-1). Although many classic problems were generated, some of which were reviewed in Chapter 10, there were fewer suggestions on how to overcome sets and counteract rigidity. In the long run understanding and a more open attitude toward seeking alternatives should effectively combat rigid sets; in the short run, a change of scene and activities seem to work. What they involve is getting away from the immediate problem and doing something else, preferably something mindless and physical such as garden work or vigorous activity (running or swimming). This procedure of "taking a vacation" from a problem often has the effect of allowing incubation to occur. *Incubation*[9] refers to a hypothesized process, which at one time was assumed to be a necessary stage of problem solving, a period away from the problem during which some unconscious processing appeared to continue with the result that at some later time a solution, or some idea leading to it, occurred. It may be that working on a problem over a period of time sensitizes one to relevant material or inclines one to consider everything as potentially relevant to the problem. In any event, time away is by no means "empty" time.

FOSTERING CREATIVITY IN THE BROAD SENSE

Whether creativity in the broad sense is subject to training or by how much it can be increased are questions to which there are no satisfactory answers at present. Certainly if creativity can be increased in meaningful magnitudes, it is unlikely that the effective procedures will be so simple and relatively mechanical as those described in the preceding section. There is some presupposition that

BOX 12-5

Variations Upon the Laocoön Theme

WHAT'S YOUR GRIEF?

Rutgers, the State University of New Jersey.

Drawing by Chas. Addams;
© 1975 The New Yorker Magazine, Inc.

"Come off it, you guys."

Drawing by O'Brian; © 1962 The New Yorker Magazine, Inc.

outstanding creative geniuses, such as da Vinci, Mozart, Newton, or Einstein, are born, not made. But we know only of the "born geniuses" who achieved preeminence; we don't know about possible equally endowed geniuses who didn't make it (such as the sister of Mozart or of Galton). One might suspect that filtering factors were at work in view of some notable similarities among geniuses of the past—for example, they were all male and most came from families with sufficient wealth and position to give them a good education and early encouragement. Hayes and Bond (in Hayes, 1981) present a stimulating evaluation of some of these filtering factors for women, Jews, Asians, Blacks, and American Indians. As a result of these comparisons, they identify five social and familial conditions, all of which must be present to foster creative attainments: (a) valuation of intellectual activity, (b) encouragement of individual interest, (c) encouragement of individual belief in ultimate success, (d) availability of educational opportunities, (e) freedom from occupations that preempt time for individual development. The last is especially important for girls who are saddled with responsibility for household chores in many societies. A possible sixth condition, noted in the biographies of many eminent achievers, is the presence of a good role model/mentor who might be a family member or a teacher.

Given that one is of at least average and preferably above average intelligence and that one is not blocked at the outset by insuperable, unfavorable circumstances preventing personal advancement (of the sort described in the preceding paragraph), are there controllable factors that can facilitate the development of creativity? The probable answer is that there certainly are but none provides a "quick fix" of the sort discussed in the preceding section. I shall discuss them under three headings: attitude, commitment, and problem-finding procedures.

The Imaginative Attitude. The facilitating attitude or background orientation for becoming a creative person is a complex combination of many ingredients, most of which have been inferred from biographies and studies of creative persons as well as from the nature of high-level creativity as defined earlier. One ingredient that operates as a precondition is a value system in which intellectual activity is assigned top importance and value, above being loved, for example. There must also, obviously, be strong personal interest in the particular area of endeavor: a belief that it is not only important but absorbing and personally rewarding. I am tempted to add that it is fun, and it is, although the intense exhilaration of those intervals when the work goes well and everything seems to "fall into place" can be counterbalanced by the despair of the more frequent and longer-lasting periods when that is not the case.

Perhaps the major ingredient of a creative attitude is a very strong personal independence. Independence manifests itself in many ways, in charting one's own course, in setting one's own goals, in resisting discouragement and counterpressure from environment, peers, and family. One facet of independence is self-confidence; another is detachment. Detachment comes into play not only in rising above immediate circumstances and influences but also in allowing imagination to come into play in the first place. If, for example, you give in to immediate impulse and respond to a chilling comment with an angry retort, the opportunity for a witty put-down or a cool correction has been foregone. It takes time and some intellectual effort to come up with a superior response. Part of creativity lies in foregoing the obvious, easy response and in consistently seeking for a better one by generating and testing alternatives and by placing a premium on responses that are novel, insightful, fanciful, or amusing. For example, in order to counteract interference from the immediate and the obvious, it could help to create a fantasy context for unfettered exploration (for example, imagine a world where mundane constraints don't apply). It also helps to view yourself as an imaginative person and to act as such as often as possible.

Creative Commitment.   I have differentiated commitment from attitudes to emphasize that creativity has its costs as well as its rewards. It is not sufficient to identify yourself as creative and to be strongly motivated for success in your chosen field. It is necessary, in addition, to be ready to devote the time and effort required for success and to realize that it is a long-range commitment, perhaps the major commitment of one's life. In any area a minimal level of knowledge and skill are prerequisite; as noted earlier, high-quality creativity involves levels beyond the initial entry level, a period—generally long—of apprenticeship. What is required for sustained creativity beyond commitment of time for most of your waking life may differ depending on the field in question. In the arts prime time appears to be solitary time in a place consecrated to work and under conditions free from distraction, the study or studio. Virginia Woolf (1935) is especially eloquent on the importance of a room of one's own.[10] In the sciences it seems to be increasingly the case that no one can work in isolation because there is too much going on and a certain amount of exchange of ideas and information with colleagues is essential to keeping abreast. To the extent that no one person can be a master of all techniques and knowledge in a specific area, collaboration may be required, preferably with other creative individuals.[11]

In addition to commitment of time and energy in large amounts over long time periods, there must also be a commitment to excellence. The creative individual typically challenges himself or herself by posing difficult problems and by refusing to accept facile or inadequate resolutions of them. A continuing goal of the creative person is to exceed previous records and reach new heights of achievement.

Problem Finding.   Creativity in the broad sense was earlier characterized in terms of finding meaty and challenging problems rich with potential for insight and advancement. Where do such problems come from? Although the literature is replete with advice on problem solving, there is no comparable glut of advice on problem finding. In part that is because it is a harder question, in part because there is no general answer that holds across domains of creativity. Because of that limitation artistic and scientific creativity will be discussed separately. There is one common thread, however, in the sense that a would-be creator does not launch naked into the void. He or she starts with some organizing plan, theme, or hypothesis, however provisional, as an orienting thread through the maze of subsequent ideas and revisions.

1. *Artistic problem finding.* In the beginning is the theme, the central guiding idea of the enterprise. Although Tolstoi insisted that his guiding idea in writing *War and Peace* was to entertain, most artists acknowledge the importance of a theme and of variations upon a theme. The theme itself might be very simple—a few bars of melody, a poem to be set to music, or an idea. The idea as a literary launchpad need not be novel or imaginative; in fact, most of the best are universal themes heavily explored in the past. Creativity lies in development and realization of the theme. Shakespeare, for example, derived almost all of his plots from extant works by other writers or from events in history. Nevertheless, the indecision of Hamlet, the jealousy of Othello and Iago, are now landmarks of character depiction. And the Shakesperian themes are continually reworked in opera, in ballet, and in other plays (Romeo and Juliet is a prime example). Similarly, the Faust theme was not novel when Goethe used it. It, too, has been reworked many times since in music and literature and most recently in a Japanese film, *Ikuru,* about a civil servant dying of stomach cancer. One possible problem, by way of example, would be to explore the Faust theme with other unlikely protagonists, such as a woman. Similarly, in the visual arts and in music it is not uncommon for the artist or composer to rework the material of some earlier artist or composer (including himself or herself). The two cartoons in Box 12-5 are an amusing reworking of a Roman sculpture with very different content that is used literally in the example labeled "What's your grief" to advertise a college service for dealing with red tape. They are a lighthearted but illustrative example of reworking a theme. You can find dozens of additional examples with little effort. Picasso, for example, frequently reworked the material of other artists; he also found inspiration in the conventions of African art. Examine your examples and note to what extent your appreciation of the reworking is dependent upon comparison with the original, that is, you derive intellectual pleasure from partly retracing the intellectual activity of the artist.

Another important aspect of artistic creativity is the evolution of an individual style so unique as to be instantly recognizable. Style *per se* is not creative, its import arises in the development of the theme. How style evolves is an interesting question well beyond the scope of this discussion, but one component of artistic style is unquestionably a careful study of the work of fellow artists to understand the means they used to attain artistic ends. There is, in other words, a good deal of intellectual problem solving in the evolution of artistic style along with, no doubt, a good deal of trial and error, much of which is destroyed along the way. If you have never paid explicit attention to artistic style before, look at the works of several artists, listen to the music of several composers, and read the works of several writers from the standpoint of identifying their particular style and analyzing how it enhances the effect of the complete work. Notice also how work with no pretension to creativity signals that fact by deliberate avoidance of style, for example, the bland homogeneous descriptive style of textbooks or the prose of news reports. Imaginative breaks from convention, such as an artistic advertisement or an amusing commercial, instantly draw attention for that very reason.

   2. *Scientific creativity.* No one doubts that scientists address themselves to problems, what is less commonly recognized is that there is a good deal of creativity involved in the formulation of problems, the interpretation of evidence, and the process of theory construction. The problem directing any specific bit of research must, of course, be explicitly formulated in advance and possible outcomes, along with interpretations to be placed upon them, anticipated in the advance planning of the research. In putting evidence in a broader perspective, however, there is much need of detachment in two respects: (a) the need to avoid hasty acceptance of the obvious or the voguish explanation and to consider other alternatives, some of them possibly "far out" in terms of current thought; and (b) the acceptance of uncertainty and ambiguity, recognizing that none of an array of alternative explanations satisfactorily answers the question and that a firm conclusion is premature. The writings of great scientists[12] often contain accounts of mulling over a problem for a very long time realizing that something more was needed and sometimes supplying the missing part with a sudden insight in unlikely circumstances.

   A third aspect of detachment arises in a characteristic point of view or kind of orienting question with which the scientist approaches his or her area. For example, Einstein tried to free himself from the subjective by performing thought experiments such as imagining how the universe would appear to an observer traveling at near the speed of light. The ethologist, Tinbergen (in Krebs & Shelley, 1975, p. 38), reports that he gets insights into animal behavior by rephrasing the traditional question "What could be the survival value of this behavior?" to "What would go wrong, and why, if the animal were to do something different?" Elsewhere in the same volume he describes the value in understanding animal behavior of trying to think like the animal in question; in this particular example, of thinking like a plover in order to locate the nest sites of ringed plovers. Contemporary cognitive psychologists take as their orienting question "How could one program a computer (or, more generally, design a machine) to perform this behavior?" As an exercise in understanding the notion of orienting questions and procedures, you might read the writings of scientists for additional examples[13] and try to formulate the orienting approach that you bring to frequently occurring problems. Could you, like Tinbergen, develop a more imaginative version of it?

SUMMARY

The cream of thinking, creativity and imagination, has been saved for last. The chapter began with the observation that creativity is not a single unitary quality that is present or absent in behavior, but rather, a quality that can be present in varying degrees and that is attainable by all individuals. In support of that assertion, two senses of creativity were differentiated: *creativity in the narrow sense,* which is typically associated with fluency, flexibility, and divergent thinking; and *creativity in the broad sense,* where additional requirements of originality, value, and sustained production are imposed. Creativity in the broad sense tends to be defined in terms of properties of creative individuals. Some of the characteristics that have been identified include intelligence (where it is likely that variation beyond a requisite minimum level is not crucial), appropriate background knowledge/skill and sustained effort, and a number of personality characteristics such as independence, detachment, commitment, and seeking of challenge. When creativity in the broad sense is viewed as a process, the process is best described as *problem finding*: setting and solving hard problems.

Techniques to foster creativity in the narrow sense tend to focus upon an *increase in fluency*—the production of many alternatives and the *removal of barriers*. Among the techniques developed to achieve these goals are (a) brainstorming, in which evaluation is withheld in the service of enhancing production of alternatives; (b) a variety of checklist methods; and (c) incubation, or time out from solution attempts, as a specific technique for overcoming barriers.

In suggesting techniques for promoting creativity in the broad sense, it was first noted that several social and familial conditions appear to be prerequisite to the development of singular talent: (a) valuation of the talent, (b) encouragement of its development, (c) development of self-confidence, (d) availability of educational opportunities, and (e) freedom from time-consuming, mindless activities. An additional contributory factor is the existence of a good role model or mentor. Additional contributory factors that can be developed by the would-be creative individual include (a) an imaginative attitude, (b) commitment to effort and to excellence, and (c) skills at problem finding. To the extent that problem-finding techniques may be domain related, problem finding in the arts (development of themes and style) was considered separately from problem finding in science (detachment, openness to experience, and systematic orientation).

EXERCISES

1. There are many available tests of creativity, some of which, for example, unusual uses, were presented in this chapter. Take some of them in class or, as a variation, invent new tests of your own. Here are some formats to get you started.
   (a) List all the uses you can think of for each of the following: a nail, a match

box, scotch tape, milk carton, old socks, pop tabs (from beverage cans), a plastic bag. Having generated as long a list as you can without special assistance try to augment it by use of one of the techniques described (for example, an attribute list or brainstorming).

(b) Creating amusing story titles or cartoon captions. You might, as a class, bring in stories or cartoons for this purpose (for example, a contest for the best title where all of you use the same story or cartoon). Alternatively, you might want to look at cartoon collections of a particular artist (Chas. Addams, G. Booth, R. Chast, W. Hamilton, Cobean, E. Koren, S. Harris, G. Larsen, G. Price, Wm. Steig, Thurber, and G. Wilson are all possible candidates; each has not only a unique style but also some recurrent themes). Identify the stylistic feature or theme that makes these cartoons funny and see if you can, by use of the K–J method or morphological forced choice, create some cartoon ideas of your own.

(c) Mednick, S. A., and Mednick, M. T. (1967). This work presents noun triplets for which the common association is to be identified, for example, for Cottage Rat Green, the common associate is Cheese; for File Head Toe, it is Nail. Take the Remote Associates Test or create a remote associates test of your own.

(d) Take a simple form such as a circle, oval, triangle, or square and create as many objects as possible by minimal elaboration of it. Here, too, after completing the task, you might try to augment it by application of a checklist technique.

2. Return to Exercise 4 of Chapter 2 for which you assembled examples of clichés. Transform some of the examples into an imaginative expression of the same idea by application of one or more of the techniques for promoting creativity (such as an attribute list). An interesting sidelight on this exercise is a report in *Forbes* (1984, September 10, p. 27) of proverbs created by a fourth grade class:

Original Proverbs	*Fourth Grade Proverbs*
One man's meat is another man's poison.	One man's meat is a cow's death.
Strike while the iron is hot.	Strike while the ball is there.
An idle mind is the devil's playground.	An idle mind is better than none.

3. Although this chapter has focused on intellectual aspects of creativity, many of the techniques for promoting creativity in the narrow sense (brainstorming, synectics) arose in the context of business, making money. Two examples appear in *Forbes* (1984, May 21):

(a) A 29-year-old entrepreneur started a computer service in 1971 that matched empty moving vans around the country with shipments to be moved so vans need not return empty. The ICC called this unlicensed brokering and threatened to stop it. At the time there was a strike at Western Union which was used by trucking companies to wire money to drivers on the road. He offered a service in which a trucker presents a blank draft issued on his company's account at a truck stop. The cashier at the stop calls a toll free number to verify the trucking company's credit and the driver's ID. The service is now also available, for a fee, to gamblers at casinos and race tracks who want a cash advance on their credit card to place a bet. In essence, this is making the strange familiar (reducing a variety of different problems to the same available solution). Think up some other businesses that could be started on this principle. Alternatively, you might apply a bug list to create some ideas for new business enterprises.

(b) A successful entrepreneur offers two suggestions on creating business opportunities: go to parts of the world that are ahead in a given area and ask what they are doing that is not done in your area but could be done (for example, gourmet cookies); and look systematically at any business to find what makes it work and ask what might happen if some things changed in the product or the marketplace. One example could be the creation of term insurance. Regular life insurance provides savings and protection, but there is no reason why a person desiring one or the other should have to pay for both. Term insurance provides only protection, at a reduced price. Consider how either of these two principles could be applied to creation of a new business or service, or how they might be applied noncommercially. You might also note the similarity of the second problem-finding technique to Tinbergen's question for understanding biological adaptation.

4. List all the techniques you can devise for stimulating imagination. Both Adams and McKim recommend a technique proposed by DeMille in his book, *Put your mother on the ceiling*, in which one is to relax completely and imagine something bizarre and aversive such as breathing in a goldfish and allowing it to swim around in your lungs, then breathing in a lot of tiny goldfish, or rose petals, fire, hot desert wind, steam, etc. For another lead, you might watch children at play to observe what stimulates their imagination. Some other leads might be obtained from earlier chapters, for example, techniques of detachment (Chapter 4) or application of nontraditional models (Chapter 8). DeBono asserts that logic is inimical to imagination; you might consider whether that assertion is necessarily true. Finally, you might want to analyze what works for you in freeing your own imagination.

5. This exercise derives from one devised by Rae Carlson in which 24 short vignettes are given and the reader is to imagine each of the presidential and vice-presidential candidates of the 1984 election as the central character. After doing that with each of the vignettes below, write some additional vignettes and devise your own cast of characters to star in them. This might be more fun as a class exercise.

(a) Told in flashbacks, this story portrays our central character as a promising young musician preparing for a major recital. Scenes with a dedicated teacher, and in solitary practice, establish the importance of a musical career. An accident leads to temporary paralysis of the right hand; the recital must be canceled. How does the star cope?

(b) Based on a true incident, this program portrays the devastation of a community when a dam breaks, flooding and destroying a semirural community. Our central character, leading a rescue team, is seen in vivid episodes providing food, comfort, and shelter to victims. An important point is the central character's human motivation rather than his or her official responsibility.

(c) Vacationing in another part of the country, our central character impulsively telephones a childhood friend and arranges an evening together. The outcome is disastrous: a once-loved friend has turned to a career that betrays all of the values they once shared. Disgusted, our central character departs with mingled emotions to be supplied by you, the director of this drama.

(d) Set in contemporary urban life, this drama represents a conflict of values. Our central character is invited by friends to attend a showing of an art film. It turns out to be a thinly-veiled (no pun intended) bit of pornography. Scenes portray the character's surprise and disgust. You supply the resolution of this drama.

6. Inspired by the last exercise, you decide to write and direct your own drama which is to be based upon your favorite film with an entirely new cast of characters and whatever plot revisions you care to introduce (for example, you might want to change the ending, make an opera of it, turn a tear-jerker into a parody, and so on). Outline the storyline, the cast of characters, and at least one memorable scene.

7. Redesign your room so that it is optimally geared to your life-style (promotes doing what you like to do). Do not assume that unlimited funds are available for this purpose, or that your present interests will become permanent ones.

8. Many of the techniques described in this chapter for promoting fluency or removal of blocks have a somewhat mechanical aspect to them. Assuming that you adopted one or more of these techniques and applied them repeatedly, what might be the long-range implications for developing creativity in the broad sense? Discuss your answers in class.

9. Suppose you lived in a desert region where it rained infrequently (or a very wet region with yearly monsoons). What sort of housing, clothing, and other consumer products would be most ideally suited to this environment? To stretch your imagination a bit more, you might imagine living in an era before electricity or antibiotics, or in a world where a dust cloud from a volcanic eruption leads to the eradication of plant life. What consequences would result?

10. What sorts of projects might you give a scout troop under your charge (as a result of Exercise 8, Chapter 10) to promote creativity? If you prefer, you

might also answer this question in terms of curriculum revisions in your own major, such as, how could training be changed to produce more creative practitioners? In this connection a recent article, or some of the references in the following notes section, may give you some leads (Stewart, 1985).

11. Invent some Laocoön theme cartoons of your own. One that comes to mind is the electrocution of Redikilowatt. After having attained your goal, consider how you did so (for example, did you think of a likely ingredient, such as a garden hose? of a theme? a central character?).

Thinking as a Way of Life: The Pursuit of Understanding

T he completion of any enterprise provides an occasion to organize one's understanding, not in the sense of tying it up to be placed in a figurative box of mementos but, rather, to revise and expand it for use in future endeavors. In this instance, a final summary and evaluation should provide both motivation and guidance for future independent adventures in thinking. My device for achieving a final summary will be to return to Chapter 1 to reconsider the nature of understanding and to use that as a focus for organizing what you have learned in the interim. As an additional guideline for future independent exploration on your part, I shall offer summarizing observations. You may want to compose a set of your own better attuned to your own needs.

Observation 1: It is enlightening to revisit past thinking, especially thinking about topics about which you may feel especially sure and knowledgeable. *Observation 2:* In order to review one's past thinking it is necessary to have a record of it to provide a basis for comparison; a journal entry provides a convenient record for this purpose. Sometimes, on rereading an earlier entry, you will be pleasantly surprised at the degree of change that has taken place. On other occasions, you may be surprised to find that you knew more than you thought you did: all the ingredients were there, but they had not yet been organized to capture the nascent insight explicitly. For a concrete example of the rewards of review, consider your earlier answers to Exercises 3 and 4 of Chapter 1 in light of how you would answer them now. Compare them in detail to identify changes in what you include as well as changes in the emphasis placed upon your inclusions.

UNDERSTANDING REVISITED

Thinking was initially defined as symbolic activity directed toward understanding. At that stage understanding could not be clearly defined because a full discussion would involve additional concepts to be clarified later. As a temporary expedient, understanding was treated in the context of self-awareness and self-direction of thought. In that framework understanding was identified as the highest level of awareness, a level in which thought precedes and directs practice rather than accompanying or resulting from practice. Two lower levels were also identified. At the lowest level, one may stumble upon a successful solution without prior planning or knowledge. Having once done so, it is possible to note the antecedent conditions that led to success and to reinstate them whenever the occasion arises. That path leads to ritualization of technique. It will work, but it does not make for flexibility or innovation. It may also be wasteful to the extent that some components play no contributory role but are there solely as a result of fortuitous correlation. Let's summarize those observations as *Observation 3:* Attainment of success is not an exclusive goal: how one gets there is as important as where one ends up.

Understanding presupposes knowledge, but knowledge in and of itself need not lead to understanding. It is how knowledge is represented and organized that determines its influence in directing action. A collection of facts, or of practical rules, cannot serve as a basis for directing action unless one or more of the facts or rules is directly relevant to the situation at hand. In that case one can do what worked in the past. But suppose none of the collection of facts and rules is directly relevant, then what? A model or theory, on the other hand, not only provides an economical summary of knowledge but also a basis for extrapolating to situations not previously encountered. It can also lead to developing new contexts in which to test the model. This leads to *Observation 4* which is also the title of an influential paper by Karmiloff-Smith and Inhelder (1974/5): "If you want to get ahead, get a theory."

But, how does one get a theory? That question was discussed earlier. Theory building, or the construction of organizing frameworks more generally, requires classification. Classification, in turn, presupposes evaluation of what is important, essential, defining, or intrinsic as a basis for classification. Evaluation, as you are now well aware, is inherently subject to error, as are the theories and models that eventually result. For this reason, and this is *Observation 5:* Be open to revision of evaluations and of theories. You are also reminded that a theory is tested by generating hypotheses that can be shown to be false. One never proves a theory or a hypothesis.

A second inherent feature of evaluation is that it implies a criterion which should be made explicit. It is rarely, if ever, the case that only one criterion for evaluation is uniquely applicable. Even for so seemingly straightforward a judgment as a contest for the best jam, best dog in show, or Miss America, there are alternative criteria that could be applied and alternative weightings of those criteria. I shall return to the subject of alternative criteria in the next section. For the present we can add *Observation 6:* Be explicitly aware of your criteria and consider alternative criteria that might be equally applicable.

Another requisite of understanding is that it must be expressed in a form capable of communication. Exploring ideas, either in interchange with another person or through the medium of the written word, is a major highway to deepening and enrichment of understanding. To travel that highway one must communicate effectively. *Observation 7:* You don't understand if you can't communicate your understanding.

In revisiting the nature of understanding by way of eight observations, my aim has been to show that attainment of understanding is both a directing purpose and defining property of thought. In addition, I have tried to demonstrate that the material of each chapter shed light on the nature of understanding and the means of its attainment. It should be evident from the foregoing discussion that understanding is not a finite commodity or a static state. It is a fluid and dynamic state whose pursuit is a way of life. I conclude with one final observation anticipated in some of the earlier ones, but important enough to warrant repetition. *Observation 8:* Alternatives are always possible. Seek them.

ALTERNATIVES ARE ALWAYS POSSIBLE

Skill at generating alternatives is considered to be a defining property of creativity, but its importance is not confined to that realm. Appreciation of alternatives is important in all areas of thought. In that sense all thinking is creative. As a final justification, if any is needed, consider the meaning of "understanding"— the goal of this enterprise. "Understanding" refers not only to enlightenment, insight into the nature of reality, but also to sympathy and compassion, informed participation in the human condition. Thus, the pursuit of understanding inevitably implies the acceptance of alternatives. This conclusion is so important that it is worth considering some of the many forms of alternatives in more detail.

Alternative Purposes.   Even in so mundane an activity as selecting a commodity, such as a new shirt, although a specific occasion of its use may play a prominent role in the decision, there are other purposes that could be served as well and a consideration of them will result in the purchase of a more serviceable commodity. Similarly, in any enterprise, especially one involving other individuals, it is unrealistic to assume a unique purpose common to all participants. In understanding the behavior of others, therefore, it is generally useful to ask if an alternative purpose is being served. This consideration is frequently useful in understanding folkways of other cultures as well as disagreement within one's own. To cite one of many possible examples, changes in educational practices are to some extent the result of changing views of the purpose of education—to prepare one for life, for citizenship, for gainful employment, or for acquiring basic skills.

Alternative Evaluative Criteria.   This form of consideration of alternatives has already been touched upon. It is a ubiquitous consideration in everyday life. In fact, much of the current literature[1] on life adjustment and psychopathology can be interpreted within this context. Judgments of the form, "This is devastating," "This is catastrophic," "This is the worst thing that could happen to me," may be viewed as the result of applying gross, unrealistic, or inappropriate evaluative criteria. Within the context of that interpretation, therapy takes the form of inducing more realistic evaluations. This example may seem unconvincing when stated in so bold and compressed a fashion, but consider instances from your own experience in which you have gotten very upset for a prolonged period about something that, on later consideration, did not seem so devastating as upon first evaluation. You can also think of other instances in which some event or action that appeared to be relatively minor with respect to one evaluative criterion turned out to have serious consequences that might have been anticipated had an alternative criterion been applied at the time (a possible example is accomplishing something at the expense of alienating a friend).

Alternative Bases for Classification.　Good classification schemes utilize intrinsic and invariant properties as the basis of classification but, as was noted in the discussion of classification in Chapter 2, those properties are not always known. The subject of taxonomy in biology, for example, is still an open issue. In the field of psychology the classification of psychiatric disorders, DSM III (1980), has recently been revised and is still under discussion. If even classification schemes central to a discipline have a provisional status, it is reasonable to assume that more limited and personal classification schemes such as some of those that each of us applies in everyday life might also be subject to modification. That being the case, it is well not to become too deeply wedded to one's personal categorization.

Alternative Models.　By now you should be convinced that model building is one of the important and continuing tasks facing the serious thinker. It is worth reminding you, however, that in testing one's model, the test is always made with respect to an alternative model to determine which, if either, provides a more satisfactory explanation. Even the didactic example of comparing two alternative models is often an oversimplification. In principle, a host of alternative models may be possible as you can convince yourself by listening to any discussion of a speech or recent event by a number of different commentators or by reading several historical accounts of any given event. To look for *the* one correct interpretation is a quixotic enterprise. As a corollary of that assertion, it is rarely safe to assume that all the data are in.

Alternative Courses of Action.　Even before learning about creativity, you probably needed little convincing that there are almost always alternative courses of action in any situation. I include the category in this list partly for completeness, but also as a caution to reevaluate any situation in which you conclude that "there is no alternative."

Alternative Styles.   After introducing the subject of style in the first chapter, I have had very little to say about it. The subject of style is almost totally neglected in all treatments of thinking. To some extent, the neglect may be a consequence of the English language where style is contrasted to substance, a contrast implying that style is of lesser importance. That is too extreme an evaluation. Certainly, we are all well aware that style is an important ingredient of art even though it is not, of itself, a defining property. In all other realms of life as well, style is an important contributory factor to ultimate effect. In the first chapter it was noted that some cognitive styles are more conducive to critical thinking than others. You were warned, for example, to beware of impulsiveness and literal thinking and urged to adopt a greater tolerance of uncertainty.

At this point, however, I want to correct any mistaken impression that there is one cognitive style that is optimally suited to all tasks. It is more likely the case that there is an interaction of style and task such that some styles are conducive to some classes of tasks but not to others. An analytic style, for example, promotes success in thinking tasks such as logical reasoning where attention to form and facility with abstraction are required; it may not lead to diplomacy in interpersonal interactions. To the extent that conclusion is warranted—and current knowledge about cognitive style does not warrant many firm conclusions—it suggests that one should try to adopt a variety of cognitive styles that can be tailored to the demands of the task at hand. Certainly, it seems to be the case that people who tend to focus upon details of context have great difficulty with subjects like mathematics and logic. Moreover, overcoming context dependence does help them to tame those *bêtes noirs*. On the other hand, to the extent that propensity toward a particular style is like a personality characteristic that may not be easily modified, adaptability may have to take the form of devising means of overcoming the limitations of one's habitual style in contexts where it is less appropriate.

And, now, you are on your own. Don't be hesitant about exercising your skills and "testing your wings" as a thinker—they strengthen with use. You have the capacity and sufficient background to launch out on your own and to direct your own progress. Good-bye. Good luck. Good thinking.

Appendix on Probability

$\mathbf{B}$ecause the basic concepts of probability are so fundamental to so many areas, most students have already been exposed to them. If you have not been so blessed, or if you simply need a review, this appendix is intended to acquaint you with some basic notions. For a deeper understanding, there are many texts on probability.

Definition. Although there are alternative, possible definitions of probability, the most common definition will be used here: *relative frequency of occurrence*. To obtain it one considers the universe of all possible outcomes and partitions the universe into two sets: all those events you are interested in and its complement, everything else. For example, suppose you roll one die; the possible outcomes are 1, 2, 3, 4, 5, or 6 dots on the face showing. The probability associated with each outcome, assuming a fair die, is the number of times that particular event can occur in all possible events, $p = 1/6$. Suppose you toss two fair coins. They can land HH, HT, TH, or TT. The probability of HH, $p(\text{HH}) = 1/4$ since only one of the four possible outcomes corresponds to HH. The probability of one head and one tail, on the other hand, is 2/4, since two of the four events, HT and TH, are included. Suppose that in the area where you live there are 35 rainy days in the year on average. What is the probability that it will rain next Tuesday? $p = 35/365$. Suppose that one of the girls a boy's roommate can arrange a date with is pretty and the other four are not; what is the probability of his going out with a pretty girl? p 1/5 if he selects randomly. The probability of getting an unpretty date, $q = (1 - p) = 4/5$.

In all the examples above, we have spoken of dividing the universe into two parts as is done whenever one constructs a class and its complement. It is, of course, possible to distinguish more than one set: for example, the usual 52 card deck of playing cards may be partitioned with respect to suit into hearts, diamonds, clubs, and spades; with respect to color into red or black; and with respect to value into 1–10, K, Q, J. The corresponding probabilities are $p(\text{suit}_i)$ = 13/52, $p(\text{color}_i)$ = 26/52, $p(\text{value}_i)$ = 4/52, where the subscript i designates a particular class (red, or club, or 7). The probability of getting a card with a person on it (K, Q, J) is $p(\text{picture}_i)$ = 4/52 if a particular picture is specified and $p(\text{picture})$ = 12/52 if not. Many probability problems can be solved on the basis of the definition of probability alone. It is, therefore, worthwhile to go back to the definition in formulating one's problem.

One requirement inherent in the definition is $\Sigma_i p_i = 1$, that is, the probabilities assigned to each of the possible partitions *must* sum to one (the probability of drawing a card, or getting some face of the die, is unity). Because of this property, the probability of any outcome class may be defined in terms of its complement, $p = (1 - q) = 1 - (1 - p)$. This frequently provides an easier solution where relatively few elements are excluded from the value to be determined.

Joint Probabilities: The Multiplication Rule.   This state of affairs is called joint occurrence to refer to an event's falling into the intersection of two classes, for example, that a card is a seven *and* that it is a red suit. Consulting the Venn diagrams of Box 7-4 yields a graphic representation of set intersect, that is, the intersect of S and M is the portion common to both S and M. The joint probability is determined by multiplication of the associated probabilities of each of its components: $p(\text{AB}) = p(\text{A}) \times p(\text{B})$. In the case of the card example, $p(\text{red 7})$ = 4/52 $\times$ 26/52 = 2/52 (which can be verified by counting the number of red sevens in a deck). The multiplication rule is also used for a sequence of events, for example, the probability of tossing three heads in a row is the probability of getting heads on the first toss *and* the second toss *and* the third toss, $p(\text{HHH})$ = 1/2 $\times$ 1/2 $\times$ 1/2 = 1/8. As a final example, consider the prospects of a young man who enrolls with a dating service that has 100 women in his age range: 40 brunettes, 25 redheads and 35 blondes of which total 40 are pretty and 60 are not. What is the probability that he will be fixed up with a pretty brunette? p = 40/100 $\times$ 40/100 = 16/100.

Conditional Probabilities.   The joint probability estimates in the preceding section were computed assuming *independence* of the component events and their associated probabilities. In the case of a red seven, whether it is red or black in no way affects the likelihood of a seven and vice versa, drawing a seven does not influence the likelihood of red or black suit. In other instances, however, the assumption of independence may be unwarranted. For example, in predicting the probability of rain, one can improve on a prediction based upon the yearly frequency if one knows that rain is more likely at some season than others or that a low pressure system is headed toward the region. By taking additional information (such as, of correlations among events) into account, one can derive a probability conditional upon that information (usually expressed as the prior occurrence of some state of affairs). The estimate is called a *conditional probability*. To illustrate it let's return to the dating service example and assume that the distribution of young women with respect to hair color and prettiness is as shown in the table below:

Prettiness	Hair Color			
	Brown	Red	Blonde	Total
Not Pretty	40	15	5	60
Pretty	0	10	30	40
Total	40	25	35	100

By computing joint probabilities based on the marginal totals, you can see that hair color and prettiness are not independent: brunettes are less pretty than would be expected, 0 vs 16 expected, and blondes are prettier than would be expected, 30 instead of 21. The cell entries are observed frequencies of joint occurrence of two properties (as contrasted with predicted probabilities discussed earlier). Given prior information as to hair color, we can take the cell frequency for each particular hair color divided by the number of individuals with that hair color to obtain the probability of being pretty given a particular hair color, $p(\text{pretty/brown}) = 0/40$, or $p(\text{not pretty/blonde}) = 5/35$, generally, the number of cases of A_iB_i/number of cases of B. The resulting probabilities of prettiness contingent upon hair color are shown in the table on the left. The corresponding probabilities of hair color contingent upon prettiness ($p(AB/A)$ = number of A_iB_i/number of A_i) are shown to the right. Note that each is obtained by taking the cell frequency relative to a marginal (that is, appropriate column or row) total rather than the overall total. The cell frequency relative to the overall total gives the observed joint probability.

Prettiness	Hair Color						
	Brown	Red	Blonde	Brown	Red	Blonde	Total
Not pretty	1.00	.60	.14	.67	.25	.08	1.00
Pretty	0	.40	.86	0	.25	.75	1.00
Total	1.00	1.00	1.00				

Alternative Outcomes: The Addition Rule. The probability that *any one* of a number of mutually exclusive events will occur is the number of the probabilities of the separate events. Thus, going back to the rolling of a single die, the probability of getting three or less is the sum of the probabilities of getting a one, a two, a three, any of which satisfy the condition: $p(1v2v3) = 1/6 + 1/6 + 1/6 = 1/2$ which can be verified by going back to the definition of probability.

If the addition rule is applied to the probability that a card is, for example, red or seven, however, a complication is encountered. By adding the probability of red, $p(R) = 1/2$ and the probability of a 7, $p(7) = 1/13$ we get 15/26 or 30/52 which does not correspond with the value obtained by applying the definition of probability, 28/52. The reason for the discrepency is that the events are not mutually exclusive: a card can be both red *and* seven (whereas a die cannot be 1 and 3). Thus, the red sevens count twice (in the probability of red and in the probability of seven) and leads to a violation of the requirements that all probabilities sum to unity. This may become more obvious by consulting the Venn diagram again; what is wanted is the union of two circles—the area of one, plus the other—the intersect (the area common to both) would be included twice through addition of their separate areas. Therefore, in dealing with probabilities of one or the other of events that are not mutually exclusive, it is necessary to remove the probability of their joint occurrence from the sum, $p(A \text{ or } B) = p(A) + p(B) - p(AB)$ is the fully general form of the rule. Where A and B are mutually exclusive $p(AB) = 0$. As a test of your understanding of the addition rule, compute the probability that a date will be pretty or blonde from the joint frequency table data.

NOTES AND SELECTED ANSWERS TO
BOXES AND EXERCISES

Chapter 1

1. Solutions to problems: (a) the so-called nine dot problem is an old one. The usual solution is shown in *a*. Two additional solutions *b* and *c*, are given in Anderson (1980) and Adams (1974).

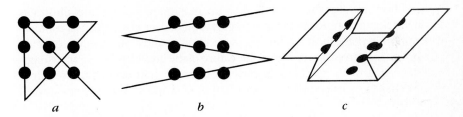

a   *b*   *c*

(b) The neurosurgeon must be the boy's mother. (c) Use all the links of one length as connectors for the remaining three lengths. This problem, the "cheap necklace problem," is from Wickelgren (1974). (d) The attendees are a grandfather, his son, and his grandson. The grandfather's son is both a father and a son. There is no requirement that each person be uniquely one or the other; if that were the case, there would have to be four persons. (e) M = 1, S = 9, O = 0, E = 5, N = 6, R = 8, D = 7, Y = 2. This is a unique solution.

2. Contemporary psychologists often use the term "metacognition" to refer both to the awareness of one's thought processes and to the deliberate direction of them. Some relevant references on this topic may be found in Bransford (1979), Halpern (1984), and Brown (1984). My treatment of self-regulation derives almost entirely from Piaget (1976, 1978).

3. Texts that relate good study skills include Gilbart (1982), Gross (1977), Jaffe (1982), Kagan (1982), and Langan & Nadell (1980).

4. How to think texts include Adams (1986), Anderson (1980), Bransford & Stein (1984), Gilhooly (1982), Hayes (1981), McKim (1972), Polya (1957), Whimbey & Lochhead (1982), and Wicklegren (1974).

5. Item A is similar to the Matching Familiar Figures Test (see Kagan, Rosman, Day, Albert, & Phillips, 1964). Item B resembles items in the Group Embedded Figures Test, in which the simple target figure is always presented separate from the embedded figure so they cannot be directly compared (see Oltman, Raskin, & Witkin, 1971). Item D is from an inventory of learning processes (see Schmeck, Ribich, & Ramanaia, 1977). An overall review of cognitive styles is available in Goldstein & Blackman (1978) and Kogan (1983).

6. Each of the vignettes illustrates literal and field-dependent thinking. In addition, each illustrates a subject that will be discussed in future chapters. (a) The young child in a family of two boys readily assents that he has a brother but will deny that his brother has a brother. Piaget cites such evidence to illustrate the young child's inability to take the view of another (Chapter 4). Here, failure to solve the initial riddle illustrates that shortcoming. The literalness is further compounded by equating "me" in the answer "It's me!" with a specific unique individual (which is ridiculous because it cannot be an answer to the riddle). (b) He assumes that his wife will read the letter aloud, much in the manner of conducting a conversation with him and, on encountering "send my slippers" will equate "my" with herself and send her own slippers. (e) This vignette, like the preceding one, illustrates an unscientific approach to the interpretation of data: changing it to conform to one's hypothesis (Chapter 9). In addition, it illustrates the effect of an implicit inappropriate model of the nature of the growth process: an assumption that growth proceeds linearly from some starting point. Growth is obviously a more complex transformation of shape and complexity as well as size.

7. These are rather standard kinds of problems. (b) The age ordering sentence identifies Jean as the oldest and Amy as the youngest. From there it is easy. (d) The general approach in series completion problems (of which this is an example) is to compare successive items of the series with respect to the transformation that could have produced them and to find a pattern in the transformations (adding or subtracting some number, n, where n may change systematically over the series; the transforming operation could also be multiplying, dividing, raising to a power, etc.). In this series one alternates subtracting, -3, -2, -3, etc. The blanks are filled with 7, 4, 2.

Chapter 2

1. The periodic table is discussed in most chemistry texts. One specifically devoted to it is Mazurs (1974).
2. Some collections of haiku include Bownas and Thwaite (1964), Henderson (1958), Stewart (1960), and Yasuda (1957).
3. There are many good books on modern art. A sampling includes Amaya (1965), Hughes (1980), Pellegrini (1966), and Pradel (1983).
4. There are many good books on memory. Some good introductions and interesting collections include Bransford (1979), Klatzky (1980), Neisser (1982), and Zechmeister & Nyberg (1982).
5. Flavell, Friedrichs, & Hoyt (1970) and Neimark, Slotnick, & Ulrich (1971) discuss the development of awareness of the demands of memorization.
6. A brief introduction to levels of memory is presented in Flavell (1985). A more theoretical analysis is offered in Tulving (1985).
7. There are a number of books on mnemonics by or about mnemonists. A few to start with include Cermak (1976), Crovitz (1970), and Luria (1968).

Chapter 3

1. In addition to the volumes from which the letters in Box 3-2 were selected, an interesting assortment of letters may be found in the following selected sources: Brockway & Winer (1941), Saintsbury (1922), and Schuster (1940). One example of a story developed through letters is Thurber (1949).
2. There are many texts on good writing. A sampling includes Baker (1966), Barnett & Stubbs (1977), Cowan & McPherson (1977), D'Angelo (1980), Guth (1980), Maimon, Belcher, Hearn, Nodine, & O'Connor (1981), McMahan & Day (1980), and Shaw (1979).
3. Some of the many interesting journals available are included here (you can find dozens more): Bucheridge (1973), Darwin (1975), Defoe (1966), Frank (1967), Hansen (1964), Hunt (1954), Irving (1969), Kemble (1970), Newton (1962), Sanderson (1974), and Swift (1948).
4. Some early research documenting the fact that children have difficulty appreciating that they don't understand was done by Markman (1977a, 1977b).

Chapter 4

1. Tasks for assessing an "egocentric" view include Flavell, Botkin, Fry, Wright, & Jarvis (1968), Huttenlocher & Presson (1973), and Piaget & Inhelder (1956).
2. Sources on adolescent egocentrism include Elkind (1967) and Elkind & Bowen (1979).
3. Ethnocentrism is discussed in many places. Some interesting discussions may be found in LeVine & Campbell (1972) and Sumner (1906).
4. This parallels a distinction made in the study of mnemonic strategies between mediation deficiency (not having the mediator in your repertoire) and production deficiency (having it but not using it). Both are discussed in Flavell, Beach, & Chinsky (1966) and Reese (1970).
5. This is a classic problem discussed in Wertheimer (1959).
6. An extensive current ethnograph series is the *Case Studies in Cultural Anthropology* series published by Holt, Rinehart & Winston, some volumes of which include Applebaum (1981), Esman (1986), Keiser (1979), Kuper (1986), and Safa (1974).

Chapter 5

1. Treatments of the area of signal detection and of its methodology tend to be quite technical. For the interested reader some good references include Baird & Noma (1978), Gescheider (1976), and Green & Swets (1966).
2. For 1 and 2 the correct answer is "equal." For 3 the (a) alternative in each pair is the more likely because (b) contains (a) plus another event. Although this is a straight-forward application of the multiplication rule of probability, more people choose (b) than (a). See Tversky & Kahneman (1983).

3. Psychological scaling is, again, a technical area. Some good references are Baird & Noma (1978), Coombs (1964), and Guilford (1954).
4. There is a wealth of relevant philosophical material going back to Plato. Some interesting sources include Bok (1978), Kahane (1983), Scriven (1966), Plato (1941), Stevenson (1944), Edwards (1955), and Westermarck (1932).
5. Some of the relevant developmental studies include Broughton (1978); Colby, Kohlberg, Gibbs, & Lieberman (1983); Gilligan (1982); Hardy-Brown (1979); Kenney & Nodine (1979); Moshman & Neimark (1982); Perry (1970, 1981).
6. These items were taken with modification from a set developed by D. Kramer. For the five items here, absolutistic choices are b, a, b, b, a. Choices a, b, c, a, b, respectively, reflect an awareness of multiple alternatives and judgmental standards. It corresponds to the stage Perry calls "recognition of multiplicity." The remaining choice in each triplet reflects what Kramer calls "dialectical thinking," an awareness that nothing is unalloyed right, good, beautiful, etc., but that from another aspect, properties of their opposites are also present.
7. Ball-Rokeach, Rokeach, & Grube (1984). The obtained rankings from top to bottom are 8, 17, 7, 2, 15, 12, 1, 3, 5, 11, 14, 13, 16, 10, 4, 18, 9, 6.
8. In reading about values there is, again, a wealth of material. The two measures referred to for this exercise are found in Allport, Vernon, & Lindzey (1960). This is a scale in which one ranks four alternatives for each of 45 questions. The resulting score reflects personal interest in each of six areas: theoretical, aesthetic, social, economic, political, and religious.

Chapter 6

1. An earlier classification scheme for statements differentiated analytic and synthetic statements (where the former refer to what are here called definitional statements and the term synthetic encompasses what are here called factual assertions). That distinction, as used by philosophers, traces back to Kant, for whom a proposition whose negation is a contradiction is analytic, otherwise it is synthetic. The distinction has been a source of controversy among philosophers and, in recent times, it has been abandoned. The present classification scheme is offered as a practical device for overcoming a common tendency to treat all assertions equivalently as matters of fact and as an occasion for exploring the fuzzy borderline sometimes separating factual assertions from conceptual ones. Assertions and their evaluation are not often discussed. One recent consideration appears in Nickerson (1986).
2. There is a good deal of interest among contemporary cognitive psychologists in the structure of concepts. The classic Aristotelian view was presented in Chapter 2. A strong opposing view is the prototype view of which Eleanor Rosch is the major exponent. It holds that concepts are organized in terms

of a prototype as the focal instance with less characteristic instances shading off into the periphery; the boundary itself tends to be fuzzy. For a comparison of opposing views, see Smith & Medin (1981) and Scholnick (1983).

3. Many texts provide a more extended examination of advertising, including Kahane (1984), whose Chapter 7 presents a lively analysis. The great grand-daddy of the genre is Packard (1957).

Chapter 7

1. There are a great variety of good texts on the more traditional treatment of formal logic, including Black (1946), Blumberg (1976), Copi (1978), Fearnside (1980), Fogelin (1982), and Salmon (1984).

2. There is currently much discussion among philosophers as to how to teach reasoning, and a new school of informal logic appears to be developing. Some useful works in this area include Beardsley (1975), Blair & Johnson (1980), Bull & Staines (1981), Cederblom & Paulsen (1982), Kahane (1984), Scriven (1976), and Thomas (1977).

3. There are many treatments of fallacies, among them Copi (1978), Fearnside (1980), and Hamblin (1970).

4. The false conservation task is described by Lunzer (1968). Spitz, Borys, & Webster (1982) report an interesting application of it.

5. There is a great deal of reported evidence showing that educated adults make consistent errors of reasoning both on formal logic tasks (Halpern, 1984 and Henle, 1962 are two examples) and their informal equivalents (Wason & Johnson-Laird, 1972). Many attempts to explain the logic of illogic have been offered. Johnson-Laird (1983) and Mayer (1983) provide but two examples of them.

6. Any premise should be translatable into standard form as shown by some selected examples in Box 7-4. Use of a Venn diagram provides an additional test of the translation. 1 (h), for example, as it stands, translates to "No doors will open." What is intended (see Box 7-4) is "Some doors will not open (and some doors will open)." In 1 (b) and 1 (i), although no quantifier is stated, "All" is intended; in 1 (j) every translates to "All." "Nearly all," like "Almost all," "Not quite all," "All but," and "Only some" all translate to "Some S are P" and "Some S are not P." 1 (d) some easy courses are not satisfying. A good set of translation rules appears in Ballard (1972). The conditional assertion, "If p then q" appears in many forms and is widely used in reasoning about causation (see Chapters 8 and 9), obligation, and contingency. Statements about cause such as "Frustration leads to aggression" or "Cholesterol deposits narrow the arteries" all translate into "If cause then effect." Application of the conditional to obligation arises in stating rules or defining classes and takes the general form "State of affairs X requires Y" ("Apologize when you burp"; "Psychology majors must take Statistics 101"). All these

examples can be translated into "If occasion X (p) then alternative Y must be done (q)." For contingency statements such as "Rain date the following Sunday," a possible hitch or contingency requiring a change in normal procedure is described. Such statements translate into "If contingency X arises (p) then do Y (q)." Note that in each of these applications (a) the major premise translates into a conditional, "If p then q; (b) valid arguments can then be constructed only by asserting the antecedent, p, or denying the consequent $\bar{q}$; (c) inverting the p and q terms of the conditional premise is a common error that leads to fallacious reasoning (see Exercise 2b). To state the last point in symbolic terms, "If p then q = If $\bar{q}$ then $\bar{p}$" but neither is equivalent to "If q then p." Construct examples until these points become clear and familiar.

7. There are three conditional syllogisms: (b), (c), (e). None is valid: (b) and (c) assert the consequent while (e) denies the antecedent. (b) is the trickiest because its first premise is "If there is someone outside, then the dogs bark." Of the categorical syllogisms, (a), (d), (f), (g), and (h), only two are valid— (f) and (h). Only (f) is sound. No invalid argument can be sound.

8. This is an instance of the ironic conditional argument.

9. If you have difficulty constructing a tree diagram of this argument then you are doing the exercise correctly. This is a poorly constructed argument. The first problem is to find the conclusion. The conclusion does not appear to be strongly connected to the assortment of other statements given. The purpose of this exercise is to demonstrate the value of diagramming an argument before making it to ensure that it is valid, sound, and convincing. "It appears to be that the word *punk* has lost its meaning and should not be used any longer," is the intended conclusion. What are the supporting arguments and how are they related to the conclusion? Scriven's procedure should be employed along with the criteria proposed by Johnson and Blair.

10. Only a sampling of the sample of fallacies is included here. (c), (d), and (e) employ *ad hominem* arguments in shifting from the substance of the issue to the person of the critic. There is some coloration of *ad hominem* in (b) as well: doctors know what is or is not good medicine because they are physicians; lawyers are in it for the money and therefore their purposes are suspect. (a) is a clear example of the fallacy of appeal to authority. (e) is an example of equivocation.

11. Numbers 7 and 8 are straightforward. For instance, the first figure takes the form M are P, S are M, S are P. There are four possible quantifiers (All, No, Some, Some are Not) for each of the three terms leading to $4^3 = 64$ possible first figure syllogisms. One way of generating them is to start with "all" as the quantifier for both premises and, holding premises constant, list all four possible forms of the conclusion. Then, holding "All" constant in the first premise, use "Some" for the second, and generate all four conclusions for that pair of premises, etc.

Chapter 8

1. My treatment of Mill and Aristotle is drawn from Wallace (1978). Hume's treatment of cause and effect is in Book One of *A treatise of human nature* (1739). It is available in Ayer & Winch (1968). Other useful treatments are to be found in Beauchamp (1974) and Sosa (1975). Einhorn & Hogarth (1986) contains an interesting recent review of theories along with a new one.

2. The Pearson product-moment correlation coefficient is perhaps most readily understood as the mean of a set of Z score products; that is, given paired measures expressed as standard Z scores, you get the product of each pair (preserving sign) and take the mean of the Z products, $r = \dfrac{1}{n}\Sigma Z_x Z_y$. This quantity will assume its highest value when $Z_x = Z_y$ so that $Z_x Z_y = Z^2$ since $\Sigma Z^2 = n$ so $r = +1$. The lowest value will obtain when $Z_x = -Z_y$ so that $Z_x - Z_y = -Z^2$; $\Sigma - Z^2 = -n$ and $r = -1$. Usual computation formulas and more extended explanations are available in any statistics text, such as Baggaley (1964).

3. If you are interested in pursuing the research on the determinants of the bee dance code, see Frisch (1967).

4. Two good probability texts are Hoel, Post, & Stone (1971) and Ross (1984).

5. Not wishing to complicate the example unduly, I compared observed and expected frequencies in terms of absolute magnitude. One could, of course, do a statistical comparison of them. In that case, the difference between the observed frequency, f_i, and the expected frequency, $\bar{f}$, is evaluated relative to the expected standard deviation: $Z = (f_i - \bar{f})/\text{s.d.}$ For probabilities $\bar{f} = np$ and s.d. $= \sqrt{npq}$. In this example, $np = (10{,}000 \times 1/365) = 27.40$ and $\sqrt{npq} = \sqrt{10{,}000 \times 1/365 \times 364/365} = 5.23$.

6. The value is determined as follows: there are two possible answers, T or F. If you select by flipping a coin, the probability of each is $p = q = 1/2$. If the exam is so constructed that questions on which T is correct are as likely to be true as items on which F is correct, then the probability of correctness for each question is 1/2. The probability of any given combination of answer, i, and correctness, j, (TC, TX, FC, FX) is $p_{ij} = 1/4$, so the probability of a correct answer is $p_{tc} + p_{fc} = 1/4 + 1/4 = 1/2$. Note that because of the assumption about grading, the same result would be obtained if you answered all questions with T (or F).

7. Attneave (1959) provides a clear simple explanation of information theory and its measurement. The great classic is Shannon & Weaver (1949). The general formula for uncertainty is $H = \Sigma p_i \log 1/pi$ or $-\Sigma p_i \log p_i$. That is also the formula for *entropy*: the randomness or unpredictability of a physical system.

8. The purpose of this exercise is to evoke examination of inferred causes and

the basis for their identification. With respect to cause, a distinction is sometimes made between causal and contributory factors. That distinction might arise naturally in (b), (c), or (d): the souring of milk, for example, results from bacterial action but cleanliness of the container will influence whether or not bacteria are present and conditions of storage (such as temperature) will influence their activity and reproduction. With respect to basis of identification, Mill's canons provide a useful identification scheme. It is likely that the first canon will be invoked most often; the third and fifth are also common. There may also be proposed causes for which none of the canons apply.

9. This exercise requires application of the relative frequency definition of probability; the last two parts require, in addition, the addition rule. There are 75 letters of which 15 are A, etc. (a) $p(D) = 4/75$. (c) $p(A \vee G) = 15/75 + 3/75$.

10. This exercise requires application of the multiplication rule, and introduces the term "sampling with replacement." (b) is a reminder that all probabilities sum to unity for the universe in question; a class or its complement comprises the universe so $p(A \vee \bar{A}) = 1$. (a) $p(A) \times p(A) = (15/75)^2 = 1/25$.

11. This question anticipates the discussion of efficient information gathering strategies in Chapter 10 (and the marble problem in the discussion of Exercise 5 of that chapter). Intuitively it should be clear that in predicting events of unequal probabilities, over the long run one is most likely to be correct by guessing the most likely outcome first (in this case, A) and proceeding to less and less likely outcomes (L, K or I, down to G).

12. This exercise calls for application of the definition of information as reduction in uncertainty. For the first two parts alternatives are equally likely; the more alternatives, the greater the information. (a) die, (b) draw of card. (c) compares equally likely alternatives, 50 cards, to unequally likely alternatives, 50 candidates for Miss America (some of whom are more attractive/talented than others). Since uncertainty is at a maximum where alternatives are equally likely, the answer is cards. (d) Invokes the interpretation of correlation in terms of improvement in prediction (which is certainly akin to reduction in uncertainty). The higher the correlation, the greater the improvement in prediction. Sign of the correlation is irrelevant.

13. This exercise calls for use of the binomial distribution as a model of chance (in essence, using the model discussed in evaluating the outcome of a true-false quiz). The two problems are identical. In each case one assumes that the two outcomes (male vs female or 1, 3, 5, vs 2, 4, 6) are equiprobable and determines the likelihood of obtaining $r = 7$ for $n = 10$ observations. From Box 8-5B one finds that the probability for $r = 7$ is 120/1024; the probability of seven or more of one outcome is $p(7) + p(8) + p(9) + p(10) = (120 + 45 + 10 + 1)/1024 = .172$. That is not particularly uncommon; for a .05 criterion for significance of a deviation from expectation (as

was used in the true-false example) one could not conclude discrimination in favor of women or an odd number.

14. Four experimental outcomes are shown for an experiment in which children who consumed one of two alternatives for each of four commodities either all got colds or all remained healthy. Comparing values of the alternative commodities for the healthy vs cold outcomes shows that type of cereal or soft drink does not differentiate the two outcomes, whereas oranges and baked potatoes always occur on healthy outcomes and apples and french fries on cold outcomes (method of agreement). It is possible that one or the other (e.g., oranges or baked potato) alone or both in combination (but not individually and independently) is responsible for each unique outcome.

Chapter 9

1. My treatment relies heavily upon Popper (1961) and Platt (1964). Influential alternative positions are those of Kuhn (1970) and Lakatos (1970). A good introductory treatment of the role of hypotheses is presented in Part Four of Johnson-Laird and Wason (1977).

2. Some examples of faulty models are illustrated in McCloskey, Caramazza, & Green (1980), Tversky & Kahneman (1974), and Gentner & Stevens (1983).

3. Karmiloff-Smith & Inhelder (1974, 1975) show that children as young as 4½ years old develop explanations for observed phenomena and use their explanations to deal with more complex tasks. They also show how the nature of theories changes with intellectual development. Another work that shows age change in knowledge structure is Carey (1985). Many mental models are presented in Gentner & Stevens (1983). Braitenberg (1984) presents an instructive, step-by-step account of the construction and testing of a model for the working of a nervous system.

4. Biologists make a useful distinction between *analogous* parts that are similar in function but differ in evolutionary origin and *homologous* parts where there is correspondence in function *and* in evolutionary origin. An example of analogous parts is the gills of fish as compared to lungs in a mammal; homologous parts are exemplified in the seal's flipper and the human arm.

5. Tables of areas and ordinates of the unit normal distribution are available in the appendix of almost every statistics text.

6. Discussions of the setting of confidence intervals and whether to select the .05 or .01 level are generally included in most statistics texts, such as Snodgrass (1977) or Welkowitz, Ewen, & Cohen (1982).

7. Students often find the difference between a standard deviation and a standard error confusing. A standard error is a standard deviation but it is the standard deviation for a distribution of *estimates*; for example, a distribution of means, rather than a distribution of raw scores. Because an estimate is

based upon a number of scores, estimates will vary much less than the scores upon which they are based. The larger the sample upon which an estimate is based the smaller the variation among repeated estimates. Where the estimate of a population parameter is based upon the entire population there will, obviously, be no variation in repeated measures, or estimates, of the parameter.

8. The logic of testing the null hypothesis is a subject that tends not to be treated clearly in most statistics texts. The two references in Note 6 of this chapter do about as well as any.

9. The best-known experiment on the testing of conditional assertions is summarized in Wason & Johnson-Laird (1972). Much literature has appeared since, largely in response to the Wason findings, but they make for difficult reading. One recent example is Overton, Ward, Noveck, Black & O'Brien (1987). The source of much work on identification and control of variables stems from the procedures and evidence of Inhelder & Piaget (1958). There has been much research since but the same kind of errors are repeatedly found. For evidence on interpretation of results, perhaps the most dramatic evidence comes from work in which scientists are subjects; see Mahoney (1986) or Mitroff (1974) for examples.

10. This is the Wason four card problem in which one is required to select those cards, and only those cards, that would have to be turned over to decide with certainty if the rule is true or false. The proposed rule, if p, E, then q,7, is disproven by observation of $p\bar{q}$, E and 2. Thus, one should turn over the card with E and the card with 2 and only those two cards. If there is a 2 on the E card or an E on the 2 the hypothesis is false; if neither is observed, it is true. Turning over either of the other two cards yields irrelevant evidence. Much research with tasks of this form shows that adults tend to turn over E and 7 (p and q) but that performance is improved when familiar content is used. The purpose of this exercise is to explore the effect of variation in content upon solution.

11. In each example there are alternative possible explanations besides that proposed. (a) One possible conclusion is that beer drinking promotes health. Another is that the population of people who drink beer is more heavily weighted with healthier people (for instance, the young or more active segments, such as students and workers outdoors). These two factors are positively correlated with health. The population of non-drinkers, on the other hand, contains the very young (children) and the old who tend to be less healthy regardless of drinking status. (b) The larger the population of a city the greater the number of daily deaths; absolute number is a meaningless measure that must be corrected by population size to yield a rate. If there is no differential rate the phenomenon is an artifact. Even for differential rates it is possible that composition of the population differs as a function of size (for instance, more older people move to the city).

12. (b) The bags are significantly heavier than advertised. The observed mean

of three pounds, eight ounces is four standard deviations above the advertised mean—a very unlikely event if the true mean were exactly three pounds.

13. (a) The answer to the penny problem is that it will be right side up. Many people guess that it will be upside down because they employ a mental model of rolling the coin 180° which would make it upside down. That model is inappropriate, however, because both rolling and pivoting about the fixed coin are involved. (b) A pull on a yo-yo to the right imparts force that can result in spinning and/or motion. Focus on the spin will lead to a prediction that the yo-yo spins counterclockwise thereby rolling away from the tug to the left. That analysis is incorrect. The yo-yo will roll to the right in the direction of the force imparting movement (diSessa, 1983, pp. 30–32). (c) The ball will fall in a parabolic arc; the plane will be directly above the ball when it hits the ground. The parabolic arc trajectory is the resultant of the combination of constant horizontal velocity and the increasing vertical velocity of gravity. Before the ball is dropped there is only a horizontal velocity equal to that of the plane. After the ball is dropped it acquires a vertical velocity from the effect of gravity. But, since the horizontal velocity is unchanged the ball continues to move horizontally at a speed equal to that of the plane, while gravity acts in a direction perpendicular to the ball's horizontal motion. No other forces are acting on the ball. Thus, according to the principle of inertia, the horizontal velocity of the ball will remain constant—the same as that of the plane which will remain above it until it hits the ground. (d) The ball rolling off the cliff problem is very similar to the airplane problem. After going off the cliff the ball will continue to roll horizontally at a constant speed of 50 mph but, in addition, it acquires an increasing vertical velocity because of gravity. The result is a parabolic arc (see McCloskey, 1983, pp. 302–305).

Chapter 10

1. Newell & Simon (1972) introduce the concept of problem space. Wickelgren (1974) describes state-action spaces.
2. For help with learning to solve mathematics problems, the following are warmly recommended: Polya (1957) and Wickelgren (1974).
3. Solutions to problems: (a) Four + Five = Nine has 72 solutions. Find an economical means of summarizing all of them. (b) Cross + Roads = Danger: C = 9, R = 6, O = 2, S = 3, A = 5, D = 1, N = 8, G = 7, E = 4. There are two solutions to Pete ate all the tripe: P = 9, E = 3 or 6, T = 1, A = 7 or 3, L = 4 or 8, H = 2 or 7, R = 0, I = 8 or 4. E is the most constrained after T, which must equal 1, and it constrains L. A chapter on cryptarithmetic appears in Newell & Simon (1972). (c) Solutions to anagrams: Sinusoidal, Symmetric, Dictionary. (d) Solutions to matchstick problems: For the first, a square with diagonals is not a solution because the triangles are right angles

rather than equilateral, but you are on the right track. The solution is achieved by thinking in three dimensions and creating a pyramid. For the second, remove both horizontal sides of the second square and the bottom of the last square and use those three sticks to create a new square adjacent to the last one, as follows:

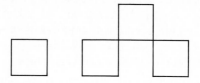

(e) Tangram solutions are shown below.

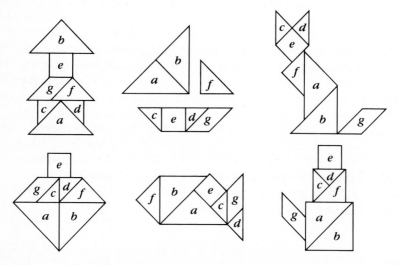

4. A good brief treatement of anagrams appears in Mayer (1983).
5. Many more matchstick problems are given in Katona (1940).
6. A treatment of the Missionaries and Cannibals problem, rechristened Hobbits and Orcs, appears in Greeno (1974)
7. Simon (1975) and Spitz, Minsky, & Bessellieu, (1984) discuss the Tower of Hanoi problem.
8. Several sources include the following: Duncker (1945), Katona (1940), Mayer (1983), and Wertheimer (1959).
9. I have borrowed Bruner's term for extrapolation. It is also the title of a paper by Bruner and of a book edited by Anglin (1973).
10. Sources on the diagnostic problem include Bruner, Olver, & Greenfield (1966), (Chs. 4 & 6); Neimark (1961); and Neimark & Lewis (1967).
11. The state-action tree diagram for the marble problem in Box 10-7 is shown below. The expected number of questions with this strategy is a weighted

mean, obtained by taking each possible number of questions to solution (1, 2, or 3) weighted by its probability and summing, as shown:

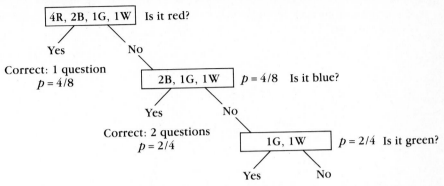

In either case, $p = 1/2$ for each, to be correct in three questions.

The expected value is computed by weighting the number of questions asked for a correct solution by the probability of a Yes or a No answer (keeping in mind the prior route to a No or Yes at any given level) and summing the values. $(4/8)(1) + (4/8)(2/4)(2) + (4/8)(2/4)(1/2)(3) + (4/8)(2/4)(1/2)(3) = 1.75$

12. Inefficiencies of information gathering are dealt with in chapters 4 and 6 of Bruner, Olver & Greenfield (1966) and Driscoll, Lanzetta, & McMichael (1967).

13. A summary of all the proposed stages of problem solution from Poincare in 1908 to Lyles in 1982 appears in Torre (1984). The sequence described here is that of Hayes (1981).

14. For more extended discussion, see Ellis & Bernard (1983) and Minuchin (1974).

15. (1a) Let H = husband's age today and W = wife's age today. Given H + W = 98; he was the age she is today (H − W) years ago. (H − W) years ago she was W − (H − W) years old so H = 2 W − (H − W). W = 42, H = 56. (1b) Dan has 8, Bob has 4, Mary has 12, Nora has 2, and Aaron has 2. (1c) Harry is 5'2" and Tom is 4'10". (1d) Jack goes to E, Dick to W, Bob to S, Tom to N, and John to C. (1e) 33.

16. Glorify, Ostrich, Grapefruit, Institute, National.

17. (4a) 31; (4b) 34FP; (4c) 16.5; (4d) 7; (4e) HS.

18. (5a) The first weighing breaks the 24 coins into two sets of 12 each. The 12 in the higher pan (one of them must be lighter) are then divided into two sets of six each and the procedure repeated (the lighter set of six is divided into two sets of three). The lighter three in that weighing are then broken into two sets of one each. If the pans do not balance, the light coin is identified directly; if they do balance, the light coin must be the one that was excluded. Number of weighings = four. (5b) An alternative procedure is to take three sets of eight coins each and weigh two of them. If one set is

lighter proceed to break it into half on each successive weighing; if the two balance, then apply successive weighings to the third set. Again, four weighings are needed. Both methods apply the tool of maximizing expected informational outcome discussed in diagnosis. For a nice treatment of problems of this type, see Rubenstein & Pfeiffer (1980).

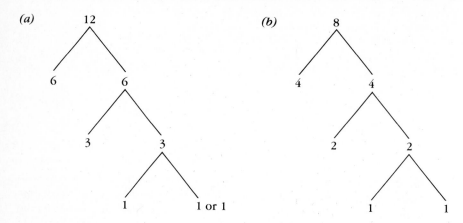

(a)   12   *(b)*   8

Chapter 11

1. Benjamin Franklin's letter to Joseph Priestly appears in Franklin (1956) and Anderson (1980) p. 211–212.
2. A good early collection of some of the classic papers is assembled in Edwards & Tversky (1967). A more recent consideration appears in Kahneman & Tversky (1982, January).
3. See Bross (1953). The classic treatment of game theory can be found in von Neumann & Morganstern (1947).
4. Hayes (1981) and Rubinstein & Pfeiffer (1980) provide good discussions of decision criteria.
5. Goldman, Weinberg, Weisberg, Olshen, Cook, Sargent, Lamas, Dennis, Wilson, Deckelbaum, Fineberg, Stiratelli, and the medical house staffs at Yale-New Haven Hospital and Brigham and Women's Hospital (1982). More extended treatment of construction of decision trees is available in Breiman, Freidman, Olshen, & Stone (1984).
6. Dawes (1971) shows that decisions made on the basis of a linear combination of the three best predictors of success in graduate school are more valid and less capricious than those of a professional committee and much less expensive. Cost of the time of admissions committee members is estimated at 18 million dollars.
7. Several sources that discuss systematic errors made in decision making include Einhorn & Hogarth (1982), Nisbett & Ross (1980), Slovic, Fischoff, & Lichtenstein (1977, 1980), and Tversky & Kahneman (1974).

8. Bross (1953) gives a nice treatment of Bayes' theorem in Chapter 4. See also Hayes (1973).
9. Slovic (1982) and Festinger (1964) present interesting discussions.

Chapter 12

1. Divergent thinking as it is usually used in this context is a term borrowed from J. P. Guilford's model of the structure of intellect. (Guilford, 1967). Many creativity tests were developed by Guilford and his associates; additional creativity tests have been developed by Torrance (1965).
2. Several sources on gifted individuals and high achievers include the following: Barron (1969), Roe (1952), and Taylor & Barron (1963).
3. Studies of gifted and talented adolescents include Getzels & Jackson (1962); Stanley, George, & Solano (1977); Wallach & Kogan (1965); and Wallach & Wing (1969). Horowitz & O'Brien (1985) present a collection of papers on the developement of talent.
4. Getzels & Jackson (1962) and Wallach & Kogan (1965) both report no relation between intelligence and creativity.
5. Johnson (1972) and Lehman (1952) deal with age of achievement.
6. Taylor & Barron (1963). An exceptionally engaging discussion of the correlates of creativity is given in the last chapter of Perkins (1981). Another recent discussion appears in John-Steiner (1985).
7. Osborn (1957) is the father of brainstorming. Parnes & Harding (1962), and Parnes, Noller, & Biondo (1977) deal with later applications of it.
8. Both Adams (1986) and Koberg & Bagnall (1981) provide lively treatments of creativity in the narrow sense.
9. The source of the concept of incubation as part of a problem-solving sequence of preparation, incubation, illumination, and verification is Wallas (1926).
10. Spender (1955) speaks of the role of concentration: "It is evident that a faith in their vocation, mystical in intensity, sustains poets," (pg. 57) and "The problem of creative writing is essentially one of concentration, and the supposed eccentricities of poets are usually due to mechanical habits or rituals developed in order to concentrate," (pg. 57).
11. Two sources include Amabile (1983) and Zuckerman (1977).
12. Perhaps the best-known example is Kekule's dream from which he drew the model of the benzine ring. It is accounted in Koestler (1967). Another of Kekule's insights is described on page 170. Koestler's theory of creation, in Book 1, is full of other interesting examples. Gruber (1974) traces the course of Darwin's development of the theory of evolution.
13. One of the most notorious accounts of the process of discovery is Watson's (1969) account of developing a model of the DNA molecule. Other accounts appear in Krebs & Shelley (1975), Ghiselin (1955), Roslansky (1970), Summerfield & Thatcher (1960).

Conclusion

1. The particular school referred to here is the rational-emotive theory of Albert Ellis which is presented in a popular style that makes it accessible to students (see Ellis & Bernard, 1983). Reference was made to this theory earlier in Chapter 10. Another excellent brief summary is available in Tyler (1983). One view of personality, which assumes that people develop concepts and theories that direct their adjustment to life, a view very similar to that proposed here, is proposed by George Kelly (1955, 1966). Many other recent personality theorists place great stress on the individual's construction of reality, in other words, the cognitive determinants of personality. Any good personality text, such as Pervin (1985), can be used as an introduction to them.

REFERENCES

Adams, J. L. (1986). *Conceptual blockbusting* (pp. 110, 111, 114, & 115). Reading, MA: Addison-Wesley Publishing Company, Inc.

Allport, G. W., Vernon, P. E., & Lindzey, G. (1960). *A study of values* (3rd ed.). Boston: Houghton-Mifflin.

Amabile, T. M. (1983). *The social psychology of creativity* (pp. 146–149). New York: Springer-Verlag.

Amaya, M. (1965). *Pop art—and after.* New York: Viking.

Anderson, B. F. (1980). *The complete thinker* (pp. 39–61, 145–146, & 211–212). Englewood Cliffs, NJ: Prentice-Hall.

Anglin, J. M. (1973). *Beyond the information given.* New York: W. W. Norton.

Applebaum, H. A. (1981). *Royal blue: The culture of construction workers.* New York: Holt, Rinehart & Winston.

Attneave, F. (1967). *Applications of information theory to psychology.* New York: Holt, Rinehart & Winston.

Ausuble, N. (1948). *A treasury of Jewish folklore.* New York: Crown.

Ayer, A. J., & Winch, R. (Eds.). (1968). *British Empirical philosophers.* New York: Simon & Schuster.

Baggaley, A. R. (1964). *Intermediate correlational methods.* New York: Wiley.

Baird, J. C., & Noma, E. (1978). *Fundamentals of scaling and psychophysics* (Chs. 8 & 10). New York: Wiley.

Baker, S. (1966). *The complete stylist.* New York: Thomas Y. Crowell.

Ballard, K. E. (1972). *Study guide for Copi: Introduction to logic* (4th ed., pp. 122–126). New York: Macmillan.

Ball-Rokeach, S. J., Rokeach, M., & Grube, J. M. (1984, November). The great American values test. *Psychology Today, 18,* 34–41.

Barnett, S., & Stubbs, M. (1977). *Practical guide to writing* (rev. ed.) Boston: Little Brown.

Barron, F. (1969). *Creative person and creative process.* New York: Holt, Rinehart & Winston.

Barron, F. (1972). *Artists in the making.* New York: Seminar Press.

Beauchamp, T. L. (Ed.). (1974). *Philosophical problems of causation.* Encino, CA: Dickenson.

Beardsley, M. C. (1975). *Thinking straight: Principles of reasoning for readers and writers* (4th ed.). Englewood Cliffs, NJ: Prentice-Hall.

Blair, J. A., & Johnson, R. H. (Eds.). (1980). *Informal logic: The first international symposium.* Pt. Reyes, CA: Edgepress.

Black, Max. (1946). *Critical thinking.* New York: Prentice-Hall.

Blumberg, A. E. (1976). *Logic: A first course.* New York: A. A. Knopf.

Bok, S. (1978). *Lying.* New York: Pantheon Books.

Bownas, G. R., & Thwaite, A. (1964). *The penguin book of Japanese verse.* Baltimore: Penguin.

Braitenberg, V. (1984). *Vehicles.* Cambridge, MA: MIT Press.

Bransford, J. D. (1979). *Human cognition.* Belmont, CA: Wadsworth.

Bransford, J. D., & Stein, B. S. (1984). *The ideal problem solver.* New York: Freeman.

Breiman, L., Freidman, J. H., Olshen, R. A., & Stone, C. J. (1984). *Classification and regression trees.* Belmont, CA: Wadsworth.

Brockway, W., & Winer, B. K. (Eds.). (1941). *A second treasury of the world's great letters.* New York: Simon & Schuster.

Bross, D. J. (1953). *Design for decision* (pp. 43–53). New York: Macmillan.

Broughton, J. (1978). Development of concepts of self, mind, reality, and knowledge. In W. Damon (Ed.), *Social cognition.* San Francisco: Jossey-Bass.

Brown, A. L. (1984). Metacognition, executive control, self-regulation, and other even more mysterious mechanisms. In F. E. Weiner & R. H Kluwe (Eds.), *Learning by thinking.* West Germany: Kulhammer.

Bruner, J. S., Olver, R. R., & Greenfield, P. M. (1966). *Studies in cognitive growth* (Chs. 4 & 6). New York: Wiley.

Bucheridge, N. (1973). *Journal and letter book of Nicholas Bucheridge, 1651–1654.* Minneapolis: University of Minnesota Press.

Buhler, J., & Graham, R. (1984, Jan/Feb). Fountains, Showers, and Cascades. *The Sciences,* 44–51.

Bulbrook, M. E. (1932). An experimental inquiry into the existence and nature of "insight." *American Journal of Psychology, 44,* 409–453.

Bull, P. B., & Staines, P. J. (1981). *Reasoning and argument in psychology.* Boston: Routledge & Kegan Paul.

Carey, S. (1985). *Conceptual change in childhood.* Cambridge, MA: MIT Press.

Cederblom, J., & Paulsen, D. W. (1982). *Critical reasoning.* Belmont, CA: Wadsworth.

Cermak, L. S. (1976). *Improving your memory.* New York: McGraw-Hill.

Chi, M. T. H., Glaser, R., & Rees, E. (1982). Expertise in problem solving. In R. Sternberg (Ed.), *Advances in the psychology of human intelligence* (Vol. 1). Hillsdale, NJ: Erlbaum.

Colby, A., Kohlberg, L., Gibbs, J., & Lieberman, M. (1983). A longitudinal study of moral judgment. *Monographs of the Society of Research in Child Development, 48* (1–2, Serial No. 200).

Collins, A. M., & Quillian, M. R. (1969). Retrieval from semantic memory. *Journal of Verbal Learning and Verbal Behavior, 8,* 240–247.

Coombs, C. H. (1964). *A theory of data.* New York: Wiley.

Copi, I. M. (1978). *Introduction to logic.* (5th ed.). New York: Macmillan.

Cowan, G., & McPherson, E. (1977). *Plain English rhetoric and reader* (2nd ed.). New York: Random House.

Cox, C. M. (1926). The early mental traits of three hundred geniuses. *Genetic Studies of Genius* (Vol. 2). Stanford, CA: Stanford University Press.

Crovitz, H. F. (1970). *Galton's walk: Methods for the analysis of thinking, intelligence, and creativity.* New York: Harper & Row.

Curtis, H. (1983). *Biology* (4th ed., pp. 376). New York: Worth.

D'Angelo, F. J. (1980). *Process and thought in composition.* Cambridge, MA: Winthrop.

Dart, F. E., & Pradhan, P. L. (1967). Cross-cultural teaching of science. *Science, 155,* 649–656.

Darwin, C. (1975). *The voyage of the Beagle.* New York: Dutton.

Dawes, R. M. (1971). A case study of graduate admissions: Applications of three principles of human decision making. *American Psychologist, 26,* 180–188.

DeBono, E. (1984). *Tactics: The art and science of success.* Boston: Little Brown.

Defoe, D. (1966). *Journal of the plague year.* Baltimore: Penguin.

di Sessa, A. A. (1983). Phenomenology and the evolution of intuition. In D. Gentner and A. L. Stevens (Eds.), *Mental Models.* Hillsdale, NJ: Erlbaum.

Driscoll, J. M., Lanzetta, J. T., & McMichael, J. C. (1967). Preference for information under varying conditions of outcome uncertainty, intensity and delay. *Pychological Reports, 21,* 473–479.

DSMIII: Diagnostic and statistical manual of mental disorders. (1980). American Psychiatric Association.

Duckitt, M., & Wragg, H. (Eds.). (1913). *Selected English letters, XV-XIX centuries* (pp. 118–121, 378–380). London: Oxford University Press.

Duncker, K. (1945). On problem solving. *Psychological Monographs, 58 (5, No. 270).*

Edwards, P. (1955). *The logic of moral discourse.* New York: Free Press.

Edwards, W., & Tversky, A. (Eds.). (1967). *Decision making.* Baltimore: Penguin.

Einhorn, H. J., & Hogarth, R. M. (1982). Behavioral decision theory. *Annual Review of Psychology, 33,* 53–88.

Einhorn, H. J., & Hogarth, R. M. (1986). Judging probable cause. *Psychological Bulletin, 99*(1), 3–19.

Elkind, D. (1967). Egocentrism in adolescence. *Child Development, 38,* 1025–1034.

Elkind, D., & Bowen, R. (1979). Imaginary audience behavior in children and adolescents. *Developmental Psychology, 15,* 38–44.

Ellis, A., & Bernard, M. E. (Eds.). (1983). *Rational-Emotive approaches to the problems of childhood.* New York: Plenum.

Esman, M. R. (1986). *Henderson, Louisiana: Cultural adaptation in a Cajun community.* New York: Holt, Rinehart & Winston.

Fearnside, W. W. (1980). *About thinking* (pp. 216–233). Englewood Cliffs, NJ: Prentice-Hall.

Festinger, L. (Ed.). (1964). *Conflict, decision and dissonance.* Stanford, CA: Stanford University Press.

Fisher, R. (1983). *Getting to yes: Negotiating agreement without giving in.* New York: Penguin.

Fisher, R. A. (1951). *The design of Experiments.* Edinburgh: Oliver & Boyd.

Flavell, J. H. (1985). *Cognitive development* (pp. 207–231). Englewood Cliffs, NJ: Prentice-Hall.

Flavell, J. H., Beach, D. H., & Chinsky, J. M. (1966). Spontaneous verbal rehearsal in a memory task as a function of age. *Child Development, 37,* 283–299.

Flavell, J. H., Botkin, P. T., Fry, C. L., Wright, J. W., & Jarvis, P. E. (1968). *The development of role-taking and communication skills in children.* New York: Wiley.

Flavell, J. H., Friedrichs, A. G., & Hoyt, J. D. (1970). Developmental changes in memorization processes. *Cognitive Psychology, 1,* 324–340.

Fogelin, R. J. (1982). *Understanding arguments.* New York: Harcourt Brace Jovanovich.

Frank, A. (1967). *The diary of a young girl.* New York: Washington Square Press.

Franklin, B. (1956). *The Benjamin Franklin Sampler.* New York: Fawcett.

Frisch, K. L. V. (1967). *The dance language and orientation of bees.* Cambridge, MA: Bellnap Press of Harvard University Press.

Furth, H. G. (1968). *An inventory of Piaget's developmental tasks.* Washington, DC: Catholic University.

Gentner, D., & Stevens, L. (Eds.). (1983). *Mental models.* Hillsdale, NJ: Erlbaum.

Gescheider, G. A. (1976). *Psychophysics method and theory* (Ch. 3). Hillsdale, NJ: Erlbaum.

Getzels, J. W. (1979). From art student to fine artist: Potential, problem finding and performance. In A. H. Passow (Ed.), *The gifted and the talented: Their education and development* (78th yearbook of the National Society for the Study of Education). Chicago: University of Chicago Press.

Getzels, J. W., & Jackson, P. O. (1962). *Creativity and intelligence.* New York: Wiley.

Ghiselin, B. (Ed.). (1955). *The creative process.* New York: Mentor.

Gilbart, H. (1982). *Pathways: A guide to reading and study skills.* Boston: Houghton Mifflin.

Gilhooly, K. J. (1982). *Thinking.* New York: Academic Press.

Gilligan, C. (1982). *In a different voice.* Cambridge, MA: Harvard University Press.

Glucksberg, S., Krauss, R. M., & Weisberg, R. (1966). Referential communication in nursery school children: Method and some preliminary findings. *Journal of Experimental Child Psychology, 3,* 333–342.

Goldman, L., Weinberg, M., Weisberg, M., Olshen, R., Cook, E. F., Sargent, K., Lamas, G. A., Dennis, C., Wilson, C., Deckelbaum, L., Fineberg, H., Stiratelli, R., and the medical house staffs at Yale-New Haven Hospital and Brigham and Women's Hospital. (1982). A computer-derived protocol to aid in the diagnosis of emergency room patients with acute chest pain. *New England Journal of Medicine, 307,* 588–596.

Goldstein, K., & Blackman, S. (1978). *Cognitive style.* New York: Wiley.

Gordon, W. J. J. (1961). *Synectics.* New York: Harper & Row.

Green, D. M., & Swets, J. A. (1966). *Signal detection theory and psychophysics.* New York: Wiley.

Greeno, J. G. (1974). Hobbits and Orcs: Acquisition of a sequential concept. *Cognitive Psychology, 6,* 270–292.

Gross, R. (1977). *The lifelong learner.* New York: Simon & Schuster.

Gruber, H. E. (1974). *Darwin on man: A psychological study of scientific creativity.* New York: Dutton.

Gruber, H. E. (1981). *Darwin on man* (2nd ed.). Chicago: University of Chicago Press.

Guilford, J. P. (1954). *Psychometric methods* (2nd ed.). New York: McGraw-Hill.

Guilford, J. P. (1967). *The nature of human intelligence.* New York: McGraw-Hill.

Guth, H. P. (1980). *Words and ideas* (5th ed.). Belmont, CA: Wadsworth.

Halpern, D. F. (1984). *Thought and knowledge* (Ch. 3). Hillsdale, NJ: Erlbaum.

Hamblin, C. L. (1970). *Fallacies.* London: Methuen.

Hansen, T. (1964). *Arabia Felix: The Danish expedition of 1761–1767.* New York: Harper & Row.

Hardy-Brown, K. (1979). Formal operation and the issue of generality: The analysis of poetry by college students. *Human Development, 22,* 127–136.

Hayes, J. R. (1981). *The complete problem solver* (Chs. 8 & 11). Philadelphia: Franklin Institute Press.

Hayes, W. L. (1973). *Statistics for the social sciences* (2nd ed.). New York: Holt, Rinehart & Winston.

Helson, R. (1971). Women mathematicians and the creative personality. *Journal of Consulting and Clinical Psychology, 36,* 210–220.

Henderson, H. G. (1958). *An introduction to haiku.* Garden City: Doubleday.

Hoel, P. G., Post, S. C., & Stone, C. J. (1971). *Introduction to probability theory.* Boston: Houghton Mifflin.

Hogarth, R. M. (1980). *Judgement* (sic) *and choice: Strategies for decisions* (pp. 124–125). New York: Wiley.

Horowitz, F. D., & O'Brien, M. (Eds.). (1985) *The gifted and talented: Developmental perspectives*. Washington, DC: American Psychological Association.

Hughes, R. (1980). *The shock of the new*. New York: Knopf.

Hume, D. (1968). A treatise of human nature, Part I. In A. J. Ayer & R. Winch (Eds.), *British empirical philosophers*. New York: Simon & Schuster.

Hunt, J. B. (1954). *The conquest of Everest*. New York: Dutton.

Hurwicz, L. (1953). What has happened to the theory of games? *American Economic Review Supplement, 43,* 398–405.

Huttenlocher, J., & Presson, C. C. (1973). Mental rotation and the perspective problem. *Cognitive psychology, 4,* 277–299.

Inhelder, B., & Piaget, J. (1958). *The growth of logical thinking from childhood to adolescence*. New York: Basic Books.

Irving, W. (1969). *Journals and notebooks*. Madison, WI: University of Wisconsin Press.

Isaacs, J. (Ed.). (1928). *Familiar letters on important occasions* (pp. 10, 11). New York: Dodd, Mead.

Jaffe, I. L. (1982). *Achieving success in college*. Belmont, CA: Wadsworth.

Johansson, G. (1973). Visual perception of biological motion and a model for its analysis. *Perception and Psychophysics, 14,* 201–211.

Johnson, D. M. (1972). *Systematic introduction to the psychology of thinking* (Ch. 7). New York: Harper & Row.

Johnson, R. H., & Blair, J. A. (in press). Fallacy theory revisited: In defence of fallacy theory as an instrument of critical evaluation. In E. P. Maimon, B. F. Nodine, & F. W. O'Connor (Eds.), *Thinking, reasoning, & writing*. Boston, MA: Longmans.

Johnson-Laird, P.N. (1983). *Mental models*. Cambridge, MA: Harvard University Press.

Johnson-Laird, P. N., & Wason, P. C. (Eds.). (1977). *Thinking* (Part IV). Cambridge: Cambridge University Press.

John-Steiner, V. (1985). *Notebooks of the mind*. Albuquerque, NM: University of New Mexico Press.

Kagan, C. E. (1982). *Coping with college: The efficient learner*. New York: McGraw-Hill.

Kagan, J., Rosman, B. L., Day, D., Albert, J., & Phillips, W. (1964). Information processing in the child: Significance of analytic and reflective attitudes. *Psychological Monographs, 78,* (1, Whole No. 578).

Kahane, H. (1983). *Thinking about basic beliefs*. Belmont, CA: Wadsworth.

Kahane, H. (1984). *Logic and contemporary rhetoric* (4th Ed.). Belmont, CA: Wadsworth.

Kahneman, D., & Tversky, A. (1982, January). The psychology of preferences. *Scientific American*. 160–173.

Karmiloff-Smith, A., & Inhelder, B. (1974–1975). If you want to get ahead, get a theory. *Cognition, 3,* 195–212.

Katona, G. (1940). *Organizing and memorizing*. New York: Columbia University Press.

Keiser, R. I. (1979). *The vice lords: Warriors of the streets*. New York: Holt, Rinehart & Winston.

Kelly, G. A. (1955). *The psychology of personal constructs*. New York: Norton.

Kelly, G. A. (1963). *A theory of personality*. New York: Norton.

Kemble, F. A. (1970). *Journal of a residence on a Georgian plantation in 1838–39*. New York: Knopf.

Kenney, J. L., & Nodine, C. F. (1979). Developmental changes in sensitivity to the content, formal, and affective dimensions of painting. *Bulletin of the Psychonomic Society, 14,* 463–466.

Klatzky, R. L. (1980). *Human memory: Structures and processes* (2nd ed.). San Francisco: Freeman.

Koberg, D., & Bagnall, J. (1981). *The all new universal traveler.* Los Altos, CA: William Kaufman.

Koestler, A. (1967). *The act of creation* (pp. 118, 170). New York: Dell Books.

Kohlberg, L. (1976). Moral stages and moralization: The cognitive developmental approach. In T. Lickona (Ed.), *Moral development and behavior.* New York: Holt, Rinehart & Winston.

Kogan, N. (1983). Stylistic variation in childhood and adolescence: Creativity, metaphor, and cognitive styles. In J. H. Flavell & E. M. Markman (Eds.), *Handbook of child psychology* (4th ed., Vol. 3). New York: Wiley.

Krebs, H. A., & Shelly, J. H. (1975). *The creative process in science and medicine* (pp. 35, 38). New York: American Elsevier.

Kuhn, D. (1986). Coordinating theory and evidence in reasoning. Paper delivered at the 16th annual symposium of the Jean Piaget Society, Philadelphia, PA.

Kuhn, T. S. (1970). *The structure of scientific revolutions* (2nd ed.). Chicago: University of Chicago Press.

Kuper, H. (1986). *The Swazi: A south African kingdom* (2nd ed.). New York: Holt, Rinehart & Winston.

Lakatos, I. (1978). *The methodology of scientific research.* New York: Cambridge University Press.

Langan, J., & Nadell, J. (1980). *Doing well in college.* New York: McGraw-Hill.

Lehman, H. C. (1952). *Age and achievement.* Princeton, NJ: Princeton University Press.

Lenat, D. B. (1984, September). Computer software for intelligent systems. *Scientific American, 251*(3), 204–213.

LeVine, R. A., & Campbell, D. T. (1972). *Ethnocentrism: Theories of conflict, ethnic attitudes, and group behavior.* New York: Wiley.

Luchins, A. S. (1942). Mechanization in problem solving. *Psychological Monographs, 54,* (No. 248).

Lunzer, E. A. (1968). Formal reasoning. In E. A. Lunzer & J. F. Morris (Eds.), *Development in learning: Vol. II. Development in human learning.* New York: American Elsevier.

Luria, A. R. (1976). *Cognitive development* (Ch. 4). Cambridge, MA: Harvard University Press.

Luria, A. R. (1968). *The mind of a mnemonist.* New York: Basic Books.

Mahoney, M. J. (1986). *Self-deception in science.* Paper presented at a meeting of the American Association for the Advancement of Science (AAAS), Philadelphia, PA.

Maimon, E. P., Belcher, E. L., Hearn, G. W., Nodine, B. F., & O'Connor, F. W. (1981). *Writing in the arts and sciences.* Boston: Little Brown.

Maltzman, I., Belloni, M., & Fishbein, M. (1964). Experimental studies of associative variables in originality. *Psychological Monographs, 78,* (No. 580).

Markman, E. M. (1977a). Realizing that you don't understand: A preliminary investigation. *Child Development, 46,* 986–992.

Markman, E. M. (1977b). Realizing that you don't understand: Elementary school children's awareness of inconsistencies. *Child Development, 50,* 643–655.

Mayer, R. E. (1983). *Thinking, problem solving, cognition* (Ch. 3). New York: Freeman.

Mazurs, E. G. (1974). *Graphic representation of the periodic system during 100 years* (rev. 2nd ed.). University, Alabama: University of Alabama Press.

McClosky, M., Caramazza, A., & Green, B. (1980). Curvilinear motion in the absence of external forces: Naive beliefs about the motion of objects. *Science, 210,* 1139–1141.

McKim, R. H. (1972). *Experiences in visual thinking.* Monterey, CA: Brooks/Cole.

McLuhan, M. (1964). *Understanding media.* New York: McGraw-Hill.

McMahan, E., & Day, S. (1980). *The writer's handbook.* New York: McGraw-Hill.

Mednick, S. A., & Mednick, M. T. (1967). *Remote associate test: Examiners manual.* Boston: Houghton Mifflin.

Miller, G. A. (1956). The magical number seven plus or minus two: Some limits on our capacity for processing information. *Psychological Review, 63,* 81–97.

Minuchin, S. (1974). *Families and family therapy.* Cambridge, MA: Harvard University Press.

Mitroff, J. J. (1974). *The subjective side of science.* New York: Elsevier.

Moshman, D. S., & Neimark, E. D. (1982). Four aspects of adolescent cognitive development. In T. M. Field, A. Huston, H. C. Quay, L. Troll & G. E. Finley (Eds.), *Review of human development.* New York: Wiley.

Neimark, E. D. (1961). Information gathering in diagnostic problem solving: A preliminary report. *Psychological Record, 11,* 243–248.

Neimark, E. D. (1975). The natural history of spontaneous mnemonic activities under conditions of minimal experimental constraint. In A. D. Pick (Ed.), *Minnesota Symposia* (Vol. 10, pp. 84–117). Minneapolis, MN: University of Minnesota Press.

Neimark, E. D., & Lewis, N. (1967). The development of logical problem solving strategies. *Child Development, 38,* 107–117.

Neimark, E. D., Slotnick, N. S., & Ulrich, T. (1971). Development of memorization strategies. *Developmental Psychology, 5,* 427–432.

Neisser, U. (1982). *Memory observed.* San Franciso: Freeman.

Newell, A., & Simon, H. (1972). *Human problem solving.* Englewood Cliffs, NJ: Prentice-Hall.

Newton, J. (1962). *The journal of a slave trader.* London: Epworth.

Nickerson, R. S. (1986). *Reflections on reasoning.* Hillsdale, NJ: Erlbaum.

Nisbett, R. E., & Ross, L. (1980). *Human inference: Strategies and shortcomings of social judgment.* Englewood Cliffs, NJ: Prentice-Hall.

Oltman, P. K., Raskin, E., & Witkin, H. A. (1971). *The Group Embedded Figures Test (GEFT).* Palo Alto, CA: Consulting Psychologists Press.

Osborn, A. F. (1957). *Applied imagination.* New York: Scribners.

Osgood, C. E. (1962). Studies on the generality of affective meaning systems. *American Psychologist, 17,* 10–28.

Overton, W. F., Ward, S. L., Noveck, J. A., Black, J., & O'Brien, D. P. (1987). Form and content in the development of deductive reasoning. *Developmental Psychology, 23,* 22–30.

Packard, V. (1957). *The hidden persuaders.* New York: D. McKay.

Parnes, S. J., & Harding, H. F. (Eds.). (1962). *A source book for creative thinking.* New York: Scribners.

Parnes, S. J., Noller, R. B., & Biondi, A. M. (1977). *Guide to creative action: Revised edition of creative behavior guidebook.* New York: Scribners.

Pauker, S. G., & Kassirer, J. P. (1980). The threshold approach to clinical decision making. *New England Journal of Medicine, 302,* 1109–1117.

Pellegrini, A. (1966). *New tendencies in art.* New York: Crown.

Perkins, D. N. (1981). *The mind's best work.* Cambridge, MA: Harvard University Press.

Perry, W. G., Jr. (1970). *Forms of intellectual and ethical development in the college years: A scheme.* New York: Holt, Rinehart & Winston.

Perry, W. G., Jr. (1981). Cognitive and ethical growth: The making of meaning. In A. W. Chickering and Associates, *The modern American college.* San Francisco: Jossey-Bass.

Pervin, L. (1985). *Personality: Theory and research* (4th ed.). New York: Wiley.

Piaget, J. (1970). Piaget's theory. In P. Mussen (Ed.), *Carmichael's manual of child psychology.* (Vol. 1, pp. 703–732). New York: Wiley.

Piaget, J. (1976). *The grasp of consciousness.* Cambridge, MA: Harvard University Press.

Piaget, J. (1978). *Success and understanding.* Cambridge, MA: Harvard University Press.

Piaget, J., Inhelder, B. (1956). *The child's conception of space.* London: Routledge and Kegan Paul.

Piaget, J., & Inhelder, B. (1969). *The psychology of the child.* New York: Basic Books.

Plato. (1941). *The Republic* (Cornford, Trans.). Oxford: Oxford Press.

Platt, J. R. (1964). Strong inference. *Science, 146,* 347–353.

Polya, G. (1957). *How to solve it.* Garden City, NY: Doubleday.

Popper, K. R. (1961). *The logic of scientific discovery.* New York: Basic Books.

Pradel, J. L. (1983). *World art trends in 1982.* New York: Abrams.

Reese, H. (1970). Imagery and contextual meaning. *Psychological Bulletin, 73,* 404–414.

Roe, A. (1952). *The making of a scientist.* New York: Dodd, Mead.

Roslansky, J. D. (Ed.). (1970). *Creativity.* Amsterdam: North-Holland.

Ross, S. (1984). *A first course in probability* (2nd ed.). New York: Macmillan.

Rubinstein, M. F., & Pfeiffer, K. (1980). *Concepts in problem solving* (pp. 26–28 & 102–117). Englewood Cliffs, NJ: Prentice-Hall.

Safa, H. I. (1974). *The urban poor of Puerto Rico: A study in development and inequality.* New York: Holt, Rinehart & Winston.

Saintsbury, G. (1922). *A letter book.* New York: Harcourt Brace.

Salmon, M. H. (1984). *Logic and critical thinking.* Orlando, FL: Harcourt Brace Jovanovich.

Sanderson, I. T. (1974). *Green silence: Travels through the jungles of the Orient.* New York: D. McKay.

Schatten, G., & Schatten, H. (1983, Sept./Oct.). The energetic egg. *The Sciences,* 28–34.

Schmeck, R. R., Ribich, F. D., & Ramaniia, N. (1977). Development of a self-report inventory for assessing individual differences in learning processes. *Applied Psychological Measurement, 1,* 413–431.

Scholnick, E. K. (Ed.). (1983). *New trends in conceptual representation.* Hillsdale, NJ: Erlbaum.

Schuster, M. L. (1940). *A treasury of the world's great letters.* New York: Simon & Schuster.

Scribner, S. (1977). Modes of thinking and ways of speaking: Culture and logic reconsidered. In P. N. Johnson-Laird & P. C. Wason (Eds.), *Thinking.* Cambridge: Cambridge University Press.

Scriven, M. (1966). *Primary philosophy.* New York: McGraw-Hill.

Scriven, M. (1976). *Reasoning.* New York: McGraw-Hill.

Shannon, C. E., & Weaver, W. (1949). *The mathematical theory of communication.* Urbana: University of Illinois Press.

Shaw, H. (1979). *A complete course in freshman English* (8th ed.). New York: Harper & Row.

Sheils, M., Deutschman, A., Kelley, T., Sherwood, B., & Knox, K. (1986, April). Tips: How to write better. *Newsweek on Campus.* pp. 46–47.

Simon, H. (1975). The functional equivalence of problem-solving skills. *Cognitive Psychology, 7,* 268–288.

Skinner, B. F. (1953). *Science and human behavior.* New York: Macmillan.

Slovic, P. (1982). Toward understanding and improving decisions. In E. A. Fleishman (Ed.), *Human performance and productivity.* Hillsdale, NJ: Erlbaum.

Slovic, P., Fischhoff, B., & Lichtenstein, S. (1977). Behavioral decision theory. *Annual Review of Psychology, 28,* 1–39.

Slovic, P., Fichhoff, B., & Lichtenstein, S. (1980). Perceived risk. In R. C. Schwing & W. A. Albers, Jr., (Eds.), *Societal risk assessment: How safe is safe enough?* New York: Plenun.

Smith, E. E., & Meden, D. L. (1981). *Categories and concepts.* Cambridge, MA: Harvard University Press.

Snodgrass, J. G. (1977). *The numbers game* (Ch. 9). Baltimore: Williams & Wilkins.

Sosa, E. (Ed.). (1975). *Causation and conditionals.* Oxford: Oxford University Press.

Spender, S. (1955). *The making of a poem.* London: Hamish Hamilton.

Spitz, H. H., Borys, S. V., & Webster, N. A. (1982). Mentally retarded individuals outperform college graduates in judging the nonconservation of space and perimeter. *Intelligence, 6,* 417–426.

Spitz, H. H., Minsky, S. K., & Bessellieu, C. L. (1984). Subgoal length versus full solution length in predicting Tower of Hanoi problem-solving performance. *Bulletin of the Psychonomic Society, 22,* 301–304.

Stanley, J. C., George, W. C., & Solano, C. H. (Eds.). (1977). *The gifted and creative: A fifty year perspective.* Baltimore: Johns Hopkins University Press.

Stevenson, C. (1944). *Ethics and Language.* New Haven: Yale University Press.

Stewart, D. (1985, August). Making the familiar strange. *Smithsonian, 16* (J), 44–55.

Stewart, H. (1960). *A net of fireflies.* Rutland, VT: Charles E. Tuttle.

Summerfield, J. D., & Thatcher, L. (Eds.). (1960). *The creative mind and method.* Austin, Texas: University Texas Press.

Sumner, W. G. (1906). *Folkways.* New York: Ginn.

Swift, J. (1948). *Journal to Stella.* Oxford: Clarendon Press.

Swinburne, R. (1974). *The justification of induction.* London: Oxford University Press.

Taylor, C. W., & Barron, F. (Eds.). (1963). *Scientific creativity* (Ch. 31). New York: Wiley.

Terman, L. M., & Merrill, M. A. (1937). *Measuring intelligence* (p. 37). Boston: Houghton Mifflin.

Thomas, S. N. (1977). *Practical reasoning in natural language.* Englewood Cliffs, NJ: Prentice-Hall.

Thurber, J. (1949). *Thurber country* (Chs. 9 & 23). New York: Simon & Schuster.

Torrance, E. P. (1965). *Rewarding creative behavior.* Englewood Cliffs, NJ: Prentice-Hall.

Torre, C. A. (1984). *Problem solving and decision making.* Chicago: Northeastern Illinois University Press.

Tulving, E. (1985). How many memory systems are there? *American Psychologist, 40,* 385–398.

Tversky, A., & Kahneman, D. (1974). Judgment under uncertainty: Heuristics and biases. *Science, 185,* 1124–1131.

Tversky, A., & Kahneman, D. (1983). Extensional versus intuitive reasoning: The conjunction fallacy in probability judgment. *Psychological Review, 90,* 293–315.

Tyler, L. E. (1983). *Thinking creatively.* San Francisco: Jossey-Bass.

Von Neumann, J., & Morganstern, O. (1947). *Theory of games and economic behavior* (2nd ed.). Princeton: Princeton University Press.

Wallace, W. A. (1978). *Causality and scientific explanation.* Ann Arbor, MI: University of Michigan Press.

Wallach, M. A., & Kogan, N. (1965). *Modes of thinking in young children.* New York: Holt, Rinehart & Winston.

Wallach, M. A., & Wing, C. W., Jr. (1969). *The talented student.* New York: Holt, Rinehart & Winston.

Wallas, G. (1926). *The art of thought.* New York: Harcourt Brace.

Wason, P. C. & Johnson-Laird, P. N. (1972). *Psychology of reasoning.* Cambridge, MA: Harvard University Press.

Watson, J. D. (1969). *The double helix.* New York: New American Library.

Welkowitz, J., Ewen, R. B., & Cohen, J. (1982). *Introductory statistics for the behavioral sciences* (3rd ed., Ch. 10). New York: Academic Press.

Wertheimer, M. (1980). *Productive thinking* (Ch. 1). New York: Harper & Row.

Westermarck, E. (1932). *Ethical relativity.* New York: Harcourt Brace.

Whimbey, A., & Lochhead, J. (1982). *Problem solving and comprehension* (3rd ed.). Philadelphia: Franklin Institute Press.

Wickelgren, W. (1974). *How to solve problems* (pp. 17–20 & 56). San Francisco: Freeman.

Wilson, J. (1969). *Thinking with concepts.* Cambridge: Cambridge University Press.

Woolf, V. (1935). *A room of one's own.* London: Hogarth.

Yasuda, K. (1957). *The Japanese haiku.* Rutland, VT: Charles E. Tuttle.

Zechmeister, E. B., & Nyberg, S. E. (1982). *Human memory.* Monterey, CA: Brooks/Cole.

Zuckerman, H. (1977). *Scientific elite: Nobel laureates in the U.S..* New York: The Free Press.

COPYRIGHTS AND
ACKNOWLEDGMENTS

Chapter 7   **7–5A** O'Connor, F. W. (in press). The logical, the valid, and the methodical. In E. P. Maimon, B. F. Nodine, & F. W. O'Connor, *Thinking, reasoning, and writing*. New York: Longman, Inc. Reprinted by permission of F. W. O'Connor. **7–5B** Beardsley, M. C. (1975). *Thinking Straight: Principles of reasoning for readers and writers* (pp. 18–20). Copyright © 1975. Englewood Cliffs, NJ: Prentice-Hall. Reprinted by permission of Prentice-Hall.

Chapter 8   **8–3C** Karl, T. R., Livezey, R. E., & Epstein, E. S. (1984). Recent unusual mean winter temperatures across the contiguous United States. *Bulletin of the American Meteorological Society, 65*, 1302.

Chapter 9   **9–1** Schatten, G., & Schatten, H. (1983, Sept./Oct.). The energetic egg. *The Sciences*, 28–34. New York: The New York Academy of Sciences. Copyright © 1983 by the New York Academy of Sciences. Reprinted by permission of the publisher. **9–2A** This publication is adapted from Terman, L. M., & Merrill, M. A. (1937). *Measuring Intelligence*. Copyright © 1937. Reprinted with permission of the publisher, The Riverside Publishing Company, Chicago, IL 60631. All rights reserved.

Chapter 11   **11–5** Pauker, S. G., & Kassirer, J. P. (1975). Therapeutic decision making: A cost-benefit analysis. *New England Journal of Medicine, 283*, 229–234. Reprinted by permission of the *New England Journal of Medicine*. **11–6** Goldman, K. et al. (1982). A computer-derived protocol to aid in the diagnosis of emergency room patients with acute chest pain. *New England Journal of Medicine, 307*, 588–595. Reprinted by permission of the *New England Journal of Medicine*.

Chapter 12   **12–2A** Taylor, C. W., & Barron, F. (Eds.). (1963). Scientific creativity: Its recognition and development. *Selected Papers from the Proceedings of the First, Second, and Third Utah Conferences on the Identification of Creative Scientific Talent*, 385–386. New York: Wiley. Reprinted by permission of the University of Utah Press. **12–2B** Barron, F. (1969). *Creative person and creative process* (pp. 91–92). New York: Holt, Rinehart & Winston. Reprinted by permission of the author. **12–2C & D** Barron, F. (1972). *Artists in the making* (pp. 49, 111). New York: Seminar Press. Reprinted with permission from the author and Academic Press. **12–2E** Helson, R. (1971). Women mathematicians and the creative personality. *Journal of Consulting and Clinical Psychology, 36*, 210–220. Copyright 1971 by the American Psychological Association. Reprinted/Adapted by permission of the author. **12–3C** D'Souza, D. (1986, Jan. 15). How to join the intelligentsia without trying. *The New York Times*, p. 23. Copyright © 1986 by the New York Times Company. Reprinted by permission. **12–4A** Adams, J. L. (1986). *Conceptual blockbusting* (pp. 110, 111, 114, & 115). Reading, MA: Addison-Wesley Publishing Company. Reprinted with permission. **12–4C** Crovitz, H. F. (1967). The form of logical solutions. *The American Journal of Psy-*

chology, 80, 461–462. Reprinted by permission of the University of Illinois Press. **12–4D** Anderson, Barry F. (1980). *The complete thinker* (p. 131). Englewood Cliffs, NJ: Prentice-Hall. © 1980 by Prentice-Hall, Inc. Reprinted by permission of the publisher. **12–4E** Adams, J. L. (1986). *Conceptual blockbusting* (pp. 110, 111, 114, & 115). Reading, MA: Addison-Wesley Publishing Company. Reprinted with permission.

ILLUSTRATION CREDITS

Page **9** Hovey Burgess, New York. **33** Michener, James A., *The Hokusai Sketchbooks: Selections from the Manga,* Charles E. Tuttle Co., Inc., Tokyo, Japan, p. 74. **34** (bottom) Muybridge, E., *The Human Figure in Motion,* 1955, Dover Publications. **53** Quillian, M. R. (1969). Retrieval time from semantic memory. *Journal of Verbal Learning and Verbal Behavior, 8,* 240–247. **90–91** Furth, H. G. *An Inventory of Piaget's Developmental Tasks,* 1968. **194** (top and bottom) Reprinted from Karl von Frisch: *Bees: Their Vision, Chemical Senses, and Language.* Copyright © 1950 by Cornell University. Used by permission of the publisher, Cornell University Press. **197** From Carroll, K. K. and H. T. Khor, "Dietary Fat in Relation to Tumorigenesis," in K. K. Carroll, (Ed.), *Progress in Biochemical Pharmacology: Lipids and Tumors,* 1975, S. Karger AG, Basel, pp. 308–345. **210** After Kuhn, D. **216** The Bettmann Archive. **218** © The Society for Research in Child Development, Inc. **323** From the book *The Complete Thinker* by Barry F. Anderson. © 1980 by Prentice-Hall, Inc. Reprinted by permission of the publisher, Prentice-Hall, Inc., Englewood Cliffs, New Jersey 07632.

INDEX

n refers to footnotes.